S0-AEG-611

CHICAGO PUBLIC LIBRARY
SULZER REGIONAL
4455 N. LINCOLN AVE. 60625

ML
410
.B15
G313
1994

Gartner, Heinz,
 1922-

John Christian Bach.

$29.95

DATE			

CHICAGO PUBLIC LIBRARY
SULZER REGIONAL
4455 N. LINCOLN AVE. 60625

MAR 1996

BAKER & TAYLOR

John Christian Bach

Heinz Gärtner

John Christian Bach

Mozart's Friend and Mentor

Translated by Reinhard G. Pauly

Amadeus Press
Reinhard G. Pauly, General Editor
Portland, Oregon

Translation of this book into English
was made possible in part by a grant from the German Government.

Sources of Illustrations

All illustrations taken from the author's collection, except:
Archiv für Kunst und Geschichte, Berlin (1); Bildarchiv Preussischer Kulturbesitz,
Berlin (4); British Museum (5); Conservatorio Giuseppe Verdi, Milan (1); Deutsches
Theatermuseum, Munich (1); dpa (1); e. r. a. Photo News Agency, Milan (1); Gleim-
Haus, Halberstadt (1); Hohenzollern Museum, Berlin (1); Neue Mozart-Ausgabe,
Bärenreiter, Kassel (2); Staatliche Galerie Moritzburg, Halle (1); Staatsbibliothek
Preussischer Kulturbesitz, Berlin (1); Stadtgeschichtliches Museum, Leipzig (4).

Copyright © 1989 as *Johann Christian Bach*
by Nymphenburger Verlagshandlung
in der F. A. Herbig Verlagsbuchhandlung GmbH, Munich

**Translation copyright © 1994 by Amadeus Press
(an imprint of Timber Press, Inc.)**
All rights reserved

ISBN 0-931340-79-9
Designed and composed by Carol Odlum
Printed in Singapore

Amadeus Press
The Haseltine Building
133 S.W. Second Ave., Suite 450
Portland, Oregon 97204-3527 U.S.A.

Library of Congress Cataloging-in-Publication Data

Gärtner, Heinz, 1922–
[Johann Christian Bach. English]
John Christian Bach : Mozart's friend and mentor / Heinz Gärtner ;
translated by Reinhard G. Pauly.
p. cm.
Discography : p.
Includes bibliographical references (p.) and index.
ISBN 0-931340-79-9
1. Bach, Johann Christian, 1735–1782.   2. Composers—Biography.
I. Pauly, Reinhard G.
ML410.B15G313 1994
780'.92—dc20
[B]   94-16931
                                                                        CIP
                                                                        MN

RO1065 06982

"As you well know, I love him with all my heart, and
I have the highest regard for him."

The twenty-two-year-old Mozart
to his father (27 August 1778)

CHICAGO PUBLIC LIBRARY
SULZER REGIONAL
4455 N. LINCOLN AVE. 60625

Contents

Preface ix

1 Childhood Years in Leipzig 1

2 Life in Berlin Under King Frederick the Great 59

3 Apprenticeship and Mastery in Italy 109

4 Years of Fame in London 163

5 Bach and the Mozarts in London 203

6 Bach, Abel, and Gainsborough 247

7 John Christian Bach and Mannheim 275

8 Last Triumphs 299

Notes 335

List of Works with Opus Numbers 361

Bibliography 365

Discography 369

Chronology 381

Index 391

Preface

Less than a decade after Johann Sebastian Bach's death, when people talked about "the famous Bach," they did not mean the cantor of St. Thomas Church in Leipzig; he had been virtually forgotten by then. Most likely they were referring to Johann Christian Bach, Sebastian's youngest son. Yet historians have paid far less attention to Johann Christian (later widely known as John Christian) than to his half brothers Wilhelm Friedemann and Carl Philipp Emanuel or to his brother Johann Christoph Friedrich, the "Bückeburg Bach." I shall soon try to establish the reasons for this neglect.

While there have been some specialized studies by German scholars, it is primarily non-German authors who deserve the credit for having rediscovered the youngest Bach son and for having reestablished his rightful stature. Thanks are especially due to Charles Sanford Terry, whose biography, published in 1923, was revised in 1967 and supplemented with a detailed preface and numerous corrections by H. C. Robbins Landon.

As an Englishman, Terry understandably emphasized Christian's years in London and his successful career as a composer of opera. However, he did not neglect Christian's years in Italy, which were significant for his sacred compositions and because of his extensive correspondence with Padre Martini, translated in the present biography from the original Italian.

Terry touches only briefly on the years that Christian spent in Berlin with his brother Emanuel—years that were important in the young composer's development. Berlin's musical life was flourishing, along with its social life, under the active support of King Frederick II, and it was there in a musical atmosphere dominated by the composers Graun, Quantz, and Benda that Christian, under Emanuel's tutelage, penned his first compositions. Even more cursory is Terry's coverage of the preceeding fifteen years, which Christian spent in Leipzig, looked after by his aging father. Christian was the apple of Sebastian's eye and his favorite pupil; later the devoted father gave him no less than three keyboard instruments. Undoubtedly the son benefited from his father's rigorous instruction, which must have given him a good start on his road to success as a clavier virtuoso. But he must also have sensed the dawning of a new age of music to which the "old Bach" no longer belonged. Thus Christian came to experience two worlds, both musically and socially: the solid, frugal, middle-class household of the Leipzig cantor and the splendor of the aristocratic courts where he later achieved such brilliant success.

Finally, Terry spends little time on Wolfgang Amadeus Mozart's visit to London and on the import, both personal and artistic, of the eight-year-old child's acquaintance with the thirty-three-year-old Bach son. On this and related subjects the two French musicologists Theodore de Wyzewa and Georges de Saint-Foix had done extensive research as early as 1911. They thoroughly investigated Mozart's childhood and clarified the extent to which the young prodigy's first compositions were guided by his mentor, John Christian Bach.

American Edward O. Downes pays tribute in his masterful dissertation on Christian Bach's operas to the composer's significance for the development of opera in the second half of the eighteenth century. Another American, Marie Ann Heiberg-Vos, provides information about his church music, including an inventory of manuscript copies that exist today, many of which are housed at Einsiedeln monastery in Switzerland.

Since 1985, the 250th anniversary of Christian's birth, work on a complete edition has progressed rapidly. Its forty-eight volumes (Christian was the most industrious of the Bach sons!) will make available to professional and amateur musicians this varied oeuvre: operas, sacred music, orchestral works, chamber music, songs, and keyboard sonatas. Among the latter are three that Mozart found so pleasing, he arranged them as keyboard concertos. Credit for the monumental undertaking of the complete edition must go to Ernest Warburton of Oxford University and to the Garland Publishing Company in New York. Thanks to their initiative, Christian's work is at last available in printed form, a precondition for its becoming generally known and appreciated.

With all this pioneering work abroad, what has been done at home in Germany? The answer is: embarrassingly little. The proverb about a prophet's not being honored in his own country very much applies to John Christian Bach. It may be that the nineteenth-century (Sebastian) Bach renaissance caused us to ignore whatever did not seem to be in harmony with our cherished image of Father Bach, the exemplar of stalwart

German Protestantism and master of polyphony. Generally speaking, the nineteenth-century Bach cult, tinged with patriotism, could not warm up to a Bach son who had left his homeland to seek his fortune abroad. By those standards, Christian was inevitably found lacking and, at best, received faint praise: "Amidst frivolity and modish taste, one might catch a glimpse of his father's immense stature" (Christian Friedrich Daniel Schubart). Bach's musically conservative biographer, J. N. Forkel, mistakenly claimed that Christian unfortunately did not benefit from his father's instruction, that he "composed for the people and was generally liked in his day" but that none of his music showed "the true Bach spirit." C. H. Bitter (see bibliography) belittles even that popularity, declaring that "only his being the son of the great Sebastian saved [Christian], once greatly admired, from oblivion."

Without engaging in a fruitless comparison of father and son, one ought simply to acknowledge Christian's accomplishment in emerging from the shadow of his towering father and, rather than copying him, successfully going his own way.

Yet both Emanuel and Friedemann Bach were less than cordial toward their successful half brother, and Emanuel accused him of turning apostate when he converted, for reasons of convenience, to Catholicism.

A few German scholars during the twentieth century have been able to recognize Christian as a major composer in his own right. Both Fritz Tutenberg and Heinrich Schökel provided excellent studies, as did Hermann Abert and Max Schwarz (see bibliography). None of their works, however, has substantially increased the public's awareness or appreciation of John Christian Bach's music. And yet another effort, which might have had more influence, was cut short when fate intervened. Heinrich Miesner, a capable researcher who had unearthed much valuable information about both Emanuel and Christian, died before he was able to carry out his pre–World War II plans to translate Terry's book and to write a new biography himself.

That a major breakthrough has not yet occurred should not be attributed to the quality of Christian's work. Mozart's great esteem for this music, much of which is still extant, suggests that it would stand up well under our scrutiny today—incentive enough, perhaps, to study it in depth. The publication of the complete edition will greatly facilitate such a study.

Translator's Preface

IN ITS ORIGINAL GERMAN EDITION, Gärtner's biography was subtitled "Mozart's friend and teacher" (*Lehrmeister*). Indeed, John Christian Bach's relation to young Wolfgang (who was eight years old when they first met in London) soon became that of a mentor and good friend. Many years later, the twenty-two-year-old Mozart would write to his father: "As you well know, I love him with all my heart, and I respect him greatly. As for him, there is no doubt but that he has praised me warmly . . . in all seriousness" (27 August 1778).

It has often been stated that Mozart's music contains many style characteristics also found the the compositions of the youngest son of Johann Sebastian Bach. Yet it would be an injustice to the "London Bach" to think of him only as someone who played a significant role in the development of the great Salzburg composer. John Christian Bach was a major artist in his own right. His true stature has been recognized in our time, as evidenced by a complete edition of his works and numerous recent recordings.

In the original edition, Gärtner quotes extensively, in German, from eighteenth-century English sources, including letters, memoirs, travel diaries (especially of the great Dr. Burney), newspaper articles, and concert announcements. Whenever I was able to locate the original documents, I have quoted from them; only in a few instances did I provide my own retranslation into English.

R. G. P.

I

Childhood Years in Leipzig

> *Pure melody, with noble simplicity and
> clarity, can move the heart in a way that
> exceeds all the artifices of harmony.*
>
> Johann Lippsius (1585–1612)

JOHANN SEBASTIAN BACH's youngest son was born in Leipzig on
5 September 1735. Shortly after his fiftieth birthday, the cantor of
St. Thomas had become a father for the eighteenth time. The child,
whose mother was Bach's second wife, Anna Magdalena, was baptized
two days later. Johann Christian was named after his two godfathers—
Johann August Ernesti, the young rector of St. Thomas School who soon
would be embroiled in quarrels with Father Bach, and Johannes Florens
Rivinus, a professor of law at Leipzig university. His middle name was
chosen (and this was unusual at the time) in honor of his young godmother, Christiana Sybilla Bose, daughter of Georg Heinrich Bose, a
deceased merchant and neighbor.

Sebastian seems to have chosen these godparents with care. They
represented both intellect and money, assets that apparently seemed
desirable for young Christian's future. Blessed with so many children,
Bach had had ample experience in choosing godparents. But little Christian's arrival was not hailed by all seventeen brothers and sisters, for
many of them had died early. From Bach's marriage to Maria Barbara,
only four of seven children survived, among them Catharina Dorothea,
the eldest. When Christian was born, she had already reached the age of
twenty-six and was thus only a few years younger than her stepmother,
who was about to celebrate her thirty-fourth birthday.

By this time, the surviving sons from Bach's first marriage—Wilhelm
Friedemann, Carl Philipp Emanuel, and Johann Gottfried Bernhard—
had left home in search of careers elsewhere. Friedemann, especially
beloved by his father, had been employed for two years at St. Sophie's

Church in Dresden. Emanuel and Bernhard were also abroad when their youngest half brother was born. Emanuel was studying law in Frankfurt an der Oder, earning his tuition by working as a musician. Bernhard (who was to cause much grief to his family) had obtained, with the help of his father, an appointment as organist at St. Mary's Church in Mühlhausen, the same church where Johann Sebastian had officiated—with dubious results in both cases.

The Bach family, then, offered an unusual appearance: two parents far apart in age, the spinsterish Dorothea from Bach's first marriage, and the children from his second marriage: eleven-year-old Gottfried Heinrich, feeble-minded and a constant source of worry; his nine-year-old sister, Elisabeth Juliane Friederike, called Liesgen by her fond father; and three-year-old Johann Christoph Friedrich, later to be known as the Bückeburg Bach.

Only these three survived. Anna Magdalena had also had to bury many children—seven within the nine years just past. Crowded living quarters in the building, which also housed St. Thomas School, and the resulting unsanitary conditions may have played a part in the loss of these children. At that time, before 1732 when the building was renovated and enlarged, not every student had his own bed. Three classes were often taught in one room, which also served as dining room. It was a *schola pauperum*, a school for the poor.[1]

Contagious diseases were bound to spread quickly under these conditions, and they did not stop at the door to the Bachs' living quarters, where births and deaths of children, joys and sorrows, were common occurrences. But things improved after the renovation. Then additional space for student dormitories became available, and the danger of contracting sometimes fatal illnesses decreased. Young Christian may have benefited from these improvements. Not only did he survive, but he enjoyed good health all his life.

Let us take a walk through the house in which he was born. The Bachs lived in the southern wing of St. Thomas School near the Thomaspförtchen, the "little gate" that gave access through the town wall to the River Pleisse and the public gardens, the Vergnügungsgärten. In addition to his family, Father Bach boarded a number of pupils, as good schoolmasters often did in those days.

The middle wing of the building was taken up by the school, and the northern tract was occupied by the school's director, or rector, who at that time was Rector Ernesti, Christian's godfather and later Sebastian's adversary.

Johann Sebastian Bach at the time of Christian's birth.
Based on an oil painting by Gottlieb Friedrich Bach, c. 1736/37. Private collection.

St. Thomas School was located in the western part of the city. Like a
bulwark, it was connected with the town's old fortifications. The building
formed a right angle with the church, a rather plain structure whose high,
steep roof could be seen from afar. Church and school together enclosed
the former St. Thomas Cemetery, the city's principal burial site until the
city fathers, tired of constant disputes with the monks, had decided to
relocate the graveyard outside the city walls. The courtyard had then
been paved with cobblestones, a small well gracing its middle. Whenever
the students, the "Thomaner," went from school to church and back,
they would cross this square, behaving more or less properly under the
watchful eyes of the immediate neighbors.

The entrance to the cantor's house was through a separate door from
the cemetery square into a small hallway, from which a door led to two
rooms facing the Thomaspförtchen. Friedemann and Emanuel may have
slept and studied in these rooms, for later, during the demolition, Friedemann's school notebooks were discovered there. Another room on the
ground floor probably served as a guest room.

A narrow staircase led to the second floor. Here were the larger and
better rooms: the parlor and Bach's study, the kitchen, the dining room,
and the parents' bedroom. From the parlor and study one had an unob-
structed view across the river and the Promenade to the elaborate public
gardens, about which Goethe had raved in a letter to his sister Cornelia:

> The gardens are as magnificent as anything I have ever seen. I may send
> you a picture showing the entrance to the Apel gardens; they are fit for
> a king. When I first saw them I thought I was entering the Elysian
> fields.

Such variety of views was both charming and appropriate: on one
side were the "Elysian fields" and the view into the distance where, on a
clear day, one could see neighboring villages. On the other side, in front,
were the venerable church and the cemetery square. For his study, Bach
had chosen the garden view; he may have found that it provided more
inspiration for composing.

From this second floor a winding staircase led to the top floor, with
additional bedrooms for Bach's younger children and boarding students.
From here, Bach could reach his place of work, the school, in no time.

One door of these living quarters opened to a long corridor, which
separated the music room from the conference room and led, at the other
end, to the rector's quarters. Thus rector and cantor not only lived under
the same roof but were separated by only a hallway; arrangements that

The room in which Sebastian Bach composed, on the second floor of St. Thomas School.

St. Thomas School, remodeled and enlarged in 1732.

Mit vieler Verbesserung erbauete Thomas Schule A⁰ 1732.

may have aggravated the disagreements that were soon to erupt. On the other hand, the proximity of the music room was a blessing for Bach, enabling him to have his compositions performed by his students practically before the ink was dry.[2]

In all, it was not the home of poor people. The cantor's quarters, with eleven large and small rooms, were an adequate place to live. Later, when Sebastian's estate was divided among the children, mention would be made of household silver and implements of copper and tin, to say nothing of the large collection of instruments. All this evinced a fairly comfortable living standard. A cantor's son could hardly expect more.

Financially, Bach's position as cantor at St. Thomas Church was a significant step down from his previous appointment as court Kapellmeister in Köthen, where his income had been four times his base salary in Leipzig. Moreover, as a singer at the Köthen court, Anna Magdalena had been able to earn two hundred taler, which helped with the household expenses. But as a cantor's wife, she was not allowed to perform in public.

Bach, to be sure, had opportunities for additional remuneration. There were minutely regulated fee scales for his officiating at weddings, funerals, and other occasions. There were also compositions commissioned by the university, and there was increasing demand for his services as inspector of new organs, all of which produced extra income. When, in 1716, he inspected the organ at Our Lady's Church in Halle, he had to be content with six taler. Eight years later, he received twenty-six taler from the city of Gera for similar services. And by 1732, when he journeyed to Kassel to inspect the organ in St. Martin's Church, his honorarium was fifty taler, plus twenty-six taler for travel expenses, two taler for the porters who would carry him in a sedan chair from the inn to the church, and one taler for his servant.

Thus Sebastian was not exaggerating when he wrote to Georg Erdmann in Danzig, a friend from his school days, that his present income amounted to seven hundred taler. What remained unsaid was that some of these earnings required much toil and many struggles to obtain certain coveted assignments. At that, the total earnings were modest, for at the same time in Dresden, the capital, the elector paid a yearly salary of six thousand taler to his Kapellmeister, Hasse, and his wife, the famous singer Faustina, augmented by five hundred taler for travel expenses. Things also looked rosy in Berlin, where young Frederick had just ascended the throne. The king lost no time sending his Kapellmeister, Carl Heinrich Graun, to Italy, instructing him to hire singers for the Berlin opera and authorizing him to offer a singer up to two thousand taler a year.

Such salaries make Bach's income look quite meager by comparison; moreover, it was by no means guaranteed. In the same letter to Erdmann, Bach complained that during the past year the income he normally derived from "ordinary funerals" was reduced by one hundred taler because "a healthy climate" had prevailed. In general, he continued, he did not benefit from "many incidental fees" normally derived from such a position, and in addition, Leipzig was "an expensive place."

Of course, Bach did not admit that he was to blame for certain emoluments not coming his way. Many of these depended on the good will of the authorities, which was not always extended to him. Bach was argumentative, tenaciously insisting that he was right whenever disagreements arose over real or imagined injustices, and once he had made up his mind, he was unlikely to change it.

From the beginning, the Leipzig elders had been less than enthusiastic about his appointment. Bach had only been their third choice after Telemann and Graupner, both of whom had declined the position. The town fathers would have preferred either of the two well-known music directors from Hamburg and Darmstadt over the Kapellmeister from the insignificant court at Köthen. Their disappointment is reflected in the minutes, signed by one Dr. Platz, which contain the now-famous sentence: "Since the best candidates turned out not to be available, we shall have to be satisfied with a mediocre one."

As time went on, the town fathers realized that, whereas Bach was an organist of indisputable stature, as a cantor he was less proficient. They took his compositions for granted as merely expected of someone employed by them, and his reputation throughout the region as an outstanding organist interested them only insofar as it tended to increase the reputation of Leipzig, site of a university and of important fairs.

Thus it happened, a few years before Christian's birth, that a memorable meeting of the town council took place in which the stubborn cantor was subjected to a formidable array of accusations. In the minutes it is reported that

> the said Bach did not deport himself as he should. . . . Without the mayor's knowledge he sent one of the choristers to the country. He left Leipzig without having obtained proper leave. . . . Councillor Lange: All the complaints about the cantor were true; he should be reprimanded. . . . Councillor Steger: Not only is the cantor lazy but he refuses to give explanations. He does not teach the singing lessons, and there are other complaints. It is time for a change; a breaking point has been reached; it would seem proper to make other arrangements. . . .

Interior of St. Thomas Church before it was remodeled in 1885.

Herr Hölzel: agrees.... It was resolved to reduce the cantor's salary. (Several express agreement.) Alderman Job: agrees, for the cantor has become incorrigible. Everyone agrees.

A dim view of the cantor's abilities and behavior! It might prompt us to remember that from the beginning Bach himself had not been entirely happy with his appointment. He confessed to his friend Erdmann that "at first it did not seem proper to change from Kapellmeister to cantor" but that he was willing to do so, hoping that this would enable his sons to study in Leipzig.

Kapellmeister? Cantor? These weren't mere questions of titles. They involved social standing and important professional interests. Such issues had for years caused heated debates that continued during Bach's tenure in Leipzig.

The meaning of these titles was explained by Mattheson, Bach's great opponent in North Germany. According to Mattheson, a cantor is

> a learned musician serving church and school. He gives thorough instruction to the young, teaching them the rudiments of music, especially of singing. He should be an experienced composer, well versed in church music, which he directs, to the glory of the Highest, the edification of the congregation, and the students' proper education.[3]

Bach never considered himself a servant of the school. Though a thrifty head of his household, he hired someone for an annual fifty taler, soon after he became cantor, so that he would not have to teach Latin to the third form. Most of his life he did not use the title "cantor," except in official correspondence. He preferred the title "Kapellmeister," which Mattheson defined as follows:

> A learned official at court and a highly accomplished composer. He supplies both sacred and secular music to an emperor, king, or other great ruler. He is in charge of such music, supervises and conducts it, to the glory of God, the delectation of his ruler, and for the benefit of the entire court.

Bach equally valued the title "director musices," although Mattheson frowned on this title:

> Some will belittle the beautiful title of cantor or organist.... Some who are unable to obtain the position of Kapellmeister through begging or insisting [a slur against Bach] would rather be called music director than cantor or organist. Some would settle for "chamber composer" or "court compositeur," though these are poor, patched-together, and un-German terms.

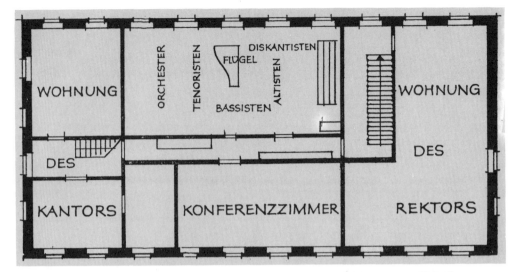

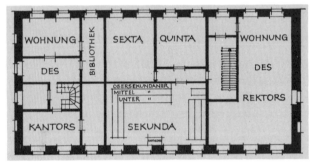

Floor plan of St. Thomas School, showing the close vicinity of Bach's, the cantor's, quarters to the class rooms and to the rector's living quarters. From bottom to top: ground floor, second and third floors.

Right: staircase in Bach's quarters.

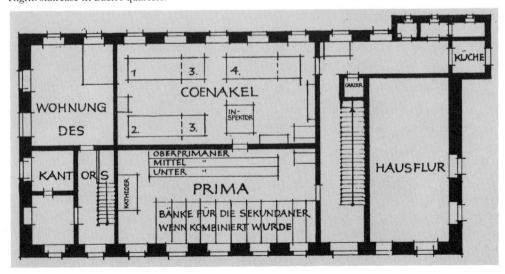

These were not Bach's feelings. He valued such titles and was always eager to be on good terms with the nobility. Though he had moved to Leipzig long ago, as cantor, he continued until 1728 to use the title of Kapellmeister to the Prince of Anhalt-Köthen. When that title expired with the prince's death, Bach was able to obtain the title of Kapellmeister to the prince of Saxony-Weissenfels. His good connections to the Weissenfels court helped, as did his marriage to a Weissenfels citizen. After the death of Duke Christian and the dissolution of the court chapel, Bach's wish of many years was granted: the Saxon elector bestowed on him the title "court composer." Henceforth Bach called himself "Court Composer and Kapellmeister to the King of Poland and Elector of Saxony; Kapellmeister and Director Musices in Leipzig."

No reference in this endless title to "cantor"! Was it vanity or self-aggrandizement? For a man like Bach this is unlikely. Impressive titles were a necessity when he looked for sources of income beyond what the cantor's position offered. He had many mouths to feed, Christian's now among them. An imposing title, and the social standing it implied, were apt to lead to extra commissions.

In a sense, such a title also offered the kind of protection Bach could well use in his tentative situation. The elector seldom interfered in such quarrels among his subjects, yet the title he had granted to Bach implied his esteem, causing the town fathers to exercise some caution.

The conflict almost put an end to Bach's work in Leipzig. Had it done so, young Christian's life might have taken a different direction. But, amazingly, a kind of armed truce was reached between town council and cantor. Although the elector's protection may have helped, Bach was probably saved by the man to whom he owed his happiest years at St. Thomas.

The man of the hour was Johann Matthias Gesner. Born in Roth, near Nürnberg, Gesner had accepted the rector's position in 1730, the year of crisis. He may have made his acceptance conditional upon the town council's refraining from further interference in Bach's work. Or maybe the town fathers hoped that Gesner's appointment would provide one last opportunity to establish a workable arrangement with the obstinate cantor.

Gesner was enthusiastic about the singing and playing of the Thomaner (whereas his successor, Ernesti, would refer to them as "beer fiddlers"). A superior who was appreciative and tolerant—this was exactly what Bach needed for his professional well-being and survival. Without Gesner's backing, it is unlikely that Bach would have dared to offer the elector his services as composer for the court chapel, which was Roman Catholic. This Bach did in his application of 27 July 1733, requesting that he be granted an appointment as Saxon Court Composer.[4] The possible repercussions, had the elector approved Sebastian's request, may be better appreciated in light of the accusations of "treason" to which Christian was later subjected when he became a Roman Catholic. At the very least, it would have resulted in a situation that would have been somewhat absurd for the time: Father Bach would have been supplying compositions to the Catholic court chapel in Dresden while his son Friedemann was employed as organist at the Protestant St. Sophie's Church in the same city.

Gesner's tenure, which was so advantageous for Bach, unfortunately lasted only four years, after which the rector accepted a prestigious position in Göttingen.

At the time of Christian's birth, Bach was still hoping that Ernesti would be another congenial superior. Upon his appointment, Bach had duly honored him with the cantata *Thomana sass annoch betrübet*. He had previously chosen Ernesti as the godfather of another child, the son Johann August Abraham, who died two days after his birth. To have Ernesti serve once more as godfather, this time for Christian, could have established a lasting friendship between rector and cantor; but it soon appeared that this was not to be. Bach's personality was not entirely to blame; there were other causes, related to the changing times. In the age of the Enlightenment, the old-fashioned *Kantorei* was on its way out as an institution, so whether Bach was a good or a bad cantor was not particularly significant. A confrontation with Ernesti was bound to occur, as he was one of the Enlightenment's foremost representatives. In spite of his youth, Ernesti was considered a major philologist, writer, and editor of the classics, a capable individual who was to impart new life and new directions to St. Thomas School. For him, St. Thomas was primarily an institution of learning. He had ambitious plans for the school, and he did not want them jeopardized by the traditional emphasis on music. The primacy of music was indeed a threat to academic excellence, for the students' musical obligations to the church were many. Singing at weddings and funerals, and the widespread "singing for alms," occupied too much of the youngsters' time and energies. Running from one such service to the next was tiring and resulted in canceled or postponed classes.

Moreover, cantors traditionally required their students to copy music, and Bach seems to have been no exception, for years later his successor Doles defended himself for doing so by pointing out that in Bach's time

Top left: Rector Gesner, who compared the singing of the St. Thomas schoolboys to "angelic choirs."

Top right: Gesner's successor, Ernesti, who compared them to "beer fiddlers" and objected to the students' singing for alms (below), one of the poorer students' chief sources of pocket money.

"[the students] were expected to copy music far more frequently than they do now." Given Ernesti's vision of the school, it comes as no surprise that he did not approve of the practice. Bach, on the other hand, was unwilling to forgo any extra income that depended on using students for copying, and this inevitably led to quarrels with his rector.

According to school regulations, Bach was also entitled to use student prefects as substitute teachers, thus freeing his own time. His good business sense made him reluctant to miss out on any opportunity to have his music performed. But there was a problem: Bach's compositions were so difficult that they required extra rehearsals. If these were not to be granted (and Ernesti took a dim view of them), his works might receive substandard performances. When it came to standards, Bach was unwilling to make any concessions; after all, his reputation was at stake. And since Ernesti was aiming for similarly high academic standards, a clash was unavoidable. Ten months after Christian's baptism, an altercation began in which both sides fought fiercely. The conflict that set it off was actually quite trivial, but it turned into what became known as the battle of the prefects, seeming to prove that great men can get excited and fight over small matters. The real issue, however, was whether the mission of the school should be musical or academic excellence. How unfortunate that no middle ground could be reached, for men of Bach's and Ernesti's caliber might have accomplished much had they worked together instead of against each other.

The story of the battle is quickly told. Basically it was a question of who had the authority to appoint prefects, the rector or the cantor. This disagreement was aggravated when Ernesti dismissed a student named Krause, who had been Bach's favorite. For his part, Bach wanted nothing to do with Ernesti's favorite, whose name, curiously enough, was also Krause. Bach's ire did not subside at the church door. Ernesti's Krause twice attempted to direct the chorus primus, and twice Bach chased him away, the second time "with much screaming and yelling," declaring that he "would not stand for it, no matter what." Such a row, needless to say, greatly amused the Thomaner, who gleefully observed the dispute among their superiors.

At the height of this affair, Ernesti did not hesitate to resort to innuendo and calumny. Bach, he stated, "treated the truth so casually that one cannot always rely on his testimony. Was it possible for a taler to produce a descant singer who is no more qualified [to sing high notes] than I am?" The implication was that Bach had accepted bribes from parents who were eager to have their sons admitted to the school. Nothing could be substantiated, but we can note the bitterness and anger that motivated both sides.

No victor emerged in this affair, which had both serious and comical aspects. The quarrels continued until the spring of 1738. Only then did the elector's intervention result in some satisfaction for Bach, so that the authorities let him alone while they waited impatiently for a more tractable successor.

One should not overestimate the impact of these squabbles on Bach. From what we know about him, they are not likely to have upset him profoundly. To the contrary, they merely stimulated the fighter in him and kindled the desire to vindicate himself. But these events did cast a shadow over Christian's formative years. Since they occurred during his early childhood, he may have not have been conscious of their effect, but they surely left an impression on his sensitive personality, especially as further clouds were brewing on the horizon, this time affecting the father more personally.

First there was the sad story of Bach's third-eldest son, Johann Gottfried Bernhard, whom Christian was never to know. Among the Bach children, Christian's lot may have been the happiest and Bernhard's the saddest. Bach probably came to reproach himself for having allowed Bernhard to enter a professional career before he had acquired a solid education at the university as Friedemann and Emanuel had done.

Father Bach may have had his reasons. Young Rector Ernesti had been in office for just a year when the conflicts began. Bach's position was thus less secure than ever, his future uncertain. It seemed important for him to know that Bernhard was taken care of, professionally and financially, and he did everything to smooth his way.

In 1735, a few months before Christian's birth, the position of organist at St. Mary's Church in Mühlhausen, Thuringia, became vacant when the incumbent died. Bach's thoughts went back twenty-five years to when, as young organist, he himself had been employed at St. Blasius Church in the same town. Mühlhausen was a free city, administered by six mayors and forty-two city councillors. Bach had started his family there with Maria Barbara; they had had many friends. But his tenure had come to an end when disagreements surfaced among the church elders on matters of dogma. A poor organ and other obstacles had also contributed.

Yet Bach's connections to Mühlhausen were still good, and Bernhard was invited to come for an audition, even though the application deadline had long passed, and town officials who were active in the church would have preferred a local applicant. Withal, Bernhard was appointed, but his tenure turned out to be ill-fated and short-lived, characterized by constant quarrels.[5]

Troubles arose immediately involving the widow of his predecessor, Johann Gottfried Hetzehen, who came from an old Mühlhausen family whose members were still influential on the town council. Hetzehen's son-in-law Bernigau was a town councillor and administrator of St. Mary's. All along, he and his followers had favored a certain Götze, who had become the acting organist after Hetzehen's death. This remained a source of friction.

Hetzehen's widow claimed the traditional half-year's salary of her deceased husband, to which she was all the more entitled, it would seem, having initially paid a substitute organist out of her own pocket. Bernhard, however, claimed the entire salary for himself, retroactively, out of which he intended to pay the former substitute. There was some legal validity to Bernhard's claim, but it was a matter of interpreting church law, and it would certainly have looked better had Bernhard assumed a more conciliatory attitude toward an old, bereft widow. Instead, he antagonized most of the council members and suffered an unnecessary defeat, at the same time giving the impression of being a hard-hearted young man who thought only of his own advantage.

The inevitable consequence soon fell out: barely three months after Bernhard's appointment, members of the town council filed a complaint. "Too many overlong organ preludes" were reducing the time allotted to the service as such. The organist did not pay enough attention to "the beautiful hymns to which the local congregation were accustomed," and he "interfered in their singing with [unsuitable] organ playing." Councillor Werneburg even feared that "if Herr Pache [sic] continues to play in his customary manner, the organ will be ruined in two years and most parishioners will be deaf."

In this and other ways Bernhard seems to have been very much his father's son. Sebastian, too, had been fond of "pulling all the stops, playing with the fullest possible sound." Other council members, remembering the famed Johann Sebastian, sided with Bernhard. Mayor Petri declared:

> We should thank the Lord that we have a talented, skillful organist, and we should neither order him to cut short his preludes nor to play in a less artful manner. If we had wanted a blunderer, we should not have looked for an artist from out of town. Such artistic playing neither ruins the organ nor causes anyone to become deaf.

But conflicts refused to abate. When it became necessary to renovate the organ and Bernhard's wishes were ignored, he asked for his father's help in obtaining a new position in Sangerhausen. What he did not tell his father was that he had other reasons for wanting to leave Mühlhausen. He had incurred debts (something unthinkable for Father Bach), and his creditors were pressing him.

Unsuspecting, Bach turned to Mayor Klemm in Sangerhausen, with whose family he had been on good terms for many years. Klemm put in a good word for Bernhard, who, in his organ audition in St. James Church, once more showed himself to be superior to all other applicants. Surprisingly, we would think, his Mühlhausen employers furnished a statement testifying to his good conduct, and nothing stood in the way of his appointment.

Things augured well for a new beginning, or so Johann Sebastian thought. It therefore came as a severe blow when news reached him, a mere ten months after Bernhard's appointment, that his son had disappeared overnight, leaving behind debts of various kinds, as in Mühlhausen, including overdue rent payments. For the father, a good Christian and a solid citizen, this news amounted to a catastophe. A Bach son an impostor? Bitterness and great disappointment speak from his letter to Klemm:

> I hear with utter dismay that [Bernhard] has again incurred debts, has not changed his ways at all, and has absented himself without revealing to me his present whereabouts. What can I say or do? No admonitions, no loving care and assistance, are of any avail, and so I must bear my cross patiently and leave my derelict son to God's mercy.

When Klemm's wife pressed Bach about the money Bernhard owed for rent, Bach's reply reveals both pride and despair:

> May the noble, much-honored lady not take it amiss if I cannot respond to her communication in the affirmative. Before I can do so, there needs to be a written confirmation [of the debt] from my (alas, derelict) son. I must also know whether he has returned, so that I can then act accordingly. As for myself, I have not seen him since I came to Sangerhausen a year ago.

But Bernhard never came home. The Sangerhausen authorities reported his disappearance to the consistory in Leipzig, and Bach, to his embarrassment, had to beg for a period of grace for his son, since the town council had decided to look for a new organist. The grace period was granted—surprisingly, in view of the anti-Bach sentiment in

Title page of the song collection *Singende Muse an der Pleisse* by Sperontes (1736), praising popular music-making in Leipzig's coffee gardens.

A student serenade. J. S. Bach wrote music for such occasions.

The Leipzig Promenade, a social meeting place located directly behind St. Thomas School.

Leipzig—and the authorities in Sangerhausen continued, unsuccessfully, to search for Bernhard until 15 October 1738.

Bernhard was actually staying in Jena, not far from Leipzig. A relative, Johann Nicolaus Bach, had taken him in. The fugitive now registered at the university as a law student. Johann Nicolaus, organist in Jena and getting on in years, had recently lost his only son, and he may have considered it providential when the young relative appeared at this time.

Bernhard never again resumed contact with his father. Perhaps he wanted to put the past behind him and to embark on an academic education, presenting himself to his father only when he could show that he had changed his ways. But on 27 May 1739, according to church records, he died "from a fever." His brief life ended sixteen days after his twenty-fourth birthday. Not a single one of his compositions has been preserved.

It was a grievous loss for Bach, not only personally but also professionally. Among his sons, next to Friedemann, Bernhard seems to have been closest to him artistically. At that point it would have been helpful if there had been someone else in the family who sided with him in musical matters. It was a time of drastic change in musical taste, in the ways people listened and responded to music. Sebastian had reason for concern: for the first time, voices were repeatedly heard in public that seriously criticized "old Bach," his compositions, and his view of the musical world in which he lived.

One of the voices was that of Ernesti's contemporary, the twenty-nine-year-old Johann Adolph Scheibe. Bach knew and highly esteemed the young man's father, organ builder Johann Scheibe in Leipzig, but it was the son in Hamburg who set off a barrage against Bach. Inspired by his teacher Gottsched and his *Critische Dichtung*, Scheibe, who was himself well-read and a good writer, had begun in 1737 to publish the weekly *Critischer Musikus*, which appeared every Tuesday and became a mouthpiece for his new views on music.[6]

When the *Musikus* was barely two months old, Scheibe began a frontal attack on Bach, in the form of a fictitious letter. Though Bach was not at first mentioned by name, it soon became obvious that he was the intended target. Scheibe began the letter by respectfully referring to "the most illustrious among musicians," to "an extraordinary performer at the clavier and at the organ." It defies comprehension, he continued,

> that his fingers and feet could move and cross each other with such amazing agility, making the widest leaps without missing a single note and without upsetting his equilibrium by such violent motions.

Having paid tribute to Bach the virtuoso, Scheibe got down to business. "This greatness," he continued, "would gain the admiration of entire nations if he did not deprive his compositions of being natural by imbuing them with bombast and confusion, obscuring their beauty by excessive artifice." He accused Bach of being the victim of his own great skill when expecting singers and instrumentalists to produce the sounds that he could produce on the organ. Bach's habit of writing down with notes even the most minute ornaments not only robs his music of the "beauty of harmony" but also "obscures the melody."

Scheibe's clever strategy of praising the performer as a means of all the more violently attacking the composer caused one contemporary to say that Scheibe had "patted Herr Bach with one hand while scratching his face with the other." In fact, the chronicler continues, he had not only scratched Bach but "stabbed him fiercely" at the end of his diatribe. There Scheibe had compared Bach to Caspar Daniel von Lohenstein, a seventeenth-century writer of heroic tragedies:

> What Herr Lohenstein is in literature, [Bach] is in music. Bombastic writing caused both to stray from what is noble to what is obscure. We can only admire their hard work, taking so much trouble—but it is in vain, for it is an affront to reason.

This is strong language, but Scheibe was not alone in his thinking. He had only stated, with youthful abandon, what was generally preached as the gospel of new music during this age that coincided with Christian's childhood. The natural beauty of a single voice, of melody in general, was to take the place of "artificial" polyphony. The confusion caused by hearing different voices at the same time was to be replaced by simple, expressive, easily comprehended melody. This view was well set forth in another publication, the *Wöchentliche Nachrichten und Anmerkungen* (Weekly News and Commentary):

> It is melody that enchants us, moves the soul, and at times evokes indescribable pleasure. Melody is to music what beautiful thoughts are to a well-executed speech, what expression is to painting, animating every part with gentle feelings. Melody is beautiful as nature is beautiful. Without melody, music would be coarse and dry, like uncultivated fields in which only thorns and thistles grow.[7]

"Back to nature!" was the catchword of the day, and naturalness was expected to counteract the alleged deterioration of traditional counterpoint. Concern with such decline and decay was voiced in many places,

especially in Italy. Count Benvenuto di San Raffaele, royal school director in Turin, enveighed against the previous

> barbaric fondness for fugues and canons, for all confusing contrapuntal
> webs. Such disgusting boasting about harmonic artifice, this gothic cus-
> tom of constructing musical riddles . . . , this music, which looks good
> but has a repulsive sound . . . , void of taste and melody, only observing
> the rules . . . , unpleasant, cold, confused, and lacking expression, mel-
> ody, and charm: what can it accomplish except boring the sleepy lis-
> tener to death?[8]

Even some of Bach's faithful followers conceded that during his lifetime contrapuntal artifice had indeed been carried to extremes and that
polyphony was threatening to become routine, turning much music "into
empty, meaningless noise." So said Forkel, the Bach biographer, who had
translated Count Benvenuto's essay. But in a conciliatory footnote, Forkel added that "such abuses do not deprive counterpoint of its essential
worth, as long as it is properly employed."

Two factions developed. Some writers, such as the cantor Petri, considered "the musical changes that evolved around 1740 and continue" to
be a "great catastrophe," while to others they heralded "a new age of
music." The latter view was held by Johann Elias Bach, a cousin of
Johann Sebastian, who urged one of his relatives to choose Berlin as a
good place for a musician.

Traditional counterpoint coexisted for some time with the new reign
of melody; indeed, it was never considered completely invalid. But adherents of the new music did not think it essential, and the balance was definitely tilted towards "singing melody." Why polyphony, with many parts,
when what was most important could be expressed in one part—the top
part? As the learned Adlung put it, "the right hand might include some
polyphonic elaborations . . . but melody is best."[9]

Many writers on music theory now embraced the new emphasis on
melody and squarely opposed Bach as the leading practitioner of counterpoint. Among the first of these writers, Scheibe is now known to have
been an advocate of melody long before he stated his views in the *Critischer Musikus*. His *Compendium Musices*, a treatise written around 1730,
was only recently discovered in a private library. In it, Scheibe called
melodia naturalis the principle, the essence, of all music and asserted that
man has an inborn tendency to listen for melody. The purpose of music is
to "delight the ear," and this is accomplished by music that is "altogether
agreeable, especially by featuring concise melody (*bündiger gesang*)."[10]

In his *Compendium*, Scheibe compared German, Italian, and French composers and asked "whether it might not be possible to combine the fairest qualities of these three nations in one single musical composition." He then answered his own question in the affirmative:

> The Italians strive for pleasantness and for spirited embellishment of melody, for good taste. The French favor lively and free expression, while the Germans stress good and thorough harmony. Whoever can combine these three is bound to produce a beautiful work.

His praise of German composers is combined with some reservations. They may be able to write "French and Italian music as well as the French and Italians, but they often include too much artifice and elaboration ... at the expense of melody." These words anticipate Scheibe's later diatribe against Bach in the *Critischer Musikus*.

It seems ironic that Scheibe's concept of *melodia naturalis* and his prophetic vision of a "European" composer prepare the ground on which Christian was later to celebrate his greatest triumphs—he, the youngest son of the man Scheibe had attacked so vigorously.

Given Scheibe's concordance with the spirit of the times, it is not surprising that the famous Lessing considered him to be the leading writer on music. Even in our own century Scheibe has been called "with Mattheson the most intelligent of the German musicologists."[11]

Mattheson, four years older than Bach and just as versatile, was in a far better position than Scheibe to become Bach's greatest adversary. Whereas Scheibe's words and tone might be written off as the typical outbursts of an angry young man, Mattheson's opinions were bound to be taken more seriously.

Mattheson never attacked Bach by name; he was too much of a diplomat for that. He was also a man of many talents and accomplishments: opera singer, composer, Kapellmeister, keyboard player, director of church music—and author, which may have made Bach feel somewhat ill at ease. Bach was not given to wordy, theoretical discourse. He wrote no treatises, no polemic pamphlets, only annotations to a few of his own works.

Mattheson said of himself that the number of books he had written was equal to his age. At the time, this amounted to no less than eighty-two (among which he may have included the translations he prepared while in the diplomatic service). He opposed Bach in a field often considered Bach's very own: church music. His writings on the subject were not personal but took the form of theses that must have seemed revolutionary

Above right: Title page of Scheibe's *Critischer Musikus*.

Above right: Johann Mattheson, author of *Der vollkommene Capellmeister.*

Below: A page from Chapter Five of the *Capellmeister:* "On the Art of Writing a Good Melody."

Fünfftes Haupt = Stück.

Von der Kunst eine gute Melodie zu machen.

*** *** ***

§. 1.

Die Melopöie ist eine wirckende Geschicklichkeit *) in Erfindung und Verfertigung solcher singbaren Sätze, daraus dem Gehör ein Vergnügen entstehet.

§. 2.

Diese Kunst, eine gute Melodie zu machen, begreifft das wesentlichste in der Music. Es ist dannenhero höchstens zu verwundern, daß ein solcher Haupt=Punct, an welchem doch das grösseste gelegen ist, bis diese Stunde fast von iedem Lehrer hintangesetzet wird. Ja man hat so gar wenig darauf gedacht, daß auch die vornehmsten Meister, und unter denselben die weitläuffigsten und **) neuesten, gestehen müssen: es sey fast unmöglich, gewisse Regeln davon zu geben, unter dem Vorwande, weil das meiste auf den guten Geschmack ankäme; da doch auch von diesem selbst die gründlichsten Regeln gegeben werden könnnen und müssen: im eigentlichen Verstande frage man nur geschickte Köche; im verblümten die Sittenlehrer, Redner und ***) Dichter.

§. 3.

Also legen jene Verfasser ihre Schwäche und schlechte Einsicht, betreffend das allernothwendigste Stück melodischer Wissenschafft, mehr als zu viel an den Tag. Andre hergegen, die doch sonst alles wissen wollen, handeln in diesem Fall noch etwas klüger, indem sie in ihren grossen Büchern lieber gantz und gar still davon schweigen.

in the Hamburg of 1728. In his essay *Der Musicalische Patriot*, Mattheson demands that "theatrical style" be used in church music. Just as the world resembles a theater, church music must also be "theatrical" if it is to induce "virtuous feelings." Who could deny that "both music and theater had been invented and introduced solely to serve religion?"[12]

These were unusual demands from a German, and from a director of church music at that. But Mattheson also practiced the progress he preached. In 1715, during a Christmas service in the Hamburg cathedral, it was he who allowed women to sing publicly in church for the first time.

John Christian Bach was four years old when Mattheson published the *Vollkommene Capellmeister*, his most important work and greatest accomplishment. At the age of eighty-five, completely deaf, he penned his theses, almost five hundred pages of them. They were the work of an authority, based on the experience of half a century in the service of music. No fewer than 164 paragraphs are devoted to his favorite topic: "On the art of writing a good melody." He justified this emphasis by telling the reader that he believed, "still, and above all else, that a single melody is the most beautiful and most natural thing in the world." With a glancing blow against the contrapuntists, and against Bach as their leader, he continued: "Everyone strives for many voices [polyphony], yet what is lacking most in the works of these highly accomplished practitioners is melody."[13]

At the beginning Mattheson formulated the "basic precept of all music: Everyone must sing well!" After all, we often "derive more pleasure from listening to a single, well-modulated voice singing a pure melody than from hearing twenty-four at the same time without understanding what it is all about." After expounding on various aspects of melody, Mattheson proposed seven rules:

1. All melodies must contain something that is familiar to all.
2. Everything that is forced, far-fetched, and heavy must be avoided.
3. One must follow nature above all, and only then, custom.
4. Avoid that which is overly artful; at least, do not let it stand out.
5. In this it is better to follow the French than the Italians.
6. A melody must be within the reach of [singable by] everyone.
7. Brevity is preferable to length.

The advocates of melody now had their manifesto, and it was to remain in effect for a long time. Forty years later, an anxious father wrote his son a letter in which Mattheson's ideas are repeated almost verbatim.

It was Leopold Mozart in Salzburg, writing to Wolfgang in Paris, citing
Christian Bach as a model.

> Short—light—popular: . . . do you really consider that kind of writing
> demeaning? Not at all! [Christian] Bach in London published nothing
> but such small things. What is *little* is *great* if it is natural, if it flows
> along smoothly and is well put together. It is more difficult to write that
> way than to produce complicated harmonies that are *difficult to perform*
> and *not understood* by most listeners. Good writing, well ordered, *il
> filo*—that is what distinguishes a master from a bungler, even in small
> things.[14]

When Mozart received this letter he was twenty-two years old. His
reply indicates that he intended to take his father's admonitions to heart.
He wrote from Paris that most of his symphonies are not according to the
local taste, continuing that

> if time permits, I shall revise several of my violin concertos, shortening
> them. In Germany we like things to be long, but short and sweet really
> is better.

We should remember that this exchange of letters took place fourteen years after Mozart had met Bach's youngest son. As a person and as
an artist, Christian had made a strong impression on the eight-year-old
Mozart. A direct line leads from Scheibe's and Mattheson's concept of
melody to the great melodists of the second half of the century, that is, to
John Christian Bach and Mozart.

Returning to Father Bach: in spite of Mattheson's writings, Bach felt
attacked only by Scheibe, and so his defense was aimed only at him.
Interestingly enough, Bach, who corresponded effortlessly and at length
with princes and other authorities, showed no interest in engaging in a
scientific dispute to defend his cause, even at the risk of being charged by
Scheibe with a lack of knowledge. He left his defense to others, in this
case to Johann Abraham Birnbaum, a professor of rhetoric at Leipzig
University. While Birnbaum played the piano passably well, he was no
match for someone like Scheibe who was well versed in theoretical and
practical music. With Birnbaum as his champion, a sweeping victory for
Bach was out of the question.

Nor did it help much to have Lorenz Mizler, another Bach admirer,
offer the platform of his *Musicalische Bibliothek* for the publication of
Birnbaum's *Unparteyische Anmerkungen über eine bedenkliche Stelle im sech-
sten Stück des critischen Musikus* (Impartial Remarks Concerning a Problematic Passage in Part Six of the *Critischer Musikus*). The long title is

Instrumental accompaniment of church music in Bach's time.

indicative of the author's labored approach; he provided a wordy, tiresome piece intended to set Scheibe straight.

Birnbaum consistently referred to Bach as "Herr Hofcompositeur" and went on, page after page, to prove that the term *Musikant* [a practicing musician, usually an instrumentalist—trans.] would not do justice to a man of Bach's stature. Even *artist* seemed inadequate. Quibbling about words was the forte of Birnbaum the rhetorician, but this made it all the easier for Scheibe to shine when it came to music.

In his eagerness to defend "the honor of the Herr Hofcompositeur, as well as my own," Birnbaum stooped embarrasingly low: he accused Scheibe of "one-eyed intellect," a tactless allusion to the fact that Scheibe, as the result of an accident at age six, had lost the sight in his right eye.

Bach seems at first to have been amused by the battle of words. Later, when Birnbaum's defense did not have the desired results, amusement must have given way to disappointment. At any rate, when Birnbaum died a few years later, Bach, in a letter to Elias, merely mentioned as an afterthought that "Master Birnbaum was buried six weeks ago."

Bach did make efforts to adjust to the changing times—early efforts at that. In a memorandum to the Leipzig town council, dated 23 August 1730, he requested better conditions for his pupils at St. Thomas School. This was necessary because

> in recent times music has changed greatly. It has risen a great deal, and there are remarkable changes in taste. Thus the old kind of music no longer sounds good to our ears.

We also learn from Emanuel that "in recent times" (that is, during Christian's youth) Bach had come to appreciate contemporary composers who really belonged to the other camp: Hasse, the Graun brothers, the two Bendas, and "in fact, all who were highly esteemed in Berlin and Dresden."

Nor was Bach the composer out of touch with the trends of the time. Lorenz Mizler mentions a Bach cantata, unfortunately lost, "performed by local students during the Leipzig Easter fair [of 1738] in the presence of His Majesty, the King of Poland." Whoever heard this cantata would confirm that "it represented in every detail the most modern taste and found unanimous approval. It is clear that the Herr Kapellmeister is well acquainted with his audiences' tastes."

Essentially, however, Bach continued to opt for tradition. After Christian's birth the flood of his works diminished. As much as he could, he relied on earlier compositions to fulfill his obligations as cantor at St. Thomas and channeled his energies into sorting out and putting in order his life's work, assembling manuscripts and preparing them for the engraver. The few new major works were instructional in purpose; perhaps he wanted to provide a monument of established and time-honored polyphony for the adherents of the new, melodic style (which he did not think would last).

The rift, stylistically speaking, went right through Bach's own family. Friedemann, as could be expected, followed in his father's footsteps. He was sure enough of himself to defend their common cause, to go publicly on record for "the honor of harmony" and against the "ear-tickling" and "bouncing" melodies of the others. Comments from Dresden about Friedemann's early works always refer to him as "the true, respected son of Sebastian." Emanuel, too, found words of praise for his older brother: "More than any of the rest of us, [Friedemann] could easily take the place of our father." This may be a dubious compliment from Emanuel, who was physically farthest away, having entered the service of the young Prussian king in Berlin, for he had also gone his own way as a composer, and neither Sebastian nor Friedemann were enchanted. When Emanuel's keyboard sonatas were published, Friedemann dismissed them as "pleasant little things," while Father Bach, also not impressed, talked of "colors that will soon fade." As we see, members of the Bach family did not mince words when discussing each other's compositions. Even Christian, a little later, would not be exempt from his family's candor.

Friedemann soon found that he was in the wrong camp—a bitter experience for the young composer. Having written a number of keyboard sonatas, he was careful to begin by publishing only one, in 1746. It was a failure. As Forkel reported, with regret: "No one bought it because no one could play it." Friedemann was thus subjected to the same criticism as his father: that what he put down on paper merely represented his own virtuoso style of performing, with every single embellishment, even the most minute, written out.

It is true that members of the Dresden court chapel would always congregate whenever "the old Bach" gave one of his legendary organ recitals in that city. And they would even gladly accompany Friedemann to Leipzig, considering it an honor to participate in one of Bach's famous house concerts. But these actions merely reflected their high opinion of Friedemann's father. Friedemann himself was a loner. He was cast out less because of his personality than because of his style of composition, in which this oldest Bach son closely followed the road his father had traveled. By the time Friedemann was admitted to St. Thomas School, Sebastian had already taken care of his preliminary enrollment at the university. Only after four years in Leipzig studying law, philosophy, and mathematics did Friedemann turn to a career in music. He may have been encouraged in the pursuit of mathematics by Lorenz Mizler, a fellow student and frequent visitor at the Bachs' home. Not unlike the mathematician and philosopher Leibnitz, Mizler viewed music as "mathematics in sound." He went on to lecture on music history at the university and later founded the Society of Musical Science, which Sebastian Bach eventually joined, after much hesitation.[15]

But for Friedemann the academic education proved less help than hindrance to his career as a composer. With so much erudition, he did not have close ties to the Saxon court, where a different kind of music was in vogue. August the Strong, the previous ruler, had also acquired the crown of Poland and had converted to Catholicism. During his reign, the Dresden court—formerly given to the cultivation of rather unassuming Protestant church music—had turned into a center of resplendent music making. Catholic Masses were performed on a grand scale, and lavish opera productions were mounted.

August's son Friedrich August had married the music-loving Austrian archduchess Maria Josepha. Under him the court chapel orchestra developed into an ensemble of European standing, on a par with Berlin's. Its members included the foremost string and wind players of Germany, Bohemia, and Italy. Their leader was Pisendel, the violin virtuoso who, it was said, would not allow any composition to be performed until he had carefully marked all orchestral parts, so that even the first rehearsals had virtually the quality of a performance. The result was a felicitous combination of Italian musical élan and German thoroughness as reflected in disciplined rehearsing. No wonder even Italians raved that whoever wanted to hear Italian music performed to perfection should go to Dresden.

Given these circumstances, Dresden was not the place for Friedemann; his compositions were too modern for the old but too old-fashioned for the young. He was even unable to make a name for himself in the field of church music, the traditional domain of the Bachs. At one point the position of organist at the Church of Our Lady became vacant. It commanded a larger salary than the post at St. Sophie's, and it carried special prestige because of the organ, built by Silbermann and inaugurated by Johann Sebastian Bach. But Friedemann's application was turned down in favor of Gottfried August Homilius, a pupil of Sebastian.

Above left: Elector Friedrich August II of Saxony, patron of opera in Dresden.

Above right: Bach's friend Johann Adolf Hasse, the uncrowned king of opera.

Below: Interior of the Dresden opera house.

Friedemann was always glad to visit his paternal home. Cousin Elias said of gatherings there that

> some specially fine music would then be heard. [Friedemann] stayed [in Leipzig] for four weeks, along with the famous lutenist Weis [sic, Sylvius Leopold Weiss, 1686–1750] and Herr Kropfgans [both members of the Dresden court chapel]. We heard them several times.

These visits by Friedemann (who, like his father, seems to have over-stayed his leave) were among Christian's first musical impressions, enriched by the presence of other colleagues and admirers of Bach. Emanuel noted with pride: "Few masters of music would pass through this city without paying a visit to my father and playing for him."

If we count the many lessons given in the family home and the rehearsals of sacred and secular works, which continued to be Bach's responsibility, that took place next door, Christian grew up surrounded by music. At times the father may have taken Christian along to various musical events such as concerts by the Collegium Musicum, which Sebastian used to direct and for which he still supplied compositions. And we need not exclude the possibility that Christian accompanied his father to Dresden, as Friedemann had done, "to listen to the nice little songs," as Bach jokingly described attending the opera.

True, the musical impressions Christian received in public were man-ifold, but what he heard at home generally bore Sebastian's imprint. Father Bach looked increasingly backward and considered himself the last representative of a glorious past, a guardian of the art of polyphony. His rhetorical question "what is left of art if it is no longer artful?" amounts to a statement of his creed. He may have realized that he was not the right one to train his youngest son as a musician according to the most recent precepts; he therefore concentrated on providing him with a solid foundation—with the tools of the trade as practiced by proponents of the old school.

Biographer Forkel described Bach's teaching technique, basing his account on reports by Friedemann and Emanuel. According to these, Bach first instructed his pupils "in his own method of touching the keys." To learn this, "they spent several months solely on practicing individual pieces for all ten fingers, always striving for a clean and clear touch. No one could complete these studies in less than a few months. Bach himself thought they should be continued for at least six to twelve months."[16]

These were rigorous preliminary exercises for mastering the traditional polyphonic style of playing, of which Bach was such a supreme exponent. They required so much patience, perseverance, and industry that they must have turned away many a pupil. But Bach tolerated no compromises. When someone asked him about the beginnings of his own road to mastery, he modestly replied, according to Forkel, "I had to be industrious. Whoever is equally industrious can accomplish just as much." It seems, however, that Bach was willing to bend a little after all, for Forkel goes on to say that

> if after a few months a student seemed ready to give up, Bach would encourage him by writing for him small, connected pieces in which the exercises would be applied. The *Six Little Preludes for Beginners* are of this type, and even more so the fifteen *Two-Part Inventions*. Bach wrote these down during the lessons, mindful of the particular needs of the student in question. Later he revised them, crafting them into small but beautiful, expressive works of art.

Only after the basics had been mastered would Bach introduce his students to his own larger works, playing them and remarking, "This is how it should sound." At times when he felt like it, Bach would deviate from formal teaching. Ernst Ludwig Gerber, the editor of the *Historisch-biographisches Lexicon der Tonkünstler* (1791), recalls:

> Among my father's [a Bach pupil] most delightful memories were the times when Bach, claiming not to be in the mood for teaching, would sit down at one of his magnificent instruments. Then the hours passed as though they were minutes.

Quite likely Christian experienced some such teaching, except when his father was away from Leipzig or preoccupied with engraving one of his compositions. On those occasions one of the advanced students, such as Altnikol, who was later to become Sebastian's son-in-law, would act as substitute.

Although one might suppose that Sebastian would have introduced his then-favorite son to music at an earlier age, he did not actually begin giving lessons to Friedemann until the boy had reached his ninth birthday. It is doubtful, however, that he waited so long with Christian. In the last decade of his life, Bach concentrated on what seemed most important to him. Perhaps realizing that his time was running out, he probably opted for an earlier start for his youngest son—a supposition substantiated by the fact that Christian, as a youth, was already able to amaze the public with his masterful performances at the keyboard.

Only once, some thirty years later, did Christian himself comment specifically on his childhood. His opera *Temistocle* had achieved a brilliant success on the Mannheim stage, and he had been invited to one of the sumptuous receptions that the elector Karl Theodor was fond of giving at his summer residence, Schwetzingen. Talking to Cannabich and Wendling, members of the famed Mannheim orchestra, Christian recalled that once, when he had been improvising at the keyboard, he had, "without thinking," improperly ended his playing on a six-four chord. His father, presumably asleep, had abruptly risen, boxed Christian's ears, and "resolved" the six-four chord.[17]

This amusing little incident does suggest that young Christian, during the years under Sebastian's tutelage, was subjected to the customary strict supervision as an instrumentalist and as a budding composer. The earliest known example of Christian's musical handwriting is an entry in the album of someone whose identity is unknown. The thirteen-year-old Christian arranged the polonaise from his father's Orchestra Suite in B Minor, in a version for clavier, transposed to D minor. He added the words: "With this small token of my esteem I recommend myself to the owner of this album. Johann Christian Bach."

Another copy of this D-minor polonaise exists in what may have been in one of the "Clavier-Büchlein" that Father Bach was fond of preparing for members of his immediate family. It is likely that Bach assembled such a small instruction book for his youngest son, as he had done for Friedemann and for his young wife, Anna Magdalena.[18] This particular collection, which is incomplete, contains keyboard pieces by Bach and his sons, including Christian.

As Christian's mother, Anna Magdalena must have been delighted when her young son displayed the first signs of musical talent. She came from a family of town musicians and organists and was the daughter of a court trumpeter. She sang at the Köthen court when she was a mere fifteen years old. Because of her deep admiration for her considerably older husband, she must have been saddened that none of her own children had so far seemed destined to follow in the footsteps of her stepsons Friedemann and Emanuel, whom Bach had proudly described in a letter to his school friend Erdmann as born musicians. "I can arrange a fine concert, with voices and instruments, using [only] members of my family."

But those days ended when the older sons left home. The children who remained were Dorothea, a somewhat older daughter from Bach's first marriage who was not without musical talent, and Anna Magdalena's issue: a boy who was mentally handicapped, a nine-year-old girl, and

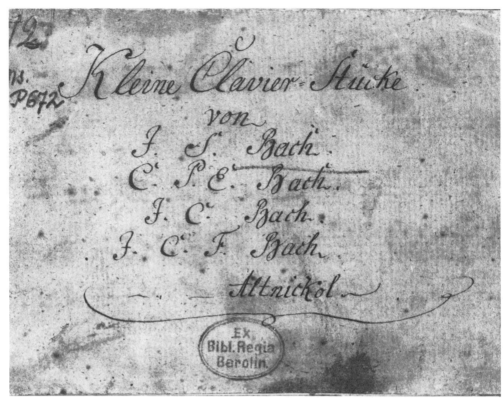

A collection of short keyboard pieces assembled by J. S. Bach. Aside from his own pieces there are compositions by Emanuel and Friedrich Bach, J. S. Bach's pupil Altnikol, and small pieces by John Christian Bach.

The first known music autograph by Christian Bach, then thirteen years old. The identity of the dedicatee is not known.

three-year-old Christian. "A fine concert" could hardly be arranged with their participation.

Now, with Christian's talent promising much for the future, things were bound to improve. But given the serious, severe father and the strictness of his instruction, one might well wonder how Christian came by the serene, easy, and gracious qualities of his personality that were later reflected in his music. The answer, in all likelihood, is found in what he inherited from his mother.

We would know just as little about Anna Magdalena as we do about Bach's first wife, Maria Barbara—and we would know equally little about the environment in which Christian grew up—were it not for the drafts of letters by "Cousin Elias."[19]

Johann Elias Bach (1705–1755) was born in Schweinfurt, Franconia. Though he called Sebastian Bach "cousin" and Anna Magdalena "Frau Muhme" [an archaic term for either aunt or cousin—trans.], he was actually the son of one of Bach's cousins. Of his first thirty-three years we know only that, according to his own account, he "moved around a great deal, away from home." After that "God's inscrutable wisdom" led him to Leipzig "to improve [himself] through useful studies." As he wrote to his mentor in Schweinfurt, Dr. Segnitz, he planned to teach school, though "without making music [his] main subject, as people might assume."

Thirty-three years old and without a profession or domicile—that suggested a footloose student or, at any rate, a young man from a poor family, unable to establish himself. Nevertheless, his arrival in the Bach household was providential. He proved himself to be so useful that Bach, anxious not to lose him, signed a formal contract with him for the years 1739–1742, requiring three months' notice for cancellation. The arrangement turned out to be beneficial for both parties: Elias, as an impecunious student of theology, saved money by living with the family; and Bach was glad to have a secretary who relieved him of the burden of correspondence, either by drafting letters for Bach's signature or by handling them himself. Even more important was the education of the youngest sons: their training at the school having been put in question by the notorious battle of the prefects, they were entrusted to Elias. Though Leipzig boasted many churches, there were few schools. For those of the thirty thousand inhabitants who were planning to enter the university, there were only the schools of St. Thomas and St. Nicholas. There were no public grade schools as we know them; their place was taken by private schools, popularly known as *Winkelschulen*—operating, so to speak, in back alleys. Their staff would include young clerics who instructed small children in the Christian faith and "other needed subjects." Additional teachers might come from among those who had failed in other callings. Since no exams or licences were required, some were self-styled teachers who eked out a living by also working as clerks, book lenders, dancing masters, or barbers.[20]

Thus it was good to have a theology student in the house who took his tasks seriously and who declined other offers by saying that he was "in charge of close relatives who badly needed solid and faithful instruction, especially the oldest one among them." This referred to the feeble-minded fifteen-year-old Gottfried Heinrich. A later remark by Elias that the education of the children required great patience most likely applied to him as well.

Christian was three years old when Elias arrived. Neither he nor the six-year-old Christoph Friedrich is likely to have caused problems, given what we know of them as adults. It is not known whether they attended St. Thomas School, since the relevant documents from this period were destroyed by fire. In view of the quarrels with Ernesti, Bach may have been torn between avoiding all but the most necessary contacts with the rector and assuring the best possible education for his two youngest sons, which they could only obtain at St. Thomas. It is likely that the loving and concerned father opted for the latter.

One way in which Bach compensated for the unpleasant situation at school and church was to undertake various journeys. Elias, always agreeable and ready to help, would then take over as head of the family. During one such occasion, a serious crisis occurred. On 5 August 1741, Elias sent an urgent letter to Bach in Berlin where he was visiting his son Emanuel, harpsichordist to the king of Prussia. He urged Bach to come home at once, for "our dearest mother has been very ill for a week," and Elias feared the worst. Furthermore, the election of the town council was imminent, and as cantor, Bach was obliged to compose an appropriate work for this solemn occasion.

That Bach had to be reminded of the election says something about his enthusiasm for his work. But Anna Magdalena's illness had to be taken seriously, especially since four days later Elias sent another alarming letter, reporting that her weakness was increasing. "For two weeks there has not been a single night during which she had an hour's rest. She can neither sit nor lie down. Last night she was so poorly that I was summoned, and we feared we might lose her."

Would this turn into another tragedy like the one that had already befallen the Bach family? Bach's first wife, Maria Barbara, had suddenly

taken ill while he was on a journey. By the time he returned, she had died
and been buried, and the children had been forced to spend a long, ago-
nizing time alone in the house of the deceased.

Being deprived of their mother must have been devastating for
Friedemann, Emanuel, and Bernhard. The oldest sister, Dorothea, was
hardly able to take the mother's place, and the young stepmother whom
Bach brought home a year later was fully occupied taking care of her own
numerous children.

Thanks to Elias, Christian and his brothers were spared such a fate.
His urgent letters brought their father back in time, and Anna
Magdalena recovered. We can gather from Elias's letters what a painful
loss the early death of Christian's mother would have been. Anna
Magdalena is pictured as a kind and loving mother, always anxious to use
the family's limited means to turn their home into a cheerful place.
According to Elias, she was a devoted gardener, which caused him to ask
his mother and sister in Schweinfurt to send her some yellow carnation
plants. When they did not arrive, Elias insisted: "This will show whether
you still love me." Anna Magdalena must have been very fond of yellow
carnations, for Elias also wrote to a certain Herr Mayer in Halle with the
same request. When the plants arrived, Elias thankfully described Anna
Magdalena's delight: "She appreciates this gift more than children love
their Christmas presents; she takes care of the flowers as though they
were her own small children, doing everything possible to make them
flourish." Another time she wished for a songbird, and he again tried his
best to comply.

The young man's letters reveal by inference that Anna Magdalena
was a softhearted person, and no doubt Christian benefited from her
warmth, and that of Elias, too. Personality traits established in Christian's
childhood followed him into later life, when his employer in Italy, Count
Litta, and his teacher, Padre Martini, referred to him as "our much-loved
Giovannino," and the English royal couple, in a testimonial letter, called
him "our John Christian Bach who has everyone's confidence and is
loved by all." Still later in England, Christian's pupil Mrs. Papendiek
would say of him: "He was too kindhearted to know what jealousy
means." Such a fond statement bespeaks the amiable influence of his
mother.

Christian's music, of which it was said that "he conveyed tender and
amorous moods better than the lofty and tragic,"[21] tells the same story.
Rochlitz, who wrote the article in question, explained Christian's "closeness to the fashionable taste of the time" by his "great weakness for the

fair sex," suggesting parallels to Mozart. But even Rochlitz, who in 1806 felt duty-bound to defend Johann Sebastian Bach's honor, had to admit that "in the midst of [Christian's] light, modish creations, the gigantic spirit of his father shines through."

That spirit was not totally negated by the progressive composers. Bach continued to be acknowledged as the great master of polyphony, but he was considered legendary—a timeless figure. Some commentators employed a conciliatory tone, and one even included Carl Philipp Emanuel in his reflections:

> If Sebastian Bach and his admirable son Emanuel, instead of being musical-directors in commercial cities [Bach in Leipzig, Emanuel in Hamburg], had been fortunately employed to compose for the stage and public of great capitals, such as Naples, Paris, or London, and for performers of the first class, they would doubtless have simplified their style more to the level of their judges; the one would have sacrificed all unmeaning art and contrivance, and the other been less fantastical and recherché, and both, by writing in a style more popular, and generally intelligible and pleasing, would have extended their fame, and been indisputably the greatest musicians of the present century.[22]

This statement points to a man who was later to play a decisive part in Christian's life: Carl Friedrich Abel. Having studied both the old and the new styles at the source, Abel would meet Christian in London; together they would found the famous Bach-Abel concerts. His father, Christian Ferdinand Abel, had been a gamba player in the Köthen court chapel, directed by Sebastian Bach. There were also personal ties to the senior Bach, who had been godfather at the baptism of Carl Abel's sister Sophia Charlotte. Carl Friedrich had then attended St. Thomas School, presumably as an extern since he is not listed among the boarders. He must have soon become an outstanding gamba player himself, for Bach put him to use in his church music, having him accompany, as a solo player, the recitatives in his cantatas.

Young Abel was still a Bach pupil when, on 13 October 1743, an important event occurred in his life. The Grosses Concert was a society of musical amateurs, "administered by the honorable merchants of the city." Only two days after its founding, Carl Friedrich appeared as gamba player, along with some other soloists. His playing was a resounding success, as a contemporary reports:

> All [the other] soloists received applause, but especially Monsieur Abel, playing the viola da gamba. His performance in a trio and in a solo fan-

tasy was greatly admired, so that on the following day he gave a command performance, solo, for His Royal Majesty. As a result he was fortunate enough to be appointed, by the grace of the King, to the royal chapel.[23]

As a member of the Dresden court chapel, Carl Friedrich could acquire firsthand knowledge of new music. Having received a strict musical education from his father and from Bach, he was now a member of an ensemble known everywhere for its mellifluous, Italian sound, that had been trained by the "divine Saxon," Johann Adolf Hasse, the leading representative of the new melodic style.

The twenty-year-old Abel's salary as a gambist in the court chapel was modest enough: 180 taler, later raised to 280. His earnings seem especially modest compared with those of oboist Besozzi, who was paid 1200 taler, or with the truly princely fees commanded by singers. But the musical and social setting in which Abel now found himself made up for this. Especially during carnival, the capital city provided a glamorous array of Italian operas, comedies, and ballets, along with such popular entertainments as target shooting, sleigh rides, and dances. It was a musically stimulating setting, like the one Abel and Christian Bach would encounter again in the London amusement gardens.

Abel was not the only artist who succeeded in making the move from Leipzig to Dresden. The singer Regina Mingotti was discovered and engaged for the Dresden opera, beginning a stellar career. She and Christian would meet later in London. In 1744, when she was still a member of Mingotti's opera company, she had sung (under the name Valentini) in the new Reithaus Theater in Leipzig, where she attracted the court's attention. During the spring of 1747 (by which time she had married Pietro Mingotti, the company's director), she again appeared in Leipzig, and she soon became one of "His Majesty's opera singers."[24] This appointment caused much excitement in Dresden, for it threatened the undisputed role of Hasse and his wife, the singer Faustina. The first opera not composed by Hasse to premiere in Dresden was Nicolo Porpora's *Filandro*. And the first young singer to offer some serious competition to the aging Faustina was Regina Mingotti.

Father Bach, who continued to visit Dresden (perhaps with young Christian) long after Friedemann had moved to Halle, could witness this struggle for supremacy on the stage. Perhaps Regina Mingotti held it against Bach that he sided with his friends Hasse and Faustina. Some fifteen years later, when she became the director of the London opera, she had her chance to get even. She managed to keep Christian Bach out of the picture for an entire season, thus temporarily interrupting his brilliant career as a composer of opera.

The actions of another Dresden resident, Count Carl Hermann von Keyserlingk, were more positive. It was he who arranged the event that was probably the most impressive to take place during Christian's childhood: Bach's visit to King Frederick II of Prussia.

Keyserlingk was the Russian ambassador to the Saxon court. Under his auspices, Bach had been appointed composer to the royal court chapel, just in time for a needed boost in his quarrel with Ernesti and the town council. Godfather to Emanuel's youngest son (a future painter named Johann Sebastian), Keyserlingk had also given Bach a lucrative commission: a set of thirty variations to be played by Johann Gottlieb Goldberg, the count's chamber musician. The "Goldberg Variations," as they are still called today, were intended to help Keyserlingk pass away the hours when he was suffering from insomnia. Bach's reward for this work was a precious box filled with one hundred louisd'or.

No sooner had Keyserlingk been appointed Russian ambassador to the Prussian court than he arranged the memorable meeting of the sixty-two-year-old cantor and the thirty-five-year-old Prussian ruler. Some later chroniclers grandiosely referred to the event as the Day of Potsdam. Actually the event turned out to be Bach's last bitter disappointment.

According to Forkel, who relied on Friedemann's none too accurate recollections, the king at first merely remarked casually to Emanuel, his harpsichordist, that it might be nice to have the father visit him in Potsdam. As time went on, Frederick supposedly became more insistent, asking why Bach did not come.

> Thus the son felt obliged to report the king's question to his father, who at first was unable to comply, being greatly overworked. But when the king's request was repeatedly mentioned in Emanuel's letters, Bach finally, in 1747, made arrangements to undertake the journey, accompanied by his oldest son, Wilhelm Friedemann.[25]

A reluctant Bach, and an impatiently waiting Prussian king? The facts suggest a different scenario. Bach had been in Berlin on several previous occasions without ever having been invited to appear at court—in 1745, for example, when he "once again" visited Berlin for the baptism of his grandson. Emanuel, who had been in the king's service for four years, had married the daughter of a wealthy wine merchant. A son, Johann August, was born. The little family celebration might have furnished a good occasion for Bach to call on the king, had he been invited.

The music room in Potsdam castle in which King Frederick II received J. S. Bach. Insert: The king.

At that time, Frederick may have been preoccupied with the Second Silesian War. Possibly no one made a point of informing him that Bach was present in Berlin. Emanuel, after all, was only a musician in the king's service and as such was not in a position to arrange a royal audience for his father. Moreover, Emanuel was not on the best of terms with the king.

In other words, it took someone in Keyserlingk's position to facilitate Bach's appearance at court, especially since there are other reasons to suspect that King Frederick was not all that eager to meet the aging composer. When conversation turned to strict counterpoint, he was quick to say, "that smacks of the church." Earlier, while still crown prince, he had made up his mind about Handel, Bach's great contemporary in London: "Handel is past his prime; his head is empty and his taste old-fashioned."

His own musical horizon was limited. He had little interest in music other than Italian operas (all by German composers), flute concertos by his instructor Quantz, and of course his own compositions. Given these tastes it seems highly unlikely that the young king forever tried to meet the old Bach. Today we no longer know whether Bach's visit (on 7 May 1747) went as Forkel described it, or whether his account is exaggerated:

> At this time there was a nightly chamber concert, during which the king usually played several flute concertos. One evening, when the musicians were all assembled and the king was getting ready to play, an officer brought the list of visitors who had just arrived in town. Still holding the flute in his hand, the king glanced at the list, immediately turned to the musicians and said, with some excitement: "Gentlemen, the old Bach has arrived!" He put his flute away, and Bach, who was staying at his son's, was immediately commanded to appear at the castle.

Bach supposedly did not even have time to exchange his traveling clothes for his black cantor's coat. Apologizing for this, he became engaged in a "veritable dialogue" with the king. It is an attractive picture: Bach, in his modest traveling coat, standing before the king in the ornate music room of Potsdam castle, surrounded by the respectful musicians, with Friedemann and Emanuel modestly remaining in the background.

Perhaps it was like that. But if we consider the rather disappointing results of this "Day of Potsdam," the sober account in the *Berlinische Nachrichten* seems more convincing:

> His Majesty was informed that Capellmeister Bach had arrived in Potsdam and that he was requesting most gracious permission to listen to the music. Whereupon His Majesty gave the order to let him attend.

Court chronicler Rödenbeck merely records, laconically: "Bach at the king's concert in Potsdam."[26]

To be sure, Frederick showed himself during Bach's visit to be an attentive host who readily acknowledged Bach's mastery of organ and harpsichord. At the king's request, Bach tried out the new Silbermann pianos that had recently been installed in the palace. On these, and later on the organs in Potsdam's Garnisonkirche, Bach displayed his supreme mastery of improvisation. But the king must have expected no less. He may even have been induced to receive the "old Bach" not so much by an appreciation of his compositions as by the desire to find out for himself to what heights the contrapuntal art had been developed—to see and hear a demonstration of Bach's skills. It gave Frederick a glimpse into a musical world to which he did not really relate. He must have reacted more with curiosity and amazement than with genuine admiration.

At the end of the visit there was no reward—neither an honorarium nor a gift. There is no indication in the exchequer's records that even Bach's traveling expenses were refunded. But what must have hurt Bach most deeply was this: he failed to be granted the title of Prussian Court Composer. Added to the Saxon appointment, this would have been his life's crowning achievement.

Bach, however, was not easily discouraged. To the last he tried to obtain a sign of royal favor. As soon as he returned to Leipzig, he took the fugue theme given him by the king and based on it a written, more elaborate composition, with all contrapuntal artifices (not without making use of some of his earlier writing). He then had the score beautifully engraved by Schübler in Zella, printed on expensive paper, and lavishly bound. All this far exceeded Bach's financial resources.

Exactly eight weeks after his visit with Frederick, this magnificent score was dispatched to Berlin, with a dedication that went beyond even the deferential, self-effacing mode of expression customary at the time. Bach speaks of a "musical offering" he is presenting to the king, saying that the theme was "truly regal" and deserved to be known "throughout the world." He had now accomplished this to the best of his ability and had "no other intention than the proper one of glorifying the fame of a monarch . . . whose greatness and ability, in music as in the sciences of war, everyone must admire."[27]

All these exertions brought no results. Nor did a second manuscript, intended as a supplement to the *Musical Offering*, bring about any recognition. By that time Bach must have considered his Berlin journey a failure. To have been received by the king and treated with respect was fine but hardly sufficient, though Bach may have found some consolation in the *Offering's* favorable reception by connoisseurs. The one hundred engraved copies, at one taler apiece, were much in demand. But Bach did not derive much financial benefit from the "Prussian Fugue," as he called it, for according to his own statement, most copies were "given away, gratis," to friends.

There was, however, one positive outcome: the *Offering* served to establish contact between Christian and his future teacher, Padre Martini, in Bologna. It so happened that court Kapellmeister Pauli in Fulda sent one copy of the work to the renowned theorist, which caused Martini to reply: "It is unnecessary for me to describe the singular merits of Herr Bach, for he is well known and admired, not only in Germany but also throughout our Italy."[28]

It may in fact have been this work of Bach's that prompted Padre Martini to open his door to Christian and accept him as a student. Other than that, few positive results can be credited to Sebastian's journey to Berlin and Potsdam. But it must have made some lasting impression on King Frederick, for Baron van Swieten reports a conversation he had with the king thirty years later, during which Frederick sang with a loud voice the fugue theme he had given to "the old Bach." And on this occasion—Friedemann Bach was giving an organ recital in Potsdam— the king was said to have thought more highly of the father's artistry than of Friedemann's, although Friedemann was generally considered the most accomplished organist of his day.

On the other hand, we do not know of a single Bach work that was heard at any of the king's nightly concerts of chamber music. Several of the flute sonatas would have been entirely appropriate—above all, of course, the Trio Sonata in C Minor, which Bach had added to the *Musical Offering* as a token of respect for the flute-playing king. Like all other works sent to Berlin, it was not acknowledged. Not even Count Keyserlingk seems to have succeeded in obtaining the slightest royal response to the *Offering* on which Bach had spent so much effort and expense.[29]

Having returned to Leipzig with neither a new title nor a monetary reward, Bach turned to a kind of composition that he had not previously undertaken. Among the major works of his last decade are not only the *Musical Offering* and the *Art of Fugue* but also the canonic variations on the chorale "Vom Himmel hoch da komm ich her." Bach originally had called it "Dr. Martin Luthers Kinderlied auf die Weynacht" (Luther's Christmas Song for Children). He chose a children's song to show how he could transform an unassuming melody into an artistic, polyphonic edifice. In the painting of Bach by the Dresden artist Haussmann, he holds a page with the music of the opening bars for all to see.

Bach subsequently presented this painting to Mizler's Society of Musical Science (the Societät), as required by their statutes, when he joined that organization. This was another landmark event during Christian's childhood. Though Sebastian had repeatedly been invited, he did not become a member until nine years after the society's founding. His sudden decision to join, only four weeks after he returned from Berlin, might be interpreted as an expression of his disappointment over the outcome of that journey.

Mizler had founded the "Corresponding Society of Musical Sciences" (to give its full name) in order to restore to music the "scientific principles" that had been so important in earlier ages. Once more there were vociferous debates about whether music was an art or a science. Mizler opted for science, following Wolff and Leibnitz for whom music was a kind of sounding mathematics. But Mizler went one step further, including in the science of music "history, knowledge of the world's wisdom, mathematics, rhetoric, and poetry."[30] He even held that the laws of mathematics applied to the creative process, the "inventing" of music, and he constructed a "thoroughbass machine for beginners." This invention prompted derisive comments from Scheibe, who ridiculed Mizler in the *Critischer Musikus*. Scheibe facetiously claimed to have invented a machine "that can evaluate all musical compositions, decide whether they are good or bad, and determine who was the composer. It can also teach us the rules of composition, along with everything else that constitutes beauty in music."

Mizler did not deserve that kind of ridicule. He attempted what several other theorists in the Enlightenment had done, namely to provide a scientific foundation for music. But he did not deny the importance of melody and even emphasized that "melody is the most important ingredient in music. Melody determines harmony, and harmony was invented for the sake of melody, which it emphasizes, supports, and accompanies."[31] Both factions could subscribe to such a statement.

Nevertheless, ridicule can kill. Mizler did not succeed as a university instructor. He attracted few students to the lectures on music that he had reintroduced in Leipzig and thus did not make a favorable impression as head of his society, especially since he then left Leipzig and settled near Warsaw as "court mathematician" to a count. From there he attempted, without much success, to keep the Societät alive.

The society received a new lease on life when Handel and, a year later, the Berlin Kapellmeister Carl Heinrich Graun joined it. Handel, however, was merely an honorary member, and Graun (whom Christian would later meet in Berlin) freely admitted that he had joined only because he wanted to be spared attack by the "satirical pens of incompetent critics." Graun's own views were far removed from Mizler's "sounding mathematics." "Experience so far," Graun wrote to Telemann in Hamburg, "has taught me that a mathematical composer and one who strives to write beautiful, touching music are incompatible."[32]

Telemann did his share to maintain division within the Societät. Soon after joining it he proceeded to poke fun at Mizler and the society's statutes. In the preface to his collection of odes, he satirically remarked that he did not plan his songs "with compasses and ruler, according to the precepts of wise men, astronomers, and palmists." Rather he "treated with contempt the trash of new, heretical rules, even if proclaimed by a Mattheson or a Mizler." With this, Telemann lashed out against both sides, the protagonists of melody and of mathematics.

Bach apparently took these quarrels in stride, along with the knowledge that the society was about to expire. By this time Mizler had been promoted to doctor of medicine in Warsaw and did little to keep the society alive. After Bach, only one first-rate musician became a member: Leopold Mozart. Thus its roster for the first time combined the names of Bach and Mozart—linking the fathers before the sons had met.

The society quietly succumbed when Mizler realized that there was no hope of his returning to Leipzig. To the end, he was beset by misfortune. Unaware of what they were, his wife sold all his manuscripts as worthless old paper. His death failed to be noted by any scientific or musical journal.

If, towards the end of his life, Bach joined a society whose founder looked upon music solely as "mathematics in sound," he must have done so out of spite. Though the world of numbers and music symbolism fascinated him, he was "no friend of dry, mathematical stuff," as Emanuel put it.[33] Nor could he accept the idea of relegating music to a place of less than supreme importance, whereas Mizler's view of music as but one element of "the world's wisdom" did just that.

Only once during his three years of membership did Bach turn to the Societät for support, and then he obtained it indirectly, from one of its members. In 1750 Christoph Gottlieb Schröter of Nordhausen backed him in a dispute that opened old wounds but showed Bach as ready to fight as ever.

The conflict, which originated in the rivalry between a cantor and a rector, evoked memories of Bach's own battle with Ernesti. If this were not incentive enough, one of the adversaries was Johann Friedrich Doles, one of Bach's former pupils. Hence, shortly before his death, Bach was prompted to get involved in the case.

As cantor at the *gymnasium* in Freiberg, Doles was subordinate to the rector, Johann Gottlieb Biedermann. Like Ernesti, Biedermann was a highly regarded scholar. To commemorate the centennial of the peace treaty of Westphalia, Doles had put on a very successful performance of a singspiel. Biedermann feared, as Ernesti had done, that this success might have an adverse effect on academic work and lead to an unwanted emphasis on music. (Biedermann's reaction might be explained more simply, however, if there had in fact been irregularities in accounting for the receipts.)

At any rate, in the next issue of the school bulletin, Biedermann launched an attack that was so sweeping, it infuriated those concerned. Reaching into antiquity, Biedermann stated that Horace had already lumped musicians together with dancing girls, quack healers, and mendicants. Small wonder, he continued, that the early Christians had excluded musicians from their devotional meetings and had allowed them to partake of the Lord's Supper only once a year. In all, this was a vociferous diatribe against music at a time when music was beginning to rid itself of its dependency on school, nobility, and clergy, and to assume its place in a society where free artists were able to appear in concerts accessible to all.

Bach may have learned from Doles about Biedermann's excesses. As in his earlier confrontation with Scheibe, Bach did not at first become personally involved. Instead, he passed on a copy of the bulletin to Schröter, a fellow member of the Societät. Bach was so impressed with Schröter's reply that, on 10 December 1749, he forwarded it to his pupil Einicke in Frankenhausen. In the accompanying letter he said:

> Schröter's reaction is well stated and expresses my views. It will soon be printed. I expect there will be additional refutations; I do not doubt that the author's dirty ear [*drecksohr*] will thus be cleansed, becoming more suitable for listening to music.[34]

The reference to "the author's dirty ear" proves that even half a year before his death Bach was quite ready for a fight. It may not have bothered him that Mattheson took offense, considering the expression unsuitable for use by a Kapellmeister and believing that it should be replaced by "rector." [Since Biedermann was a rector, the similar-sounding *drecksohr* was probably intended as a pun—trans.]

Johann Gottlieb Biedermann.

Christoph Gottlieb Schröter.

The Leipzig city hall.

So far, these salvos amounted to little more than amusing banter. But the squabble soon degenerated into the "Biedermann affair" because of revisions to the wording of Schröter's statement that were made without the author's knowledge. It is not clear who was responsible, but the printed version was considerably more acrimonious than the original, fairly restrained, wording. In fact, "it no longer resembled in the slightest what Herr Schröter had written. . . . Much had been added, and much changed," as Einicke later wrote to Mattheson in his own defense.

The altered version accused Biedermann of being more concerned with heathen literature than with the Word of God, an accusation that explains the article's new title, also supplied without Schröter's knowledge: "Christliche Beurtheilung des von Herrn M. Biedermann Freybergischen Rectore im Monat Mai des 1749sten Jahres edirte Programmatis de Vita Musica" (Christian Evaluation of the "Programma de Vita Musica," Edited in May 1749 by Magister Biedermann, Rector in Freiberg).

Enraged, Schröter turned to Einicke. He assumed Bach to be the culprit and was all the angrier because it was Bach who had asked him to reply to Biedermann, since Bach "could not think of anyone hereabouts who was able to do so." He was especially offended by the new title, for although, as he said, "[his] casual piece of writing contains nothing un-Christian, such an epithet hardly suited the occasion."

It was a veritable merry-go-round. Einicke forwarded Schröter's protest to Leipzig, causing Bach to reply briefly: "Please pay my respects to Herr Schröter. When time permits me to answer, I shall apologize for the changes in his review. However, I am guiltless; only the printer is to blame."

That attribution of guilt seems questionable, though Bach was indeed unable to write at this time. His letter is dated 26 May, but at the end of March he had undergone his first eye operation by the traveling oculist John Taylor. On 1 April the *Berlinische Priv. Zeitung* had reported prematurely that the operation had been successful.

> On Saturday and last night, the chevalier Taylor gave public lectures in the concert hall, attended by numerous scholars and other persons of high standing. An astounding number of people are turning to him for help. One of them is Herr Kapellmeister Bach who, due to constant, heavy use, had lost his eyesight almost completely. His operation had the hoped-for success, so that his sight has been completely restored. It is an immeasurable fortune for the world-famous composer; thousands of people rejoice in it and will be forever grateful to Mr. Taylor.

But Schröter, unaware that after a second operation Bach's condition had worsened, was not satisfied with the reply and insisted on a written apology. He wrote to Einicke that the "Herr Kapellmeister remains the guilty party, no matter how much he may twist and turn. But he could bring the whole matter to a good conclusion by publicly admitting that he was the author of the 'Christliche Beurtheilung.'"

Schröter was not to be vindicated, for Bach's death put an end to the entire unfortunate affair. The accusation therefore remained that Bach had falsified the essay he had requested from one of his supporters, a fellow member in the Societät, and that he had never admitted it. In the long run Einicke, completely guiltless, was the one who suffered. He became embroiled in a battle of words that continued after Bach's death and in which Friedemann also participated.[35] When Biedermann's adherents accused Einicke of having pulled the wires while remaining in the background, he finally came forward and revealed the role that Bach had played, a role that was unclear and perhaps not laudable.

Christian, too, may have been involved, more or less unwillingly, since he attended to some of his father's correspondence. During the first half of 1749 Bach had suffered a stroke and was apparently no longer able to write. As early as Easter of 1749, the thirteen-year-old Christian issued a receipt, no doubt authorized by his father, signing it "Johann Sebastian Bach."

From this time on, no writing of any kind by Sebastian has been preserved. (Some autographs are lost; other works were copied by others.) Therefore it is likely that Christian took care of the correspondence relating to the Biedermann affair. He issued other receipts at Michaelmas (29 September) of the same year, and at Easter 1750. Using his father's initials, Christian also acknowledged the endowment provided by a rich widow named Nathan, who had donated five gulden a year to pay for funeral motets sung by the Thomaner. One month before his father's death, he acknowledged receipt of another endowment by one Maria Lobwasser to compensate the custodians of St. Thomas School and Church.[36] When Bach's second-youngest son, Johann Christoph Friedrich, left to enter the service of Count Wilhelm von Schaumburg-Lippe in Bückeburg, Bach supplied him with a letter of introduction. It must also have been written by Christian. The handwriting is the same as that in a petition by Anna Magdalena, prepared at the time of the execution of Bach's testament, in which she requests that a guardian be appointed for her minor children.

The fact that Father Bach relied on Christian to take care of important correspondence, even at a time when Friedrich, three years older, still lived at home, would seem to refute Friedemann's malicious claim that their father had said, "little Christian will make his way by relying on his stupidity."[37] Evidently Sebastian had a higher regard for the intelligence of his youngest, who was soon to demonstrate his own worth. Surely the highly educated Padre Martini would not have accepted a dullard as a pupil and continued teaching him for years. Nor would a learned man such as Diderot have taken pride in his friendship.[38]

One of the few rays of light at the end of Bach's life was provided by his knowledge that his son Friedrich had found a position. Another happy event was the wedding of his daughter Liesgen to his pupil Altnikol. Bach was still able to participate in the ceremony, on 20 January 1749, in St. Thomas Church. He could also rejoice in the birth of his youngest grandchild in October, but that joy soon turned to sorrow when the infant died barely three weeks later.

Both events involved a departure. Early in 1750, Friedrich moved to Bückeburg, taking along a Luther Bible with a dedication from his loving mother.[39] And Elisabeth and Altnikol moved to Naumburg, together with the mentally handicapped Heinrich, whose care they were assuming. Christian was now the only son to remain in the parental home.

Bach had helped Altnikol obtain the position of organist at Naumburg's St. Wenceslaus Church. The minutes of the council record that Altnikol had been chosen "especially since Herr Kapellmeister Bach in Leipzig had recommended him as a capable, well-qualified individual." In spite of the changing times and musical styles, Bach's name still carried some weight.

Proof of Father Bach's enduring influence can also be seen in the appointment of eighteen-year-old Friedrich to the Bückeburg court. Everyone knew that Count Wilhelm cared only for Italian music. Why then did he settle for a son of Johann Sebastian Bach? His decision may be explained by earlier events. Soon after the count began his reign in 1748, he had paid the obligatory visit to Potsdam to introduce himself to Prussia's King Frederick II, whom he greatly admired. On this occasion he made the acquaintance of Emanuel, the king's harpsichordist. To find a Bach son among the king's excellent musicians may have encouraged Wilhelm to follow that example.

Even Bach's youngest sons benefited from their father's training in more ways than is generally recognized. He equipped them with more than just the rudiments of music, the basic technical and formal skills. He also taught them, for example, the cantabile manner of playing:

Christian became famous, as we shall see, for his "singing allegro." To Sebastian, the cantabile manner meant bringing out the individual, equal voices above the thoroughbass, which for him was the "most perfect foundation of music." But when he was giving a lesson, he would often play the bass line himself, so that the pupil could concentrate on the cantabile playing of the upper parts.

Furthermore, as Forkel relates, Bach

> played his own compositions at a brisk tempo. And he introduced so much variety in his playing that, in his hands, every piece acquired a speechlike eloquence. . . . Bach thought of the individual voices in a composition as persons who conversed with each other.

Such an analogy might be extended to the modern style. In Bach's kind of "conversation," all voices participated equally. In the new style one might say that one person was the speaker who had the floor. The others present might, at best, interject a comment here and there. "[A composer] at times might write something pleasant in the bass part, but the listener will hardly notice it, paying attention only to the melody."[40] This view might be contrasted with Forkel's more conservative view: "Many believe that the best melody is the one everyone can repeat immediately. I would say: the melody that everyone can repeat immediately is of the most ordinary kind."[41]

Here we have two seemingly incompatible points of view. Yet we must not exaggerate the degree of polarization when it comes to individual composers. Certainly the young Christian was not aware of such opposing factions. We might think of him as a connecting link, as one who built something new on the solid foundation supplied by his father.

At this point it seems appropriate to touch up, in some places, the traditional popular picture of Sebastian Bach. Fate had not been kind to him during the last decade of his life. There had been Bernhard's death, Scheibe's attacks, the battle of the prefects, the unsuccessful visit to Berlin. Nevertheless, Bach did not turn into an embittered, introverted recluse as later generations imagined him. To the contrary: until he suffered his first stroke, a year before his death, he was extremely active and traveled a great deal to play recitals, to dedicate new organs, and to visit relatives. As we have seen in the Biedermann affair, he remained quite ready to take on a fight. Nor did his creative energy diminish, although it was channeled in other directions. Bach became more concerned with demonstrating his skill at polyphonic writing than with engaging in the futile struggle with the melodists.

To Christian, therefore, his father was not a broken old man (apart from his failing eyesight); rather he was a person who continued to command respect and who, full of energy, could pass on to the son all that he viewed as essential for composing and performing any kind of music. This included a "singing" quality and lively, varied playing. Above all, there was rhythm—a dancelike character that was important to Father Bach in his own playing but was quickly forgotten by later generations of performers who often settled for a dry, mechanical style of playing Bach.

Forkel tells us that "even in his fugues, artful as they were, [Bach] created a striking light, rhythmic quality, as though they were minuets." In this, however, Bach was alone—"so alone that the world around him seemed like a desert." Forkel's views were echoed by Matthias Gesner, the rector of St. Thomas School, who harbored friendly feelings towards Bach and who called him *omnibus membris rhythmicus*, a man with rhythm in his blood.

Numerous pieces with dance rhythms are included in the little notebook Sebastian began composing for Anna Magdalena in 1725. He thought it important that dance rhythms become second nature to his students, and he included dance movements—minuets, polonaises, musettes, and others—in many of his compositions. Each of his more than thirty suites contains at least four dance movements, although in stylized forms.

Even Bach's sacred music contains elements of the dance. Hugo Riemann pointed this out in the church cantatas, especially in the many arias whose dancelike quality "remains no matter how slow the performance tempo. The comfortably graceful, ländlerlike appearance of some movements is especially notable."[42] Riemann's remarks were prophetic of today's somewhat revised view of Bach: he is no longer seen as the "fifth evangelist" or the "pious voice of Lutheranism," whose outlook is primarily that of a church musician. To be sure, Bach was not the only musician to weave secular elements into sacred music. Then, too, there was Mattheson, who thought "theatrical style" was needed in church music so that wordly splendor might arouse "virtuous feelings" in the faithful.

We can easily detect these characteristics in Christian's sacred music. The works he would soon write in Italy not only made an impression in that country during its golden age of vocal music but also found favor in the north. "[Christian's] Te Deum is among the most beautiful found anywhere in Europe," according to the reviewer for the Leipzig *Allgemeine Musikalische Zeitung*. He admired the "natural flow of musical ideas," qualities that are similar to the "free, easy flow" Forkel had praised in

Sebastian's music. The Leipzig reviewer found words of special praise for the fugues that Christian, as a matter of course, also included in his church music. They displayed "great art, while avoiding the pedantic."[43]

One quality of his father's that Christian did not assimilate, however, was his deeply-rooted faith. To the day of his death, Sebastian's attention was devoted to a sacred work. He had completed fifteen of the *Eighteen Leipzig Chorales* by himself. The remaining three were dictated to his son-in-law Altnikol, who had hurried to the dying man's bedside to fulfill his last wish. For the concluding chorale, "Wenn wir in höchsten Nöten sein" (When We Were in Deepest Misery), Bach used the words of an earlier chorale, "Vor Deinen Thron tret ich hiemit" (Forthwith I Come Before Thy Throne). The manuscript breaks off abruptly in the twenty-sixth measure.

In his *nekrolog* (obituary), Emanuel relates the events leading to his father's death:

> Ten days before his death his eyes suddenly seemed to improve, so that in the morning he was again able to see quite well, nor did the light bother him. But a few hours later he suffered a stroke, followed by a violent fever. In spite of all the skill and care of two of Leipzig's ablest physicians, he died on 28 July 1750, after 8:45 in the evening, in his sixty-sixth year. He died peacefully, secure in his faith in his Savior.

Bach was buried three days later in St. John's Cemetery, outside the city walls. The Thomaner accompanied their cantor on his last journey. No tombstone marks the place where Leipzig's most famous son was laid to rest. The occasion was marked only by the usual perfunctory oration from the pulpit of St. Thomas Church, and the minutes of the town council merely record: "The cantor of St. Thomas School, or rather, the director of chapel music, Bach, also passed away." Here one notes the pointed reference to the "director."

Eight days later, when a successor was to be chosen, Mayor Stieglitz indicated at least some appreciation:

> Herr Bach was a great musician, but not a school teacher. In replacing him as cantor of St. Thomas School one should therefore look for someone with both skills. I believe that Herr Harrer fulfills these requirements.

Within a week of Bach's death, then, the matter had been settled. Gottlob Harrer, with the backing of the almighty Count von Brühl, succeeded in his second attempt.[44] The local authorities were so intent on appointing Harrer that a decision was reached before a second letter of recommendation from the count had arrived from distant Warsaw.

Emanuel Bach had been among the other applicants. This is surprising, for he had firsthand knowledge of his father's disagreements with the town council. Nevertheless, he had applied at once—during his father's final illness, or perhaps immediately after his death. At any rate, Emanuel's name appears in the minutes of 7 August among those applying for the post. His chances of succeeding were just as small as those of the others, in view of Count Brühl's favoring of Harrer. Moreover, Emanuel had stated in his application that he did not wish to teach at the school, which was not acceptable to the town fathers. After their experiences with the intractable (as they saw it) father, they were not inclined to favor the son, another potential troublemaker.

After his unsuccessful application (he applied again five years later, again without success), Emanuel lost all interest in coming to Leipzig for the settlement of the estate. He authorized Friedemann to represent him.

Friedemann was glad to visit his home town, all the more so because he was again having disagreements with the authorities in Halle. In violation of the rules, he had lent the church's timpani to the Collegium Musicum, an infraction for which he was threatened with dismissal. According to the minutes of the council, he had left Halle "before Michaelmas" and had not returned to his place of work until Christmas Eve. The town fathers were furious and demanded an apology. When rendered, it was not very abject:

> The organist Bach, having been summoned, appeared and apologized, saying that, owing to his father's death in Leipzig, he had traveled there without reporting his absence. He then came down with a fever, which forced him to remain there until Christmas, but he said that he had made arrangements for the organ [playing] and [other] music.[45]

These had been difficult weeks for Friedemann, whether or not he had been ill. Because his father had left no will, Friedemann believed that he needed to be especially alert during the settlement in order to safeguard Emanuel's interests as well as his own. Anna Magdalena had wisely secured the services of a guardian for her minor children: Johann Christoph Friedrich, 18; Johann Christian, 15; Johanne Carolina, 12; and Regine Susanna, 9. They were represented by Johann Gottlieb Görner, the university's director of music. The mentally handicapped Gottfried Heinrich, now twenty-six years old, was also represented by a

Authentic and forged portraits of Bach and his sons. Those of Carl Philipp Emanuel (top left) and Wilhelm Friedemann (top right) are authentic. Bottom left: a portrait, painted by D. G. Mathieu in 1744, initially was claimed to be of John Christian, later of Johann Christoph Friedrich, the Bückeburg Bach, who at that time would have been only twelve years old. Most likely it represents Emanuel, to judge by the similarity to his portrait above. The other portrait (bottom right) has been claimed as a picture of the young Sebastian Bach. The portrait of Friedemann on page 294, however, makes it more likely that it shows that son in his youth.

guardian, a certain Herr Hesemann. The presence of so many representatives assured a conscientious distribution of assets but also led to some
disputes.

Friedemann was prominently involved in the conflict. Even before
an inventory had been carried out, he took possession of all his father's
music, claiming that Sebastian had promised it to him and Emanuel.
This, however, did not prevent Friedemann from objecting when Christian made a similar claim for three of his father's keyboard instruments.
The issue was argued back and forth, in typical legalistic language. Bach's
children from his first marriage did not want to acknowledge the validity
of Christian's claim, while the other heirs were willing to do so.[46]

The bequest of three keyboard instruments to his youngest son, the
only one who remained at home until the end, would indicate Sebastian's
fondness for Christian. It can also be seen as a vote of confidence in his
pianistic talent and promise. Perhaps these were symbolic gestures: he
may have left his compositions to his older sons in hope of keeping them
mindful of the tradition their father represented, while he willed his
favorite instruments to Christian in hope that they might open up for
him the world of new music.

The settlement of Bach's estate took until 11 November 1750. With
a few of his father's linen shirts in his luggage, and with exactly thirty-
eight taler, fourteen groschen, and six pfennig in his pocket,[47] Christian
left his native Leipzig, never to return. Besides these worldly possessions,
he also took with him a solid technical foundation and a musical heritage
such as no other young musician of his day could call his own. Building
upon this groundwork, he would master the musical style of a new age.
The road to success first took him to his half brother Emanuel in Berlin.
Friedemann accompanied him there, glad to extend his own "leave" by a
few days that would actually turn into weeks.

2

Life in Berlin
Under King Frederick the Great

> *Music ceases to be music*
> *when it ceases to give pleasure.*
> Christoph Martin Wieland (1733–1813)

ccompanied by Christian, Friedemann arrived in Berlin on 22 November 1750, just in time to celebrate his fortieth birthday with Emanuel and his family. Being a bachelor, Friedemann may have appreciated all the more his brother's well-ordered family life[1] from which Christian was also to benefit.

At the age of thirty, Emanuel had married into a family of innkeepers and merchants; his wife, Johanna Maria Dannemann, was ten years younger. By 1750, he had fathered three children and was hopeful that one of these, in the family tradition, would become a musician. His youngest seemed most likely to fulfill that hope. Emanuel had named him Johann Sebastian and had been able to line up a number of distinguished persons as godparents.[2] As it turned out, Emanuel was to be disappointed in that regard, for the son took after his mother's side of the family, which included no musicians. Emanuel's oldest son, Johann August, became a lawyer. Daughter Anna Carolina Philippina never married; her contact with music was limited to helping her mother dispose of Emanuel's musical estate. Even the youngest son embarked on a nonmusical career, going to Italy to live in Rome as a painter. He died at the early age of thirty.

Emanuel, coming from a family so blessed with musicians, would find it hard to accept that his own children, as they grew up, displayed no musical talent whatsoever. But at the time of Christian's arrival in Berlin, Emanuel had no such concerns, for his children were still young—five, three, and two years of age. Christian became a kind of older brother whose help with caring for them was welcomed by the entire family. Emanuel, moreover, was happy to have his young brother's help with music copying and music lessons, making it possible for Emanuel to earn some extra income. Previously Emanuel had been too busy for these activities because of the Prussian king's many demands.

Emanuel thus derived some advantages from taking Christian in, while for the younger brother the arrangement was both beneficial and pleasant. Although the environment in Berlin was very different from that of Leipzig, Christian did not arrive in the Prussian metropolis as a total stranger. Aside from his brother, he knew friends and former students of his father, which made it easier to adjust to the new environment. And his friendly, outgoing personality no doubt helped him make new acquaintances quickly.

The city itself, however, must have startled if not frightened him. Around 1750, Berlin had about seventy thousand inhabitants, including musicians and writers of many nationalities engaged in lively pursuit of their arts. They loudly proclaimed their ideas about true art, and they cherished an imaginary world of the pastoral and idyllic as an escape from the rationalistic ideas of the Enlightenment. All this ferment took place under the wings of a sovereign who, having won two wars with Silesia, was now engaged in freely pursuing his own intellectual and artistic interests. Six years later, Berlin's musical life would come to a standstill with the outbreak of the Seven Years' War.

Leipzig seemed far away. Compared with Berlin, Christian's native city must have seemed gray and unimposing to him—narrow and bourgeois, lacking in cosmopolitanism and cultural splendor. Leipzig was a provincial city of about thirty thousand; its character was defined by trade, the university, and the church. Its musical life would hardly have attracted attention had it not been for Johann Sebastian Bach.

Three of his father's former students that Christian saw frequently in Berlin had come directly from their training by the cantor of St. Thomas—training of which they were proud. They contributed significantly to the musical life at the Prussian court.

During his years as a student at the university in Leipzig, Johann Friedrich Agricola must have known Christian, then a child. As a pupil of Bach, Agricola often participated in concerts by the university's collegium musicum. (It was Agricola who, together with Emanuel, wrote Sebastian Bach's obituary, not published until four years after the death, in Mizler's *Musikalische Bibliothek*.) Having been brought to Berlin by Quantz, the king's flute teacher, Agricola composed for the court chapel. When Kapellmeister Carl Heinrich Graun died, Agricola was appointed

Right: Carl Philipp Emanuel Bach.
Below: title page and beginning of Preface to
C. P. E. Bach's famous *Essay* (1753).

Versuch
über die wahre Art
das Clavier zu spielen
mit Exempeln
und achtzehn Probe-Stücken in sechs Sonaten
erläutert
von
Carl Philipp Emanuel Bach,
Königl. Preuß. Cammer-Musikus.

Berlin, in Verlegung des Auctoris.

Gedruckt bey dem Königl. Hof-Buchdrucker Christian Friedrich Henning.
1 7 5 3

Vorrede.

So viele Vorzüge das Clavier besitzet, so vielen Schwürigkeiten ist dasselbe zu gleicher Zeit unterworffen. Die Vollkommenheit desselben wäre leichte daraus zu erweisen, wenn es nöthig wäre, weil es diejenigen Eigenschafften, die andere Instrumente nur einzeln haben, in sich vereinet; weil man eine vollständige Harmonie, wozu sonst drey, vier und mehrere Instrumente erfordert werden, darauf mit einmahl hervor bringen kan, und was dergleichen Vortheile mehr sind. Wem ist aber nicht zugleich bekannt, wie viele Forderungen an das Clavier gemachet werden; wie man sich nicht begnüget, dasjenige von einem Clavierspieler zu erwarten, was man von jedem Instrumentisten mit Recht fordern kan, nemlich die Fertigkeit, ein für sein Instru-
* 2   ment

his successor. His contemporaries called Agricola "one of our most thoughtful composers." In 1751, during Christian's stay in Berlin, he married the Italian singer Emilia Molteni, with whom he journeyed to Italy. He was well qualified to take part in the discussions about the new "mixed taste," for he was an authority on the "learned" Bach tradition but was also familiar with the cantabile style, which he had studied at the source, with an Italian singer at his side.[3]

Christoph Nichelmann, another Bach pupil in the king's service, would fare less well. An alumnus of St. Thomas School, he had studied with Bach as early as 1730. In Bach's absence he had been taught by Friedemann, and Nichelmann may therefore have given the two brothers a warm welcome on their arrival in Berlin. His relation to Emanuel, however, was problematic. In 1745 Nichelmann had been appointed by royal decree as second harpsichord player to the king. It is not clear whether his rank was equal to or below Emanuel's, but his salary of five hundred taler was substantially higher than Emanuel's. Just how relations between them deteriorated and how Nichelmann left, more or less against his own will, and how he eventually died in poverty—all this is considered later in this chapter when Emanuel's personality is investigated in relation to Christian's education.

The third former Bach pupil in Berlin, Johann Philipp Kirnberger, was to have his troubles with one of the Bach sons, in this case, Friedemann. Following his years as a student in Leipzig, Kirnberger spent ten years writing fashionable music in the service of several Polish counts. After he was engaged as a violinist for the Prussian court chapel, he published a pamphlet about composing polonaises and minuets. It amounted to a clear endorsement of the gallant style. More than other Bach pupils, he displayed the stylistic ambivalence of the time, for he turned to writing fugues and arranging chorales. In this he was so successful that theorists like Marpurg were glad to quote him. Kirnberger loudly proclaimed that "in today's music, the bass is the most important of all voices." This old-fashioned opinion displeased the king, a believer in the new, melodic style, so when Kirnberger entered the service of the king's sister, Princess Anna Amalia, Frederick was glad to be rid of him.[4]

Kirnberger's collision with Friedemann occurred at this time. Kirnberger, who had supported Friedemann in times of need, now became the victim of an intrigue. Kirnberger wrote to Forkel that "Herr Bach, unmindful of my good feelings toward him, allowed himself to be persuaded to go to the princess, slandering me in the worst manner. In that way he hoped to have me dismissed, so that he could obtain my position."[5] This happened during 1778–1779, but as a result, Friedemann fell out of favor with the princess—another step on his path to perdition.

Since these quarrels occurred after Christian's years in Berlin, he was not involved in or affected by them. To him, his father's former pupils were friends who reinforced his positive memories of Johann Sebastian and his solid teaching. Such reinforcement was valuable for the young musician, faced with the confusion of frequently opposing factions that championed the old or the new. It was also to the good that there was no great age difference between Christian and the three: Nichelmann at thirty-three, Agricola at thirty, and Kirnberger at twenty-nine were even younger than Emanuel, who was then thirty-six, and there was no real generation gap between them and Christian.

Other circumstances helped to smooth the transition from Leipzig to Berlin. It was not surprising that the three former students greatly respected Christian's father, but this attitude was not to be taken for granted among Berlin's leading musicians: Quantz and the Graun brothers. Yet Sebastian's visit, having occurred only three years earlier, was still alive in the memories of those musicians, even if they did not subscribe to the same musical creed.

Quantz, then fifty-five years old, unquestionably ranked highest with the king, who valued his teacher's opinion above all others. Quantz's treatise on playing the transverse flute is far more than its title would imply. Only 40 of its 334 pages deal with the flute per se. Most of the book discusses musical practice and describes the musical taste of the day, from his perspective as the king's instructor.

In the chapter about keyboard players, Quantz refers to Johann Sebastian Bach as "one of the greatest." Elsewhere he speaks of "the admirable Bach," who in recent times had brought organ playing "to its greatest perfection." There is not a trace of the air of superiority with which other contemporaries referred to Father Bach.

Such praise must have been a source of satisfaction to Christian, even though he, too, according to some, had once spoken disparagingly of his father. In Berlin people might disagree with or even criticize Bach, but they did not belittle his achievements. In his essay, Quantz stresses the importance of serious, comprehensive musicianship.

> Whoever wants to excel in music must be diligent and spare no effort. His love and devotion must be untiring; he must be willing to bear all the hardships that the life of a musician entails. Whatever is done in music without thinking and careful reflection, as though music were a mere pastime, is useless.[6]

Surely Christian eagerly absorbed such thoughts from Quantz's treatise, published in 1752. He may have thought of the work as his Bible, especially since Quantz had studied the much-touted Italian music at the source and surely spoke with authority.

At the age of twenty-seven, Quantz had traveled to Rome in the company of the Saxon ambassador. He had studied composition with the famed Gasparini and had experienced opera in Naples, one of its main centers. Having made the acquaintance of Johann Adolf Hasse, whom the Italians venerated as "the divine Saxon," he lived in his house. The friendship between Quantz and Hasse, formed at this time, was later renewed in Dresden and Berlin.

On his return journey, Quantz made a detour to Paris, where he became familiar with French music, and to London. Handel, then at the height of his operatic fame, urged him to stay in London. Quantz declined, saying that his king "should not be deprived of the fruits of his journey." (At this time, Quantz was still referring to the Saxon king.)

The fruits of Quantz's journey were his ability to combine the characteristics of Italian and French music with the *gearbeitete Stil*, the well worked out style of German polyphony. We may recall that this was exactly what Scheibe had considered the ideal achievement of a "European composer" (see page 23). According to Quantz, the heart should converge with the mind in the "mixed taste" or style; that is, the champion of melody should converse with the champion of counterpoint.

When Quantz returned from Italy, he had not entirely submitted to the mellifluous sounds of the south; rather, he stressed a composer's need for industry, thoroughness, and solid contrapuntal technique. To those who viewed Italy as the promised land of music, Quantz declared: "No aspiring musician should go to Italy until he has learned to distinguish the good from the bad in music. Unless he takes some musical know-how with him, he will hardly bring any back when he returns, especially at the present time."

Young Christian could subscribe to this point of view, secure in the knowledge that his father had imparted to him such "musical know-how." And he would also heed Quantz's demand that instrumental music should also be songlike. In Part Eighteen of his treatise, entitled "How to judge musicians and music," Quantz advocates "good singing" as important in instrumental music, too, and he takes to task the Italians who "praise a singer when he sings clearly and with expression but who see nothing wrong with playing that is murky and without feeling." Such views appealed to Christian, who later became famous for the "singing

The Bohemian composer Franz Benda, active in Berlin.

Johann Joachim Quantz, flute instructor to King Frederick II, who performed his flute concertos.

allegro" in his instrumental writing. Here, too, Quantz and others contributed to Christian's development.

Just which of Quantz's works would Christian be likely to have
heard? Though Quantz composed some five hundred concertos, sonatas,
trios, and quartets, all were written "in the line of duty," that is, for the
personal use of the king. Musical soirées at the court were conducted for
the pleasure of the ruler and with his participation; the public, for the
most part, was excluded. Thus it is not surprising that few of Quantz's
works reached print: a mere six duets in 1759 and the *kirchenmelodien*
(hymns) in 1760. Not a single one was published during Christian's stay
in Berlin.

Outside the royal palace, Quantz's music could be heard at some of
the many private concerts given by members of the court chapel, other
professional musicians, and amateurs. These concerts added greatly to
Berlin's musical life. For example, there was a group called the
Musikübende Gesellschaft (Musical Society), which had been founded in
1749 and was directed by cathedral organist Philipp Sack. Every Saturday
they gathered in Sack's home across from the royal palace—at six o'clock
in summer, five in winter. There they would make music for three hours
in the presence of a select audience. On Fridays there was an "akademie"
at the residence of Johann Gottlieb Janitsch, a member of the court
chapel, and on Mondays a musical "assemblée" was held in the quarters
of cellist Johann Christian Schale, another court musician. An additional concert took place on Saturdays, the same night as the Musical
Society, under the direction of court composer Agricola.[7] In all, Berlin
boasted a busy calendar of musical events.

Besides hearing chamber music at any of these concerts, Christian
may also have attended meetings of the Monday Club. Such clubs were
based on an English model. As the leading organization of its kind, the
Monday Club (which in Christian's time was actually the Thursday
Club) had many distinguished members, including Quantz. By belonging
to this select circle, Quantz extended his influence to middle-class audiences, who were impressed with his personality, appearance, and compositions.

Quantz was not gentle and self-effacing—an obsequious courtier,
bathing in his master's reflected glory—as one might imagine the king's
flute instructor to be. Rather, he had an imposing appearance, which
inspired the great Dr. Burney to quote Shakespeare:

> The son of Hercules he justly seems,
> By his broad shoulders, and gigantic limbs.

Burney, who met the seventy-five-year-old Quantz, described him as having a blustering, robust manner, open and frank in a way that impressed King Frederick.[8]

Quantz's colleagues respected him but were not averse to humor when it came to acknowledging Quantz's special relationship with the king. With his proverbial sharp tongue, Emanuel posed the question: "Which is the most feared animal in all of Prussia?" When everyone was baffled, Emanuel provided the answer: "It is Madame Quantz's lap dog. It is so fierce that even Madame Quantz is afraid of it. But Herr Quantz is afraid of her, and the greatest living monarch is afraid of Quantz." The Marquis d'Argens is said to have reported this joke to the king, who laughed and replied: "Dear Marquis, make sure that Quantz will not get wind of this, or he will dismiss us all from his service!"[9]—a clever royal repartee, if indeed ever made. At any rate, such anecdotes do tell us something about the respect Quantz enjoyed, even from the king.

When reading or listening to one of the king's compositions, Quantz sometimes "voiced" his criticism by discreetly clearing his throat. He once resorted to this tactic to call attention to a faulty harmonic progression in Frederick's score. Several days later the king asked Franz Benda, a violinist-composer of whom he also thought highly, whether Quantz's criticism seemed justified. When Benda answered in the affirmative, the king corrected the passage in question, remarking that "after all, we don't want Quantz to catch a cold."

At times the king responded less positively to criticism. When Quantz introduced one of his other pupils to the king, Frederick praised him somewhat faintly and then reproached the teacher: "You have neglected me! The young man proves it; he certainly is not as industrious as I am!" "With him I employed a very effective teaching device," said Quantz. "And what was that?" asked the king. Quantz hesitated, but when Frederick insisted, the teacher moved his arm as if beating with a cane. "I see," said the king, "let's stick to our accustomed method."[10]

Given Quantz's stature, Carl Heinrich Graun, the other star in the Berlin musical firmament, was less firmly established. Frederick was unsure whether Graun was to be esteemed chiefly as a composer or as a singer. (Because of Graun's beautiful, expressive performance, Frederick called him his "adagio singer.") On a personal level, the king was closer to Graun than to Quantz; but then Graun's forte was opera, a field in which the king felt quite secure, whereas in the realm of chamber music, he was sometimes subjected to his underling Quantz's criticism.

When it came to opera, the king ruled, as Burney put it, "like a field

marshal in battle." During rehearsals, and sometimes even during a public performance, he would stand immediately behind Graun, keeping an
eye on the score. Woe to anyone who took liberties with the music!

> In the opera house, as in the field, his majesty is such a rigid disciplinar-
> ian that if a mistake is made in a single movement or evolution, he
> immediately rebukes the offender; and if any of his Italian troops dare
> to deviate from strict discipline, by adding, altering, or diminishing a
> single passage in the parts they have to perform, an order is sent, in the
> name of the king, for them to adhere strictly to the notes written by the
> composer, at their peril.[11]

This may have been a strict regime, but because of it Christian experienced opera in all its splendor. What Mingotti's opera troupe had produced in Leipzig, on an improvised stage, had been merely a pale
imitation of what Christian now saw and heard in Berlin. This was Italian opera at its best, musically and visually. Vocal and orchestral discipline were outstanding, while costumes, scenery, and ballet were
unequalled anywhere in Europe.

During his years as a student at the Dresden Kreuzschule, Graun had
received an introduction to Italian opera by participating as an occasional chorus member. At that time Frederick, then still crown prince,
developed great enthusiasm for Italian opera. When he became king, this
enthusiasm produced tangible results. One of his first official acts was to
send Graun to Italy to recruit singers for the Berlin opera (see page 6).
Graun's own singing pleased even the hard-to-please Italians. After nine
months he returned to Berlin with five male and three female singers
whom he had recruited in Rome, Milan, Naples, Venice, Bologna, and
Brescia.[12]

The results of Graun's scouting trip left something to be desired. In
his defense, it should be pointed out that while he could offer his recruits
good money, he could not entice them with a good theater, for at the
time Berlin had no opera house. Thus the new arrivals could at first
present themselves in concert only. A small provisional theater was hur-
riedly installed in the palace, but not until a year later could Baron von
Knobelsdorff report to the impatient king that the new opera house was
ready. The hall was inaugurated on 7 December 1742 with a performance
of Graun's *Cesare e Cleopatra*.

A few days earlier the *Berlinische priviligierte Zeitung* had announced
the winter's weekly calendar: assemblies and masked balls on Saturdays,
operas on Mondays and Fridays, and French comedies on Wednesdays. It

Above left: Carl Heinrich Graun, the king's favorite opera composer.

Above right: Francesco Algarotti, one of the king's close friends, author of an essay advocating opera reform.

Below: the Berlin Opera, c. 1770. Engraving by Johann David Schleuen.

was a season of brilliant spectacles, lasting through the carnival season from late November to March, rich in entertainment and joie de vivre. It wasn't a bad life for the singers; they had to perform only twice a week and were on vacation for half a year. For that their salaries amounted to several thousand taler, far more than those of the orchestra members. Among the latter, Quantz and Graun fared best with two thousand taler each. The salaries of most others, Emanuel included, ranged between one hundred and four hundred taler. No wonder that, after the modest premier season, first-rate Italian singers were attracted to Berlin, among them Salimbeni from Milan and Signora Astrua from Turin. They signed long-term contracts for yearly salaries of four thousand and six thousand taler, respectively. The dancer Barbarina (Barbara Campanini) commanded seven thousand taler, a salary that was unusually high, even for Frederick, leading to rumors that other, nonartistic considerations were involved.

Among temperamental artists, too much free time inevitably led to boredom and dissatisfaction. "Malcontents," the king called them, and when their demands became too obnoxious he sent word to them that they had been hired "for the king's pleasure, not to vex him." If such reprimands failed, he did not hesitate to hint that they might spend a summer "behind the iron lace curtains of Spandau prison."

The king could afford to make such threats. The opera was closed during the summer and the singers were not needed. But since the monarch did not want to do without any theater or lighter musical fare, the "Intermezzo" was established on the stage of Potsdam castle's small theater. A troupe was engaged, at first for one season only but eventually as a standing company, to perform once a week, even during the regular season. The king liked Italian opera buffa, which he referred to as "silly stuff—but . . . pleasant when sung well." These productions provided a welcome change from the two serious operas that Graun customarily wrote each year for the large house. Perhaps to make it more palatable, Graun's work was coupled on at least one occasion with a magnificent display of fireworks.[13]

By the time Christian Bach arrived in Berlin, Graun had become a fixture there. Of the thirty-three operas he wrote in all, twenty-two had been given by then. It was no easy task to be the favorite composer of a king who insisted on Italian operas but would tolerate only German composers. Aside from Graun, only Hasse and Agricola were acceptable. Frederick liked Graun's vocal writing, which reflected the composer's own ability as a singer. But the king had his own ideas about operatic reform and instructed Graun to devote special attention to the cavatina, a shorter type of aria.

His Majesty interfered in many other ways. When one of Graun's arias displeased him and Graun refused to write another one, the king thought nothing of ordering it replaced with one by Hasse. Another time, when Graun decided to perform a fugue that his friends considered "most artistic" as the opening number for his opera *Lucio Papirio*, Frederick summarily commanded that it be replaced by a traditional overture.

In spite of all this, Frederick harbored warm feelings for Graun and even displayed an interest in his church music, a genre he usually approached with suspicion. He actually liked Graun's oratoio *Der Tod Jesu*. On the day following its performance, the monarch sent a letter: "Yesterday I heard your cantata *Der Tod Jesu*. I am sending you a tobacco box filled with thirty ducats. But from the pieces that pleased me I exclude the aria "Ihr weich geschaffene Seelen." Graun was disturbed by this apparent criticism until his wife suggested that he look at the other side of the letter, where the sentence continued: "for it is priceless."[14]

All in all, the king appreciated his court composer. No one else would have been able to satisfy his insatiable craving for Italian operas. For Christian's development this was all to the good, for Graun's Italian operas made a lasting impression on him—not only for their lyric, cantabile qualities but also for their visual aspects, their elaborate staging. They may have served Christian as a basis for comparison when he later established himself as an opera composer of repute in Italy, England, France, and Germany, including Mannheim.

Of the eleven remaining operas Graun wrote for Berlin, Christian may have seen five, assuming that he was in the audience for *Mitridate*, staged in mid-December 1750. During the following years he may have heard *Armida* (27 March 1751), *Britannico* (17 December 1751), *Orfeo* (27 March 1752), *Il giudizio di Paride* (a special pastoral play written for the wedding of Prince Heinrich, 26 June 1752), and *Silla* (27 March 1753). He may also have been among the citizens who sat in the third balcony to see Graun's twenty-third opera, *Semiramide*. Since it was given on 27 March 1754, Christian would have been able to hear it before he departed for Italy.[15]

At any rate, Christian had the opportunity of attending these performances, for by royal decree the opera was open to any and all, provided they were "decently attired." By this, Frederick showed himself to be a true "citizens' king," especially since there was no admission charge, though tickets were often sold on the black market.

An evening at the opera was a great event. A contemporary writer well describes the experience of a friend, a young visitor from the country, with whom he attended a performance of Graun's *Alessandro e Poro.* They arrived an hour early, in good time to look around.

> So far, the object of his curiosity was hidden by the curtain. Only a few lamps had been lit; only a few boxes were occupied. But soon the house was filled completely. Soldiers from the Garde du Corps stationed themselves at the parterre entrance. Ladies in makeup and bedecked with jewels occupied the crowded boxes. With their ribbons and flowers they attracted much attention. The light of many candles that had now been lit was reflected in their jewels.
>
> Now the orchestra began to tune, to the fascination of my friend who could not take his eyes off the players. Two musicians stood out among the rest, due to their red coats: the two Grauns. Carl Heinrich, the Kapellmeister, sat at the first harpsichord, while the concertmaster [Johann Gottlieb] took the first chair among the violinists. As princes and other members of the nobility arrived, they took pleasure in conversing with the Kapellmeister, who responded to their friendly condescendence in a dignified manner.
>
> Soon the royal family entered their boxes, causing some stir among the spectators. The Garde du Corps presented arms as the king made his entrance, bareheaded, through the crowd. They were elated by his appearance, as the earth welcomes the rising sun. He stood next to the two Grauns, eyeing the crowd through his opera glasses. Meanwhile two alternating groups of kettledrums announced the arrival of the king's mother, following which the opera's opening chorus was heard. After a few measures, my friend found himself transported to another world.[16]

Strict etiquette was not always observed. Once, on 1 April, an expectant public had filled the hall for the "Intermezzo," waiting for the curtain to open. Cricci, the director of the Potsdam theater and the ensemble's basso buffo, stepped up to the footlights, looked around in feigned surprise, and began to laugh. The audience, a little perplexed but in a good mood, also started to laugh. Their disappointment was all the greater when Cricci asked for silence and announced, in his broken German: "Ladies and-a gentlemen: is-a today the first of April—HA, HA, HA!" With that the curtain closed, lights were extinguished, and the spectators, more or less annoyed about their ruler's April Fools' Day joke, left for home.[17]

Yet opera in Berlin amounted to more than social diversion, for Frederick sought three qualities: beautiful melodies, true and profound emotion, and solid musical construction. The "learned" quality (which to the king was not synonymous with counterpoint) had up to then been represented by Quantz and his instrumental music; soon Emanuel was to follow with his *Essay on the True Art of Playing Keyboard Instruments*. In opera, the intellectual leader was Francesco Algarotti, who was a good friend of the monarch. Late in life Frederick declared that he "was always pleased when intellect and music went hand in hand. Music that is both beautiful and learned pleases me as much as good conversation at the dinner table."

Algarotti had established himself with lightning speed at the Prussian court. Soon after his accession to the throne, Frederick had called the twenty-eight-year-old Italian to Berlin and at once raised him to the nobility. Algarotti made a good personal impression, was well educated, and had the king's tastes in arts and belles lettres. He was just the right person to act as artistic adviser. One of his assignments was to overhaul the stereotyped old librettos, even Frederick's own, before they were exposed to public scrutiny. He also acted as the king's secretary. When Frederick was deeply moved by the aria "All'onor mio rifletti" from Hasse's opera *Lucio Parpirio*, he had Algarotti write a congratulatory letter to the composer who, next to Graun, was his favorite.

Except for a temporary estrangement from 1742 to 1746, their friendship continued even after Algarotti, for reasons of health, retired to Italy in 1753. When Algarotti died, Frederick commissioned a monument for his tomb in faraway Pisa; a unique gesture for a Prussian king.

In Berlin, Christian probably acquainted himself with some of the ideas that Algarotti would publish in his famous essay, the *Saggio sopra l'opera in musica*.[18] For Christian's career as an opera composer, this exposure was all to the good. Algarotti represents one of the ironies in music history: an Italian, making use of experiences gathered at the Prussian court, sets out to reform Italian opera, demanding "discipline" to "bring order to its musical realm."

In his introduction to the *Saggio*, Algarotti states:

Among all the entertainments enjoyed by men and women of spirit, opera may be the most perfect and most meaningful. In opera, all the charms of poetry, music, pantomime, dance, and painting are felicitously combined to charm our senses, to enchant our hearts, and to produce a pleasing illusion.

After this encomium, Algarotti turns to more critical observations:

Yet those gentlemen who today take charge of our pleasures do not

bother to make the efforts needed to create a good opera. They devote
little attention to the selection of text and poetry; they do not care
whether the music expresses the text, and they are completely indifferent to truth in spoken and sung words. Whether the dances are related
to action, whether the sets are suitable, and even whether the theater
building itself is faultily constructed—none of these concerns enters
their minds. As a result, a performance that might have been the most
perfect of all becomes as trite and boring as one can imagine. . . .
Whoever wants to return opera to its former glory and dignity must
begin where the need is greatest: he must restore order in the musical
realm. The virtuosos, as in former times, must submit to discipline and
authority.[19]

Discipline and authority on the stage were the king's personal concern, but in the orchestra Johann Gottlieb Graun, the older of the two
brothers, was in charge. Frederick had engaged him as early as 1732,
while still crown prince, for his ensemble in Rheinsberg. Later he
appointed him concertmaster of the court chapel, an ensemble of forty
musicians.

Gottlieb had also been to Italy, where he had studied with no less a
master than Tartini.

To tell the truth, upon his return to Dresden his playing found far less
favor than before, so that, in order once more to receive applause, he
had to return to the tasteful playing of the famous Pisendel, his former
teacher.

Thus reported the anonymous author of *Thoughts About Italian Artists*
(1751).[20] Gottlieb, following in Berlin the example Pisendel had set in
Dresden, lead a well-disciplined orchestra, all of whom were virtuosos in
their own right. It was as good as, if not better than, the Dresden model.

Gottlieb Graun's relation to the Bach family was close. While Graun
had been in Merseburg, Father Bach had entrusted Friedemann to his
care, anxious to have his son receive a well-rounded education. Friedemann continued to be fond of his former violin teacher, and Johann
Sebastian Bach, always interested in music from the court of the Prussian
king, made copies of two of Graun's trios.

Gottlieb Graun also forms a link to an important group of musicians
coming from Bohemia. Many gifted Bohemian instrumentalists left their
homeland to seek employment all over Europe. Berlin saw a regular invasion of them, headed by Franz Benda, who had attracted Frederick's
attention when he was still crown prince. In his lively autobiography
Benda recalls the occasion:

I arrived in Ruppin on 17 April 1733 and took a room at an inn. I was just warming up on the violin when His Highness the crown prince passed by the inn. He stopped and listened for a while, then sent for me. I immediately came downstairs and presented myself. His Highness instructed me to call on him in the evening. He himself most graciously accompanied me on the clavier, and this is how I entered his service. I then also met the present concertmaster, Herr Graun, whom to this day I count among my dearest friends.[21]

A lifelong friendship united Graun, instructed by Tartini, and Franz Benda, who always pointed out that he had learned more from a blind Jew named Löbel, with whom he played at country dances, than from any "real" teacher.

Benda was devoted to his king. When Gottlieb Graun died in 1771, surviving his younger brother Carl Heinrich by twelve years, Benda succeeded him as concertmaster of the court chapel. He remained in the king's service until his death, a full fifty-three years.

Christian's high opinion of Bohemian musicians (an opinion he shared with Mozart) was based on his familiarity with Franz Benda and the many musicians in Benda's family, and also with the many other Bohemians at court: Czarth, Hock, Horzizky, and Mara, to name only some. In his famous account of his journey through Germany, Charles Burney confirms this for 1773:

I had frequently been told, that the Bohemians were the most musical people of Germany, or, perhaps, of all Europe; and an eminent German composer, now in London, had declared to me, that if they enjoyed the same advantages as the Italians, they would excel them.[22]

The "eminent German composer" was none other than John Christian Bach whose experiences can only have been gained in Berlin. Other contemporary reports confirm these opinions. "More than once, Benda's playing of an Adagio moved his listeners to tears." Again it was the cantabile playing that touched people's hearts, and Benda's mastery of the style comes as no surprise since he, like Carl Heinrich Graun, had begun his career as a singer.

Specific Bohemian influences in Christian's music are difficult to identify, but there are traces everywhere in his instrumental music, in expressive, songlike passages that occur in both slow and fast movements. Berlin and Bohemia were important to Christian's career in more ways than one.

Both Emanuel Bach and Benda were favored by the patronage of Fer-

dinand Philipp Joseph, Prince von Lobkowitz, a high-ranking nobleman
who came from an old Bohemian family with a tradition of patronizing
the arts. He became one of Frederick's closest friends—an intermediary,
as it were, between the Austrian imperial house and the royal Prussian
court, to which he had turned after Austria lost the Silesian wars. Frederick heaped honors on him, making him a member of the Academy of Sciences in 1749, and establishing him as feudal lord of Sagan, an estate in
Silesia. Prince Lobkowitz harbored friendly, familial feelings toward his
fellow Bohemians at the Prussian court. Franz Benda instructed him in
violin playing, and the prince was godfather to the son of Benda's brother
Joseph who was also a member of the court chapel.

Emanuel Bach, too, was close to the prince—musically speaking,
perhaps closer than Benda. Later, in Emanuel's will, there is a reference
to a "symphony written, measure for measure, together with Prince
Lobkowitz," a testimony to the informal nature of their relationship and
perhaps the product of lively composition lessons. Though details are
lacking, we can assume that Emanuel instructed the prince in both piano
playing and composition,[23] just as years earlier he had given composition
lessons to Lobkowitz's relatives Prince Karl Eugen, the later regent, and
his brother, Friedrich Eugen. Their grandmother was a Lobkowitz by
birth; quite likely the family had been satisfied with Emanuel's services,
which may have helped him in his association with Prince Ferdinand
Philipp.

In spite of their common patron, Emanuel and Benda were not particularly close, which brings to mind Emanuel's relations to other musicians and his criticisms of their works. More generally it leads to the
question: what kind of a person was Emanuel, who watched over Christian during the crucial years of his development from age fifteen to eighteen?

Burney described his physical appearance:

> He is now fifty-nine, rather short in stature, with black hair and eyes,
> and brown complexion, has a very animated countenance, and is of a
> chearful and lively disposition.

Others said that he had an "almost southern" temperament. "Imagination and sobriety, quick repartee but also great sensitivity; a cheerful and
witty manner, a practical outlook; purposefully searching for what is new
and daring in art" were qualities he "combined in an unusual way."[24]

Such observations allude to the two faces of Emanuel, to the strange
split personality also found in his music. Predictably, those who knew

him reacted in different ways. He commanded attention and respect as the son of the great Johann Sebastian and as a teacher, a keyboardist, and a composer, in that order. But there were also negative opinions, alleging that he seemed satisfied with composing "pleasant little things" and that he displayed a tendency toward the trivial, which seemed at odds with his own insistence on quality.

People enjoyed his company because of his wit and lively mind, but they were also on guard, because his wit could turn into irony and sarcasm, giving rise to biting, malicious comments. He had shown these traits even in childhood. Friedrich Rochlitz, editor of the *Leipzig Allgemeine Musikalische Zeitung*, reports that Emanuel, "more than other physically and mentally agile boys, suffered from a compulsion to tease others mercilessly." The king was not pleased with these qualities, seeing in them a certain stubborn and rebellious nature. Emanuel, it was said, would beat time most emphatically whenever the king himself wanted to set the tempo.[25] On one occasion, the story goes, a listener praised the king's flute playing to high heaven, exclaiming "what wonderful rhythm!" To which Emanuel, in his usual, satirical way, replied: "Yes, many rhythms!"

Another anecdote relates that Emanuel did not think much of the king's understanding of music. "If you think the king loves music, you are wrong; he only loves to play the flute. But if you believe that he loves to play the flute, you are wrong again; he only loves his flute."[26]

Emanuel, one realizes from these stories, was not his ruler's most devoted subject. In that way he resembled his father, often at odds with his superiors. Karl Friedrich Fasch, second court harpsichordist, took a more conciliatory view:

> Carl Philipp Emanuel and Graun had opposite artistic personalities. Emanuel, spirited and full of originality as a composer, was fond of the king as a person of keen intellect and a great ruler but would not accept his autocratic claims to genius and expertise in art. The king, Emanuel contended, was the ruler of his kingdom but not of the kingdom of the arts, where only gods ruled. All talent came from them and would return to them. . . . Such views were hardly within the limits of the great Frederick's tolerance, nor did Bach's compositions meet with approval.[27]

This lack of approbation must have disappointed Emanuel. His bitterness led to sarcasm, which in turn brought further ill will from the king—truly a devilish circle. It was a depressing state of affairs: concerts of chamber music took place daily except on Mondays and Fridays, which were opera days. But Emanuel was never given a chance to shine.

It wasn't that he didn't try. Back in his Leipzig days he had already composed five trios and a solo for flute, the king's own instrument. The flute pieces he wrote while in Frankfurt on the Oder suggest even more strongly that Emanuel composed them in order to attract the attention of Frederick, then still crown prince. This was certainly the motivation behind the two flute concertos he wrote in Berlin in 1738, but to no avail. Even the six sonatas for harpsichord, written in the king's service and containing a lengthy Italian preface and dedication to him, would not put Emanuel in the monarch's good graces.

Such rejection cannot be entirely attributed to Emanuel's stubborn and brusque demeanor. It is true, and stands to reason, that in his early works he still adhered largely to his father's style. "In composition and keyboard playing my father was my only teacher," Emanuel said in his autobiography. Such a remark not only reflects the son's pride in his famous father; it also suggests that there had been strong bonds between father and son. In his *Essay*, Emanuel relied closely on his father's technique. Throughout his life he never lost his fondness for counterpoint. It seems symbolic that among his contributions to Marpurg's *Historisch-kritische Beiträge* he included an "Invention in double [invertible] counterpoint at six measures," a somewhat mathematical tour de force. He also exchanged riddle canons with Kirnberger, a kind of writing of which his father had been very fond.[28]

There is something tragic in all this. His talent notwithstanding, Emanuel lacked the lightness and spontaneity with which others, especially his brother John Christian, embraced the new style. Among his colleagues in Berlin, Emanuel was not wholly accepted as a composer. Although Christian Gottfried Krause, a member of the Monday Club, harbored no ill will toward Emanuel, he expressed his reservations about one of Emanuel's trios in a letter to a friend: "Try hard not to reject this trio immediately. Bach's music requires study. One has to become quite familiar with his melodies; then they may please." In his chief work, *Von der musikalischen Poesie*, written in 1750 at a time when Emanuel was by no means a beginner in composition, Krause defends Emanuel against the accusation that his music is difficult to understand. "A keyboard concerto by the esteemed Berlin Bach is no less perfect than one by Herr Kapellmeister Graun. The latter may please more listeners more readily, yet both concertos are well written for the clavier, keeping in mind the ability of the player."[29]

Twenty years later, Heinrich Wilhelm von Gerstenberg, a music critic and friend of Emanuel, wrote to the publisher Friedrich Nicolai that "Emanuel's cantabile writing is as good as that of any other German, not only in vocal music but also in compositions for the clavier. They are difficult, I admit, but melodious."[30] He was apparently responding to Nicolai's concern that Emanuel's works were hard to understand and lacked melodic appeal.

Emanuel himself had stated, at the end of his autobiography, that his "chief endeavor in recent years has been to play and write for the clavier in as cantabile a manner as possible, in spite of the instrument's inability to sustain tones." This, he admitted, was a challenge.

Emanuel's rather mediocre salary reveals something about his position at the Prussian court. The payroll records for 1744–1745 list Emanuel among those appointed in 1741 with a salary of three hundred taler. Whereas eighteen musicians received lower pay and eleven the same (including some long-forgotten names such as Hesse, Spehr, and Pfeiffer), no fewer than twenty-four were paid more—considerably more in some cases. Besides the highly paid singers and the dancer Barbarina mentioned earlier, there was the singer Porporino, who received two thousand taler.

Among the instrumentalists we find Quantz and Carl Heinrich Graun with salaries of two thousand taler plus some extra benefits. Graun's brother Johann Gottlieb received a respectable twelve hundred, while Benda earned eight hundred, well over twice Emanuel's salary. It must have been especially demoralizing to Emanuel that in all of fourteen years he did not receive a single raise, and he had to swallow the fact that, as first harpsichordist, he earned two hundred taler less than Nichelmann, the second harpsichordist.

Not that he had to suffer deprivations. He had married into a family of well-to-do merchants, he earned additional income as a composer, and he was much in demand as a teacher, even during the Seven Years' War when the king's musicians were not paid in cash but were given nearly worthless certificates. Zelter recalled that, by 1758,

> Bach had acquired an excellent reputation throughout Germany and had had good success [in deriving financial benefit from his composing]. He was so well paid for this, and for teaching, that he had no financial worries.[31]

Emanuel's business acumen was one of his less attractive traits, as noted by his contemporaries. According to the *Musikalmanach von 1796*, he was ever mindful of his own financial gain, even as a teacher of eager young artists, and "this avarice was also the motivation for some of his recent compositions."[32]

A story about the copper plates of his father's *Art of Fugue* also belongs here. Emanuel had received them from his father's estate. Since only thirty engraved copies of the music had been sold, Emanuel decided to dispose of the plates as quickly as possible and published the following advertisement:

> I hereby inform all music publishers that I intend to sell very cheaply the copper plates, cleanly and accurately engraved, of the fugue compo-sition of my late father, Kapellmeister Joh. Seb. Bach. There are about sixty plates, altogether weighing 100 pounds. . . . Any interested music lovers may write to me here in Berlin; they can be assured that I shall reply immediately to the first acceptable offer, and shall turn over the plates without any delay or formalities.[33]

The announcement brings to mind Emanuel's obituary in which it is said that "he did not lack an appreciation of money and the monetary worth of things." One would like to think that in selling the plates he hoped someone else would publish the *Art of Fugue*, but his wording con-veys the impression that Emanuel was above all eager to divest himself of the plates as quickly as possible, without regard for assurance of later pub-lication. Moreover, the pointed reference to the weight of the copper plates suggests that he may have hoped someone would buy them for their metal value. His motivation, therefore, seems to have been material gain rather than the desire to preserve for posterity his father's last instru-mental work.

The reason for dealing with Emanuel in such detail is that, after his father's death, it was he who was in charge of Christian's education dur-ing the youth's formative years. In answering the question of what one Bach son passed on to the other, the Nichelmann affair must also be mentioned.

Nichelmann's essay on melody, which was dedicated to the king, had received much praise. The learned Marpurg spoke of "a fine piece of writ-ing, the result of much thinking and industry," adding that "the author's profound insights are evident throughout."[34]

Others were less impressed. Using the pen name Kaspar Dünkelfeind [= foe of arrogance—trans.], an anonymous writer launched an attack on Nichelmann's essay. In sixteen pages entitled "Thoughts of a Music Lover About Nichelmann's Treatise on Melody," the writer denied with insult-ing irony that Nichelmann had any qualifications whatsoever for publishing such a work.

> Our well-meant advice to Herr Nichelmann is that instead of writing
> books (for which he has as little talent as for composing), he would do
> better to stick to playing gentle, pleasant little pieces that do not
> require nimble fingers. We sincerely regret that he lacks the ability to
> rise to such heights as his self-love caused him to attempt.

A mean, cutting attack, which should require no further comment. Believing that he knew who was hiding behind the pen name, Nichelmann addressed his refutation of the attack to Emanuel Bach, in full knowledge that this rendered impossible any further working together. He consequently tendered his resignation in December 1755, the attack having been published in July of the same year.

Nichelmann was still carried on the 1754–1755 payroll with a salary of five hundred taler (while Emanuel was earning only three hundred), but there is a notation that Nichelmann's salary would be reduced by two hundred taler, which amount would be added to Bach's pay. The next year's records show that Nichelmann had resigned and that from now on Emanuel was to be paid the amount saved due to Nichelmann's resignation.

The anonymous attack strikingly resembles the Biedermann affair in which Father Bach had been involved, but there is a difference. The old Bach had been fighting for a cause, the place of music in the school curriculum, whereas the central issue for Emanuel was self-interest.

There was such a world of difference between the personalities of Christian and Emanuel that it is hard to think of them as having the same father. But these two sons from Bach's first and second marriages were probably more influenced by their mothers. Of Maria Barbara, mother of Friedemann, Emanuel, and Bernhard, we know next to nothing. In the *nekrolog*, Emanuel wrote that his father "spent thirteen years in a happy marriage" but said little about the wife. Emanuel, of course, was not yet six years old when his mother died.

The similarities between Christian's temperament and Anna Magdalena's likeable personality, however, are clearly evident. His manner was cheerful, ingenuous rather than calculating or devious, and accomodating rather than quarrelsome. When compared with the egotism and shrewd business sense of his brother Emanuel, Christian's character seems pure and naïve.

In monetary matters Christian was generous to a fault, a quality that was evenutally to bring him to the brink of ruin. His housekeeper in London would obtain credit at the stores and keep for herself the money he had given her to cover household expenses. By the time the unpaid merchants remonstrated with Christian, she had long disappeared, leaving him with debts amounting to a thousand pounds. We shall come back to these matters in a later chapter.

The dispositions of the brothers differed in more than just their attitudes toward material things. Emanuel, for example, relished his role as a strict teacher. In the score of a keyboard concerto that Christian had composed in Berlin, Emanuel added his seal of approval: "Riveduto [revised or inspected] dal Sign. C. P. E. Bach," as though the work required his approbation. By contrast, Christian was far more casual. Another keyboard concerto in D major, also written in Berlin, contains the note, scribbled between the lines of the score: "I have written this concerto—isn't it beautiful?"[35]

It may have been a casual comment, quickly jotted down, but it is symbolic of an outlook on life that was to characterize Christian for the rest of his life. To him, as to Mozart, "beauty" was what mattered most in music, and next to beauty came naturalness, even though he would be reproached by Emanuel for excessive simplicity. To Emanuel's "don't be a child," Christian would reply: "I must speak simply, so children will understand me."

Such an exchange points up Emanuel's fear that music might "only fill the ears, but leave the heart empty,"[36] that melodiousness might interfere with the expression of emotion, of the affects. He touches on these ideas in his textbook, the *Essay on the True Art of Playing Keyboard Instruments*:

> One should take advantage of every opportunity to hear talented singers; *one learns thereby to think through singing [singend denken]*. It is wise to sing one's own musical thoughts to arrive at their proper rendition.

The performer, he continues, should also appeal to the heart:

> A musician cannot move others unless he himself is moved. He must therefore be able to experience all the emotions he wants to kindle in his listeners. . . . When we consider the many affects that music can stir, we realize what special gifts an accomplished musician must possess, and with what wisdom he must use them.[37]

The affects, then, must be considered, but they must be governed by the intellect. To be sure, Emanuel treats the concept of affection rather loosely in some of his small keyboard works. According to a contemporary writer:

While still in Berlin, C. P. E. Bach wrote keyboard pieces that portrayed several women of his acquaintance. I was told that their dispositions and behavior were very aptly described in them, but one would have to hear them played by Bach himself.[38]

These miniatures formed part of what Christian may have heard in Berlin; short pieces with titles such as "l'Herrmann," "la Buchholz," "la Boehmer," "la Stahl," and "l'Aly Rupalich"—pieces that were included in the collection *Musikalisches Allerlei*. Bitter described them thus:

L'Herrmann (G minor, 2/4, Allegro moderato) describes a woman of gentle, sensitive disposition, tinged by grace and longing and not without some passion. La Buchholz (D minor, 3/4, Allegro) is chiefly melancholic and sentimental; her easily stimulated imagination leads to choleric outbursts, though she does not lack subtle humor.... l'Aly Rupalich, however (C major, 2/4, Allegro assai), is restless, extroverted by nature, given to changing, passionate feelings, proud but not majestic, lacking depth, and given to only fleeting expressions of grief or pain.[39]

Miniatures of this kind are still recalled in pieces such as Beethoven's "Rage over a Lost Penny, In the Form of a Caprice," though on a somewhat larger scale. The melodists of Emanuel's circle preferred to express the "gentle and tender affects" mentioned by Krause in his *Von der musikalischen Poesie*,[40] in which he distinguishes between "virile grace" and "effeminate weakness." According to Krause and his circle, tragic and desperate emotions, "whatever evokes fear and terror, cannot be expressed in music." Such strong emotions would be more than listeners could bear. He cites Mattheson, who "would gladly have voted in favor of banning overly gruesome subjects from music."[41]

Nor did the melodists approve of what their opponents espoused in the name of variety: the frequent and abrupt changes of affect, of emotional state. Quantz, for instance, had declared that "the charm of music lies not in sameness or similarity but in variety," and "the more our ears are bewitched by new invention, the more they like it." All music should contain "a mixture of thoughts."[42]

Emanuel seems to have been aware of the contradiction inherent in the concept of music with constantly changing affect, or perhaps he had been taken to task for employing that style. At any rate, he appears to be defending himself in his autobiography when he says that he has never been fond of monotony in any field, including composition, and has always believed that one should accept whatever is good wherever one finds it, even if in a composition it occurs in small doses. This, he continues, may account for the variety that has been observed in his music.

It would seem that Emanuel, unlike Christian with his different temperament and pronounced melodic gift, did not turn wholeheartedly to the cantabile style. Consequently, one wonders what Emanuel could have contributed to the musical development of his brother and pupil. Let us consider areas that would be of importance in view of Christian's later stay in Italy.

As for opera, Emanuel never wrote one. Given the king's preference for Graun, and on occasion for Hasse and Agricola, there simply may not have been an opportunity. Emanuel may also have been unfavorably impressed by the superficiality he thought existed in the world of opera and its singers. At home, neither his father nor his brother Friedemann had had much use for opera and its "nice little songs," though occasionally they did journey to Dresden to hear some of this "ear-tickling" music. At any rate, when it came to opera, Christian received no instruction or inspiration from Emanuel.

The story was much the same for sacred music, a field that was important for Christian, who, to the surprise of many, turned to it in Italy before taking up instrumental music and opera. But by the time Christian arrived in Berlin, Emanuel had written only one sacred composition, a Magnificat in eight movements, which was finished in Potsdam on 25 August 1749. At the end of the score Emanuel added the letters "S. D. Gl."—Soli Deo Gloria.

That he should have written a sacred work while involved in the predominantly secular life of Berlin may seem surprising. Does the pious notation at the end align the work, and the composer, with the venerable tradition of the Bach family? Though some consider it doubtful, there are indications that Emanuel included this Magnificat with his application to succeed his father at St. Thomas in Leipzig. At any rate, he wrote no other sacred works until the Easter cantata of 1756.

The Magnificat's date of completion is significant, for on 25 August, Father Bach was still alive. It is likely that when Bach's eventual successor, Harrer, played an organ audition on 8 June, Emanuel decided to write a work in support of his own application, to be ready and available at the time of his father's death. There can hardly be another explanation for the existence of this single sacred work. Moreover, its resemblance to Johann Sebastian's great Magnificat in E-flat major (1723) is obvious and may have been intentional. Perhaps Emanuel hoped that his work would remind the selection committee of his distinguished father, causing them to give special consideration to his own application.[43] But, as we know, Emanuel's efforts were not successful.

The Magnificat was not printed during Emanuel's lifetime, not even after he became director of church music in Hamburg. Indeed, it is surprising how few of his works had appeared in print up to that time: only four before, and two after Christian arrived in Berlin. Emanuel mentions them in his autobiography:

1. *Anno* 1731: a minuet for clavier, calling for hand crossing. This clever effect was very popular at the time. I engraved this minuet myself.

2. 1742: Six keyboard sonatas, engraved and published by Schmidt in Nürnberg.

3. 1744: Six keyboard sonatas, published by Hafner in Nürnberg.

4. 1745: A harpsichord concerto in D major, with accompaniment, published by Schmidt in Nürnberg.

5. 1751: Also published by Schmidt: Two trios. The first, in C minor, for two violas and bass, with annotations [= figured bass]; the second, in B-flat major, for flute, violin, and bass.

6. 1752: Also published by Schmidt: A harpsichord concerto in B-flat major, with accompaniment.

[Translator's note: this list differs from that given by Burney, *The Present State* . . . 2:264f.]

This is a rather modest showing, not altogether due to the small amount of music that reached print in those days. Emanuel's serious works were not popular, and Krause was right in saying that his compositions "had to be studied and practiced at length before they might please."

The seventh entry on the list is a work that showed the side of Emanuel through which he exerted the strongest influence on Christian, that of teacher. This well-known work is the previously mentioned textbook whose full title is *Essay on the True Art of Playing Keyboard Instruments, With Examples and Six Sonatas Engraved on Twenty-Six Copper Plates. Part I, Published by the Author* (1753).

Christian was bound to have profited from Emanuel's teaching—though not so much in matters of technique, where their father had laid a solid foundation, as in artistic questions concerning musical interpretation. Here Emanuel may have provided much to which the father's more practical teaching merely alluded.

"To think through singing"—this was Emanuel's concept of the cantabile style, and this Christian could readily understand and apply. In his essay, Emanuel had established what was important; for example, in paragraph eleven: "Every step must be taken to remove the accompanying parts from the hand that performs the principal melody so that it may be played with a free, unhampered expression."[44]

Witnesses confirm that Emanuel practiced what he preached and that only after having heard him play his own works could one properly judge them. If Christian later became a celebrated keyboard soloist, Emanuel deserves credit for helping to show him the way.

The aforementioned Gerstenberg wrote to a friend, the poet Matthias Claudius, recalling how in Hamburg he had needed Lessing's help to persuade Emanuel to sit down at the keyboard. "The best way I can describe his playing of an Adagio is to compare him to a speaker who has not memorized his speech. Full of what he wants to say, such a speaker does not hurry but quietly communicates, one sentiment at a time, what wells up from his soul."[45]

The analogy recalls Johann Sebastian Bach, who thought of the individual parts in his own compositions as persons who conversed with each other. But whereas Sebastian was thinking of the multiple voices in a polyphonic composition, the description of Emanuel's playing refers to a single speaker.[46]

Christian could relate quite readily to the vocal qualities Gerstenberg detected in Emanuel's playing, especially when they reflected the lighter side of his brother's personality. Emanuel, unlike Friedemann in Dresden, was a gregarious man. In spite of his propensity for sarcasm and irony, his was not a gloomy disposition. He participated freely in the lively social activities of Berlin's "strong minds,"[47] which were not restricted to court circles, and he included Christian in these gatherings.

At first the circle was small. In 1747, Christian Gottfried Krause, then legal secretary to Count Rothenburg, met with two friends, the poets Ludwig Gleim and Ewald von Kleist. In time, the trio grew to a "whole colony of friends, all of the same mind," as Ramler, one of the new members, wrote to Gleim. They met in their homes, sometimes at Krause's, or in the cafe across the street from the opera house. There was plenty to talk about, this being the age of the Encyclopedists—educated men who wanted to gain a comprehensive understanding of the arts and sciences. They knew about Diderot, d'Alembert, Voltaire, and Rousseau in Paris. In Berlin, Krause, Sulzer, and Ramler had similar ideas. Sulzer was readying his *Allgemeine Theorie der schönen Künste*, modelled on the

Encyclopédie Française, the first volume of which had just appeared in Paris. Sulzer's mentor was his teacher Kirnberger; he also received inspiration and suggestions from this circle of friends.

The gatherings were informal,[48] taken up with casual debates and exchanges, with versifying, and with spirited battles of words. In a letter to his friend Gleim, who by then had moved to Halberstadt, Ramler describes such an evening at Krause's:

> It was a large gathering, but as usual, since all could not participate in the same conversation, they split up into groups of three or four, standing around or sitting. If one conversation lags and I hear something witty elsewhere, I join that group. . . . [The evening] ended with the lightness of conversation being transferred to hands and feet. The dancer M. Dubois was one of us, and his lightness infected the others.[49]

Having grown to eight members, the group became known as the Thursday Club. Although they at first met on Thursdays, they later changed to Mondays. According to its statutes, the purpose of the club was "free and spirited conversation." Members gathered at six, took supper at eight, and ended the evening at ten o'clock. No games were allowed except chess. To achieve "the desired variety in conversation," the group accepted "not only scholars but also businessmen, jurists, physicians, poets, musicians, and those engaged in the fine arts." The club soon became the most prominent in Berlin and also attracted the king's musicians: Quantz, Agricola, Nichelmann, the two Grauns, Franz Benda, and Emanuel Bach.

Music seems to have played the principal part. In his letter to Gleim, Ramler stresses that at Krause's, in the company of Lessing and others, he had heard "several beautiful excerpts from Telemann's *Messiah.*" Another time he commented on "the jolly and honorable musicians: Quantz, Agricola, Nichelmann, and our dear father Krause."[50]

According to Christian's mother, Krause had been particularly close to Christian in his youth, a true kindred spirit. Like Emanuel, Krause had studied law at Frankfurt on the Oder, but then, unlike the Bach son, he had chosen law as his principal profession. His career would not interfere with his fondness for music, he wrote to Kleist, no matter how "stiff" the legal profession was apt to make him. "When I am tired of [the law] I think about music, and that again puts me in a good mood." According to Ramler, Krause "was always harmonious, in good spirits," and "really knew how to live." For Kleist, given to depressions, Krause was "the only one with whom I now socialize; he knows how to dispel my moods with his talking and fiddling."

Christian Gottfried Krause, music amateur and writer. Christian Bach thought highly of him.

Promenading in Berlin's Tiergarten, a mid-eighteenth-century view.

Poets and musicians got along famously. Nicolai, the publisher, even described this cheerful atmosphere in a poem.[51] Full enjoyment of life speaks from this union of music and poetry during Christian's time in Berlin, an idyllic setting in the spirit of the Anacreontics who, around the middle of the century, dreamt of such joie de vivre and undisturbed bliss. The group was fortunate in that Krause, the connecting link between poets and musicians, was well-to-do. At the age of thirty he had already settled down as a lawyer in Berlin and Potsdam. His annual income of a thousand taler impressed his friends and made it possible for him to be a gracious host. He employed five servants and had a garden "outside the king's gate." His town house, complete with an artistically decorated music room, was one of the sights of Potsdam. It was open to all good musicians and to those who discussed music intelligently.

In his youth, Krause had been taught by his father "to play the violin and to accompany at the keyboard; he had also learned to play the kettle drums expertly."[52] According to Ramler, he was "a virtuoso on this thundering instrument." Krause had a special talent for formulating his thoughts about music. His *Von der musikalischen Poesie*, which set forth his creed about the inseparability of music and poetry, had been completed in 1747 and published in 1752, years before Quantz and Emanuel Bach published their essays. Christian could readily relate to Krause's chief postulate: "True music must both move and delight the listener." "Delight," Krause maintained, is engendered by the sheer beauty of tones; it is not a specifically musical quality. But that which "moves" represents a more profound satisfaction, conveyed to the soul by that same "delightful" sound. Music that contains both qualities will affect most people, because nature "has made us receptive to it."

The judges of "what is truly expressive" should therefore be, not professional musicians, but "amateurs, who judge only by what their ears and hearts tell them." Professionals, after all, have their own "intellectual music," which gives them pleasure "without much appeal to the heart."[53] Krause urges them "not to look for true beauty in that which is artful and farfetched," words with a familiar ring. Did not Scheibe also warn that "too much art will always lead from what is clear and natural to what is obscure"?

In Krause, Christian encountered a man who considerably enlarged his horizon by extending it to include the poetic aspects of music, which were to remain dear to the young composer. Not that Krause condemned polyphonic music altogether. He conceded that it was majestic and resplendent and that, "with due moderation," it was suitable for sacred music. In this he saw eye to eye with Quantz, who would soon express virtually identical thoughts in his treatise.

To explain and illustrate the changing taste of the day, Krause turned to the visual arts. "Formerly we loved those paintings that require us sit to in front of them for a half hour before we detect a certain beauty in them. . . . Today we love all the more that which is pleasant and lively." After the "excesses of the Gothic," we now prefer "a less opulent" style in architecture. Listeners are most likely to detect clearly defined senti-ments in "melodic, especially vocal, " music. Many emotions can inspire us to sing, "even to invent musical [= melodic] instruments. Next to "pleasant and tender emotions," "noble simplicity" is most desirable.[54]

The genre in which these notions could most easily be demonstrated was song. Having stated his theories in ways that convinced many, including Christian, Krause turned to practical matters. In 1753 he pub-lished, together with Ramler, Part I of his *Odes With Melodies,* a collec-tion of poems in several stanzas, using the same melody of twelve to fourteen measures for each stanza. The collection was dedicated to Prince Lobkowitz as "the greatest connoisseur of spirited writing." The preface refers back to this dedication, noting that the chief purpose of the collec-tion was to provide "pleasure and amusement."

> If our German composers would sing while writing their songs, away from the keyboard, and without thinking about a bass [= accompani-ment] to be added, then more of our people would develop a taste for singing, for pleasure and sociability.

Such songs should be attractive, of a certain naïveté, but "not so highly poetic that a beautiful songstress cannot understand them. On the other hand, they should not be so facile and flowing that they would be unattractive to persons of esprit." Krause freely admits that he wants to emulate the French, "those born friends of song."[55]

France had been the forum of similar discussions at the time of Jean-Jacques Rousseau. The controversy in Germany between those loyal to the Johann Sebastian Bach tradition and the "progressives" around Mat-theson and Scheibe (now endorsed by Krause) can be compared to the situation in Paris where the venerable Jean-Philippe Rameau clashed with Rousseau, then barely forty years old.

At the root of the dispute were Rameau's operas. Rousseau, eloquent and eager to fight, accused Rameau of "abuses in his instrumentation." The accompaniments were "far too heavy, so multifaceted as to be con-fusing. They deafen our ears and neither delight nor stir our souls." After a recitative, a single, unexpected chord played by the strings would usu-ally "capture the attention of even the most distracted listener, but the great noise produced by Rameau's orchestra does not accomplish this." In general, his "very elaborate music" does not hold our attention. In com-paring it to light Italian opera, Rousseau concludes: "a fat goose cannot fly like a swallow."[56] In the example he promptly introduces, his own *Le devin du village* is, of course, the swallow. The work presents his own ideal, in poetry and music, of a return to the unsullied natural state. The music is simple and folklike—so much so that Rousseau was accused of having borrowed too much from street songs. The plot, having only three roles, is equally simple: two young lovers, shepherd and shepherdess, their affections having wavered, are reunited by the clever village soothsayer.

Compared with Rameau's elaborate operas, this is simplicity personi-fied, and the very contrast led to the spectacular success of Rousseau's lit-tle play with music. The king and his mistress, Madame Pompadour, attended the performance in Fontainebleau on 18 October 1752; both were enchanted. The king granted Rousseau an audience (Rousseau did not take advantage of the invitation) and Mme Pompadour sang the part of the shepherdess in a subsequent performance.

Le devin du village was still in the Paris opera repertoire in 1829. Throughout Europe, both text and music of this unassuming little play were viewed as the very models of simplicity, naturalness, and cheer. Whereas Italy had previously provided a model of the light genre in Per-golesi's *La serva padrona*, Rousseau's work was now in the limelight, testi-fying to his victory over Rameau.[57]

In Germany, the Berlin school of song writing, embodied in the cir-cle around Krause, produced similarly simple fare in the *Odes with Melo-dies*. Owing to King Frederick's love for everything French, the connection was there. Krause had read Rousseau diligently, not only his articles in the *Encyclopédie* but also his *Lettre sur la musique française* of 1753, in which Rousseau landed heavily on the "narrow-minded" follow-ers of Rameau.

Perhaps the Berlin composers were not altogether sure of themselves, for some of their contributions to the collection were anonymous. In his *Historisch-kritische Beiträge* of 1754, Marpurg provided names. According to him, the first part of the *Odes* contained five odes by Krause, four each by Franz Benda, Quantz, Agricola, and the younger Graun, three each by Emanuel Bach and Nichelmann, and two each by the elder Graun and Telemann. Thus all the major Berlin composers were represented (as well as Telemann, from Hamburg); but perhaps not all of them were enthusiastic about contributing. The younger Graun is reported to have considered such odes to be "trifles," though admitting that "to compose such a trifle is no small task if it is to be successful."[58]

Remarks by Emanuel suggest that he felt obliged to contribute. Referring to his compositions in general, including the odes, he recalled that he had written most of his works for specific persons, which had "tied him down" more than the few works he had written for himself. Such circumstances caused him to write some things that otherwise would not have occurred to him. Enough collections of odes were published to indicate that there was a market for such music. The first volume of *Odes with Melodies* was so successful that Krause and Ramler followed it with a second. Poets and composers were again anonymous, but we do know that the last ode, No. 30, was composed by John Christian Bach. The ambitious, though not scintillating, amorous poem[59] presented quite a challenge to the eighteen-year-old composer. The melody is basically simple but does contain ornamentation. It consists of twenty-six measures; the marking at the beginning is *angenehm* (agreeable, pleasant). This was Christian's first published composition. The poet for his next effort as a composer of odes was Friedrich Wilhelm von Hagedorn, one of the leading spirits of the Berlin circle. The setting appeared in Marpurg's *Neue Lieder zum Singen* (1756), and this time Christian was not only mentioned by name but was prominently listed in the Table of Contents, right after Graun and before Quantz and his brother Emanuel.

Hagedorn's text is an engaging fable about an imaginary animal kingdom in which the animals carry out human functions. This time Christian wrote only twelve measures—a single, jaunty melody to serve for no less than ten stanzas. It was still a timid early effort by the youngest Bach son, but to be published in Marpurg's collection was tantamount to having been accepted into the guild of the Berlin masters.

And there was more. Marpurg relates that Christian had appeared before the Berlin public "with several compositions that received applause."[60] Since it was customary at that time for a musician to introduce himself with his own works, Christian is likely to have performed keyboard concertos that he had written. From the inventory of Emanuel's estate, one obtains the impression that Christian already displayed the industry that was to characterize him throughout life. Specified as Christian's works in the listing prepared by Emanuel's widow is "a parcel of compositions written before the author left for Italy, consisting of five keyboard concertos, one cello concerto, two trios, and three arias." Heading the list is a "clavier concerto in the manner of Tartini," an indication of the strong influence then being exerted by Italian instrumental music on Berlin's musical life and on Christian.[61]

A glance at Christian's manuscripts (publication of an instrumental work was out of the question at this stage) clearly reveals the schooling he had received from father and brother. The minor mode prevails, a dolorous, somewhat tragic mood as we know it from works by his elders. The harpsichord concerto in F minor ("Riveduto dal Sign. C. P. E. Bach") shows this heritage; there is still a grave, earthbound quality. With its three broadly conceived, strongly rhythmical movements, this concerto is far removed from the easy-going serenity that would later characterize Christian's style.

The other four keyboard concertos have a more distinctive flavor. Heinrich Schökel undertook a detailed analysis of Christian's works from the Berlin years and concluded that they already demonstrate qualities we associate with his later writing:

> Gentle, dreamy feelings, beauty of sound, carefully worked out homophonic technique. The five concertos can hold their own in comparison with the best of his later compositions. They are quite modern for their time, quite subjective in expression. There are no strong contrasts, which accounts for their conservative impression in regard to form. In the mellow timbres of the keyboard part they go beyond Emanuel's manner, and there are many dynamic gradations. . . . Here we already encounter Christian's outstanding melodic gift.[62]

Another work from this period, the cantata *L'Olimpe: Choeur pour l'anniversaire de la naissance du roi*, must have been written for the Prussian king's fortieth birthday in 1752. Whether this choral ode was ever performed is not known. If so, it would mean that Frederick's birthday was honored by a young composer whose father, five years earlier, had impressed the king merely as some giant belonging to an unfamiliar musical world.

Among the important musicians to influence Christian during his Berlin stay, Giuseppe Tartini ranks high. He provided the Italian ingredient of the "European" style to which Scheibe had alluded. The excellent reputation of the composer from Padua had reached Berlin, where the king and those around him thought highly of Tartini's works.

Two common misconceptions or stereotypes should be dealt with at this point. Tartini was far more than a virtuoso, famous for bravura pieces such as his "Devil's Trill" sonata. Nor was Italy (then or ever) inhabited by naïve, carefree people who love to sing but cannot be bothered with

Title page of the collection *Oden mit Melodien*, Part Two.

Ode 30, the last of the collection, was composed by the eighteen-year-old Christian Bach.

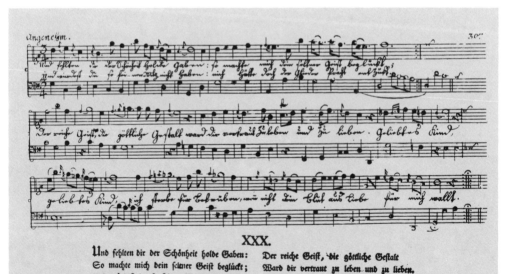

XXX.

Und fehlten dir der Schönheit holde Gaben:
So machte mich dein seiner Geist beglückt;
Und würdest du so feinen Witz nicht haben:
Mich hätte doch der Glieder Pracht entzückt.

Der reiche Geist, die göttliche Gestalt
Ward dir vertraut zu leben und zu lieben.
Geliebtes Kind, ich sterbe für Betrüben,
Wenn nicht dein Blut aus Liebe für mich wallt.

theoretical, profound problems. Tartini, the "Maestro delle nazione," gives the lie to both notions. He wrote at least 125, and probably more than 200, concertos[63] that show him to have been far more than a paragon of finger dexterity. A singing manner of playing was a matter of course for him. "Per ben sonare bisogno ben cantare," he used to tell his pupils: good playing requires good singing. To achieve this singing quality he employed unusual means. He would open a composition with a written motto, or he would provide a text or epigram—poetic thoughts he wanted to be expressed in sound. The principal moods in music were *allegria* (happiness) and *mestizia* (sadness), with many gradations in between. In his *Saggio*, Algarotti, who had established the contact between his friend Tartini and the Berlin music establishment, left us a description of how Tartini put himself in the right mood for composing. Reading Petrarch or Metastasio, Algarotti tells us, "gave wings to his imagination and inspired his soul." Some of the texts chosen by Tartini reveal good literary taste, while others, such as the motto at the beginning of Concerto No. 118 in B-flat Major, may strike us as banal: "Do not weep if I no longer love you, if your beauty no longer pleases me." Sometimes he quoted contemplative lyrics; for example, he introduced the slow movement of his fiftieth concerto, in G major, with "submerge your wings in Lethe [the river in Greek mythology whose waters caused oblivion— trans.], o silent, peaceful sleep!"

Tartini's principal employment was at the church of San Antonio in Padua. Fearing that such lyrics might be regarded by some as too worldly for any music (including concertos) destined to be heard in church, Tartini resorted to cryptography, the key to which has only recently been found.[64] Through these purely instrumental works, then, Tartini was able to express the close link between poetry and music.

In Tartini's writing, musical interest is concentrated in the melody to such an extent that his accompaniments seemed thin and drab, even to some of his fellow Italians. One of them, Stefano Arteaga, thought it necessary to come to Tartini's defense:

> [Tartini] has been accused of excessive restraint in his accompaniments. True enough: when we compare them with those of others, there is a great difference. But the accusations cannot be maintained if we remember that Tartini's music, with its delicate shadings, might lose all its charm and grace under the onslaught of many heavy chords.[65]

Given that J. S. Bach was Tartini's elder by only seven years, it is remarkable that the two lived in such different worlds. While Bach was building a monument to polyphony with his *Well-Tempered Clavier* and

Art of Fugue, Tartini's melodic style, his *genere cantabile*, was being met with wide acclaim.

Although Tartini was involved primarily as a composer in the great stylistic change that affected much of Europe during the age of the Enlightenment, he was also among the musicians who investigated the scientific foundations of music. It is not surprising that Tartini, the great master of the violin, should have published a method of violin playing. (Leopold Mozart followed in 1756, the year of W. A. Mozart's birth, with his own *Versuch einer gründlichen Violinschule*, in which he did not hesitate to borrow from Tartini.[66])

More unexpected, however, is Tartini's treatise in which he opposed the excessive use of embellishments, a practice that had become mannered and rigid. In their place he advocated "good taste," which in his opinion depended not on the use of trills, appoggiaturas, and other embellishments but on the performer's ability to "produce tones gracefully." He conceded that moderate use of embellishments is often appropriate but went on to say, "I could never understand their application to *all* melodies. I am convinced that a melody that faithfully expresses the affections of the text must have its own characteristic manner and therefore must contain its own appropriate embellishments."[67]

He expressed these convictions in his *Trattato di musica*, the work of a lifetime that he presented to the public at the age of sixty-two. It contains much that the public did not understand—not in the portion dealing with embellishments and other practical or esthetic questions but in those sections where the aging author provided a curious mixture of science and mysticism.

During the early stages of writing this work, Tartini had submitted it to Padre Martini and to the mathematician Balbi in Bologna, hoping that they would confirm his theory of "combination tones." He explained the concept in one of the many letters he wrote over the years to Padre Martini, Christian's future teacher, indicating that it was not intended for practical musicians but for scholars[68] and explaining that before his death he wanted to arrive at an understanding of the art he had practiced all his life.[69] Neither Martini nor Balbi fully understood Tartini's argument, while in France the musician-philosopher Rousseau considered it quite intelligible "if read attentively." Resorting to simple language, Rousseau outlined the differences, as he saw them, between the two epochs of music represented by Rameau and Tartini:

> While Rameau sees the high notes as generated by the bass, Tartini takes the opposite approach. Rameau derives melody from harmony,

Jean-Jacques Rousseau.

Giuseppe Tartini.

A scene from Rousseau's *Le devin du village*.

Tartini's harmony comes from melody. Rameau's melody exists for the accompaniment, the opposite is true for Tartini.[70]

In Berlin, still Christian's home, Krause and his friends from the Berlin school of song writers had arrived at similarly simple formulations. The influence of Rousseau was felt there, but so was that of Tartini, who included among his friends Count Algarotti and Prince Lobkowitz. The king also thought highly of Tartini, though he showed less interest in the man's theories than his music.

Tradition has it that Tartini presented the king with several "short violin sonatas" and a concerto, probably for the flute. Frederick, by way of thanks, reciprocated with an aria of his own composition. With his customary great modesty, Tartini asked his friend Algarotti not to praise him too highly to the king, who had already shown him "far greater kindness than deserved."[71] He acted with similar self-effacement toward Prince Lobkowitz when in 1750 he delivered six violin concertos commissioned by the prince. Tartini asked, through Algarotti, that Lobkowitz let him know if he found the solo violin part too difficult, for he would be glad to make appropriate changes. But he extended that offer to two or three concertos only; "all others should remain as they are."[72]

Among those in Berlin who were less than enthusiastic about Tartini's music was Quantz, who claimed in his treatise that Tartini's compositions contained "hardly anything but dry, simple, and common ideas, more suitable for light than serious music." In this harsh criticism, Tartini was referred to not by name but rather as "a celebrated violinist from Lombardy." Quantz found fault with the thin accompaniment in not only the works of Tartini but those of Italians in general:

> Their basses are neither majestic nor melodious, and have no particular connection with the principal part. Neither the fruits of labor nor anything venturesome is apparent in their middle parts; you simply find dry harmony. And even in their solos they cannot endure a bass that occasionally has some melodic motion. . . . They pretend that in this fashion the soloist is least obscured.[73]

Quantz's derogatory remarks extended even to Tartini's violin playing, which had been universally admired. "His playing did not move, his taste was not noble; his performing lacked a good, singing manner." Considering that Quantz had not heard Tartini in more than thirty years (since the coronation of Emperor Charles VI in 1711), some jealousy may well have been involved. At the Prussian court, Quantz thought of himself as the undisputed ruler in the realm of music and did not welcome interference from abroad. During this age of change he opposed the Italian style and advocated instead a compromise, "an admixture of the cantabile," as the most beautiful manner.[74] "The old deplore the melodic excesses of the young, who in turn make fun of the dry music of their elders."[75]

In Berlin, Christian was thus introduced to music and musicians representing greatly differing styles—old, new, and "mixed." For the budding composer, this broad exposure was an advantage, and Christian made good use of it. Soon he would bid farewell to Emanuel and his family, and to the city in which he had taken his first steps as a composer. The reason for his departure has been the subject of much guesswork, as have the specific circumstances of his leaving. As for the year, however, statements by Emanuel and Marpurg point to 1754.[76]

At this time Emanuel was seriously considering leaving Berlin. After all, he had never been on good terms with the king: he rightly felt that he was underpaid and that, as a composer and a son of Bach, he was not sufficiently appreciated. Furthermore, neither he nor the other musicians had direct access to the monarch, who had entrusted all dealings with the musicians to his former chamberlain Fredersdorf.[77] Correspondence between Fredersdorf and the king testifies to the tense atmosphere.

For one thing, there were disagreements about special pay. On becoming king, Frederick allegedly promised his musicians that they would receive additional pay for any concerts in Potsdam. When he seemed to have forgotten that promise, the musicians, led by Emanuel, complained bitterly. Their place of employment, they argued, was Berlin, and the long journey to Potsdam, over bumpy roads, was not one of their obligations. Emanuel, it is said, even threatened with refusal to work, saying to the majordomo: "Tell our ruler that neither honor nor money would sufficiently reward us for such dangerous service."[78]

The king, highly incensed, complained to Fredersdorf: "These musicians are driving me crazy with their demands for extra pay! They think they are entitled to it according to their contract, which is not true! Let me know the total annual music expenses." Fredersdorf, whom Voltaire had called "le grand factotum du roi Frédéric," dutifully supplied an itemized account and added the remark: "The musicians are most unhappy!"

Unmoved, Frederick replied: "It is proper that [the musicians] who come [to Potsdam] for the Intermezzo should receive extra compensation. But why should I pay people twice? I am here all year, but in Berlin I need them only for the opera, so *that* is where extra pay is in order."[79]

Since Emanuel acted as spokesman for the musicians, neither the

king nor Fredersdorf was partial to him. This became apparent when
Emanuel complained about his own pay, pointing out that both Agricola
and Nichelmann received six hundred taler, far more than he did, though
they were his "former students." Apparently Fredersdorf submitted this
complaint to the king, adding his own observations, for the royal reply
shows unusual anger. "Bach lies. Agricola receives only five hundred
taler. Bach played in only one concert; that seems to have gone to his
head."

Though the king's memory may have been faulty, Emanuel's position
was weak. He threatened to leave, then changed his mind, which caused
the king to observe with obvious sarcasm: "Mr. Bach has kindly agreed to
remain here until Nichelmann returns." It was no secret at court that
Bach was looking for a change. An earlier attempt (in 1750, when he
applied for his father's post at St. Thomas) had failed.

Three years later another opportunity came along when the position
of music director and organist in Zittau became available. The selection
process turned out to be complex, as the minutes of the Zittau town
council show. At first both Emanuel and his brother Friedemann were
among those considered.[80] The magnificent organ by Silbermann must
have been a great attraction, for among the other applicants were Homilius in Dresden, Sebastian's son-in-law Altnikol, and two Bach pupils,
Krebs and Trier.

In the end it was Trier who was appointed, which is surprising in
view of the two Bach sons and other quite prestigious applicants. The
decision against Emanuel may have been influenced by the fact that he
had not played the organ for some time,[81] but this cannot have been the
reason in Friedemann's case.

Emanuel's popularity and reputation evidently left something to be
desired. Later, when he applied to become Telemann's successor in Hamburg, it was only after a second ballot that Emanuel won out over Rolle
from Magdeburg, and then by only one vote. One wonders, therefore,
about Burney's statement that

> frequent opportunities arose, during this period, for him to establish
> himself very advantageously elsewhere, some of which he wished to
> accept; but he could not obtain his dismission: however, his salary, after
> many years services, was augmented.[82]

These remarks call for some corrections. Today's scholars do not know of
many "advantageous" opportunities during these years, and as to the
augmented salary, this was late in coming and was only granted because

The quarrel about the musicians' pay. C. P. E. Bach (left) complained about the long journey to Potsdam. He had an adversary in the king's chamberlain Fredersdorf (right) whose views in this matter influenced the king (below).

of the savings that resulted from Nichelmann's departure.

The king's thrift, to be sure, extended beyond Emanuel. It was dictated by the general political situation, which had become increasingly threatening with the Seven Years' War on the horizon. To the demands of musicians and dancers the king would now reply, "I need money for cannons, equipment, pontoons, and so on; there is not much left to waste on entertainers." He spent more and more time with his troops, taking part in maneuvers outside Berlin. At times the palace seemed deserted; it was said in 1755 that "not a visitor" was to be seen.[83]

Berlin no longer provided the stimulating, lively environment from which Christian had benefited so much. Moreover, he now had constantly to consider the possibility that Emanuel would pull up stakes in Berlin and move to Zittau (where the possibility of a position at first seemed good) or to the country in order to escape the dangers of the impending war.

Emanuel continued to feel responsible for Christian, for he obtained for him a position as organist away from Berlin. Christian, however, was not interested. Having begun a promising career in cosmopolitan Berlin, he understandably did not want to "get stuck" in some provincial backwater, as long as there were other opportunities. One of these presented itself in Italy.

Christian's departure gave rise to a variety of romantic stories, all involving one or more female singers whom he is said to have followed to Italy. Thus we read in Gerber's *Lexikon* of 1790 that "his desire to see Italy was kindled by several Italian singers." Gerber based his account on Forkel, whose almanac of 1783 had mentioned Christian's friendships with many Italian singers, "one of whom persuaded him to accompany her to Italy." Bitter took up this version and added, with some embarrassment, "the Italian singers whom he met at the Berlin opera had a rather bad influence on him, so that at the age of nineteen he left his brother's home and instruction in order to accompany one of them to Italy."[84]

A highly imaginative account, no doubt less fact than fiction, was given by one Elise Polko, who found it quite understandable that young Christian was not averse to the charms of "these Italian song birds" whose music "sounded sweet to the ears of a sixteen-year-old [?]"; that "young John Christian Bach was more charmed by an Italian aria than by an organ prelude." She continues that one of these singers, the beautiful Emilia Molteni, had married Johann Friedrich Agricola, and that Christian accompanied them to Italy.[85]

The only truth in Polko's fanciful tale is the marriage of Agricola and

Molteni—but that took place in 1751, whereas Christian did not depart, according to Emanuel and Marpurg, until 1754. It is more plausible that the singer he accompanied to Italy was Anna Loria Campolungo, a contralto who had belonged to the opera company since 1742. In April 1754 she was rather ungraciously released by the king, after he had written to Fredersdorf: "I don't know what is the matter with Loria. If she wants to leave, that is fine with me; it would not be much of a loss."

Consider the sequence of events: late in 1753 Emanuel applied for the position in Zittau, possibly entailing an immediate move from Berlin, and in April 1754 Campolungo received her discharge. Thus she is most likely the singer with whom Christian shared the discomforts of crossing the Alps in a stage coach.[86]

Christian's separation from his family was finally complete; he now embarked on his years of apprenticeship and mastery abroad, starting in Lombardy—enemy territory. At that time a fragile peace still reigned. But in Milan, Christian's future residence, the citizens who were loyal subjects of Maria Theresia had not forgotten the hardships inflicted on their empress by Frederick during the two Silesian wars. While one could still find followers of the Prussian king, vocally defending him as they argued in academies, cafes, and barber shops,[87] the general mood in Milan was hostile to Prussia. New arrivals from there were not likely to receive a cordial welcome—especially when the newcomer was Lutheran! To become established in Milan one needed the recommendation of someone more prominent than a singer, whether her name was Molteni or Campolungo. Was there someone else sufficiently influential to arrange for easy access to one of the most distinguished families in Lombardy, to open the door to Count Litta's palace?

Enter once more, and for the last time, Prince Lobkowitz. At this point we need to retrace our steps a few years in order to deal with the strange series of events that brought about, almost accidentally, Christian's introduction to the Litta family.

Subsequent to the deaths of his father and older brother, Prince Ferdinand Philipp von Lobkowitz became the head of the family at an early age, while still a student in Würzburg. The prince had studied music in Vienna, especially the violin. His teacher, Christoph Willibald Gluck, was soon to make a name for himself in the world of opera. Gluck's father had been a forester in the service of Ferdinand Philipp's father, and when the musical talent of young Gluck became apparent, he was allowed to take part in house concerts in the Vienna palace of Prince Lobkowitz. This opportunity became a springboard for him to the musical establishment of Count Melzi in Milan. Gluck also became a student and friend of Giovanni Battista Sammartini, who later played an important part in Christian's life. Einstein described the young Gluck as "a musical savage who breaks with the utmost unconcern through the thickets of technical practice."[88]

Gluck dedicated one of his first operas to Ferdinand's uncle Georg Christian von Lobkowitz, who resided in Milan from 1743 to 1745 as Austrian General Governor. Although the dedicatee was more interested in the science of war than the art of music, it was music that established the connection between Berlin and Milan, through a circuitous route that can be traced with the help of some yellowed papers printed in 1776.

An old register, the *Serie de' governatori di Milano . . .* , reveals that the *eccelsa real giunta di governo*, the town council led by Georg Christian Lobkowitz, also included the Marchese Don Antonio Litta, who held the rank of *commissario generale*.[89] His sons, Pompeo and Agostino Litta, were about the same age as Georg Christian's sons, Joseph Maria Karl and August Anton. These four—and here, at last, is the connection—had in common a great love of music.

Ferdinand Philipp, not much older than his cousins, was a frequent guest in Milan, in part to observe the progress of his protégé Gluck. These circumstances led to his friendship with the Litta sons. When Prince Georg Christian Lobkowitz was called back by Maria Theresia and given a military post, his nephew Ferdinand Philipp, accompanied by Gluck, embarked on a European journey that took them to England, where Gluck composed two operas for the King's Theatre. To be precise: being in a hurry, he patched the operas together using parts of earlier works. The result was a failure. (Some fifteen years later, Christian would also move from Milan to London and premiere *his* operas at the King's Theatre, but they were resounding successes.)

In London, Gluck and Prince Lobkowitz parted for good. Gluck joined the traveling opera company of the Mingotti brothers (which Christian may have heard when they played in Leipzig), whereas Prince Lobkowitz went to the Prussian court in Berlin, where he made quite a name for himself. In his *Account of the Reign of Frederick the Great*,[90] the court chronicler Rödenbeck noted, on 9 January 1749, that "the king, in a solemn ceremony, installed Prince Lobkowitz as the feudal Lord of Sagan." An entry on 25 July 1750 reports that "Prince Lobkowitz [was] with the king in Potsdam," and another, on 19 May 1751, states: "Parade in Potsdam. The king dines with Prince Lobkowitz for the first time in the palace's new marble hall." Thus it is confirmed that contacts were frequent and close. And when the prince resided at Sagan, Count Algarotti maintained the liaison with the king.[91]

Lobkowitz was admitted to membership in the Royal Prussian Academy; his loose lifestyle does not seem to have been an obstacle. Count Lehndorff referred to Lobkowitz, then thirty years old, as "a great rake who, owing to a vision, mended his ways and got rid of his mistress, the charming dancer Denis. People say that she cost him fifty thousand taler a year." Another time Lehndorff counted the prince among those who worshipped a pretty lady-in-waiting at court, Fräulein von Pannwitz.[92]

Undoubtedly Lobkowitz enjoyed his bachelor's existence; he did not marry until he was forty-five years old. Years later, in 1769, Lehndorff visited him at Sagan and described him as "one of the most peculiar of men, who leaves his house only at night. Soon he will marry a Princess von Carignac." Burney provided more detail, reporting that late in life the prince lived in virtually total seclusion, that he was very knowledgeable about music and was talented as a performer and composer.

Prince Lobkowitz never lost the good will of the Prussian king, even during the Seven Years' War when he was obliged to fight on the Austrian side. Soon after the eruption of hostilities, however, he was taken prisoner in a spectacular battle, the details of which were recorded by a chronicler.[93] None of this affected his cordial relationship with the king. After the peace treaty was concluded, Lobkowitz was one of the first to dine with the king, as though nothing had happened. Hence it is all the more surprising that even Lobkowitz did not succeed in establishing better terms between the king and Emanuel, whose special relationship to the prince is confirmed in a letter from Gleim to a fellow poet, Uz:

> Prince Lobkowitz is young and well-to-do. He is fond of the arts and sciences, understands poetry, and is quite a ladies' man. Herr Bach, a court musician, is among his closest confidants.[94]

All indications point to Prince Lobkowitz as the one who was instrumental in smoothing the way for Christian's departure for Italy. He was the only prominent figure at the Berlin court with close ties to the Littas in Milan. As a lover of music, interested in advancing the careers of talented young artists, he was the logical one to help Christian, the brother of one of "his closest confidants." Moreover, the two men had similar lifestyles—as we shall see, Christian, too, had a taste for female beauty.[95]

Christian was about to become the first member of the Bach family ever to set foot on Italian soil. He was embarking on a new venture in which he would be aided by a young nobleman, much as his father had

Prince Ferdinand Philipp von Lobkowitz, a patron of the arts and C. P. E. Bach's friend in Berlin. According to recent research, Lobkowitz helped Christian find employment in Milan (below).

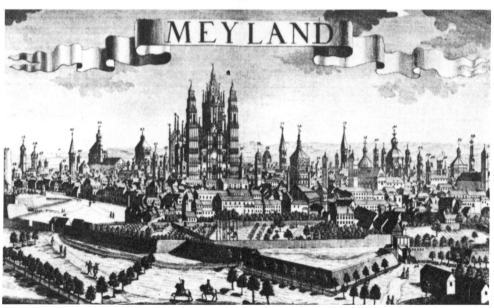

been thirty-seven years earlier.

When Johann Sebastian Bach left Weimar for Köthen, he was cordially received by Prince Leopold of Anhalt-Köthen, a mere twenty-three years old. Bach was glad to have escaped the intrigues and power struggles at the Weimar court (where, before he left, he had even been imprisoned for four weeks). Admittedly, his resounding title of Kapellmeister and Director of Chamber Music for His Highness, the Prince of Anhalt-Köthen, referred to what was really a minor German court. Yet Köthen was to provide the agreeable setting in which Sebastian's talents could fully develop.

Now John Christian Bach was leaving Berlin for Milan. There he would have the good fortune to receive a helping hand from another young nobleman, Count Agostino Litta.

3
Apprenticeship and Mastery in Italy

*Go to Italy; this will clear your
head of superfluous ideas!*
J. J. Fux (1660–1741) to
Ignaz Holzbauer (1711–1783)

THE PALACE OF MARCHESE LITTA is located on the Corso di
Porta Vercellina. It boasts an impressive, beautifully decorated
façade. Inside, the furnishings are equally resplendent, several rooms
having Brussels tapestries based on paintings by Teniers and other fine
masters. Many paintings by Provacaccini, Guercino, and other major
artists are displayed in two galleries. The owner is most hospitable.
Once introduced, visitors are free to return any day; they will enjoy
good company and an excellent cuisine.

Thus a contemporary chronicler[1] pictured what was to be the working environment of Christian Bach. Actually, the description is less than
adequate, for even today this Milan residence of the Littas, now Corso
Magenta 24, impresses us as a magnificent baroque edifice with six courtyards and extended gardens. It was built in 1648 by Count Bartolomeo
Arese, a member of the most famous branch of the Litta family, the Visconti Arese. Colonnades, simple but elegant, invite the visitor to stroll
through the courtyards. The long flights of rooms, especially the hall of
mirrors and its magnificent chandelier, easily conjure up visions of receptions filled with laughter and excitement, peopled with distinguished
guests who considered it a privilege to be invited by Milan's first family.

The Littas had arrived at that highest rung of the social ladder by the
time Count Antonio, the father of Christian's future employer, married
Donna Paola of the Visconti Borromeo family. She brought immense
wealth to the marriage, and with their combined family fortunes, Litta
could afford to open the doors of his famous, luxurious home to persons of
rank, from Italy and abroad, wining and dining them in regal splendor.

All this hospitality was suddenly interrupted when Antonio Litta, governor general of Milan and knight of the Golden Fleece, was relieved of his post. On 30 August 1747, Empress Maria Theresia convened a conference at Count Königsegg's. Due to "great irregularities, especially in the war financial accounts," Litta was dismissed as Commissario generale, "though honorably discharged," as is specially noted. In view of the Littas' great wealth, the irregularities were most likely a question of negligence rather than fraud.[2]

Thus it was now up to the sons to restore the former luster to the family crest. Pompeo, age twenty-seven, was the elder; his brother Agostino, at twenty-six, was only seven years older than Christian, whom he had engaged to satisfy his private musical ambitions. Pompeo, the head of the family, married his stepsister Elisabetta Visconti Borromeo, with whom he had many children. Meanwhile, Agostino carried on the family's musical tradition. He relied on Christian Bach to provide compositions for chamber music concerts for the edification and entertainment of his guests. Milan's patrician families held such events not only in their town houses but also at their country estates, where they spent most of their time. The Littas habitually repaired to Lainate, located about an hour's drive from Milan on the way to Lago Maggiore. It was considered "a beautiful estate where, during the fall, Marchese Litta held grand parties."[3] These events also called for music.

It appears that Christian wrote many vocal and instrumental pieces for such festive occasions in town or country—compositions that apparently met with lasting success, for twenty years later Burney still noted that he had gained entrance to one of the best "academies" [= concerts] in Milan, where almost thirty singers and instrumentalists performed. Several symphonies by J. C. Bach were heard and found much approval. Another time Burney attended an amateur concert and considered it quite good. "They executed several of our Bach's symphonies, different from those printed in London; all the music here is in MS [manuscript]."[4] These reports suggest that long after Christian had moved to London, his instrumental music, although available only in manuscript form, was still in demand in Italy.

Agostino Litta, however, had other plans for his protégé. In spite of his social pretensions, Litta was a serious young man who was fond of sacred music in the strict, polyphonic style. He also had an interest in ensuring a secure position for Christian. In the musical world of the time, composing instrumental music or opera did not provide a comfortable, secure existence. Works were often distributed in unauthorized copies,

Right: Count Antonio Litta.

Below: The Casa Litta at the time of Christian's activity there.

DISSEGNO DELLA FACCIATA DEL MAGNIFICO PALAZZO FATTO FABRICARE DALL ECC.ᵐᵃ CASA LITTA L'ANNO 1751

and operas tended to be short-lived. The situation around 1700 was well described by the French traveler Charles de Brosses:

> Unlike in France, Italian opera here is not given by an established company of regular singers, where changes in the roster are made only when necessary. Here, if someone wants to put on an opera for the winter season, he obtains the governor's permission, rents a theater, and brings in singers and players from various towns. He signs contracts with stagehands and designers; in the end he often goes bankrupt, just as our directors of third-rate provincial companies do. As a precaution, workers insist on being given certain boxes, which they then rent out for profit. . . . There are new operas and new singers every year. No one wants to see the same work, ballet, scenery, or singers they saw last year. . . . Once a text has been set to music it is considered to be free, belonging to all. There are lots of composers. For a new opera they simply appropriate a libretto that has already been composed by others, and write new music to the old text. . . . The manager gives them thirty or forty pistole; that is the only profit they derive from their music except for copies they immediately make of the arias; those bring a good price. But once the tunes have become well known, this source of income dries up, as it is too easy for others to make their own copies.

Brosses was not impressed by audience manners. It was quite normal for people to shout, praising their favorite singers.

> As soon as a singer favored by a faction of the audience begins to sing, they will applaud, sometimes even before he opens his mouth. People will comment loudly from the upper tiers of boxes; fans will recite verses in a singer's praise, or they will throw down sheets of paper containing such verses. In short, the noise is so unseemly and annoying that one has to avoid the first tier of boxes. These therefore are turned over to women of ill repute, the boxes being close to the main floor which is occupied by the common crowd.[5]

Church music presented a different picture. With 120,000 inhabitants, Milan had many churches, some of which—Sant'Ambrogio and Maria delle Grazie (home of da Vinci's "Last Supper")—were quite close to the Litta palace. "First-rate music" could be heard there, and "great virtuosos." Burney laments that on Friday, 20 July, "there was music at three different churches; I wished to be at them all during the performances, but it was impossible to be present at more than two of them." The great cathedral, the *Duomo*,

> is superior to every Gothic structure in Italy. . . . There are two large organs, one on each side of the choir. On festivals there are oratorios *a*

due cori [for two choirs], and then both organs are used; on common days only one. There are two organists; M. J. C. Bach, before his arrival in England, was one of them; at present the first organist is Signor G. Corbelli.

Giovanni Corbelli had been the first organist at the Duomo when Christian arrived in Milan. Michelangelo Caselli, the second organist, had been there since 1740 and was now in his mid sixties. Count Litta hoped to secure Caselli's position for Christian. It looked like good, steady employment, for there would be additional opportunities in church music. At this time, Giovanni Battista Sammartini was the leading figure in sacred music and would continue to be preeminent in that field. In 1770, Burney still listed him as choirmaster and organist at several churches, saying that his music was "very ingenious, and full of the spirit and fire peculiar to that author."[6] But Sammartini was well over fifty, so some fresh blood might be all to the good.

Count Litta, then, was right in steering Christian toward church music. It may also have occurred to him that this was the appropriate direction for a Bach son. But clearly Litta's plan would not have succeeded without Christian's willingness and enthusiasm. Facts give the lie to later generalizations that the youngest Bach had been nothing but a fashionable composer at best. It amounted to faint praise when people referred to his "agility" and his ability to adapt himself to the spirit of his age—to embrace the superficial melodic style of the time, as Rochlitz had put it. Christian, after all, spent eight years in Italy, and most of his studies and efforts there were devoted to sacred music, although he might have found it easier to succeed in the secular vein, writing operas and instrumental music.

Quite obviously Christian took his studies seriously, readily turning for instruction to Padre Martini in Bologna, a master of the "strict" church style, who was also the foremost theorist of his age and a declared admirer of Johann Sebastian Bach. When Count Litta inquired whether the padre was receiving adequate fees for Christian's lessons, Martini replied that the satisfaction of teaching Christian was sufficient pay![7]

Christian's earnestness is documented through the many letters he exchanged with Padre Martini in a kind of correspondence course that went on for several years after the lessons in Bologna ended. These letters reveal Christian as a likeable, cordial young man, and they also show him to be more eager for learning than any other Bach son had been. Of the many letters Christian wrote to Padre Martini, thirty-two have been preserved. That the padre kept them is an indication of how much he valued

Left: The Hall of Mirrors in the Litta Palace. Christian and his musicians performed there.

Below: The Litta Palace in Milan today.

them. Today these letters, written in fluent Italian,[8] are among the treasures of the Liceo Musicale in Bologna. The first letter, also the first written from Italy, surprisingly enough comes from Naples.

> Reverend Father and Honored Master!
> One of my first duties upon arriving in Naples is to send news to you. I have received a letter from a friend in Bologna who complains that he has lost touch with me; this causes me to fear that you, Reverend Father, might be displeased with me for my neglect. Among the letters my friend has not received is one that I had included, addressed to you, as a token of my great gratitude to you. I had intended to call on you a month ago, to kiss your hand, but Cavaliere Litta's kindness made it possible for me to extend my stay here by one month, because of the inclement weather. I hope, however, to return to Bologna by mid-February. I was surprised here to run into the "Roman" [an unidentified mutual acquaintance] wearing the uniform of a pupil at the conservatory. I do not know the reason for this change, and the "Roman" advanced no explanation. If you have any commissions for me, I anxiously await them; it would be an honor to take care of them. I kiss your hand and am always your most devoted and faithful servant.
> Naples, 18 January 1757   G. C. Bach

The date on the letter indicates that Christian had by then received most of Padre Martini's instruction—two and a half years of intensive study. Christian intended to continue, though from now on chiefly by correspondence between Milan and Bologna.

Little is known about Christian's activities in Italy from 1754 to 1756. Nor is it clear why this letter, the first one preserved, was sent from Naples. Perhaps Count Litta's generosity had enabled his protégé to gain experience elsewhere, particularly to obtain further firsthand knowledge of opera. For both opera and church music, Naples was a fine place to visit. Many organizations there offered excellent music, often trying to outdo each other in splendid performances.

The chief source of talent for both sacred music and opera were the three conservatories: San Onofrio, La Pietà dei Turchini, and Santa Maria di Loreto, with enrollments of 90, 120, and 200 students, respectively. These institutions were unequalled in all of Europe, producing the best singers, instrumentalists, and composers. Pupils would enter at the age of eight and were normally expected to stay for eight years. Anyone who proved to be without talent would be turned out to make room for another.

Students of the three schools could easily be recognized by their attractive uniforms. Those at San Onofrio wore white, at the Pietà, blue, while those at Santa Maria di Loreto sported white dress with a black scarf.

In Burney's opinion the "scholars" of the Neapolitan conservatories "have long enjoyed the reputation of being the first *contrapuntists*, or composers, in Europe." When Burney attended concerts in the churches "I expected to have my ears gratified with every musical luxury and refinement that Italy could afford." On 17 October 1770, Burney wrote in his diary:

> This afternoon I went to hear a musical performance at the church of the Franciscans, where the three Conservatorios were to furnish music and musicians for a great festival of eight successive days, morning and evening. (It is by this performance that the Conservatorios hold their charters; and, in consideration of the boys playing gratis, they are exempted by the King from all taxes on wine and provisions, which are paid by the other inhabitants of Naples.) This is a large handsome church, but too much ornamented. The architecture seems to be good, but it is so gilded that it almost blinded me to look at it; and in the few interstitial parts where there is no gold, tawdry flowers are painted in abundance.
>
> The band was numerous, consisting of above a hundred voices and instruments. They were placed in a long occasional gallery, totally covered with gold and silver gilding; but though the band seemed to be a very good one, and the leader was very careful and attentive, yet the distance of some of the performers from the others, rendered it almost impossible that the time should be always exactly kept.
>
> The composition was by Signor Gennaro Mannio, and in many movements admirable. . . . The air that was given to the base [bass] was as ingeniously written as any I ever heard; the accompaniments were full, without destroying the melody of the voice parts: instead of shortening or mutilating its passages, the instruments seemed to continue and finish them, giving the singer time for respiration.[9]

Much as he was impressed by the students' attractive uniforms and good manners in public, Burney did not like what he saw inside the conservatories. Having visited San Onofrio, Burney asked himself how any good music making could take place in so noisy a setting.

> On the first flight of stairs was a trumpeter, screaming upon his instrument till he was ready to burst; on the second was a french-horn, bellowing in the same manner. In the common practicing room was a *Dutch concert*, consisting of seven or eight harpsichords, more than as many violins, and several voices, all performing different things and in

different keys: other boys were writing in the same room. . . . The jumbling them all together in this manner may be convenient for the house and may teach the boys to attend to their own parts with firmness, whatever else may be going forward at the same time; it may likewise give them force by obliging them to play loud in order to hear themselves; but in the midst of such jargon, and continued dissonance, it is wholly impossible to give any kind of polish or finishing to their performance; hence the slovenly coarseness so remarkable in their public exhibitions; and the total want of taste, neatness, and expression in all these young musicians, till they have acquired them elsewhere.[10]

He was similarly disappointed by what he heard at the famous San Carlo opera house. The appearance of the auditorium was impressive enough: seven tiers of boxes, each box accommodating ten to twelve spectators. The box seats were "as comfortable as in a private house."

In every range [tier] there are thirty boxes, except the three lowest ranges, which, by the king's box taken out of them, are reduced to twenty-nine. In the pit there are fourteen or fifteen rows of seats, which are very roomy and commodious, with leather cushions and stuffed backs, each separated from the other by a broad rest for the elbow; in the middle of the pit there are thirty of these seats in a row. [Though it was magnificent,] it must be owned that the magnitude of the building, and the noise of the audience are such that neither the voices nor the instruments can be heard distinctly. . . . Nor did the singers, though they exerted themselves more, appear to equal advantage: not one of the present voices is sufficiently powerful for such a theatre, when so crowded and so noisy.

Things had probably been much the same during Christian's stay in Naples some fifteen years before. But in spite of shortcomings, Neapolitan composers created a style that set the tone for the epoch. Burney admired the "elegant and simple melodies, such as might be remembered and carried away after the first hearing," which he had heard in a light *burletta* by Paisiello. Christian may have had similar reactions to what he heard on the Neapolitan stages. Burney also remarked on the full orchestral writing in Piccinni's scores. "Indeed Piccinni is accused of employing instruments to such excess, that in Italy no copist will transcribe one of his operas without being paid a sequin more than for any other composer."[11]

Names such as Scarlatti, Durante, Leo, and Porpora testify to the early years of Naples's glory, followed by Pergolesi, Piccinni, and Jommelli. Two Germans, George Frideric Handel and Johann Adolf Hasse, also belong here, having absorbed much of the Neapolitan style.

Like Christian Bach, Handel had come to Italy to learn—in 1707, almost half a century before the Bach son. True, he spent only a few months in Naples, but they proved decisive for his future. When his opera *Agrippina* was performed in Venice, the duke of Manchester, then English ambassador to Venice, was so pleased with it that he invited Handel to come to England.

The success of the work must have been spectacular. As Mainwaring reports, "The theatre, at almost every pause, resounded with shouts and acclamations of *viva il caro Sassone!*" With such an achievement, Handel provided a model for the Germans who were to follow him, at first Hasse, then Christian Bach. Handel, Mainwaring continues, had "a thorough acquaintance with the Italian masters, to whose delicate and beautiful melody he added indeed still higher touches of expression, at the same time that he united it with the full strong harmony of his own country."[12]

As fate would have it, Christian, like his father before him, never met Handel. In the year of Christian's first preserved letter to Padre Martini, the seventy-two-year-old Handel drew up his will in England. Two years later Handel would die, and Christian would follow in his footsteps as music teacher to the royal family.

Hasse was the other German who, before Christian, contributed substantially to the success of Italian opera throughout Europe. He, too, was feted as "divino Sassone"; in his case the "Saxon" referred to Dresden, the city of his operatic triumphs. Actually, Hasse had been born in Bergedorf, near Hamburg. He always defended Italian opera vigorously, at times even violently. Charles de Brosses relates that Hasse once "almost strangled him" when Brosses dared to make some remarks gently defending French music. He asked Hasse, "Have you ever heard any of our music? Do you know any operas by Lully, Campra, Destouches? Have you as much as looked at our Rameau's *Hippolyte?*" To which Hasse replied, indignantly, "May God preserve me from looking at or listening to any but Italian music; Italian is the only singable language. Your language [French] is full of hard, unmusical syllables that sound awful when sung. I am not interested in any language but Italian." Hasse, he continues with humor, was nearly choked with rage, and if his wife, the singer Faustina, had not interfered, he might have "stabbed me with a sixteenth-note or knocked me down with some sharps."[13]

Whereas Christian had never met Handel, he had meet Hasse at least twice before. There had been several meetings in Leipzig between Johann Sebastian Bach and the Hasses, and Christian was there when

Hasse's archenemy Porpora and his protégé Regina Mingotti dared to challenge Hasse, the uncrowned king of opera, and his wife Faustina. At the time, Christian's father had taken the side of Hasse. The Dresden public may have been amused by all this, but the incident was later to cause Christian some problems in England.

In March 1753, Christian probably met Hasse again, in Berlin. While the young Bach was only starting his career at that time, Hasse was a star; in the eyes of Frederick the Great, he was the only opera composer who ranked equal to, or perhaps even higher than, Graun. Hasse's opera *Didone abandonnata* had made a great hit just before, with nine successful performances in January alone. Hasse's next opera, *Cleofide*, was to be given later in the same year.

During his visit to Berlin, Hasse had appeared at one of the king's private concerts, together with Monticelli, a male mezzo-soprano of the Dresden opera. On that occasion Hasse reportedly spoke highly of Carl Philipp Emanuel Bach. No doubt the king did not share this opinion, but he continued to admire Hasse. During these days in March 1753, Hasse apparently renewed his friendly contacts with the Bach family by visiting Emanuel, and on that occasion he probably also met Christian.

Somewhat later, in 1757, the two may have met at Padre Martini's in Bologna. According to Hasse's letter to Algarotti,[14] Hasse intended to visit the padre in the fall of that year. At about this time Christian wrote a letter to his teacher in which he exclaims, "How much I would like to return to Bologna, to benefit from your valuable instruction!" If he did return, a meeting between Hasse, Martini, and Christian may indeed have occurred.

Hasse's wife, Faustina Bordoni, came from Venice. Hasse had taken a position there, as director of the conservatory Degl'Incurabili. His most famous sacred composition is a Miserere that was performed every year during Holy Week. Padre Martini called it a "magnificent work." Burney discussed it, raving about the beautiful voices of the girls who, as illegitimate children or orphans, were customarily taken into the conservatories and performed in all sacred music. They were instructed by the best teachers, were "absolute nightingales," and played the organ, violin, flute, cello, and even the French horn.[15]

According to contemporaries, Hasse's sacred music differed little in style from his operas, and it was no less esteemed. Opinions varied, however, as to its suitability: what some viewed as inappropriate mirth in a solemn liturgy, others considered a sincere hymn of praise. A writer belonging to a later generation saw it this way:

Hasse's unique, immortal church style forms a beautiful, extreme contrast to the Palestrina style. Together, and in combination with Handel's and Bach's church music, these styles bring unity and perfection to
the entire field of religious music. Hasse is the Correggio of sacred
music. That great painter knew how to depict heaven, filling it with
beautiful figures, expressing delicate, tender sentiments. Hasse also
knew how to move us, giving us a foretaste of the joys of heaven by
writing tender and beautiful music.[16]

Sacred music was then flourishing in Italy, thanks in part to Handel's
and Hasse's contributions, and Christian undoubtedly felt at home in this
genre. Thus there is nothing unusual in Christian's turning to sacred
music at this time, even though his immediately prior experience in Berlin had been gained in opera and concert music. The problem, if such it
can be called, lay in the situation of church music in general. The practice of utilizing elements of theater music in sacred music was being
widely questioned. Was such a mixture of styles at all permissible, and if
so, to what extent?

In furthering the efforts of the Counter-Reformation, the Council of
Trent had taken the position that music, in principle, was "worthy of
God" and that "all music of our time" should be included. What was
important was the "active participation of the people" so that the faithful
would not attend divine service "as though they were strangers or spectators." Furthermore, Mass, including the sermon and the music surrounding it, should convey to the worshippers the thoughts and emotions of
religion so that they, "overwhelmed by the liturgy's beauty, would participate actively, through singing," mindful of the old adage "who sings well,
prays doubly."

Some of these ideas implied a new concern with the individual wor-
shipper. Music should appeal to him, increasing his faith; he therefore
should understand the text of what was being sung. This was best accomplished by a solo singer, and thus the aria found its place in church.[17]

There was, of course, resistance to what some considered the secular-
ization of church music. Advocates of the "stile moderno" pointed out
that music was the language of the heart and, in sentiments expressed
through an aria, also the language of the church. Opponents such as Giovanni Antonio Ricieri, a valiant Franciscan monk and teacher of Padre
Martini, replied forcefully. In a letter to his pupil written in 1740, he
lamented:

> In our time, the house of God, because of the lack of restraint in music,
> has been changed into a noisy house of ill repute. . . . I do not mean to

say that the composers are bad, but they no longer induce worshipful feelings.[18]

The Catholic church faced a dilemma. Its political power had been weakened and challenged by the Reformation; it was worried about the decline of its authority and the loss of many believers. To recapture these, church music had to be allowed to move with the times, despite concerns that such changes might be made at the expense of piety and devotion. The new music seemed attractive to many. Even in the later nineteenth century, when the Cecilian movement was advocating a return to "pure" church music, Cardinal Bartolini expressed his concern that the faithful might be bored by the music they heard in church. In order to recapture their hearts, the church was now urged to enlist the help of all the arts, including music. Such statements bring to mind Mattheson, who as early as 1728 had advocated the "theatrical style" in church music. Thoughtful people, he claimed, took offense when "mindless hypocrites would say of some harmless little work of church music that it was 'theatrical'— people who knew nothing about it and who acted as though 'theatrical' were a swearword." Was there a difference between music for the church and for the theater? Mattheson answered his own question in the negative. "If worldly things can sadden me, so can spiritual things, and both can also cause me to rejoice. Music that delights me in the theater can affect me the same way in church; only the subject is different."[19]

Convictions of this kind, one might think, could lead a composer to write sacred music that was carefree or easygoing, but Christian thought otherwise. During 1757 and 1758, he submitted his many sacred works to the scrutiny of Padre Martini. Mattheson had recommended that church music should not be "resplendent" but should show "thoroughness and inner strength." Christian was eager to incorporate those qualities in his sacred writing, with the help of his continued studies under Padre Martini. Some persuasion by Count Litta, along with encouragement from his friends, may also have been involved, for the group of amateur musicians around Litta (Christian called them "eccelentissimi signori") showed remarkable interest in his training. He referred to them as "gentlemen" when informing Martini of his safe return to Milan.

> I can assure you that these gentlemen received me with great respect and treated me very kindly. They are pleased that I am studying with you and expect a great deal from me. Cavaliere Augostino [sic] Litta is already thinking about a way to show you his appreciation for the trouble you have taken with me. I would be grateful if, in a brief note, you would indicate whether in the future I might continue to benefit from

your valued advice. Trusting that you are in good health, I am always
your most faithful and obedient servant.
Milan, 30 April 1757   Giov: Christiano Bach

Count Litta wrote to Martini on the same day. His letter shows that
Christian's well-being and future had become a concern of the count and
those around him.

Reverend Padre and Maestro!
Our Bach has returned safely; he is forever grateful to you for all
the knowledge you have imparted to him. His only regret is that he
must be so far from his honored master. I hope that from now on he will
be more content here. We are giving much thought to finding a suitable
profession for him. At any rate, I am deeply indebted to you for the
inconveniences you must have had taking care of him. I remain, with
all respect, your devoted and grateful servant.
Milan, 30 April 1757   Cavaliere Agostino Litta

These letters must have crossed in the mails a letter by Martini in
which he inquires about Christian's return. Apparently he was worried
that Christian's "employers" (he also used the plural) might have taken
his long absence amiss. Christian hastened to dispel Martini's worries,
repeating that the "excellent gentlemen" had received him with respect
far exceeding his merits. He stressed again that Litta was looking for suitable employment for him, which would provide him with an assured
income, and that Litta went out of his way to satisfy him.

Christian then turned to the scientific dispute he had had with a certain Balbi,[20] who had apparently complained about him to the padre.

My relations with Signor Balbi are entirely amicable. The letter you
received from him was prompted by nothing more than an insignificant
question relating to a problem that you have already solved. . . . Signor
Balbi's opinion was the opposite of mine. I did not want to take the
matter up again, for I had the impression that Sig. Balbi might be
offended, thinking that I wanted to argue with him about music. This
will teach me in the future not to engage in such conversations. I would
not have entered into them with anyone but a friend, such as Balbi. I
consider it necessary to describe all this, so that you will not think I
tried to play the part of a scholar without having the qualifications.

This little digression suggests that Christian, like his father, was not
averse to discussing controversial subjects. Christian continues:

I shall be only too glad to take you up on your generous offer of help.
Should I need advice or, more precisely, correction, I shall not fail to

Padre Giovanni Battista Martini.

impose on you with my compositions, so that you may "purify" them. At the moment I am working on the Officio [4][21] and have completed the Invitatory and the Dies Irae. Please, Reverend Father, extend my greetings to the other padres and to the entire school. I am always . . .
Milan, 21 May 1757   Giov: Christiano Bach

The Dies Irae mentioned by Christian formed part of a Mass for the Dead in eight voices, the performance of which had been planned for 29 July. It consisted of Introit, Kyrie, and Dies Irae, but only the last-mentioned was performed. According to Christian's letters to Padre Martini, the Introit was not completed until the late fall of 1757, the Kyrie in the spring of 1758. This Requiem Mass has remained to this day Christian's most famous sacred work. It can stand comparison with the Requiem by Mozart, who was then barely one-and-a-half years old.

In his next letter, dated 24 June, Christian as always asks for Martini's advice, posing detailed questions and including sketches of music. In a movement in 2/2 time, is it permissible to write parallel fourths, even when the bass proceeds in contrary motion? He had found an example of this in "good old Perti" (Giacomo Perti, 1661–1756, one of the most famous seventeenth-century writers of sacred music) and had used this progression but was severely criticized for it.

Other questions about music theory follow. Finally Christian asks Martini to tell him why a composition in minor must always end in major. (Christian's Dies Irae in C minor also ends in major.)

Five weeks later Christian reports that the Dies Irae was quite successful at the dress rehearsal.

> Reverend Father, honored patron,
>
> No doubt a great amount of work has caused you to delay writing to me. Nevertheless I am anxious to let you know that the Mass that I began composing under your supervision has been rehearsed in Count Litta's house. The success and the general applause for the composer drive home to me how deeply I am indebted to you, Reverend Father, for all this is due to your instruction and encouragement alone. Words fail me to relate how impressed the count and his family were, along with all the musicians here. His Excellency has just received your letter. He asks me to send you his regards and wants you to know that there is no need for you to thank him. You will receive another letter from him in the next mail, along with the rest of the chocolate.[22] He hopes that you will continue to allow me to benefit from your invaluable counsel and experience. . . . Everyone in Milan who examined the eight-part composition was impressed by the unusual and specific suggestions you

had made. . . . Please continue to be generous with your letters. . . .

Your Excellency's most thankful servant and student G. C. Bach
Milan, 30 July 1757

Contemporary accounts confirm that the first performance of the Mass, on 27 July 1757, was a splendid occasion. Christian, then twenty-one years old, directed an ensemble of sixty-four singers and instrumentalists. The number of performers underscores the event's significance. Those who attended included important church musicians, Sammartini probably among them, and leading members of Milan society. Everyone was curious to find out what the youngest Bach son, Padre Martini's pupil, had accomplished.

They were not disappointed. The monsignori of the cathedral chapter, who may have been wondering about the competence of their future cathedral organist, were surely impressed. They would have been impressed, for instance, by the monumental double fugue of the final movement, which a later reviewer called "the most artful piece of contrapuntal writing from these years," and by the moving "Pie Jesu Domine" that precedes the powerful finale, which brings to mind the contrasting, tender sounds of the *Voca me* in the "Confutatis" section of Mozart's Requiem. In all, Christian had created "a work of art such as an Italian composer of the time could hardly have written."[23]

Count Litta lost no time informing Padre Martini of the work's success, also sending him the second parcel of chocolate, three weeks after the initial gift. In his letter Litta speaks of "our dear Giovannino Bach" who, thanks to Martini's instruction, had reached "perfection as a musician." He goes on to say that "the pupil's fame reflects on the teacher, for you have made him a maestro." (Letter of 13 August 1757.)

That Christian's compositions for the church continued to attract attention is confirmed by the many copies made for the most famous libraries in Europe. The story of the autograph manuscripts is complex and does not have a happy ending. The fifteen works that had reached England formed part of Christian's estate and were purchased by his friend, Miss Emma Jane Greenland. Christian had dedicated to her his Opus 16, six sonatas for keyboard, accompanied by flute or violin. (Her father's signature appears on Christian's last will and testament.) Later these manuscripts became the property of Vincent Novello,[24] who in turn passed them on to the German scholar Friedrich Chrysander. He brought them to Hamburg, where they were deposited in the State and University Library. There, during the bombings of the Second World War, they were destroyed.

Copies fortunately survived. Einsiedeln monastery in Switzerland had acquired many through the efforts of Pater Marianus Müller, later archabbott of the monastery. Müller had studied music in Milan during the time of Sammartini, who may have been his teacher. While there, he had obtained many music manuscripts for a secondary school in Bellinzona, southern Switzerland, that was operated by the monastery during the eighteenth and nineteenth centuries. Among these manuscripts were works by Sammartini and also, most likely, by Christian Bach, whose autograph scores were copied near Milan. (Most of the originals accompanied Christian to England.) Eventually, by way of the school in Bellinzona, these copies found their way to Einsiedeln and were thus preserved for posterity.[25]

Christian had intended to copy the Dies Irae for Padre Martini. During fall of the following year, he wrote to him that he had begun but that pressure of other duties had prevented him from completing the task. Now, having a little more time, he wanted to catch up. But three months later, in October, Christian had to confess that he had not progressed beyond the opening, and that he would have to hire a copyist to complete the manuscript. If Martini should notice minor errors in the score, would he please excuse them. But Christian's handwriting and that of the copyist were amazingly similar (one thinks of the like problem involving Mozart's and Süssmayr's writing in Mozart's Requiem), so that differentiation is often difficult. Martini bequeathed his copy to the Liceo Musicale in Bologna; the copy has served as the basis for several recordings of the Dies Irae. In this copy, Christian's hand can be detected at the beginning.

The work's success beyond Italy indicates that once again, following Handel and Hasse, a young German composer had achieved international recognition during the golden age of Italian church music, having competed with many Italian composers of note. At the time, few of those around Christian were even familiar with the name of his father. At best, "the old Bach" was to them a legendary figure from a distant region north of the Alps.

Three weeks after the rehearsal at the Litta mansion, the performance took place in the magnificent San Fedele church. Christian described it in his next letter to Martini, using the occasion to remind his mentor of this student's continued need for advice.

> I know my shortcomings, but I try to remember that you assured Count
> Litta and me of your intention to give me further help in music, which I
> still need badly. On 23 July I performed my composition in San Fedele;

by the grace of God and thanks to your schooling it earned much acclaim. I never doubted that it would be successful, but now more than ever I hope to benefit from your expertise. I would therefore like to send you soon a composition for eight voices on which I am now working for study purposes. Only after I have received your corrections would I dare submit it to public scrutiny without fear of being criticized even for minor details. Cavaliere Litta sends you respectful greetings, and I remain, in the hope of enjoying your continued favor, your obedient and faithful servant

Milan, 30 August 1757   Giov: Christiano Bach

The work in question, a Pater Noster, has been lost. On the day after his twenty-second birthday Christian sent it to Martini. In spite of the success of his Mass, Christian was worried about any mistakes for which he might be taken to task by the learned "professors of music" in Milan. His fear may have been due in part to the fact that, as a Lutheran (still), he was not intimately acquainted with the Catholic liturgy. In the letter to Martini accompanying the score, Christian admits that his eagerness to compose exceeds his ability.

> But I have learned that the person who doesn't embark on an adventure with courage will never get anywhere. . . . With the same mail I was going to send you a Kyrie fugue in eight voices, but I lacked the time to complete it and will have to send it another time. I beg you to look at the Pater Noster. It will be examined by the professors here, and they will not approve of it unless you have already seen it. Only then will I be so bold as to show it to everyone. Many professors have asked to be remembered to you. I remain Your Excellency's most humble and obedient servant.
>
> Milan, 2 September 1757   Giov: C. Bach

In a postscript Christian takes up several problems, citing musical examples and asking for the padre's help. He also expresses his concern about his mentor's health, specifically about a persistent leg ailment. In a letter of 8 October [26] Christian says that he had been told about the problem by "Signor Valentini." Michelangelo Valentini was the brother of Regina Valentini, a pupil of Porpora and the wife of opera impresario Pietro Mingotti. She was the one who had threatened the undisputed reign of the Hasses in Dresden; later she also would cause Christian some difficulties in London.

Other names in this letter show that by then Christian had become quite familiar with Milan's world of music, including opera. He refers to

Martini's "protégé Pietro Tibaldi"; the correct name is Giuseppe Luigi Tibaldi, a singer whom Martini had instructed in composition and whom he had apparently recommended. About a singer from Bologna, the male alto Giuseppe Cicognani, Christian reports that his reputation had become firmly established. Because of his success, he was obliged to repeat every evening "un'aria cantabile."[27] Christian was sure the Milan impresarios would engage him for the carnival season.

Christian's reports about the world of opera indicate his growing interest in that genre. In his next letter one notices some discontent with the kind of music Count Litta had urged him to compose so far.

> Let me tell you the truth about my situation here. My patron, Count Litta, always wants me to write things I have never tried before. Some time ago he asked me to write a Pater Noster in eight voices. When I told him that I had never attempted this before without some guidance, he replied: "You must try it!" I told him that I could make no headway without your help. Whenever he asked me about that piece, I told him that it had been sent to you. Right now he is away hunting and will be gone all of next week. Therefore, may I ask you to send me a few comments about it, so that I might incorporate your corrections and then show the piece to the count? Heaven knows I would love to come to Bologna and benefit from your instruction! But I depend on my superiors and cannot do as I please.

After getting this off his chest, Christian returns to practical matters. He plans to send to Martini an "Introit a 7" with "canto fermo" (20), written in the style that was customary in Milan, according to Signor Balbi and others. He is also working on an eight-part Magnificat (15), almost completed; he plans to give it to Tibaldi, who would be returning to Bologna on completing his Milan engagement. (As it turned out, Christian did not complete the Magnificat until March 1758, at which time he sent it to Martini by mail.) His further remarks about Litta are more positive:

> I try to make the most of my employment here. I compose, partly to improve my skills, partly to give pleasure to my patron. He seems very pleased with my work and never fails to encourage me. Please do send me the comments for which I have asked you, before he returns; also do tell me about the state of your health.
> Milan, October 22, 1757   G. C. Bach

Two weeks later, Christian himself is "in campagna," in the country. On 16 November[28] he writes from Lainate, the Littas' country estate

The tomb of Emperor Charles VI in the San Fedele Church in Milan. Christian's Dies Irae (below) was performed there on 23 August 1757.

some ten miles northwest of Milan. The count was expecting the duke of
Modena, and the distinguished visitor would have to be entertained with
chamber music. There is at least a hint here of Christian's duties with
regard to chamber music.

Six string trios and seven sonatas for violin and keyboard exist in
manuscript, carrying the notation "Del Sig. Bach in Milano." No doubt
these works constitute only a small portion of his chamber music from
this period. To judge by the comments he made a few years later, he was
establishing himself beyond Italy as a composer of secular music. In
another letter to Padre Martini he excuses himself for having had to
neglect his studies. "Every day I am called on to write something for the
concert hall: symphonies, concertos, cantatas, and so on—many works
for Germany and also for Paris."[29]

In his correspondence with Martini, Christian says little about his
chamber music, nor does he mention all his sacred works. He makes no
specific reference to the three *Lezioni* (12, 13, and 14), or to the equally
impressive Miserere in ten movements (18) of 1757. We hear nothing
about the "Beatus vir" (1), "Domine ad adjuvandum" (7), or "Laudamus
te" (117), all of 1758. These works may have been started before 1757,
under Martini's supervision, but in view of his many sacred works from
1757 and 1758, it is entirely possible that Christian never submitted
them to his teacher.

Christian's conversion to Catholicism must have taken place around
this time. In his appendix to the Bach family chronicle, brother Carl
Philipp Emanuel noted it with a pointed remark: "He did not do like the
honest Veit." The remark alludes to an early member of the Bach family
about whom the chronicle relates:

> In the sixteenth century Vitus Bach, a baker in Hungary, had to leave
> his home because of his Lutheran faith. He sold all his belongings and
> left for Germany. Thuringia offered safety to the Lutherans; therefore
> he settled in Wechmar, near Gotha.[30]

It was easy for Emanuel to be critical; he faced no such problems in
the liberal Prussia of Frederick the Great. To judge by Gleim's letter to Uz
(16 August 1758), life there was pleasant and easy, full of sociability.[31]
Gleim raved about life in Berlin at about the time when Christian converted to Catholicism, a step that was not all that unusual. Hadn't Hasse,
his predecessor in Italy, also changed his religious affiliation when he was
in hope of obtaining the position of Kapellmeister at the Conservatorio
degl'Incurabili in Venice? Now Bach, thirty years later, faced a similar sit-

uation. He seems to have agreed with Litta's plan to obtain for him the position of organist at the Milan cathedral—but this appointment called for a Roman Catholic![32]

Christian's next letter to Padre Martini was written after a long interval, on 22 March 1758. The great number of compositions mentioned is both confusing and impressive: confusing because of the difficulty in dating them, and impressive because they attest to Christian's industry. This time he relates that the count had honored him by asking him to provide the music for a festive service in honor of St. Nepomuc, to be celebrated in the church of the "Minori conventuali di San Francesco." As always, Christian asks for the padre's help. A while earlier he had sent him his Magnificat (15), which Martini had returned with corrections.

> If the work has some merit, this is due to the two bass parts that you have added. I would be ever so thankful if you could go over the music one more time, for I am convinced that I shall have much success with the work. May I also request you to look over the Kyrie [20] and return both whenever convenient? I have already received the Mass and the Credo [3], along with the four-part Dixit Dominus [5] that I composed under your supervision, and I shall be so bold as to send another piece for your evaluation. . . . My *Officio per gli morti* [4] was very favorably received here; with your kind help I therefore hope for similar success. . . . I also trust that you will kindly send me the first volume of your great work as soon as it is published. [Martini's *Storia della Musica*, the first volume of which was published in 1757.]
>
> Milan, 22 March 1758   Giov: Christiano Bach

Apparently Martini was not entirely pleased with the final fugue of one of these works, for in a short reply of 28 April, Christian promises to make the suggested changes in the Amen. A week later, Christian expresses his appreciation for Martini's help and asks him whether he would have any use for an old treatise on music theory. The treatise to which he referred was the *Toscanello in Musica* by Pietro Aaron, published in five editions between 1523 and 1562. Martini accepted the offer and added the volume to his famous library.

On 1 July 1758, Christian proudly reports:

> Since I owe all I know about music to you, it is my duty to tell you of the successful performance of my music in the church of San Francesco. I hope this will give you the kind of satisfaction a teacher feels when his student has distinguished himself.

At the same time he expresses his regret that he had not heard from his mentor in a long time. Indeed, the correspondence seems to have virtu-ally ceased, unless letters have been lost. We next hear from Christian in January 1759, this time with interesting news:

> Cavaliere Litta sends his regards and excuses himself for not having written. He is very busy but is quite ready to help Signor Filippo Elisi, whom you have recommended. Elisi was treated poorly here by the composer who wrote his first opera for the carnival season; as a result he did not succeed. After three or four performances, the Cavaliere com-missioned me to write an aria for Elisi, to the text "Misero pargoletto." It had the good fortune to succeed, and with it, the singer, who must now repeat the aria during every performance.
> Milan, January 1759   Giov: Christ. Bach

The composer in question was Giovanni Ferrandini, one of many who had set Metastasio's popular libretto *Demofoonte*. Apparently Elisi, who had the lead, was not satisfied, and soon after the first rehearsal refused to sing Ferrandini's arias, especially his setting of "Misero pargo-letto," a typical display aria. Perhaps his refusal was justified; perhaps it was just the kind of capriciousness also practiced by male "prima donnas" in the eighteenth century. Christian's setting, written specifically for Elisi, pleased him all the more. Later, he often sang the aria in concerts, along with cantatas by Christian. Twenty years later, "Misero pargoletto" was still so popular that it was heard (in *Demofoonte*) at the opening of the London opera season of 1778. Christian and Elisi would meet again in London, and Elisi may have been instrumental in obtaining for Chris-tian the commission to write an opera for the King's Theatre.

To return to 1759: there is a certain irony in Count Litta's asking Christian to write the aria for Elisi, thereby pointing his protégé in a direction he would have preferred Christian to avoid. Although Litta had other plans for the young composer, he actually helped Christian develop a taste for writing opera. But Christian's operas were still in the future; for 1759, plans included further large-scale sacred works.

Ties to Padre Martini were not completely severed—they continued to the end of Christian's life—but the number of letters diminished greatly. Christian's letter of 4 March is brief: he is sending Martini two volumes of Ambrosian chants [the chant, different from Gregorian, that had developed in Milan], and he requests an answer regarding a letter of recommendation for a young man from Milan who wished to be accepted by Martini as a student. Christian then apologizes for the pause in their correspondence.

The end of Christian Bach's Magnificat in the composer's handwriting.
(See his letters of 22 October 1757 and 22 March 1758.)

Reverend Father and honored patron,

I hardly dare write to you, having neglected for such a long time to send my compliments. Only because of pressing obligations did I fail in my duty to you. Be assured, however, that I esteem your friendship above anything else. I work hard, yet it takes me a long time to overcome difficulties. But I have written a Te Deum in eight voices [22] and several small fugues in three and four voices. As soon as time permits I shall send them to you, so that you can correct them. . . . I have begun to study geometrical proportions, in order to be able to follow more adequately the thoughts expressed in such an excellent work [Martini's *Storia della Musica*]. I am, etc.

Milan, 14 July 1759   Giov: Christ: Bach[33]

The Te Deum in question is dated 1758, in Christian's hand; apparently he had begun it the year before he wrote this letter. The work, preserved in the British Library, is incomplete; the orchestra parts for the last 155 measures are missing. Rochlitz called it "one of the most beautiful works of its kind to be found in Europe," but the impressive song of praise does not seem to have reached Christian's mentor in Bologna. One might infer from this that Christian by then felt more sure of himself as a composer of sacred music; yet he nevertheless continued to express interest in Martini's counsel. In his next letter, written half a year later, Christian even thinks of continuing his studies with him in Bologna.

I am afraid you will think of me as someone who promises much but delivers little, for I often said that I would send you compositions and then did not do so. Let me assure you that there is no lack of ambition, only of time. The music is ready, but I have no time to make a copy. Yet I want to copy it myself, for the copyists here do not do reliable work. The Cavaliere [Litta] has asked me to send you his compliments; he can confirm that I am extremely busy. I am composing a new Mass and Vespers for the feast of St. Joseph; I have gotten only as far as the Gloria. This morning I set the "Suscipe deprecationem nostram" as a four-part fugue. I shall take the liberty of sending it to you, along with the eight-part Te Deum, so that both works may be improved by your corrections.

Padre Lampugnani, who brought greetings from you, assured me of your continued benevolence toward me. I am relieved to know this, especially because the Cavaliere is giving me reason to hope that I may return to Bologna, that I may continue my studies under your guidance.

I hope the young student whom the Cavaliere recommended is doing well. He stopped in Milan, but I did not meet him as I was in the country at the time. I have the honor to remain Your Excellency's most devoted and thankful servant.

Milan, 18 December 1759   Giov: C. Bach

It is significant that Lampugnani's name should come up at this t
It suggests that Christian's ties to opera in Milan were gradually bec
ing stronger. Giovanni Battista Lampugnani was a master of Italian o..…
who, for more than half a century, had maintained close ties to Milan's
Teatro Regio Ducale. His activity resulted in connections not only to
Christian but also to Wolfgang Amadeus Mozart.

Let us look ahead for a moment to the year 1770. The scene is the
Regio Teatro Ducale in Milan. Young Mozart, a mere fourteen years old,
had recently arrived from Bologna, where (thanks to some help from
Padre Martini) he had been solemnly admitted to membership in the
Accademia filarmonica. Now, in Milan, he was preparing his first opera for
Italy, *Mitridate, Re di Ponto*. The many obstacles encountered by the
young composer were due, according to Leopold Mozart, to the "Virtuosa
Canalia," that rabble of virtuosos.[34] The first rehearsal was to take place
at the beginning of December, but by the end of November, Benedetti,
the primo uomo, had not yet arrived. Meanwhile, the other singers were
insisting on being given other arias that they thought would bring more
applause.

If, in spite of all this, *Mitridate* turned out to be a triumph for Mozart,
this was due to Lampugnani. He functioned as a coach during rehearsals,
using all his influence and authority to keep the rebellious singers in line.
During the first performance, he officiated at the second harpsichord
while Mozart conducted from the first. Later, when things were going
smoothly and Mozart felt free to listen from the auditorium, Lampugnani
took his place at the first harpsichord, directing subsequent performances
with Melchior Chiesa at the second harpsichord.

On 5 January 1771, Leopold Mozart wrote to his wife:

> Fifteen or eighteen years ago, when Lampugnani in England and Chiesa
> in Italy were composing so much—if anyone had then told me that
> someday these men would be expected to accompany your son's music
> when he wishes to leave the keyboard, I would have considered that
> person out of his mind and sent him to the asylum.

Leopold Mozart here alludes to Lampugnani's two sojourns in London. From 1743 to 1745, and again in 1755, he had drawn enthusiastic
crowds at the King's Theatre, the place of Christian's later activity. When
Lampugnani returned to Milan in 1758, he began to cultivate the
"dramma giocoso," a lighter kind of opera. Burney had these impressions:

> Lampugnani's is not a grand style, but there is a graceful gaiety in the
> melody of his quick songs, and an elegant tenderness in the slow, that

resemble no other composer's works of that time. . . . The music is light, airy, and pleasant. It wants dignity, as is usual with the compositions of this master, but it is never vulgar or tedious; it is the music of a light-hearted man of the world; no study or labour appear, though fashion or elegance are never wanting.[35]

Burney's remarks about "graceful gaiety" and "elegant tenderness" could have applied equally well to Christian, who may have received from Lampugnani reports about the state of music in England at this time, shortly before the death of Handel on 14 April 1759.

Another death at this time—that of his mother—affected Christian more profoundly. Though separated from her by many miles, he had been close to her all along. The event rated but a modest notice in the Leipzig register of deaths of 29 February 1760, the day of the funeral:

> Anna Magdalena Bach, née Wilckin, indigent, widow of Herr Johann Sebastian Bach, cantor at St. Thomas School, died at Haynstrasse, fifty-nine years old.

A note scribbled at the margin, "1/4," referred to the simplest category of funeral, customary for an "indigent woman" (*Almosenfrau*). It indicated that only one-fourth of the students sang at the funeral. This sad state of affairs leads to the question: were none of Bach's sons in a position to see to it that their mother received a dignified burial? At the time of her death, Friedemann was forty-nine, Emanuel forty-five, Friedrich twenty-seven, and Christian twenty-four years old.

To be sure, distances were great, and travel was hazardous during the unrests of the Seven Years' War. Hard times caused everyone to be preoccupied with their own survival. For Friedemann and Emanuel, Anna Magdalena was "only" a stepmother. In those days funerals, even within the immediate family, often were not treated with great sentimentality. Still, we look for signs of some human concern during these last, cheerless days of Johann Sebastian Bach's widow.

Friedemann would have had the shortest distance to travel. Among the brothers who were already employed, he had the smallest income, though as organist and director of music, his earnings were regular and assured. His base pay amounted to 180 taler, which could be augmented if he was willing to bestir himself as a composer. As noted earlier, after their father's death, Friedemann and Emanuel had acquired his musical estate, which in some instances Friedemann passed off as his own compositions. At other times—and not only later, when he was in financial straits—Friedemann sold his own works as compositions by his father.

As for Emanuel, hadn't he offered to sell the copper plates of the *Art of Fugue* to the highest bidder—he who, of all the sons, was most comfortably off? Thanks to his success as a composer of popular pieces and as a teacher, he had few financial worries. Yet Reichardt had claimed that Emanuel was very interested in material gain. It would seem that he had little concern for his impecunious stepmother in Leipzig.

Anna Magdalena's own sons did little more than eke out an existence. For the ten years prior to 1759, Johann Christoph Friedrich, in the employ of the count of Schaumburg-Lippe, earned no more than two hundred taler a year. That income was augmented by one hundred taler when he married Lucia Elisabeth Münchhausen; it was her income as a singer in the count's employ. The extra money did not go far, however, after two children were added to the mouths to be fed. When a substantial raise was at long last granted in 1759, it came too late to provide any support for Friedrich's mother. Moreover, to judge by the numerous petitions drawn up by Friedrich, the family's standard of living continued to be very low. All in all, he was hardly in a position to help his mother.[36]

The same applies to Christian, who was in every way dependent on Count Litta. Precise records are lacking, but quite likely he received room and board plus a small allowance, while expenses over and above his scholarship with Padre Martini were taken care of by Litta. Nor can we be sure that news of his mother's situation had traveled across the Alps to Milan.

All in all, it is sad to contemplate how little concern was shown by any of the sons; certainly a reflection on them, but perhaps also on the general status of women at the time.

For Christian in Italy, important changes were in the making. After some lapses in the correspondence, he now wrote to Padre Martini, telling about the realization of operatic plans. This may not have been a complete surprise to the padre, considering Christian's aria for Elisi and his acquaintance with Lampugnani. Christian seems to have been feeling somewhat guilty, to judge by his letter of 17 June 1760. He admits that he deserves censure for not having kept his promise to visit Bologna, but

> I had hoped from one week to the next to be able to visit Bologna, until there was no longer any possibility of doing so. It is true that last week I was in Reggio, but I was in such a hurry that I could stay only one night in order to hear the last performance of the opera. I then immediately left for Parma, where I remained for only two nights before returning to Milan. In all I was gone only six days, and I had to travel by mail coach to make better time. The purpose of my journey was to hear two singers

in Reggio who had been engaged by the Turin opera for the coming carnival season. Since I had also been engaged by that theater, it was very important for me to acquaint myself with the abilities of these singers.

His next sentences clearly show the conflict Christian faced at this time. Opera exerted a strong attraction, yet he did not want to write off church music altogether. Quite to the contrary, he again assures Martini that he intends to continue his studies with him—part-time, one assumes:

> As soon as time permits I shall make copies of my compositions and send them to you, Reverend Father, for corrections. I don't want this spring to go by like last year's. I have decided to visit Bologna at all cost and to stay a few months in order to make use of your manuscripts [the padre's famous library], if you will still allow me to do so. The Cavaliere asks me to send you his best regards . . .
> Milan, 17 June 1760   Giov: Christ: Bach

Christian had good cause for expressing an interest in sacred music: Count Litta had achieved his goal of obtaining for Christian the position of second organist at the Milan cathedral, reason enough for Christian's making sure once more of Martini's support. But when a few days later he informs him of his appointment, the tone of his letter is somewhat unenthusiastic:

> Reverend Father, honored patron:
> I was glad to receive your letter and immediately delivered your message to Signor Fioroni [the cathedral maestro di cappella]. He sends you his respects and wants you to know that he has received the five compositions but will be unable to decide which one he considers best. [We do not know what compositions were involved.] And now I can tell you that I have been appointed organist at the Milan cathedral. The position pays 800 lire annually and is not very demanding. I hope you have received my letter [of 17 June] in which I informed you of my stay near Bologna where, owing to the pressure of time, I could tarry only one day. I remain, etc.
> Milan, 28 June 1760   Giov: Bach

Christian's apparent lack of enthusiasm may have been because the second organist, Michelangelo Caselli, had agreed to retire only on condition that, until his death, he was to be paid Christian's salary. The document, preserved in the Milan cathedral archives, reads as follows:

> Michelangelo Caselli, organist at the cathedral and devoted servant of

The Milan Cathedral and its organ.

the cathedral chapter, in view of his age and physical frailty, wishes to turn over his position to Signor Giovanni Bach. He does this with the understanding that this meets with the approval of the venerable cathedral chapter and that the said Giovanni Bach agrees to turn over to him his entire salary as organist, and to execute all other obligations pertaining to the position. This income is to be paid to the said Caselli as usual, through the "Veneranda Fabbrica," as long as he lives. If, however (which may God forbid), the said Bach should die before Caselli, or should suffer an accident, then all rights to the position should revert to the said Caselli. Assuring the said chapter that the church will be competently served by the person recommended, Michelangelo Caselli asks for consent to this proposal.[37]

Such "buying into a position" was not unusual among organists at the time in both Italy and Germany. We may recall that when Sebastian Bach was considering becoming Buxtehude's successor in Lübeck, he demurred because a condition of his appointment was that he marry the incumbent's elderly daughter.

In view of all that Count Litta had done for him, Christian had no choice but to accept the arrangement with Caselli. There was, in fact, some income, for at times he had to take the place of the first organist, Corbelli. On feast days, when oratorios *a due cori* were given, Christian played the second organ. He was not obliged to compose sacred works for the cathedral, since that was the prerogative of maestro Fiorini. As it turned out, Christian was not deprived of his salary for long; just a few months later, on 15 January 1761, Caselli died at the age of seventy-one.

From then on Christian was able to pursue two kinds of activity. He had passed the audition as organist, on 22 August 1760, *valde laudabiliter* (with great distinction). Having the secure position of cathedral organist, he could now turn also to opera. It is significant that, out of his twenty-eight preserved sacred works,[38] only three were written after his appointment: a "Domine ad adjuvandum" (6) and a Magnificat from 1760, and a Te Deum (23) from 1762. Compared with the earlier wealth of sacred compositions, this is not much.

During the second half of 1760, Christian was a busy man. Not only was he composing an opera for Turin but he was still obliged to keep writing the kind of secular music for which Count Litta had employed him: compositions for the count's chamber music events and for public concerts. Christian refers to all this in his next letter to Padre Martini.

> Reverend Father, highly esteemed maestro,
>   It was wrong of me to wait this long to carry out my obligation; I

admit my guilt. I only hope that you will forgive me when I tell you the reasons. Not only do I have to write the opera for Turin, . . . but I also have been ordered to travel soon to Casal Maggiore and to Mantua. There I am to direct two major concerts of instrumental music given by the city of Milan in honor of the princess of Parma, who is passing through both places. You will understand, Reverend Father, that writing so many symphonies and concertos has kept me more than busy, especially since I have a serious competitor, San Martino [Sammartini?]. You probably know him by name; he is an expert at this kind of composing. God only knows what kind of an impression I shall make. I find comfort in the thought that I do not have to establish my reputation with these compositions.

Signor Lolli [Antonio Lolli, violinist, ca. 1730–1802] has given me your letter. I would have done everything possible to assist your protégé, but unfortunately the Cavaliere was out of town. Moreover, Signor Lolli was in Milan for a short time only. However, I did not fail to give him a good letter of recommendation as he left for Parma. . . . I can assure you, Reverend Father, that [Lolli] is indeed one of the best violinists to be heard today. . . . I intend to spend all of the coming carnival season in Bologna, but only with your permission and if you will allow me the use of your precious sources. I am, etc.

Milan, 30 August 1760   Giov: Bach[39]

Once again, nothing came of the visit because of "pressing obligations," as he wrote to Martini six months later. Strangely enough, Christian mentioned nothing about his opera *Artaserse*, which was performed with great success early in 1761 and no doubt represented one of the "pressing obligations." In the few letters still to follow, Christian avoids any references to his operatic activities. He gives only one "weighty reason" that prevented him from going to Bologna: his obligations to Count Litta, who was not pleased by his absences.

Throughout the carnival season, concerts that I must direct are held in the Litta palace. You will agree that I must respect my employer's wishes. Still, I am grieved by all this, I assure you. I almost had an altercation with the Cavaliere because of my insisting on going to Bologna, having neglected my studies for so long. Every day I am expected to provide for musical events—symphonies, concertos, and cantatas, also for Germany and for Paris [see note 29 on page 345], but you know that my studies do not benefit from all this. I am, etc.

Milan, 14 February 1761   Giov: Bach

The visit with Padre Martini actually did take place sometime before

10 April 1762. His fatherly friend and mentor was as kind and helpful as ever, which we can tell from Christian's last, short letter:

> With God's help I returned safely to Milan where this morning I resumed my activities. My most cordial thanks go to you, Reverend Father, for all the kindnesses you extended to me during my stay in your city. I am at your disposal for any commissions you may have for me. Please give my respects to Sig. Francesco de Majo.[40] I am, etc.
>
> Milan, 10 April 1762   Giov: Bach

This was indeed Christian's last letter to the padre. (Previously there had been an insignificant message, dated 22 February 1761, in which he asked Martini to receive a certain Carlo Dassio.) The correspondence is historically important not only because the two writers were musicians of stature but because it substantiates how seriously Christian endeavored to live up to his father's image. For many years he diligently sought to master the learned church style, having realized its validity for every genre of music. Later generations, always with a respectful bow to Sebastian, too readily labeled Christian as superficial if not frivolous, thus showing ignorance of the facts manifest in Christian's years of apprenticeship with Padre Martini.

At about this time, the period of Christian's life that was characterized by his involvement with church music came to an end. He would go on to achieve his European fame as a writer of operas.

In retrospect, it is not clear why opera was hardly ever mentioned in Christian's correspondence with his revered teacher. Martini was by no means a scholar who lacked contact with the world of opera. He had even done some writing for the stage: an "Azione Teatrale" and four intermezzos, spirited satires dealing with the theater world of his day. Of these, *Don Chisciotte* is musically the most attractive. We know nothing about any performances, and it is entirely possible that Martini just wrote these incompletely preserved scores for his own amusement. Or perhaps they were intended for an impresario who hoped to benefit from these casual pieces without having to name the composer, for Martini, after all, was a member of the clergy.[41] In fact, it would have been surprising if this open-minded priest had not concerned himself with the theater, for we know that no clear lines of demarcation then existed between theater and church. Besides, we know of other Martini pupils, some of them German like Christian, who had turned to opera.

One of these was Johann Gottlieb Naumann, whom Christian must have known personally.[42] As the traveling companion of a Swedish vio-

linist, Naumann had first gone to Padua, where he had studied with Tartini, before going on to Bologna. A letter of recommendation by Tartini
introduced him to Padre Martini. Having benefited from the famous
padre's instruction for half a year, he made his debut as an opera composer in Venice in 1763. A year later, on Hasse's recommendation, he
found employment at the court in Dresden, his native city. Eventually he
was appointed for life as the elector's Kapellmeister, at a high salary. From
Naumann's memoirs we learn something about the high esteem Martini
enjoyed everywhere.

> Not only in his own country, but in all European countries where Ital-
> ian music is venerated, [Martini] enjoyed universal esteem. One might
> say that like a magnet he attracted students from everywhere. Some
> who had already served faraway princes as Kapellmeister made the pil-
> grimage to Bologna and were not ashamed of starting out once more, as
> his students. An endorsement from him was worth more than words of
> praise from any academy. A musician who returned to Germany from
> Italy was considered an ignoramus unless he could prove that he had
> studied counterpoint, for a half or whole year, with the great Martini.[43]

In fact, Martini had become the central figure in the exchange
between north and south. Except for the Prussian king, Frederick the
Great, German princes were eager to fill their key musical positions with
Italians. Young German musicians, seeing no other way to success, made
the pilgrimage across the Alps in order to receive their musical consecra-
tion in Italy. Thus it was not merely the longing for the promised land of
music that caused German musicians to go there; it was also a question of
professional survival. In this steady stream of travelers in both directions,
we can also include writers such as the Englishman Burney and the
Frenchman Brosses.

Christian also made the acquaintance of another German (or, more
accurately, Bohemian) student of Martini: Florian Leopold Gassmann,
who had been born in Brüx. His light opera Gli uccellatori was given in
three famous theaters in Northern Italy in 1759: Venice, Bologna and, in
the fall of the same year, at Milan's Teatro Ducale.

Gassmann, too, had begun his career studying church music with
Padre Martini. He was active at the Conservatorio degl'Innocenti in
Venice; Hasse had preceded him there as maestro di cappella. Fifty-four
Masses by Gassmann have been preserved; not only is the number signif-
icant but so are the works themselves. Mozart, as a mature composer, was
impressed. After playing an organ recital in Leipzig's St. Thomas Church

in 1789, he is said to have remarked to Cantor Doles, "When I return home, I want to study [Gassmann's] sacred music thoroughly; I hope to learn a great deal from it."

Gassmann can also be credited with establishing a link to Mozart that might be considered less harmonious, for it was he who discovered the young Antonio Salieri in Venice and brought him to the court in Vienna. The imperial couple transferred to Salieri the favor they had previously bestowed on Gassmann; as we know, Salieri's status at court would also cause some problems for Mozart. The relations between Gassmann and the Mozart family were entirely cordial. Father Leopold categorically denied that he had once journeyed to Vienna solely in order to introduce Wolfgang as the possible successor to Gassmann after his death.[44]

One of the first compositions to impress young Wolfgang in Vienna was Gassmann's opera *Amore e Psiche*. King Frederick II of Prussia, a connoisseur of Italian opera, also admired a Gassmann opera. When he and Emperor Joseph II were to met at Mährisch-Neustadt in 1770, Gassmann was given the honor of being asked to write an opera for the king. He fulfilled this assignment with an opera buffa, *La Contessina*, which pleased Frederick so much that he asked the emperor to let him have this man who wrote "just the way the king liked it, and who might replace Graun," who had just died. Gassmann declined with thanks, but by way of expressing appreciation to Frederick, he dedicated a group of flute compositions to him.[45]

In 1759–1760, the Milan opera saw a veritable invasion of German composers. At that time Christian got to know two other countrymen, Ignaz Holzbauer and Georg Christoph Wagenseil, who were to influence the development of both Christian and Mozart. In general it is to be noted that Christian's and Mozart's areas of activity intersected repeatedly. Not only did they meet in person, which will concern us in a later chapter, but they had numerous mutual friends and acquaintances among singers and composers.

Ignaz Holzbauer was Kapellmeister and court composer under Elector Karl Theodor of Mannheim (a position similar to Graun's in Berlin and Hasse's in Dresden). One might say that he brought a touch of the Mannheim spirit to Milan when, in January 1759, he first appeared at the Ducale to present his opera *Alessandro nell'Indie*, a subject that Christian would compose three years later for Turin. The Mannheim musical establishment had by then earned a remarkable reputation as a kind of "musical paradise." The poet Christoph Martin Wieland raved about the church music there, saying that he would "rather lose a few fingers than miss the Christmas Eve service in the Mannheim court chapel," which for him was "a festive occasion greater than any other, including opera." Then there was the Mannheim orchestra. It was famous for its inimitable rendering of all subtle shadings of sound. As Wieland's colleague the poet Schubart put it, their forte was "like thunder, their crescendo a cataract, their diminuendo a distant stream gently rippling along, their piano a breath of spring."

High standards also prevailed in opera, which Holzbauer had led since 1753. Having earlier undertaken three study trips to Italy, Holzbauer had joined the ranks of German composers who, after entering employment, would return to Italy to polish their skills. Once there, they would write operas for various Italian cities and supervise the performances, all the while watching out for singers they could take back who would lend splendor to the musical establishments of their princely employers. An inducement for singers recruited by Holzbauer was that they would appear, as Burney put it,

> in one of the largest and most splendid theatres of Europe, capable of containing five thousand persons. . . . The mere illumination of the Mannheim Theatre, with wax lights, cost the elector upwards of forty pounds at each representation; and . . . the whole experience of bringing a new opera to this stage amounts to near four thousand. The great theatre, the ensuing winter, was to be opened with an opera composed by Mr. J. Bach, who was daily expected here from London, when I was at Mannheim [August 1772].[46]

Burney's words, written more than a decade after the composers' first meeting in Milan, are interjected here to show how Christian's acquaintance with Holzbauer was to come full circle. In 1759, in Milan, the twenty-three-year-old Christian must have been greatly impressed by Holzbauer and his opera. But by 1772, when they were to meet again at the elector's summer residence in Schwetzingen, Christian was the famous man, "daily expected from London." He had been chosen to open the season with a gala performance of his opera *Temistocle* in honor of the elector's name day. This event amounted to a triumphal return for Christian, who had been absent from Germany for nearly two decades.

Both Holzbauer and Wagenseil contributed to a broadening of Christian's horizon, the former representing the influence of Mannheim, the latter that of Vienna. After Gassmann and Holzbauer, Wagenseil was the third German opera composer within thirteen months whose work was performed at the Teatro Ducale. An excellent reputation had preceded Wagenseil when, in January 1760, he directed a successful performance of his *Demetrio*. A recent observer commented on "the profound emotion in this work of an early romantic, combined with the élan of *Sturm und Drang*. . . . His light, graceful choruses display a Rococo charm."[47] These qualities helped Wagenseil capture the Milan public and must have impressed Christian, who was in the same year readying his first opera for Turin. Wagenseil, twenty years older, may have been close to Christian on a personal level as well, in somewhat the same way as he was to the child prodigy Mozart. "Nannerl," Mozart's sister, relates a charming story about little Wolfgang's audience with the emperor.

> In 1762, when the boy was in his sixth year, he played for Emperor Franz. As he sat down at the keyboard, he asked the emperor, who was standing next to him: "Where is Herr Wagenseil? He should come here; he knows how to do things." So the emperor asked Wagenseil to come and stand next to the boy, who said: "I am going to play one of your concertos, and you must turn pages for me."[48]

At one time Father Leopold Mozart had been worried that Wagenseil might publish a violin method before he did. Later he always saw to it that both Nannerl and Wolfgang would familiarize themselves with Wagenseil, both as keyboard player and composer. Thus the little collection of pieces Leopold assembled in 1759 for "Mademoiselle Marie-Anne Mozart" (which also contains Wolfgang's first attempts at composition) included a scherzo by Wagenseil. In 1764, when the eight-year-old Wolfgang performed at the English court, in the presence of the royal family and their music master John Christian Bach, the music consisted of works by Handel, Christian Bach, Abel, and Wagenseil.

These events took place only four years after Christian's appointment as cathedral organist in Milan and his first commission to write operas. For him this was a time to sort out feelings and ambitions. The result was that, while organ playing remained a way of earning a living, opera was to be Christian's first love in the years to come.

Perhaps Christian did not make his operatic debut in Milan because these three other Germans (Holzbauer, Gassmann, and Wagenseil) had already appeared there during 1759–60. Another foreign composer may not have been welcome, especially since Lampugnani, Galuppi, and Piccinni, all first-rate native composers, were available. Besides, Turin was by no means a provincial town. It was the residence of Sardinia's king, Carlo Emanuele III. (For a short time after Italy's unification in 1860, it

Pietro Metastasio, the most prolific writer of librettos in the eighteenth century.

Autograph page from *Artaserse*, the opera with which Bach made his 1761 debut as opera composer in Milan.

even was the nation's capital.) The Turin opera could easily stand comparison with San Carlo in Naples, generally considered the leading house in Europe. Both cities were ruled by kings whose ambition it was to present the most elaborately staged and most expertly sung performances. Even Milan could not compete with this. Few of her general governors showed any real interest in the arts, so that other noble families became the chief supporters of the fine arts and music.

For his *Artaserse* and for his next two operas, Christian had chosen a text by Metastasio. At this time the grand old man of opera librettos, more than sixty years old, had passed his prime as the main supplier of opera texts throughout Europe. Yet operagoers continued to be eager to make comparisons, to see how a new composer might treat his verses. Metastasio's *Artaserse*, for instance, was composed more than a hundred times, before and after Christian's version.

Christian's predecessors, his fellow Germans Hasse and Gluck, had also introduced themselves to the Turin public with operas on Metastasio texts. Hasse had come out with *Catone in Utica* in 1731; Gluck with *Alessandro nell'Indie* in 1744. Christian followed in their footsteps, composing the same two librettos. He used *Catone* for his second opera, his debut at the Naples San Carlo, and brought out *Alessandro* as his third opera, also at this theater.

The esteem in which Metastasio was generally held is reflected in Jean-Jacques Rousseau's sentimental remark:

> If your eyes are filling with tears, your heart is pounding, shivers overcome you, or delight renders you speechless—then turn to Metastasio and start working. His creative genius will inspire yours, . . . and other eyes will soon fill with the tears that your master caused you to shed.[49]

For almost a hundred years, Metastasio was the undisputed ruler. His librettos were published, during his lifetime, in no less than twelve volumes. His first text, *Didone abbandonata*, was written for Naples in 1724. In 1730 he had become the imperial court poet in Vienna.

Christian turned to Metastasio for his first (1761, Turin) and last (London, 1778) operas; Mozart, in the year of his death, still turned to Metastasio for his *La clemenza di Tito* (1791).[50]

Though contemporary reports are lacking, Christian's *Artaserse* must have been a great success. It could hardly have been otherwise since Tanucci, the omnipotent minister in charge of the Naples theaters, gave his approval when the impresario Grossatesta recommended Christian as the composer for *Catone in Utica*. According to Grossatesta, Christian was "a composer who had been widely applauded, especially last year in Turin."

An endorsement by Count Firmian, the Austrian governor of Lombardy, was also helpful. Christian carried it in his pocket when he arrived in Naples in September 1761 to prepare the opening performance on 4 November. Addressed to Tanucci, Firmian's letter stated:

> Excellency,
>
> Sig. Bach, a famous maestro di capella, is coming to Naples, having been commissioned to write an opera for the Royal Theater. He has asked me to give him a letter of recommendation to Your Excellency. Since he is a person of great merit I am happy to comply, for I know well Your Excellency's humane spirit. I therefore am certain that you will show him the kindness that he begs you to extend him. Your very devoted, always faithful servant.
> Milan, 15 September 1761   Count C. di Firmian[51]

The words "famous" and "of great merit" are indicative of the high esteem in which the youngest Bach son was held, even at this stage of his career. Tanucci paid attention to this recommendation, which is not surprising since he had to rely on the judgment of others. Because of his complete lack of musicality—he, of all people, the head of the opera—he was the butt of many jokes in Naples.

Catone was enthusiastically received; everyone was happy. Congratulations were exchanged by Tanucci and Firmian, with Tanucci writing first, on 24 November: "Maestro Bach, recommended by you as the composer to set *Catone*, was greatly applauded for his work. As always, I cannot but admire Your Excellency's good taste and infallible judgment." Firmian replied on 7 December that he was "overjoyed to hear that maestro Bach was so enthusiastically received in a city which, in music, is far ahead of all others."

Firmian's words of praise carried special weight. As a confidant of Emperor Franz I and his chancellor, Wenzel Anton, count of Kaunitz-Rietberg (who would later be a supporter of Mozart as well[52]), Firmian was influential and politically powerful. He was a man of culture, wise and enlightened. One of his friends, the art historian Winckelmann, referred to him as "one of the greatest and most learned" of all the aristocrats he knew. Eight years later, Firmian was to smooth the way for the Mozarts on their Italian journey; now he did the same for Christian's second opera. Hasse had originally been asked to write the music for *Alessandro nell'Indie*, the second opera for the carnival season of 1762,

The Teatro Regio in Turin where Artaserse was first performed.

but he was busy in Vienna. The directors of the San Carlo then turned to Christian because, they said, "he had given proof of his ability with the successful performance of his previous opera."

But there was a problem: Christian was still employed by Count Litta and, even more important, he had his obligations as cathedral organist, which meant that he would have to return to Milan. Count Firmian was the only one who could come to the rescue, and Christian requested Tanucci to enlist the count's help. Firmian, he hoped, could intervene with the cathedral chapter in Milan and persuade them to "excuse [him] from his assigned duties since, at the king's command, he was composing his second opera." The request was granted. The esteem in which Christian was by this time held can be gauged by the fact that the rulers of two countries, Naples and Lombardy, were involved in obtaining his freedom so that he could write an opera.

Such support from the highest quarters was helpful, but Christian obtained additional support from a very different source—the singer Anton Raaff. He had added a special touch of brilliance to Christian's first Naples opera by singing the leading part. As a singer of legendary fame, he doubtless had some say in choosing the composer. As a German, Raaff had accomplished the seemingly impossible: among the Italian vocal stars he managed to reach the top rung of the European operatic ladder. From now on, his path would again and again cross those of Christian Bach and Mozart.

Raaff was born near Bonn, the son of a shepherd. He was educated by Jesuits and was destined for the clergy. When his beautiful voice was discovered, he was given a scholarship to study singing in Munich with court composer Giovanni Ferrandini. In 1753 he participated in the first performance of his teacher's *Catone in Utica*, a brilliant production for the opening of the Residenztheater. The work is based on the same Metastasio text as Christian's opera that achieved success, eight years later, with Raaff's participation.

Raaff's career then took him to Bologna, where he studied with Antonio Bernacci, a famous teacher of singing and a friend of Padre Martini. Bernacci's students included the best singers of the time. Tommaso Guarducci was one of them, singing the part of Cesare in the first performance of *Catone* while Raaff sang the title role. Some years later, both of them would appear in London, joining Christian in some opera productions.

While in Bologna, Raaff became a friend of Padre Martini. On the basis of all we know about Raaff—his kind, friendly disposition, ever ready to help others—one can assume that he, Martini, and Christian got along famously.[53] After triumphal guest appearances at German courts and in Spain and Portugal, Raaff was engaged in 1759 for the Naples San Carlo. It seems certain that Martini played an important part in bringing about this appointment, and it is equally certain that Martini and Raaff in some way helped Christian obtain the commission to write the opera. It was an important occasion for Raaff, since *Catone* was given to celebrate the king's name day. Under these circumstances, one could hardly ignore the primo uomo's preference when it came to choosing the composer. To a singer, it was essential that his most effective arias be written to order so that the best qualities of his voice would be displayed.

The only known reservations about Raaff had to do with his acting; it was, to quote Burney, "stiff and poor." But everyone agreed on the magic quality of his voice. Schubart grew ecstatic about it:

> He can rise to the high regions of the alto voice; just as effortlessly he descends to the bass register. All his tones are full and pure. He has an uncanny ability to sing everything at sight, and he can embellish an aria in several ways with indescribable art. No one can equal his ornaments and cadenzas, or his general musical taste. Whatever he sings reveals deep feeling; his renditions seem to reflect the beauty of his soul.[54]

Even Giuseppe Tartini, usually not fond of opera, grew enthusiastic about Raaff. He wrote to Padre Martini:

> We have, in Signor Raaff, two angels in one person: virtue, and music. He is not loved here [in Padua], he is worshipped, and justly so. . . . I heard him sing in the Santo, and I can truthfully tell you that I have never heard such singing. Praise be to God who endowed a mortal with such a gift.

In another letter Tartini vowed that "as long as I live I shall remember this man and his singing; he made an indelible impression on me."[55]

In view of such praise one can believe the story, fairy-tale-like as it may sound, about a Princess di Belmonte. After the death of her husband, she supposedly fell into a grieving, melancholic depression, unable to shed a single tear. A wise lady-in-waiting secretly had Raaff summoned to the park; by singing the romance "Solitario bosco ombroso," he succeeded in moving the princess to tears. "She wept and was thus cured," the story concludes.

To some it might seem that the meeting of Raaff, with his beguiling voice, and Christian, who knew so well how to express tender sentiments, was predestined rather than accidental. All his life, Christian was to write his best arias for Raaff. One of these, "Non so d'onde viene," Alessandro's aria from the opera by the same name, became what we would call a hit. It was so popular that Christian used it again in two pasticcios: *Ezio* in 1764, and *L'Olimpiade* in 1769, both given at the King's Theatre in London.

The eight-year-old Mozart had heard the *Ezio* aria there. It made such an impression on him that he still thought about it fourteen years later. On 28 February 1778, he wrote to his father from Mannheim:

> As an exercise I set the aria "Non so d'onde viene," which Bach had composed so beautifully. I know it so well that I can't get it out of my mind. Therefore I wanted to see whether, in spite of this, I could compose an aria [to the same text] that would not resemble Bach's—and mine turned out completely different.

Originally, he states, he had wanted to dedicate it to Raaff, "but the first part was too high for his voice, yet I liked it too much to want to change it. Because of the instrumental accompaniment it seemed more suited to a soprano; therefore I decided to write this aria for [Aloysia] Weber."

Mozart chose to write this aria for Aloysia rather than Constanze Weber, his later wife, for at the time Aloysia was closest to his heart. He asked his father not to give the aria to anyone else because he had written it expressly for that "dear Weber girl." In 1787, Mozart made use of this text once again, in order to please Ludwig Franz Fischer, the bass who first sang the role of Osmin in Mozart's *Entführung*.[56]

For Raaff, Mozart then wrote another aria, and later also the title role of *Idomeneo,* the work in which Raaff gave his farewell performance, at the age of sixty-seven. Actually, Raaff had taken the initiative. He had interceded with Elector Karl Theodor (who had by then moved from Mannheim to Munich), urging that Mozart be commissioned to write the opera. Before that, Leopold Mozart had written to Padre Martini, asking him to intervene with Raaff on behalf of Wolfgang. All these strategies were successful. They are typical for the time: making use of all available contacts in order for an artist to survive. One relied on good connections, on making the rounds armed with letters of recommendation.

To have succeeded with three operas in one year, two of them at the prestigious San Carlo, was a good way for Christian to enter into the world of opera, the field in which he felt most at home, though he had also proved his mettle in the realm of sacred music. He was aware of a

Anton Raaff, for whom Bach wrote his most popular aria, "Non so d'onde viene" (below left). Mozart set the same text for Aloysia Lange (below right).

problem: if he bowed to the taste of the time, he was likely to be criticized by some for lack of seriousness. He is said to have remarked once,
while improvising at the keyboard among friends, "This is the way [I]
would compose if I were allowed to," referring, perhaps, to the serious,
expressive style of his Symphony in G Minor, Op. 6, No. 6.[57]

Christian undoubtedly felt comfortable in the easygoing company of
opera singers and dancers, and he had quite a few amorous encounters.
For example, the production of his *Alessandro nell'Indie* was noted for the
spectacular stage effects, including twenty-four soldiers riding in forma-
tion on horseback, but it also gave rise to official criticism of Christian's
conduct. He had fallen in love with the dancer Colomba Beccari, an
affair in which the public took a lively interest. The authorities were displeased, claiming that his affair gave rise to idle gossip. A government
official summoned him and issued a reprimand.

Christian was not impressed, to judge by further reports that he had
been observed "joining female singers in the box reserved for them."
Once more he was instructed, through the theater secretary, that this was
inappropriate. The young composer reacted by failing to take his place at
the keyboard for the next performance, sending a substitute instead. Following this, the official reminded him a third time, "in his own interest,"
that "His Majesty had repeatedly given an order, even to the officers of
the royal guard, forbidding them to flirt backstage with any female cast
members during the performance."

Christian had no choice but to comply, though he complained that
he knew of no theater, anywhere in the world, where the maestro was not
allowed backstage. It speaks for his popularity that his followers urged the
official to allow Christian, at least one more time, to view a performance
from the artists' box, "to give the lie to all kinds of rumors that had arisen
as a result of the interdict." The offical report, however, concludes by
confirming the royal order.[58]

Count Litta, Christian's employer, must have followed all these
goings-on with some trepidation: not only his protégé's various escapades
but also his success as an opera composer. While Count Firmian was
delighted with the success of the Bach son, whom he had recommended,
it seemed to Count Litta that, in spite of his efforts on Christian's behalf,
the young man was now wasting his talent in the company of easygoing
singers and dancers. Litta's concerns, including his worries about a continued secure existence for Christian, are expressed in a letter to Padre
Martini. It clearly reflects his disappointment and annoyance.

Reverend Father, honored patron,

I wish I could agree with you and your wishes regarding "il mio Bach," for I know that you have his best interests at heart. However, I am aware of his obligations here, and this compels me to advise him to return at once and resume his duties. He holds the post of cathedral organist here, but he is not serving in that capacity, for he has been absent for almost a year. Yet he would be very unwise to forfeit a position that pays him 800 lire a year, and probably more in the future. Such a position represents security for one's old age. It therefore behooves him to show himself industrious, rather than acting in such a way that the person who recommended him for this appointment regrets having done so. People here are beginning to complain, especially the high clergy. I know that you, Reverend Father, take a lively interest in him; therefore I am confident that you will know how to counsel him, so that he can give the lie to those who (due to jealousy or ulterior motives) call him indifferent and negligent and complain about him. I am, etc.

Milan, 7 April 1762   Conte Cav. Agostino Litta

Christian did return. Three days later, as we learned, he informed Padre Martini of his safe arrival in Milan. Yet the break between Christian and Count Litta was now inevitable. Litta, as the result of this separation, seems to have turned to new pursuits. From this time on there is no indication of continued interest in the music that, with Christian at his side, had given meaning to his life for many years.

To be sure, biographical information about Litta is scarce. His older brother Pompeo had written a voluminous study about Italy's most famous families, but he did not include his own. "[Pompeo] never published a history of the Litta family, though it was one of the most famous, respected, and wealthy in Milan."[59]

The only further information we have about Count Agostino Litta deals with quite a different interest: water supply. In the *Atti della Società Patriotica di Milano* (Documents of Milan's Patriotic Society), we find a lengthy chapter devoted to Litta and his "merits regarding the utilization of the Milan canal":

> To appreciate [Litta's] merits concerning public welfare, one need only turn to the navigable canal that surrounds our city; it is a source of livelihood and many amenities.[60]

Litta's activities as an expert in canal construction were not without problems, for the chronicler reports that the count was accused of stealing intellectual property. True, he continues in Litta's defense, a device

Then and now, European opera houses were also used for occasions of state. The illustration shows a reception given by the Austrian governor Pallaviccini in honor of Prince Peter Leopold, the heir apparent, in 1747 at the Teatro Ducale in Milan.

such as Litta had advocated for regulating the water level had been in
existence for a century, but thanks to Litta's invention it had been greatly
improved.

At any rate, when Litta died in 1781 at the age of fifty-three,[61] he was
eulogized for his expertise in constructing waterways, but there was no
mention of music. After Litta and Christian parted ways, the count seems
to have lost all interest in music—the sad ending of a friendship that had
meant much for both and had been particularly important in the launch-
ing of Christian's career.

Christian's decision to embark on the career of a free, independent
musician may not have been an easy one. He was a grateful person by
nature, as shown by his lifelong devotion to Padre Martini. But we can
hardly hold it against him that in the long run he was not satisfied with
an organist's position. He had turned down such an offer while he was in
Berlin; now it seemed even less enticing, given the excellent opportunities he had for success as a composer. His years of apprenticeship lay
behind him; he was acknowledged, even in Italy, as a master in the fields
of sacred music and opera, to say nothing of instrumental music.

So far I have not said much about his instrumental works, except for
mentioning some chamber music he wrote while in the service of Count
Litta. We may recall Burney's account of attending a private concert in
Milan where symphonies by Christian were played that were different
from those published in England (see page 110), apparently early works
that existed in manuscript copies. But there were other concerts that
served to considerably enrich the musical life of Milan. Count Gian-Luca
Pallavicini, one of Count Firmian's predecessors as Austrian governor of
Lombardy, had created an institution that was unique in all of Europe:
popular open-air symphonic concerts. They were given on the steps of
the Castello Sforzesco, the former residence of the dukes of Milan. Count
Pallavicini had asked Sammartini, the city's leading composer, to write a
"symphony for large orchestra, for the entertainment of the citizens who
enjoyed themselves, on warm summer evenings, on the square below the
castle."

Sammartini had at his disposal the orchestra of the Teatro Ducale,
made up of forty-seven players. On days when there were no performances in the theater, the orchestra was expected to participate in sacred
music and in private concerts. It is easy to imagine how on such evenings
sounds from the castello drifted across to the nearby palace of the Littas.
Christian may have listened to them or perhaps even participated in the
concerts.

Special festive events called for special music. Such an occasion was the birth of Archduchess Maria Carolina of Austria on 7 September 1752. At that time, Pallavicino proudly reported to Vienna that "a large crowd circulated on the esplanade of the castello. There they enjoyed, for several hours, music by an orchestra consisting of many outstanding players, which I had ordered to perform there." To ensure the concert's success, he continued, the archbishop had even been asked whether "the service might end in time for the nobility and the people to be regaled by such noble music." The concert lasted until two o'clock in the morning.

A year later, disappointed by the only moderate success of his operas, Sammartini left the Teatro Ducale and with it the opera orchestra. But the open-air concerts at the Castello Sforzesco offered him another opportunity: he founded a new orchestra. In a petition drawn up in 1758 to establish a "philharmonic academy," Sammartini's name appears ahead of all other signatures. This academy was founded by the citizens of Milan with the purpose of maintaining a permanent orchestra, which was to have their financial support and would perform works written specially for the ensemble.

We no longer know just what works were performed. One of the academy's policies was to keep the works under lock and key; they were considered to be the academy's property. The orchestra's music librarian was strictly prohibited from making any of the performance material available to the public. No doubt this did not prevent members of the high nobility from passing music on to Vienna, Paris, or other cities where aristocratic music lovers were thirsting for new music to be played in their own salons. Influential members of Milanese society also succeeded in acquiring music for their own circle. Count Firmian, for example, a bachelor residing in the palace of Princess Antonia Maria Melzi, was always eager to lend special brilliance to her musical soirées. The palaces of Marchesa di Caravaggio and the Littas were similarly supplied. Early in the nineteenth century the Palffy family could pride itself on owning more than one hundred works by Sammartini, the most popular composer of the so-called Lombardy school, whose members excelled in instrumental music. The aforementioned Charles de Brosses, claimed that he had acquired his love of Italian music, not from listening to bel canto, the Italians' vocal artistry, but from "their magnificent symphonies and choral works, which I shall never cease praising."[62]

Although there is no record of a meeting between Christian and Sammartini, they could hardly have avoided each other in Milan. As a composer, conductor, and organist, Sammartini was equally at home in churches and in the salons of the nobility. He was also a member of the commission that appointed organists for the cathedral, and thus it is likely that he was present at Christian's audition. They may not have met at the Teatro Ducale, since Sammartini had left in 1753, but their paths were bound to have crossed on many musical occasions.[63]

Undoubtedly Sammartini was one of the composers whose instrumental music helped form Christian's own style. More than anyone else, Sammartini represented the Lombardy school, which continued to exert its stylistic influence on Christian as he started out on the journey to England. At that time, a change was in the making, though Christian at first viewed it as temporary.

Sometime between 10 April and 27 May 1762, a commission to write two operas for the King's Theatre in London seems to have reached him. In his last letter to Padre Martini, dated 10 April, Christian makes no mention of any important developments, and a commission from abroad would have been just that. Nor does Count Litta refer to it in his letter, written three days earlier. But according to the minutes of the cathedral chapter, Christian requested on 27 May a leave "for a year, beginning this July, in order to travel to England and compose two operas." These facts suggest that the offer from London must have come soon after his return.

It is clear that Christian had at first merely asked for a leave, because on 1 July of the following year his name still appeared on the cathedral chapter's payroll. Not until December 1763 did Christian resign his position as second cathedral organist. On 28 December, the accounts list for the first time the name of his successor, Antonio Terzi, who was to hold the position for the next forty years.

As Christian's first operas achieved good success in Italy, developments were also boding well for him in England. The singer Colomba Mattei and her husband Trombetta had taken over the management of the King's Theatre, the Italian opera at the Haymarket, hoping to instill new life in the run-down company. They had engaged Gioacchino Cocci as their resident composer, but his creative talents seem to have quickly disappeared. Burney thought they had never amounted to much; of one of his comic operas he said that it "was the most melancholy performance I ever heard in an Italian theatre."[64] Cocci's contract ran through the 1761–1762 season; Mattei had no interest in renewing it. There are several reasons why Mattei might have thought of Christian as Cocci's successor. There were his recent operatic successes in Turin and Naples. Also, as already mentioned, Lampugnani may have put in a good word for Christian. Lampugnani was a prominent composer of operas. As a

Giovanni Battista Sammartini.

Castello Sforzesco in Milan, where Bach heard instrumental works by Sammartini.

friend of Padre Martini, he may also have known Christian. In 1755, Lampugnani's opera *Siroe* had been presented at the King's Theatre, with Colomba Mattei as seconda donna to the eminent Mingotti. It is quite possible that Mattei, by then impresario at the Haymarket, asked Lampugnani in Milan for advice.

Even more likely is a recommendation by a member of her ensemble, Filippo Elisi, the singer for whom Christian in 1759 had written the bravura aria "Misero pargoletto." A grateful Elisi, having been hired by Mattei for the 1761–1762 season, may well have spoken in support of Christian's appointment.

Another development of a nonmusical nature has import in connection with what lay ahead for the young German composer. It was late in August of 1761 when a young German princess, the seventeen-year-old Sophie-Charlotte of Mecklenburg-Strelitz, boarded the vessel that was to bear her across the channel to England. There she would assume her place next to George III as queen of England.

4
Years of Fame in London

*Like Handel, he became the
darling of the English.*

Johann Baptist Cramer
about John Christian Bach

T IS AN AMAZING STORY: the rise of an insignificant German princess
to the throne of the queen of England. In his memoirs, Horace Walpole reflects that hardly six persons in England were accustomed to the
lifestyle of such a princess.[1] The story is worth telling because Christian,
as music master to the royal family, would enjoy the protection of the
British crown for the next two decades.

Was the crown indeed British? For two generations, since 1714, the
British throne had been occupied by Germans—members of the house of
Hanover. First was King George I, who spoke no English and whose court
was predominantly German. His unpopular successor, George II, preferred spending carefree days in Hanover to performing his royal duties in
London, which seemed drab to him by comparison. His son had died
young. The grandson who succeeded him as George III was the first ruler
from the house of Hanover to have been born on English soil and whose
mother tongue was English.

He, however, was a mere figurehead, manipulated by his widowed
mother, Princess Augusta, and her lover, Lord Bute. Both feared that the
king, madly in love with the charming Lady Sarah Lennox, might insist
on marriage, thus according a position of unwelcome influence to the
duke of Richmond and his family, who were in the opposing camp. If the
twenty-two-year-old king was to continue as a mere tool, easily managed,
a different bride would have to be found, preferably abroad. We do not
know just why the choice turned out to be Sophie-Charlotte, not a particularly attractive young woman. Colonel Graeme had been sent to Germany to look for possible candidates. In addition to Mecklenburg-

Strelitz, his list included the courts of Anhalt-Bernburg, Brunswick, Darmstadt, and Gotha. Young Sophie-Charlotte must have made an especially favorable impression not only on Graeme but also on Lord Harcourt, who then journeyed there to deliver the formal proposal of marriage. On 17 August 1761 he reported back to London:

> I reached this place on the 14th; on the 15th the treaty was concluded and despatched away to England.... This little Court exerted its utmost abilities to make a figure suitable to the occasion, and I can assure you they have acquitted themselves, not only with magnificence, but with a great deal of good taste and propriety. Our Queen that is to be has seen very little of the world, but her good sense, vivacity, and cheerfulness, I daresay, will recommend her to the King and make her the darling of the British nation. She is no regular beauty, but she is of a very pretty size, has a charming complexion, very pretty eyes, and finely made; in short, she is a fine girl.[2]

For a small duchy such as Mecklenburg-Strelitz it was quite a stroke of luck to find itself at the center of power politics, if only briefly. It was indeed a small state, measuring less than 200 by 90 kilometers, containing six towns in addition to Neu-Strelitz, the duke's residence. There were other miniature states like it, impoverished, living in the shadow of powerful Prussia. The duke's annual income was approximately fifteen thousand pounds, which corresponded to that of a second-rank English peer. An offer of marriage from London must have seemed to the duke like a gift from heaven. Love seldom entered into such arrangements, except in the case of Sophie-Charlotte's unfortunate sister Christina.[3]

The unoffical wedding ceremony promptly took place in the ducal palace. Things were not easy for the young bride who had seen little of the world. She now had to exchange her familiar surroundings for life in a strange country with a husband who was completely unknown to her. She had no idea that he had had his share of amorous adventures or that he was calm and friendly and tolerably good-looking. Nor did she know that he could hardly read or write and that there were already indications of his later mental derangement.

A great blow to Sophie-Charlotte was the death of her mother, the widowed Duchess Dorothea-Sophie, who had intended to accompany her daughter to England. After her husband's death, Dorothea-Sophie's son Adolf Friedrich IV had taken over the reins of government, but she had continued to be the mother of her country and was responsible for attracting many musicians to Strelitz. Sophie-Charlotte had inherited her mother's love of music. She played the piano and the guitar and

Princess Sophie-Charlotte of Mecklenburg-Strelitz, the future queen of England.

The ducal palace in Strelitz.

proudly called herself a pupil of Carl Philipp Emanuel Bach.

All musicians of note were welcome at the ducal residence in Strelitz, especially virtuosos from Berlin, a good day's journey away. Members of the Prussian king's court chapel had a standing invitation to visit Strelitz whenever their duties in Berlin permitted. Dorothea-Sophie had found her own concertmaster, Johann Christian Hertel, in Berlin. His son Johann Wilhelm again established ties to Berlin, where he studied music with teachers of note such as Franz Benda, Emanuel Bach, and Carl Heinrich Graun before rejoining his father in 1748 as a member of the Strelitz court chapel. Benda and Emanuel Bach often journeyed to Strelitz, the latter in order to give lessons to young Sophie-Charlotte. After she became queen, she often mentioned to her friends how important these lessons had been to her.

It is possible that Sophie-Charlotte met Christian Bach, too, on some of these occasions, for he lived in Berlin from 1750 to 1754. It was during this period that the younger Hertel had substituted as concertmaster while his father was ill, and the duchess may have particularly welcomed reinforcements from Berlin at that time. So Emanuel may have taken Christian along on his visits to Strelitz, in which case the nine-year-old Sophie-Charlotte, in a charming coincidence, would first have met the seventeen-year-old Christian ten years prior to their more celebrated meeting when she was queen of England and he, a famous composer of operas, was about to become music master to the royal household.

In spite (or perhaps because) of her youth, Sophie-Charlotte soon came to enjoy the respect of her future subjects. The Channel crossing to England was stormy, and lasted nine days instead of the usual three. To reassure her frightened travel companions, she showed herself remarkably fearless, putting her trust in God. Despite the raging storm, she sat down at a spinet and played English folk songs and Lutheran chorales, leaving open the door to her cabin and thus giving new hope to her fellow passengers who, along with the crew, had despaired of ever reaching the English shore. After the storm subsided, Sophie turned to her guitar and played "God Save the King." To her lady-in-waiting, Lady Effingham, this seemed a little inappropriate, since the king had had nothing to do with their surviving the storm.

The royal wedding took place on 8 September 1761. It provided the occasion for Christian's congratulatory cantata entitled *Thanks Be to God Who Rules the Deep. An Ode on the Auspicious Arrival and Nuptials of Her Most Gracious Majesty Queen Charlotte, by John Lockman. Set to Music by*

Mr. Bach. The surprising news of the marriage must have reached Christian while he was still in Italy, causing him to compose the ode in great haste. This leaves unanswered the question of how he obtained Lockman's text.

It is not known whether the cantata was performed in connection with the wedding and coronation festivities, but the composition could hardly have reached London in time, given the almost unseemly haste with which the marriage had been arranged. The marriage contract had been signed in Strelitz on 15 August; the wedding took place in London on 8 September.

Queen Charlotte liked the cantata, if a notation on the score (now in the British Library) is an indication: "This volume belongs to the Queen, 1788."

Charlotte continued to maintain close ties to her ducal family in Mecklenburg-Strelitz and to the Bach sons, especially Emanuel. There is a document proving Emanuel's presence in Strelitz at the very time when Christian set out for England, in the summer of 1762. This is a signed receipt acknowledging that Emanuel had been paid "100 taler, Saxon currency. Strelitz, 8 July 1762—Bach."[4] An explanatory note to the exchequer states that the amount was for travel expenses. It is unlikely that Emanuel's trip had anything to do with Christian's opera commission for London, which had already reached him in May, but perhaps Emanuel interceded in some other way. Until 1 July 1763, Christian was still bound by his contract to the Milan cathedral, which means that he was still on leave and not at all sure about remaining in England.

In this connection, it should be noted that the state of opera as Christian found it in London was far from ideal. Filippo Elisi, the star, had left the ensemble, and neither the rest of the remaining company nor those newly engaged lived up to Christian's expectations. As Burney recalls, "on his arrival here, he was extremely exasperated to find that he had no better singers to write for ... being unwilling, as a stranger, to trust his reputation to such performers."[5] Perhaps for that reason Christian at first directed only *pasticci*, works consisting of parts of other operas to which he contributed overtures and a few arias. He seems to have considered returning to Italy; at this point the queen, always in touch with her brother in Strelitz, may have asked for Emanuel's help in persuading Christian to stay.

Neither would the opera house itself be likely to impress someone accustomed to the San Carlo in Naples and the Teatro Regio Ducale in Milan. A contemporary traveler was not favorably impressed by the

King George III of England.

Royal Theater at the Haymarket:

> The street leading from Pall Mall to Piccadilly is called Haymarket
> because hay and straw are sold there three times a week. This is where
> the opera house and a smaller theater are located. The former is most
> unpreposessing; one would never suspect that it was an opera house.
> The audience occupies the sides and rear, also the parterre. On the sides
> are three tiers of boxes. The rows of seats behind the parterre are called
> galleries; their wooden ceilings act as resonators, so that the music
> sounds almost better than in the parterre or boxes. The company one
> keeps there, however, is not the best, and one is trapped in a corner
> without any light whatsoever. To be sure, a seat there costs only three
> shillings. The house accomodates approximately 1500. The boxes and
> draperies are clean; there are gilded carvings. Other than that the build-
> ing is drab and lacks sufficient lighting.[6]

Given these conditions, we can understand why Christian was at first
reluctant to stay and considered returning to Italy. But doubts vanished
when he encountered the young singer Anna Lucia de Amicis. Mattei
had engaged her for comic roles; Christian first noticed her when he conducted the pasticcio *Il Tutore e la Pupilla*, which opened the season on
14 November 1762. When, in a private concert, she also showed talent
in serious roles, Christian was convinced that he had found the singer to
star in his first London opera.

Anna Lucia, in her early twenties, had arrived in London with her
father, brother, and sister. Her debut had taken place seven years earlier
in Bologna, in one of Galuppi's light operas, *La Calamità de' Cuori*. Christian, then studying with Padre Martini, may even have heard her. She
continued to sing in comic operas until Christian cast her in an opera
seria; both profited from the change. From then on her success was
assured in both genres, so that "on Tuesday nights, she delighted the
town as the representative of Thalia, and on Saturday nights as that of
Melpomene," as reported by Burney, who was one of her admirers.

> [She] captivated the public in various ways. Her figure and gestures
> were in the highest degree elegant and graceful; her countenance,
> though not perfectly beautiful, was extremely high-bred and interest-
> ing; and her voice and manner of singing, exquisitely polished and
> sweet. She had not a motion that did not charm the eye, or a tone but
> what delighted the ear. De Amicis was not only the first who intro-
> duced *staccato divisions* on our stage, but the first singer that I ever heard
> go up to E-flat in altissimo, with true, clear, and powerful *real* voice.[7]

The King's Theatre, Haymarket, scene of Bach's triumphs and failures.

Exterior of King's Theatre, here forming the backdrop for one of Hogarth's famous satirical engravings.

Before Amicis scored her greatest London success (in Bach's *Orione, o sia Diana Vendicata*; 19 February 1763), she had introduced herself to the London public in several pasticci. Perhaps Galuppi's *La Calamità de' Cuori* belonged to this genre; Christian contributed only an overture. The choice may have been an accommodation for Amicis, who had sung her debut in this opera in Bologna.

All these pasticci were advertised in the London *Public Advertiser* with a notice that performances were "under the direction of Mr. John Bach, a Saxon master of music." One announcement refers to him as "a Saxon Professor." Although he had adopted the English name John, and few Englishmen at the time still remembered his father's name, Christian did not deny his Saxon ancestry.

Orione's first performance turned out to be a great success for both Bach and Amicis. The royal couple honored them with their attendance and even returned for the second presentation. It must have been a most lavish production. The *Public Advertiser* made special mention of the "grand choruses" along with the "several Vocal and Instrumental Performers" who had been engaged in addition to the regular cast. Burney also recorded that this was "the first time that *clarinets* had admission in our opera orchestra."[8] He further states that there had been

> a very numerous audience. Every judge of Music perceived the emanation of genius throughout the whole performance but [was] chiefly struck with the richness of the harmony. . . . The richness of the accompaniments perhaps deserve [sic] more praise than the originality of the melodies; which, however, are always natural, elegant, and in the best taste of Italy at the time [Christian] came over. The Neapolitan school, where he studied, is manifest in his cantilena, and the science of his father and brother in his harmony.

Christian wrote his best arias for Amicis, his prima donna, Burney observes, to show off to greatest advantage her "compass of voice and delicate and difficult expression and execution." Even other arias, given to other singers, did not fail to please. Thanks to Christian's skillful instrumentation "they were more admired as instrumental pieces than compositions for the voice."

Thus Burney. It was also new, and not without risk, that for *Orione* Christian had not fallen back on the customary Metastasio libretto but had chosen a text by the resident poet of the King's Theatre, Giovan Gualberto Bottarelli. Though the libretto deals with a little-known incident from Greek mythology, it is typical for the time. A synopsis may serve as an example.

The opening act takes place in Diana's temple. Orione is about to lead the warriors of Arcadia and Thebes into battle against an unnamed enemy. Priests question the oracle about the battle's outcome. The answer: Orione will be victorious, but he will die and ascend to the starry skies. His love for Candiope, daughter of Arcadia's king, will remain unfulfilled. Orione is the son of the god Mercury and the queen of Thebes. Although Orione's engaging in battle might bring down on him the wrath of the goddess Diana, neither his mother nor his beloved Candiope is able to dissuade him.

The scene changes to a grove of trees near Diana's temple, in which we find Tirsi and Nice, shepherd and shepherdess. Tirsi must accompany Orione to war; Nice laments their separation in a moving aria, "Andrò dal colle" (the aria was published the same year in a collection of "Favourite Songs" from the opera). The act closes with Orione's triumphal return; his victorious soldiers display their trophies to the people.

The following scene is quite typical for librettos of the period: it effectively contrasts the underworld, a place of terror, with Elysium, the island of the blessed spirits where, according to Homer, the fallen heroes assemble.

The opening of Act II takes place in the king's palace. Mercury tries in vain to get Diana to change her mind. She believes that Orione provoked her, that he pitted his own laws against hers and those of Thebes and Arcady. In the following scene, those around Orione urge him to pacify the goddess with a solemn ceremony of thanks, but he proudly refuses. Hardly has he left the stage when the shepherd Tirsi brings the horrible news that Orione is dead, pierced by Diana's arrows.

The scene changes again. Nice and Tirsi meet in the grove near Diana's temple and bemoan Orione's fate. They speak of a monument that Candiope wants to have erected on the grave of her beloved. Unlike Orione, shepherd and shepherdess, happily reunited, obey the will of the goddess. At the end of the act, we see Candiope at Orione's grave, shaded by cypress trees. It is a large mausoleum, decorated with weapons. Candiope believes she is seeing the ghost of her beloved. She wants to stab herself, in order to be united with him in death, but Mercury, Orione's father, intervenes, instructing Candiope instead to follow him to the land of the dead where Orione is waiting for her.

In Act III, Mercury and Candiope are on their way to the underworld. The road divides: one fork, lying in darkness, leads to the Palace of Fear; the other, bathed in brilliant light, to the Elysian fields. After praying to the gods, Mercury and Candiope choose the bright road. At its end, Orione is waiting to bid a last farewell to his beloved. He has submitted to the will of the gods and renounced earthly love. To insure his immortality, Candiope resigns herself to returning to earth with Mercury.

In the last act, all protagonists (except Orione) appear together in Neptune's temple; the sea is visible in the background. Mercury announces that Diana has been reconciled and that the gods have decided that Orione [Orion] should forever appear as a bright star in the skies. In a grand finale, soloists and chorus praise Orione's fame and the inscrutable will of the gods. To provide a magnificent conclusion, Neptune and his wife, Amphitrite, appear with a retinue of mermaids. Though the libretto does not specifically call for it, this finale may have been in the form of an aquatic ballet.[9]

The *tombeau* or tomb scene in Act II suggests Bach's familiarity with this convention of French opera. He may have encountered it in Parma, where he had gone in search of a singer for his first opera. In 1758 Tommaso Traëtta was the maestro di cappella at the duke of Parma's court. For his debut there Traëtta had set the text of Rameau's *Castor et Pollux*, translated into Italian. Traëtta's version included, according to the announcement, choruses and ballets *alla francese*. Thus Christian became acquainted with Traëtta's music, of which Einstein said, "a few of his arias show a direct link to John Christian Bach, not to say to Mozart."[10] Surely Christian noted characteristic features of French opera, such as tomb scenes, the underworld, and Elysium, and included them in his *Orione*.

At about this time another operatic master had become acquainted with Traëtta's *I Tindirati*. This was Christoph Willibald Gluck, who had attended the work's first performance in Vienna. On 5 October 1762, four months before Christian's *Orione* was given in London, Gluck had brought out his own *Orfeo ed Euridice*, which was to become the best-known version of this legend involving the descent of a lover to the underworld in order to be reunited with his beloved.

Soon after *Orfeo*, Gluck had gone to Bologna. He had written a rather routine opera for the opening of a new theater there. On the way back to Vienna with his travel companion Dittersdorf, he had made a detour to Parma in order to attend a performance of Christian's *Catone in Utica*. If we can judge by Dittersdorf's memoirs, Gluck may have been only mildly enthusiastic. According to Dittersdorf: "A few of [Bach's] arias were very beautiful, but the rest of the music had been put together hastily, as is the custom in Italy."[11] Such censure seems strange, considering that he had just been to Bologna for an opera by Gluck, on a Metastasio text, that had been put together according to a conventional formula.

The work was a disappointment to Gluck's admirers, for they had expected something along the lines of the highly innovative *Orfeo*.

We might take note of the time frame: at the same time (fall 1762–spring 1763) that Gluck was making history with his *Orfeo* (though at first the work was not highly successful), Christian was establishing himself in London as an opera composer of international renown. Burney said about *Orione* that "the Neapolitan school, where he studied, is manifest in his cantilena, and the science of his father and brother in his harmony."[12]

The only opera seria given that season at the King's Theatre was Bach's *Orione*. This is remarkable, for the general public always wanted to see and hear new works. London audiences acclaimed Christian's opera for nearly three months; they were particularly impressed by the choruses, which for the first time had an important dramatic function rather than merely supplying a decorative frame or background. Six "grand" choral scenes occur during the four acts; the *Public Advertiser* announced them as a special attraction.

Bach's second opera, *Zanaïda*, was not given until 7 May 1763; the season ended with it on 11 June. Once more Anna Lucia de Amicis, his discovery, sang the title role; once more her voice and her appearance charmed all of London. *Zanaïda*, with music by "Mr. Bach, a Saxon Professor," was given eight times. Eight arias from the opera were published and advertised, on the day of the premiere, as "Favourite Songs."

Thus it seemed as though everything was going beautifully for composer, prima donna, and management. But events took a surprising turn. On 3 March, while *Orione* was still being played, Amicis was in her glory, and the impresario Mattei was cashing in on her success, Felice de Giardini, announced that he was to replace Mattei as the theater's director. Once before, in 1756, Giardini, together with Regina Mingotti, had managed the King's Theatre, but with little success. Now, in the *Public Advertiser*, he

> humbly requests the Nobility and Gentry who have done him the Honour to subscribe to his Operas for the ensuing Season, to pay in Half their Subscription to Messrs. Drummond at Charing-Cross, to enable him to give security for the Payment of several of the most eminent Singers from Italy and other Parts.[13]

As we shall see, these were empty promises. It is not now known what had happened during those weeks and months. Did Mattei or Amicis resign, or had they become victims of an intrigue? Resignations under

Singers who were important in the careers of
Bach and Mozart: Luigi Tibaldi (left); Anna
Lucia de Amicis (below left), who sang in Bach's
first operas for England. Amicis was the prima
donna in Mozart's *Lucio Silla* (Milan, 1773),
which also featured Venanzio Rauzzini (below
right), later Bach's rival in London.

such circumstances seem unlikely. At any rate, Anna Lucia gave her benefit concert on 24 March; Giovanni Gallini, the first dancer of the Royal Opera, did the same on 21 April. On that occasion, "by public request," he danced a minuet with Amicis. Both events suggest an atmosphere of leavetaking.

It is also to be noted that Amicis was not leaving to accept another engagement. After the last performance of *Zanaïde* on 11 June, she set out on a journey. While passing through Mainz in August 1763 she met the Mozarts, who were staying there at the King of England Inn. They were on their way to England, by way of France.[14]

Nor can we ascertain the reason for Mattei's sudden departure. In London she had renounced a career as a singer in order to devote herself to a second career as the impresario of King's Theatre. She had just finished a most successful season—yet her successor, Giardini, must have had his own contract early in March, else he could not have solicited subscriptions for the coming season.

For Christian these developments were a serious setback. After all, it had been Mattei who had brought him to England, where he had discovered Amicis, his ideal prima donna. The three of them seemed like an unbeatable combination. Thus a change would not benefit Christian, especially since the new principal turned out to be Regina Mingotti.

She must have been the driving force—the one who encouraged Giardini to take on the management of the opera again. Skeptics jokingly called it the "sovereign privilege of self-ruin," for during his earlier tenure he had lost a considerable part of his fortune. On the other hand Giardini, now fifty years old, was at risk of losing the standing he had achieved before Christian appeared on the scene. Giardini's first concert in 1751, with the singer Cuzzoni, had begun a new epoch in London's concert life, as Burney reported. Beginning in 1755, Giardini had headed the opera orchestra; he had also dabbled in composition. Since Christian Bach had successfully conducted his own operas and various pasticci, along with Amicis's private recitals, Giardini may have feared losing the directorship of the opera orchestra to Christian.[15]

Mingotti, at forty-one, found herself in a similar situation. She was past her prime as a singer, and her personal life was not without problems. She had an illegitimate son named Samuel Felix Buckingham, whose father was allegedly a certain Count Piesaque de Non.[16] For both Mingotti and Giardini, taking on the directorship may have been the last chance to remain in the public eye.

Mingotti may also have had personal reasons for excluding Christian from the new season (namely, her quarrel with Faustina Hasse in Dresden, when Father Bach had sided with both Hasses), but this is merely speculation. At any rate, Christian cannot have been surprised, for even during their first season as opera directors, Mingotti and Giardini had made it clear that they did not intend to have a resident composer. They thought they would attract larger audiences with a variety of composers, and they also intended to introduce operas that already had proved successful elsewhere.

There must have been quarrels within the company, to judge by the announcement in the *Public Advertiser* that Mattei would leave England at the end of the season. It stated further that "as Mr. Crawford [Peter Crawford, in charge of sets and costumes] intends to have no further Concern with the Management of Operas, all the Cloaths used in the Burlettas and Dances, with many other Articles, being his Property and that of Signora Mattei's, will be sold." All of which suggests intrigues rather than a routine transition from one season to the next.

This interruption of Christian's career as an opera composer was unpleasant, but it did not threaten his livelihood. His operas had provided him with a good income, and he was still employed by the cathedral chapter in Milan, free to return to Italy at any time. The experience was more likely to have been a personal and artistic disappointment.

Like Mozart, Christian tended to be close to the singers for whom he wrote; indeed, he eventually married one of them. His association with Amicis was no exception. She was twenty-two years old, he was twenty-seven; she was a highly gifted singer, he was already famous as a composer of operas and was an attractive young man, not at all indifferent to female charm. After eight months of intensive working together at the King's Theatre, it would have been strange if some personal ties had not developed, in which case he must have regretted their separation.

Professionally, Christian had other irons in the fire. His first instrumental concertos were published on 17 March 1763, eight days before Anna Lucia's benefit concert. These six harpsichord concertos, Opus 1, which were dedicated to the English queen, already represent a new style in instrumental music, a genre that would turn out to be Christian's forte, ranking ahead of his operas. Though called concertos, they are quite intimate, more in the nature of chamber music. Their two-movement form suggests this, as does the modest scoring. Only a soloist, two violins, and a cello are required for their performance. Nor do the solo parts call for a virtuoso. They were intended for the abilities of the dedicatee and were meant to be heard in an informal setting. The works are little gems, full

Regina Mingotti, director of the King's Theatre.

of grace and melodic charm, and characterized by Christian's "singing allegro" manner. Some of the six may have been written while Christian was still in Italy. Two movements stand out: the Minuet of the first concerto in B-flat major, and the Andante of the last one, in G major. To the child Mozart, soon to arrive in England with his father, they represented the London Bach's style. In deference to the royal patron, Bach concluded the third movement of the sixth concerto with imaginative variations on "God Save the King."

So far, however, Bach was not yet music master to the royal family. That title is mentioned only in the edition of Opus 2, the six trio sonatas (fall 1763) dedicated to Princess Augusta of Brunswick-Lüneburg, one of the king's sisters. Earlier, in the dedication to Queen Charlotte, the composer had simply called himself "Jean Bach," just as at other times he used "Giovanni" or "John," omitting his middle name Christian. Others indicated his status in varied ways. Some, as we learned, called him "Saxon Master of Music," even "Saxon Professor." In Italy, in connection with the performance in Perugia of his *Catone*, he was billed as "Sig. D. Giovanni Bach, Maestro di Cappella Napolitana."[17]

Having dedicated his first harpsichord concertos to the queen, Bach surely enjoyed the good will and patronage of the royal couple. Sooner or later an official appointment was bound to be conferred on him, and so Christian resolved to remain in England. After a lapse of a year, he once more wrote to Padre Martini to inform him of his decision.

> Reverend Father, esteemed patron,
> I should have fulfilled my duty to write to you long ago, but I was unable to do so because of important work and illness. I earnestly hope that you will forgive me. Along with this letter you will receive two books. One of them deals with Handel's life [Mainwaring's *Life of Handel*, published in 1760], the other is Dr. Smith's *Harmonics* [containing reflections on music and philosophy, 1749]. I was unable to find *Le poesie dell'Avaro*. You will receive my package by way of Signora Carmagiani's father. [Giovanna Carmagiani sang in Christian's operas; she, too, returned to Italy at the end of the 1762–1763 season.]
> I had planned to visit Italy this year, but the great kindness of their majesties, the king and queen, obliges me to respect their wishes and to remain here. I ask you, Reverend Father, to remember me to Cavaliere D. Carlo [Dassio, a priest whom Christian had mentioned in his letter of 27 February 1761] and to all my friends, and I remain, etc.
> London, 1 July 1763   Giov. Bach

Admission ticket designed by the engraver Francesco Bartolozzi.

Title page of Bach's keyboard sonatas, Opus 5.

SIX SONATES
POUR LE
CLAVECIN OU LE PIANO FORTE,
DEDIÉES A
SON ALTESSE SERENISSIME
MONSEIGNEUR LE DUC ERNEST
DUC DE MECKLENBOURG &c.&c.
CHEVALIER DE L'ORDRE DE L'AIGLE BLANC,
ET MAJOR GENERAL DES ARMÉES
DE S. M. BRITANNIQUE,
COMPOSÉES PAR
J. JEAN CHRETIEN BACH MAITRE DE MUSIQUE
DE S.M. LA REINE D'ANGLETERRE.
OEUVRE V.

There is no mention of Count Litta; apparently that connection no longer existed.

Christian seems to have changed residences. According to the announcement in the *Public Advertiser*, his Opus 1 was available "at Signora Mattei's, in Jermyn Street, St. James," whereas Opus 2 lists "Meard's-Street, St. Ann's, Soho." It seems that after Mattei's departure Christian moved to the north of London, to Soho, a quiet and elegant residential section, quite different from the later disreputable Soho. Nearby was Soho Square, large and well kept, with inviting promenades and surrounded by elegant three-story mansions. Equally near was Oxford Street, leading to Hyde Park, then a popular destination for excursions.

Christian shared living quarters with Carl Friedrich Abel, one of the German musicians in London on whose friendship and support Christian could count. Both Christian and Abel, twelve years older, were bachelors. From their quarters in Meard's Street, they jointly made their plans for enriching the city's concert life.

Who was Carl Friedrich Abel? We met him for the first time in Leipzig when he participated as gamba player in cantata performances directed by Johann Sebastian Bach. In 1743, when he was nineteen years old, Abel appeared as soloist in the recently founded Grosses Concert. His playing was much acclaimed, smoothing his move to Dresden, where he was a member of the famous orchestra from 1748 to 1758. Allegedly because of a quarrel with Hasse, he set out for England with all of three taler in his purse, stopping along the way at various small principalities to look for employment.

Soon after his arrival in London in 1759, he acquired fame as a versatile musician. Although he excelled as a gamba player, he was also a capable harpsichordist, a performer on the recently invented pentachord, and a horn player. Abel displayed these talents in compositions of his own, the first of which, a series of six symphonies, appeared in print in 1761.[18] As musicians and as men who enjoyed the finer things in life, Christian Bach and Abel were eminently compatible.

When a German princess ascended the British throne, Abel's chances of obtaining a court position improved greatly. Indeed, on the title page of his Opus 7 of 1763 (again a collection of six symphonies), he is listed as "Charles Frederic Abel, Musicien de Chambre de S. M. la Reine de la Grande Bretagne." (Mozart copied the sixth symphony of this set, which led to the assumption that he had composed it.) Thus Abel was employed by the queen at this time, just like Christian, who is listed in his Opus 2 trios as "Maitre S. M. la Reine d'Angleterre." Both musicians found a secure existence serving the English crown—in an environment that somewhat resembled a German colony, even away from London.

Thus in Bath, a fashionable spa about a hundred miles from the city, we meet another German musician, one Friedrich Wilhelm Herschel. Writing to his brother in Hanover, Herschel reported that "we now have in London the young Mr. Bach. He is quite successful and bound to become very famous."[19]

Herschel had left the Continent during the Seven Years' War and was making a living in Bath as organist, composer, conductor, and music teacher. Years later his career took a surprising turn: he became an astronomer, exploring the universe with telescopes and mirrors he had constructed and ground himself. Probing beyond the then-known planetary system, he discovered the planet Uranus, for which he was ennobled by the king and granted a pension. The professional musician had turned to astronomy because he found, regretfully, that in music there was "not enough science."

There is no record of Herschel's having met Christian Bach, but both Bach and Abel are believed to have visited the famous spa, as Handel, Giardini, and Burney had done. Such visits are all the more likely because both Bach and Abel had a good friend in Bath: painter Thomas Gainsborough. The threesome were united by their love of music—a love, in Gainsborough's case, that amounted to passion. Furthermore, Bach's pupil Mrs. Carl Weichsell participated in Herschel's concerts, and it would have been normal for Christian to take an interest in her appearances in Bath. If no record exists of Herschel meeting Bach, it may be because of the difference in social standing between the "famous Bach," music master to the queen, and the modest musician from "the provinces."

Herschel's reference to Bach was made near the end of Christian's brilliant opera season with Anna Lucia de Amicis. In the following year (1763–1764), Mingotti and Giardini did their best to have a good season at the Haymarket, and it did offer a few great moments. One of these was the duet "Tu parti mio ben" from the pasticcio *Cleonice*, and thereby hangs a tale.

Mingotti and Giardini had opened the season with *Cleonice*, which included two versions of the said duet. One of them was by Christian, who had apparently set the text first. But Mingotti disapproved of Bach's version and asked the Venetian composer Bertoni, whom Burney considered mediocre, to provide another setting. If true, this might explain why Christian did not supply another work for the season. The fracas about the two versions of the duet, at any rate, was one bit of excitement in an otherwise lackluster season.

The season was mediocre despite Giardini's desperate attempt to save it by engaging a resident composer, the Neapolitan Mattia Vento. He was Giardini's last chance, for Mingotti made it quite clear that she was leaving the sinking ship. She headed for the Munich opera, where she remained active until 1767. Having received a pension from the elector, she spent her old age with her son in Neuburg on the Danube, where she died in 1807.

With this season, Giardini's dreams of operatic glory came to an end. He had lost everything: his fortune and his reputation as composer and impresario. To regain some financial well-being, he was forced to give benefit concerts, teach lessons, and sell stringed instruments.[20] And when Christian brought the violin virtuoso Wilhelm Cramer to London to appear in his concerts, Giardini must have feared that he might lose his position as leader of the orchestra.

Christian could afford to wait for better days on the operatic scene. Just how popular he had become is described by Burney in his *General History of Music*:

> This excellent master soon convinced us that he possessed every requisite for a great musician; by the songs he afterwards composed in every style of good singing; by his symphonies, quartets, and concertos for almost every species of instrument, as well as by his expressive and masterly performance on the piano forte. It is with pleasure I take this opportunity of doing justice to his talents and abilities. Mr. J. C. Bach having very early in life been deprived of the instructions of his father, the great Sebastian Bach, was for some time a scholar of his elder brother, the celebrated Charles Phil. Emanuel Bach, under whom he became a fine performer on keyed-instruments. . . . He assured me, that during many years he made little use of a harpsichord or piano forte but to compose for or accompany a voice. When he arrived in England, his style of playing was so much admired, that he recovered many of the losses his hand had sustained by disuse, and by being constantly cramped and crippled with a pen; but he never was able to reinstate it with force and readiness sufficient for great difficulties, and in general his compositions for the piano forte are such as ladies can execute with little trouble; and the allegros rather resemble bravura songs, than instrumental pieces for the display of great execution.[21]

Bach's alleged loss of finger dexterity sounds exaggerated in Burney's account. He was the most sought after piano teacher in London, and his pupils, mostly female, would have noted and criticized flaws in his playing, just as the public attending his concerts would have done.

At this time, keyboard instruments were undergoing drastic changes. During the first part of the century, the harpsichord had been the favored keyboard instrument; now the pianoforte was gradually and inevitably beginning to replace it. Christian played an important role in this development. The six concertos of his Opus 1 for the queen and the six trios of his Opus 2 had clearly been intended for the harpsichord, but his Opus 5 sonatas and Opus 7 concertos in their published form indicate the alternative: "Cembalo o Piano e Forte."

These structural developments take us back to Christian's homeland, Saxony, where Gottfried Silbermann, having established himself as a maker of keyboard instruments, soon became the undisputed master. Johann Sebastian Bach thought highly of his organs, with their "thundering basses" and brilliant sound. Musicians of the next generation were equally enthusiastic. Mozart considered them "absolutely magnificent instruments." Not surprisingly, Silbermann the master organ builder and Sebastian Bach the renowned organist were in close contact. They exchanged letters and also met at inspections and dedications of new organs—in Naumburg, for example, where Bach and Silbermann examined and accepted an organ built by Silbermann's prize pupil Zacharias Hildebrandt. On 27 September 1746, Bach and Silbermann appeared at the mayor's office (according to the official protocol), delivered their evaluation, and were paid eight ducats each for their "examination."[22]

Bach's pupil Agricola, whom we met during Christian's years in Berlin, was especially fond of Silbermann's fortepianos; he found them "very easy and comfortable to play." Several of these instruments had been purchased by the Prussian king for his palace in Potsdam, and when Sebastian Bach journeyed there, he was asked to try them out. Although Silbermann did not invent the Hammerklavier, he developed and improved on the design that Bartolommeo Cristofori of Padua had originated in the early eighteenth century.

Once more we have come full circle. One of Silbermann's pupils was Johann Andreas Stein in Augsburg, the founder of a famous family firm of instrument builders. Leopold Mozart (also a native of Augsburg) turned to Stein to purchase a clavier for the seven-year-old Wolfgang, "a fine little clavier, very useful for practicing while traveling." The journey, of course, took the Mozarts to England, where Wolfgang and Christian would meet. All his life, Wolfgang admired Stein—as a piano builder and as a person. Quite likely the subject of instrument builders came up in London, where another Silbermann student had established himself. This was Johann Christoph Zumpe, one of twelve builders of keyboard instruments who had emigrated to England during the Seven Years' War. Among musicians and merchants they were jokingly referred to as the twelve apostles.[23]

Christian was on good terms with Zumpe and his friend Gabriel Buntebart, a friendship in which Buntebart played a role comparable to that of Michael Puchberg in Mozart's life. He helped Christian financially when times were hard. (He was also one of the few friends who attended Christian's funeral.) Bach supported Zumpe, helping him by promoting his new square piano, a small instrument provided with additional keys, which resulted in greater evenness of tone. Bach introduced the instrument in June 1768 at a concert in St. James Street. The advertisement refers to "a solo on the Piano Forte by Mr. Bach."

The differences between the action or mechanism (and hence the sound) of harpsichord and pianoforte are quite generally known today. The strings of the harpsichord are plucked, whereas the strings of the pianoforte (or fortepiano; in German, *Hammerklavier*) are struck by hammers, resulting in an entirely different timbre. The fortepiano, as the name implies, admits dynamic variety and shading that were previously unobtainable, allowing for cantabile playing. This enrichment of the instrument's tonal palette is reflected in Christian's compositional style.

Christian the player was physically quite capable of dealing with this new keyboard technique, in spite of Burney's claim that he "never was able to reinstate [his style of playing] with force and readiness sufficient for great difficulties."[24] The changeover from harpsichord to fortepiano seems to have required even less effort for Christian the composer, as is shown in his six Opus 5 keyboard sonatas, dedicated to Duke Ernst of Mecklenburg. According to the title page, these pieces were intended for either instrument. They accommodate both techniques, including movements in different styles. Two worlds meet here, bringing together contrapuntal and melodic qualities.

The last sonata, in C minor, may be the most beautiful and expressive of the six. A majestic Grave, recalling earlier times, serves as prelude to an artful double fugue in which Christian reveals his indebtedness to his father and to Padre Martini. It may be that this music in the old style was intended as homage to George III, the monarch he served, who was a great admirer of Handel. Perhaps Christian also wanted to bring about a synthesis, for the following Allegretto, again in minor, is a gavotte en rondeau, graceful, melodiously sentimental, and somewhat melancholic.

It is possible that Christian had composed this unusual sonata earlier and then placed it at the end of the set of six to provide an effective conclusion. In general these sonatas explore all aspects of the keyboard technique of the day. Some may indeed have been intended as "lessons" for the instruction of young ladies and were therefore in an "easy and familiar style." Others are more brilliant, for performance as well as for study. But throughout them all, we sense the composer's joy of music making; we are aware of the grace and elegance of easily flowing melodies. These sonatas were to enchant the young Mozart, impressing him so much that he obtained three of them (numbers 2, 3, and 4) in manuscript form, since they did not see print until years later, and arranged them as keyboard concertos for public performance. Mozart's fondness for them must have lasted for years; much later he also composed cadenzas for the first of these concerto arrangements.

The popular success of Christian's sonatas soon led to problems in the form of unauthorized (or "pirated") editions, and of inaccurate copies and forgeries. This state of affairs is described by music professor Carl Friedrich Cramer to his publisher in Hamburg. Though written in April 1783, Cramer's complaint also applies to the period under consideration.

> One often encounters engraved editions of works by Abel and Bach— works that in Germany would be considered mediocre, below the worth of these famous men. There is an explanation for this: Those compositions that they intended to be published, Bach and Abel had engraved by Brenner and Welcker, who paid well. Everything else was issued clandestinely, without their knowledge and consent. Some works by others even appeared with J. C. Bach's name. . . . Others tried to obtain copies of small compositions Abel and Bach had written down for their students; also quartets, trios, etc. that they had composed for various recipients. These people would assemble them, have them engraved, usually with Bach's name on the title page, and sell them. Such editions then were reprinted and circulated as authentic compositions, violating the honor and good name of both composers.[25]

Bach's first works written in England suffered from this kind of piracy to such an extent that he turned to his king for help. As early as December 1763, when he had been in England for only a year and a half, Bach was honored by a proclamation issued by the monarch.

GEORGE R.

Whereas our trusty and well-beloved John Christian Bach, gent., has by his petition humbly represented unto Us that he hath, with great study, labour and expense composed divers works consisting of Vocal and Instrumental Music, and being desirous to print the same, and apprehending, unless he can obtain our Royal Licence and Privilege, other persons may be induced to print and publish the said works, and so invade his property therein, he hath therefore most humbly prayed Us to grant him our Royal Licence and Privilege for the sole printing and publishing of the above mentioned Works for the term of fourteen years agreable to the Statute in that case made and provided. We, being willing to give all due encouragement to this his undertaking, are graciously pleased to condescend to his request, and We do therefore, by these Presents, so far as may be agreable to the Statute in that behalf made and provided, grant unto him, the said John Christian Bach, his Executors, Administrators, and Assigns, Our Licence for the sole printing and publishing the said Works for the term of fourteen years, to be computed from date hereof, strictly forbidding all our subjects within our Kingdom and Dominions, to reprint, abridge, copy out in writing for sale, or publish the same, either in the like or in any other size or manner whatsoever, or to import, buy, vend, utter or distribute any copy or copies thereof, reprinted or written, for sale beyond the seas, during the aforesaid term of fourteen years, without the approbation or consent of the said John Christian Bach, his Executors, Administrators, or Assigns, under their hands and seals first had and obtained, or they will answer the contrary at their perils, whereof the Commissioners and other Officers of our Customs, the Master Wardens and Company of Stationers are to take notice, that due obedience may be rendered to our Will and Pleasure herein declared. Given at our Court at St. James the 15th day of December 1763, in the fourth year of our Reign.

By His Majesty's Command
Sandwich.[26]

The document is impressive evidence of the interest and care the young royal couple, aged twenty-five and nineteen, bestowed on the twenty-eight-year-old Christian. In a way, he was a member of the family circle, which now included the princes George and Frederick. Thirteen more princes and princesses would follow, providing the musical setting described by eyewitnesses:

The schoolroom was one of gaiety and cheerfulness. The masters [included] for music our dear and valued friend, Johann Christian Bach.

Queen Sophie-Charlotte. Painting by Thomas Gainsborough, c. 1770. Bach wrote much music for her chamber music concerts in Buckingham Palace (below).

He also gave lessons to the Queen; and of evenings, by appointment, he attended the King's accompaniment to the pianoforte by the flute.

A Mrs. Delaney, on one of her frequent visits to the palace, found the king playing on the floor with his children, while in the adjoining chamber the court musicians were waiting, ready to be told what they should perform.[27]

So far the princes were too young to receive music lessons. Christian's duties at court therefore were not overly taxing, especially since the young royal couple had preferred a quiet domestic existence ever since the turbulent weeks of coronation festivities.

Society at court, to be sure, was disappointed; they had hoped that such young rulers would lead a merry social life, in town and at their summer residences in the country. Their disenchantment is reflected in Walpole's account.

> Life in Richmond was isolated. Daily life was characterized by great thrift, so that the queen's hairdresser also had to wait on table. . . . Few guests show up for evening receptions; on Sunday night Lady Buckingham was the only one. . . . Most of those at court are uncommonly dull. The Duchess of Grafton is the only lady of high rank who will dance at public receptions at St. James. The Duchess of Northumberland becomes more and more sleepy all the time. She slept most of the time while in the drawing room on Saturday.[28]

There were reasons for such scurrilous remarks. King George III was the butt of many jokes. Awkward in appearance and having speech difficulties—harbingers of his later mental derangement—he tried to hide these deficiencies by playing the part of a country squire. His attire was often strange, and he was excessively modest, adopting the manners of the lower classes. When he tried to make conversation, stammering and asking foolish questions, people would say with some sarcasm that he was good-natured and always eager to learn; that he asked many questions but fortunately answered all of them himself.

Both the king's mother and Parliament were content with George's subordinate role; he interfered little in their governing of the country. The young queen was kept entirely out of affairs of state; both George and his mother treated her like a child. When mother and son discussed politics, which happened rarely, Charlotte was asked to leave the room. The affront may not have bothered her. She had no desire to be involved in politics, nor did she relish being the center of attention at state receptions. She was used to the simpler life at the small Strelitz court.

She spent her time reading, doing needlework, learning English, expanding her horizon and her general education. Christian's music lessons were important interludes in her quiet existence, but they were insufficient challenge to the teacher-composer, who may also have fretted about the great thrift. Fortunately there was the "other" London, that of the middle class, with many musical activities and diversions.

According to a contemporary description, any Englishman with time on his hands did not have to look far for entertainment.

> [The English] love to promenade; therefore one sees great crowds in St. James Park, in the squares, and in Hyde Park—on foot, on horseback, or in coaches. London boasts many establishments where coffee, tea, wine, and beer are served, and where one can see tightrope walkers, puppet shows, and the like.[29]

Coffee houses were an important element of the city's social life; they were frequented by Londoners from all walks of life, including the clergy. Billiards or other games were not in evidence; people mostly engaged in conversation or read newspapers, which explains why London then had seven daily and eight evening papers. Every evening thousands of citizens headed for Vauxhall and Ranelagh, the amusement parks outside the city gates, one on the south bank of the Thames, the other near Chelsea.

Amusements continued late into the night. Eight hundred cabs were for hire and operated through the night, along with three hundred sedan chairs, to transport the revelers who would otherwise have had to contend with muddy streets and with thieves. Those who insisted upon going on foot hired youths to walk ahead carrying torches. Some hundred boats were available for crossing the Thames and for outings on the river. For Christian and others, the pleasures of the metropolis compensated for the monotony of court life.

Father Leopold Mozart also raved about the pleasures of Ranelagh and Vauxhall. "There is nothing anywhere in the world like these two gardens," he wrote to his friend Lorenz Hagenauer in Salzburg.

> The Ranelagh gardens are small but attractive, with festive illumination on Mondays, Wednesdays, and Fridays. There is a large circular ballroom on the ground level, with countless chandeliers and other lights. On one side the musicians are seated in tiers, with an organ at the top level. They play from seven to ten o'clock; then, for another hour or more, quartets are played by horn, clarinets, and bassoon. There is a large central fireplace for cold weather, for this garden opens already in March or April. . . . As soon as the hot summer begins, Ranelagh will close; then everyone will head for Vauxhall.

Leopold was even more impressed by Vauxhall Gardens.

They made me think of the Elysian fields. Imagine a very large garden with many paths, illuminated by thousands of crystal lights. At the center there is a kind of tall, open summer pavilion, with a bandstand and organ. Tables with tablecloths are everywhere, also separate boxes with tables. At the ends of the paths I saw illuminated arches and pyramids. Everything was enchanting; I did not know where to look first.

People of leisure visited the gardens in the morning, breakfasting to the accompaniment of music and other entertainment. A large orchestra, placed in the balcony, played short, pleasant instrumental pieces and also accompanied soloists and choruses. If a vocal solo pleased the audience it would soon be heard in London and beyond. "People constantly moved about, elegantly dressed. Gentlemen wore silk stockings and shoes with silver buckles, carrying their three-cornered hats under their arms and their swords at their sides. Ladies wore long dresses and huge hoop-skirts."[30] Concert promoters were not happy with such apparel. Benefit concerts would draw such large crowds that gentlemen were asked, for safety reasons, not to carry swords. Ladies were requested not to wear hoopskirts, which took up so much space that attendance suffered.

We can easily imagine Christian enjoying himself, participating in the varied activities offered in the pleasure gardens. They may have reminded him of his days in Leipzig with its coffee houses, or of the open-air concerts at the Castello Sforzesco in Milan. We can think of Christian, an elegant gentleman (as portrayed by Gainsborough), mingling with strollers at Vauxhall or Ranelagh; perhaps he was busy at times directing the orchestra or playing the organ. He no doubt owed some of his popularity to compositions he wrote for the gardens. He had time for such work because the Mingotti-Giardini management had offered no new commissions since his most recent opera, Zanaïde. Always industrious, Christian made use of the opportunities offered by these open-air concerts. Looking at Rowlandson's well-known engraving, it is easy to imagine that one is listening to one of Christian's compositions. The artist gives a vivid picture of musicians and public; some of the latter elegantly, some simply, attired; some conversing, while a few actually seem to be listening to the music! People of different social standings mingle here. Leopold Mozart was impressed: "Here all people are equals; no lord expects you to take off your hat for him. All pay admission; all are equal."

The singer in the picture may well be the aforementioned Mrs. Weichsell, and Englishwoman married to Carl Weichsell, oboist at the King's Theatre, who had come from Freiberg in Saxony. She was a pupil

Musical and other entertainments at Vauxhall. The subject of the painting might well be Mrs. Weichsel singing one of Christian Bach's popular Vauxhall songs.

of Christian, as was her daughter Elizabeth, a child prodigy. Later known as Mrs. Billington, Elizabeth would acquire international fame as an opera singer. (Her benefit in 1809 was a performance of Christian's *La Clemenza di Scipione*; she thus carried his fame into the new century.)

Christian wrote his first collection of Vauxhall songs for Mrs. Weichsell. As *Favourite Songs sung at Vaux-Hall* they proved so popular that Christian provided two additional collections. His six duets of Opus 4 were dedicated to the music-loving Lady Glenorchy. Quite likely they, too, were heard at Vauxhall. Both title and dedication are in Italian. Since the texts go back to Metastasio, Christian may have written these duets in Italy, before coming to England.

There was constant demand for new vocal and instrumental pieces. James Hook, the official composer and organist at Vauxhall, allegedly wrote more than two thousand songs for the pleasure gardens. It is understandable that Christian, during his early years in England, contributed his share of such compositions, since it was a good way for him to introduce himself to a large public.

His "wind symphonies" are good examples. Actually they are quintets or quartets, usually for two clarinets, two oboes, and one or two bassoons—wind divertimentos rather than symphonies. Lively and unsophisticated, they are eminently suitable for casual, open-air performance. Even Bach's first true symphonies (Opp. 3 and 6), elegant and graceful, were probably heard not only at court or other indoor settings but also at Vauxhall or Ranelagh.

Those of Christian's keyboard concertos that were suitable for organ may also have been played in such settings. Vauxhall had been famous for its organ ever since the concessionaire Jonathan Tyers arranged for the installation of an outstanding instrument. Mrs. Papendiek recorded that Christian had written an organ concerto to be played between the acts of his oratorio *Gioas, Re di Giuda*, and that he had performed it himself, though with only moderate success. Quite possibly he also wrote for the magnificent organ at Vauxhall or adapted one of his keyboard concertos for performance there.[31]

Christian was in good company. George Frideric Handel, his predecessor as music master to the royal family, did not consider it below his dignity to write for Vauxhall. Organ concertos and arias by Handel were heard there, as was his concerto in D major for hornpipe and strings, written specifically for Vauxhall.[32] The most spectacular event, however, was the public dress rehearsal of the *Fireworks Music*, commissioned by the king in celebration of the Peace Treaty of Aix (7 October 1748). The rehearsal at Vauxhall attracted some twelve thousand people; a similar crowd then applauded Handel at the first performance in the royal palace gardens.

A statue of Handel adorns one of the promenades in Vauxhall, an indication of the success he had obtained in that venue. Though the youngest Bach son now followed suit, it is remarkable how soon he stepped out of Handel's shadow—Handel who, though in some ways controversial, had put his stamp on this period of music in England. Later on, Cramer would say it well in his necrology for Christian, printed in his *Magazin für Musik*: "In spite of the vast differences between his and Handel's music, [Christian] was just as beloved by the English people."[33]

Such a testimonial would have pleased Johann Sebastian Bach, who, in spite of his efforts, never made Handel's acquaintance. (Handel seems to have shown great reluctance over such a meeting.) But now Sebastian's youngest son was setting out to follow in the great Handel's footsteps. During these years the names Bach and Handel could easily be mentioned in one breath, along with a third name: Mozart. At the time when Christian Bach and Abel were preparing the first of their joint concerts, the Mozart children were creating a small sensation on the Continent, causing Father Leopold to think about presenting the two prodigies on the other side of the Channel as well.

We might mention at this point the rather impudent words with which the eight-year-old Wolfgang (or, more likely, his father) dedicated his six sonatas for clavier and violin or flute, K. 10, to the queen of England. He boldly anticipates what at a later time would indeed be true. The young boy declares that he is offering a present to the queen that is worthy of her and of himself, and continues: "With your [the queen's] help, I shall become as famous as any of my great countrymen; I shall become immortal like Handel and Hasse, and my name will be as famous as that of [Christian] Bach."

Such confidence seems naïve, but it was based on the Mozarts' earlier successes in Paris. There Wolfgang's incredible pianistic facility, including a few tricks at the keyboard, had amazed and delighted the French. Friedrich Melchior Grimm, a fellow German living in Paris, acted as Mozart's promoter; he was as efficient and influential as Leopold could have desired. Soon after their arrival in Paris, the boy Wolfgang had the good fortune of being featured in a story, full of praise, in Grimm's *Correspondance littéraire*. The Prussian king and the Russian Czar were among the journal's subscribers, along with readers in England. Grimm's account begins as follows:

True prodigies are so rare that when one does encounter one, one must talk about it. A Salzburg Kapellmeister by the name of Mozart has just arrived here with two most attractive-looking children. The daughter is eleven years old [Grimm's error: Maria Anna was twelve] and plays the harpsichord most brilliantly; she executes very long and difficult pieces with astonishing precision. Her brother will be seven years old next February [Wolfgang would be eight on 27 January]; he is such an extraordinary phenomenon that one can hardly believe what one sees and hears. The little boy executes the most difficult pieces most accurately, with hands that can hardly span a sixth. What is most amazing: he will play from memory for an hour without a stop, completely absorbed by the inspiration of his genius, giving free rein to a wealth of charming musical ideas which he tastefully presents in orderly succession.[34]

Grimm then turns to Wolfgang's first attempts at composition and is equally impressed:

The most accomplished Kapellmeister could not have a more profound knowledge of harmony and modulation, which [Wolfgang] applies in uncommon but perfectly correct ways. . . . He has no trouble reading whatever music one puts in front of him. He writes and composes with amazing ease; he does not have to go to the keyboard to search for chords. I wrote down a minuet for him and asked him to write down the bass line underneath. The child picked up the pen and without going to the harpsichord wrote down the bass. . . . It is too bad that here [in France] people know so little about music. The father intends to go from here to England and then to take his children through Northern Germany.

At the time, this itinerary had by no means been decided. To the contrary: the French king and queen received the Mozarts graciously, as did the nobility, especially the Countess de Tessé and Princess Marie-Thérèse Louise de Savoie-Carignan. All these attentions impressed and flattered Leopold, causing him to have second thoughts about continuing their journey to England. "When I left Salzburg, I was undecided about going to England," he admits in a letter to Hagenauer. "But since everyone, also in Paris, urged us to go to London, I decided to do so." Most likely it was, not "everyone," but the experienced Baron Grimm who caused Leopold to go on. His advice meant much to Leopold.

He managed things at court and arranged our first concert. He turned over to me eighty Louis d'or, so he must have sold 320 tickets. He even paid for the more than sixty wax candles. Baron Grimm procured the

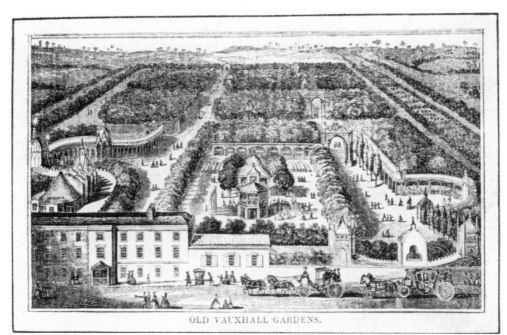

OLD VAUXHALL GARDENS.

Vauxhall Gardens.

The royal family. Portrait by John Zoffany.

permit for the concert; now he will also take care of the second concert, for which a hundred tickets have already been distributed. It shows what can be accomplished by an intelligent and kind person.

Thanks to the *Correspondance littéraire*, Grimm had contacts everywhere and was well informed, also about music in England. Since Grimm evidently did not have a high opinion of French music, Leopold may have gone by his judgment. And so it seems that Grimm, a German living in Paris, showed Mozart the way to England and to John Christian Bach—the Bach whose father Grimm had known during his student years in Leipzig.[35]

To be sure, Wolfgang's accomplishments as a composer had so far been modest, in spite of Grimm's enthusiastic report. When they arrived in Paris in mid-November of 1763, Leopold had nothing of his son's to show except a few small keyboard pieces, which Leopold had entered in "Nannerl's" music note book. By February 1764, however, he proudly wrote to the wife of his friend Hagenauer: "Four of Monsieur Wolfgang Mozart's sonatas are now at the engraver's. Just imagine what kind of excitement these sonatas will cause everywhere, since the title page indicates that they were composed by a seven-year-old child."

To exactly what extent these Paris sonatas (K. 6/7 and K. 8/9) are indeed Wolfgang's own, independent works is difficult to determine. Those found in Nannerl's notebook exist only in Leopold's handwriting. He may have made clean copies of his son's sketches, or he may have written down by ear what Wolfgang had improvised at the keyboard. We know today that no substantial compositions by the child Mozart exist that can be dated earlier than 1764.[36] Before their stay in London, Wolfgang's ability to put music on paper was so inadequate that he needed his father's help simply to write down his musical ideas in a coherent manner, let alone prepare them for print. Thus Nannerl's notebooks, which accompanied the family on their voyage, are for the most part in Leopold's handwriting.

Leopold had started the little book in 1759 for Maria Anna, who was then eight years old. He soon added little pieces as exercises for Wolfgang. They were probably based on his own orchestral compositions, which he simplified so that the children could play them on the harpsichord. Occasionally, as though he wanted to impress the public with Wolfgang's quick intellect, Leopold added marginal observations, such as: "Little Wolfgang learned this minuet and trio in a half hour, on 26 January 1761, one day before his fifth birthday, at 9:30 at night." To a

"Scherzo in C" by Georg Christoph Wagenseil, written down by an unidentified scribe, Leopold added: "Little Wolfgang learned this piece on 24 January 1761, three days before his fifth birthday, between 9 and 9:30 in the evening."

Among these instructional pieces (including an "Arietta con Variazioni in A" by C. P. E. Bach), Wolfgang is represented only once, as the composer of No. 20, a "Klavierstück in C." Even this piece may have been added to the book at a later time. Indeed, the history of Nannerl's notebook is complex; it has not been preserved in the original configuration. There is evidence that the pages were separated, reassembled, and rebound several times. Mozart's sister prized her little book, yet she saw fit to tear out leaves and present them to visitors whom she considered worthy of such a gift. After her death it belonged to her nephew, Wolfgang Amadeus Mozart Jr., the only one of the family who looked after her in her old age. In turn, Mozart's son left it to his great love, Baroness Josephine von Baroni-Cavalcabò.[37] We do not know how it then came into the possession of the Russian grand duchess Helene Pawlowa who presented it, around the mid nineteenth century, to the Salzburger Dommusikverein, today the Internationale Stiftung Mozarteum.

Owing to the book's complex history, we are faced with a number of questions. The correct chronological sequence of the leaves, for instance, can no longer be determined. But to ascertain what the child Mozart had composed before he arrived in London, one need only know which pieces found in the notebook recur in Wolfgang's four "Paris" sonatas. In all, the six months' stay in Paris resulted in only a modest amount of music.

Other musicians living in Paris helped to broaden Wolfgang's musical horizon, especially Johann Schobert and Johann Gottfried Eckard. As in London, German musicians were well represented in Paris.[38]

Leopold Mozart never could warm up to the Silesian-born Schobert. He referred to him as the "low-down Schobert," whose "jealousy and envy" kept him from admitting how well Nannerl played. Wolfgang, however, developed a lasting appreciation for Schobert as both composer and keyboard player. Other contemporaries, including Schubart, praised Schobert's "uncommonly vigorous Allegros and Prestos" but admitted that "he was not successful as a writer of Adagios, for he had not studied the clavichord enough, and he would stifle passages of great emotion with an excess of runs and embellishments." Mozart, at any rate, used Schobert's sonatas for teaching purposes when he returned to Paris in 1778.

Leopold Mozart thought more highly of the other German, Johann Gottfried Eckard. Both had been born in Augsburg. Eckard had originally

Left: Wolfgang Amadeus Mozart, seven years old, when he attracted attention in Paris. Oil painting attributed to Antonio Lorenzoni, 1763.

Right: Friedrich Melchior Grimm.

The Paris edition of harpsichord sonatas "by J(ohann) G(ottlieb) Wolfgang Mozart of Salzburg, Seven Years Old" (1764).

planned to become a painter and engraver and had demonstrated his talents while in Paris. Turning to music, he then studied Emanuel Bach's *Essay*. He had come to Paris with Johann Andreas Stein, the same builder of keyboard instruments from whom the Mozarts had bought a practice piano before they set out on their journey. In Leopold's opinion, Eckard had received the more solid training, partly because of his study of Emanuel's work. He had good success in Paris as a pianist, and (very important for the boy Mozart and for the times in general) he was the first composer in Paris to write specifically for the newly developed forte-piano, thus contributing to its acceptance in France. We know that Wolfgang's father often gave him sonatas by Eckard to play.

All things considered, Leopold may have decided that Paris did not offer enough for Wolfgang's musical growth. In spite of the furor created by the boy, his first attempts at composition were less than spectacular, and it therefore seemed that further instruction from the London Bach was called for. Such paternal considerations were no doubt reinforced by Grimm's low opinion of the musical understanding of the French, for Leopold thought highly of Grimm.

And thus, on 24 April 1764, Leopold could write home that after a stormy crossing of the Channel (he jokingly referred to it as "the little brook in Maxglan," a Salzburg suburb) the family had arrived in London.

5
Bach and the Mozarts in London

*Today, as we prize Mozart, let us also
pay tribute to the man who, due to his
outstanding creative gifts, was Mozart's
closest, direct predecessor.*

Fritz Tutenberg

HE MOZARTS AT FIRST STAYED WITH JOHN COUSINS, a hairdresser
in St. Martin's Lane. They at once adopted English dress, which
to Leopold seemed like masquerading. "Can you imagine what my wife
and daughter look like wearing English hats, and Wolfgang and I in
English clothes?" Leopold put the question in a letter, written two days
after their arrival, to his friend and landlord, Hagenauer, in Salzburg.
Throughout this journey, Leopold's letters kept Hagenauer au courant.
Perhaps the writer thought that this documentation might someday be
good source material for a life of Wolfgang. With this in mind, he had
asked Hagenauer to keep his letters.

Two days later, the Mozarts were summoned to perform for the royal
couple. (In Paris, six weeks had gone by before such an invitation was
extended.) Word of their sensational appearances—Grimm's hymn of
praise in the *Correspondance littéraire*, for example—may have preceded
them. At any rate, the gates of the royal palace in London were opened
for them so promptly that Leopold was taken by surprise; he did not mention the invitation in his letter to Salzburg.

No doubt John Christian Bach, the queen's music master, had
arranged for such preferential treatment; visiting musicians were not
likely to be introduced at court without him. In the Mozarts' case, the
reception turned out to be uncommonly friendly, as Leopold reports:

On 27 April, from six to nine o'clock, we were with the king and
queen, in her palace in St. James Park. In other words, we were received

at court only five days after our arrival. The present given us as we left was only twenty-four guineas [here, again, the royal thrift was apparent], but Their Majesties were extremely gracious. They were so friendly and unassuming that we could hardly believe we were in the presence of the king and queen of England. So far we have been treated politely at all courts, but our reception here ranks above all others.

Such royal attention evidently flattered Leopold, especially since it continued.

A week later, we were walking in St. James Park when the king and queen passed in their coach. Even though we were differently dressed this time, they recognized us. Not only did they greet us, but the king opened a window and leaned out, laughing and waving at us, especially at Master Wolfgang, as they drove by.

Leopold thought it best to introduce Wolfgang alone at what was to have been his first public appearance. The boy was the only one mentioned in the *Public Advertiser* of 9 May, in connection with a benefit concert for the cellist Carlo Graziani. The event, scheduled for 17 May, was to include a

Concerto on the Harpsichord by Master Mozart, who is a real Prodigy of Nature; he is but Seven Years of Age, plays anything at first Sight, and composes amazingly well. He has had the Honour of exhibiting before Their Majesties greatly to their Satisfaction.[1]

Unfortunately the concert had to be postponed because some of the participants had other commitments. It was rescheduled for 22 May, but Wolfgang fell ill, and the concert took place without him. It cannot have been a serious illness, for Leopold, usually a meticulous chronicler, does not mention it. Moreover, both Mozart children had played at court on 19 May. This time Leopold gave a detailed account.

I had planned to mail this letter a week ago but was unable to do so; I also wanted to wait, thinking I might have further news to report. But all I can tell you is that on 19 May, again in the evening from six to ten, we were with the king and queen. The only others present were the king's two brothers and the queen's brother. As we left, we were again handed twenty-four guineas. That's a tolerable amount if we were to receive it every three or four weeks. . . . Everything will be fine if, with God's help, we stay well, and if God will keep our indefatigable [Wolfgang] Mozart in good health.

Leopold went on to say that the king "asked Wolfgang to play not

Leopold Mozart, Wolfgang, and Nannerl in Paris. Engraving by Jean Baptiste Delafosse, 1764, based on a water color by L. Caramontelle, 1763.

London at the time of the Mozarts' visit.

only pieces by Wagenseil, but also by [Christian] Bach, Abel, and Handel, all of which he played at sight."

The king, on whose organ Wolfgang also played, thought even more highly of that performance than of the boy's harpsichord playing. (Earlier during this journey, Wolfgang had enjoyed playing the organ on several occasions.) Wolfgang then accompanied the queen, who sang an aria with flute obbligato, and then amazed the august company with his skill at improvisation. Finally, Leopold relates,

> he took the violone [bass] part of a Handel aria, which happened to be lying there, and over the bass line composed a most beautiful melody. . . . What he had known when he left Salzburg is nothing compared with what he knows now; it defies the imagination. . . . [Wolfgang] sends you his best regards; right now he is sitting at the harpsichord playing [Christian] Bach's trios.

If the boy Mozart, after four weeks in England, showed such remarkable progress beyond what he had known when they set out on their journey, John Christian Bach's caring instruction deserves much of the credit. His house on Meard's Street was full of scores and unfinished compositions, the products of his often-praised industry; this was valuable study material for his young pupil. The trios mentioned by Leopold had by then been printed, as had the harpsichord concertos dedicated to the queen. The six symphonies of Opus 3, about to be published, were probably available to Wolfgang in manuscript form. During visits to the "pleasure gardens" so much admired by Leopold, the Mozarts may have heard Christian's popular *Vauxhall-Songs* or some of his symphonies for winds.

It comes as no surprise, then, that the eight-year-old Wolfgang looked up to Christian, the successful court composer, with admiration and love. Not only Christian's music appealed to him but also his personality. Wolfgang must have felt that his talent was gladly acknowledged and nurtured, without reservations or envy, by Christian, although the latter, in view of his own fame, might have looked down on the child's musical efforts.

The opposite in fact was true. Their mutual fondness and the teacher's devotion are exemplified by a little episode, described much later by Nannerl. A year after Wolfgang's death, she contributed some of her own memories of her brother to a planned biography. Having been with him in London, she recalled that

> Herr Johann Christian Bach, music master of the queen, took [Wolfgang] between his knees. He would play a few measures; then [Wolf-

gang] would continue. In this manner they played entire sonatas. Unless you saw it with your own eyes, you would swear that just one person was playing.[2]

On 5 June, Wolfgang played his first public concert, together with his sister. It took place "at the Great Room in Spring Garden, near St. James Park," the same hall in which, three months earlier, Bach and Abel had introduced themselves to the public in their first joint concert.

The concert of brother and sister turned out to be profitable, as Leopold reported. We do not know what they played, except for a concerto for two harpsichords, since Leopold, in his bookkeeping, noted the rental price for the two instruments. On this and other occasions, Wolfgang also performed on the organ, as noted in the announcement.[3] The program also featured much music by Handel: arias and choruses from his oratorios, and the Coronation Anthem. Wolfgang had many opportunities such as this one to familiarize himself with Handel's music, of which his father did not think highly. But Leopold stressed that his son could be heard in "several fine select Pieces of his own Composition on the Harpsichord and Organ."

This brings up the question: what had the boy composed since the Opus 1 and 2 sonatas, printed in Paris? The Opus 3 sonatas, with the rather cocky dedication to the queen, were advertised by Leopold only at the end of 1764, the dedication being dated 18 January 1765. Before that, an important development that came close to threatening the very existence of the Mozart family had occurred: a serious illness of the father, on which Nannerl comments rather casually in her previously mentioned recollections:

> On 5 August, the family had to leave London for Chelsea. They rented a house in the country so that our father could recuperate from a dangerous throat ailment, which had taken him almost to death's door. When, after two months, his health was fully restored, they returned to London.[4]

Later, in a letter to Hagenauer, Leopold himself described the circumstances of his illness in more detail. During the father's confinement, Wolfgang was not allowed to play the clavier. He must have been entirely on his own, without assistance from his mother or sister with regard to his musical education. Under these circumstances, more or less to pass the time, Wolfgang began writing in a notebook that was to be of great importance, for it consisted exclusively of his own compositions, all in his own handwriting. This is the so-called London Sketch Book.

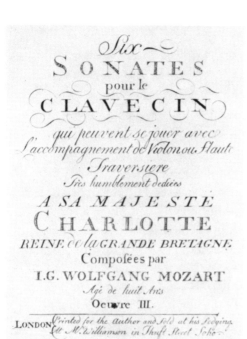

Title page of six keyboard sonatas by Mozart, K. 10–15, dedicated to Queen Charlotte.

Mozart With the Bird Nest. The eight-year-old Mozart painted by John Zoffany (authenticity doubtful).

Today we can no longer be certain when Wolfgang began or finished the sketch book. Some scholars believe that he still added to it in December.[5] At any rate, the works in it fill the gap between the sonatas printed in Paris (K. 6–9) and those printed in London (K. 10–15). It therefore throws some light on Wolfgang's activities during this important phase of his development. With this little book, some portions of it written with a blunt pencil, others with a pen, we enter into the private musical world of the child Mozart. Early in the twentieth century, when these forty-three little pieces became known, they elicited much comment and received greatly differing evaluations. They ranged from euphoria and boundless admiration for the child's genius[6] to more sober assessments,[7] the latter concluding that the eight-year-old, unaided by his father, was by no means secure in his command of musical materials. Hermann Abert, one of the outstanding Mozart scholars, shared this opinion:

> This notebook clearly contradicts the notion that the young Mozart, during the London days, already showed himself to be a master of composition. Much of the praise that has been bestowed on the son in that regard must be transferred to the father, who, in many cases, put in order what the child had written. This may disappoint those who have nothing but unquestioning admiration for Mozart. More reasonable persons may actually feel a sense of relief when they realize that Mozart developed earlier and more rapidly than ordinary mortals, but in a healthy, not capricious, manner.[8]

Given these varying interpretations, it is worth noting that not a single one of the forty-three pieces in the sketch book found its way into one of Mozart's "official" compositions, which for sketches would be normal, and which suggests that he considered them to be exercises.

In recent years, the English musician Eric Smith has orchestrated and recorded these sketches in a manner such as Wolfgang might have done, with the instruments that would have been available to him.[9] The result is surprising: much of what sounds awkward if played on the harpsichord alone displays tonal beauty that suggests a much more mature Mozart. Through these orchestrations we may find a partial answer to the question of whether the sketch book reveals any of Christian's influence from the five months when he was Wolfgang's teacher and mentor.

Wyzewa and Saint-Foix were the two Mozart scholars who first made a thorough study of Wolfgang's early compositions. They concluded that "nowhere in the works of his youth does Mozart reveal himself to us as clearly and directly as in these hastily written-down exercises."[10]

Maria Anna ("Nannerl") Mozart. Oil painting attributed to P. A. Lorenzoni, 1763.

Chelsea.

The two scholars were ahead of their time. They sought to explain Mozart's genius and its unfolding by examining his environment, including the influences to which he was exposed during his childhood months in London. Their method is in line with modern psychology, which considers the childhood period from age six to twelve as the time of acquiring mastery or control, of gaining ability to cope with the physical environment, and of becoming aware of self-identity.

> [The child] is also at this time becoming more aware of his own inner desires and impulses. . . . It is a period in which he gathers an enormous number of facts with which he can improve his ability to control his inner and outer worlds. . . . It is at this time that the shift from . . . "romantic learning" to "precision learning" takes place.[11]

The end of this period of acquiring control is also seen by psychologists as representing the end of childhood. Father Leopold, years later, was painfully aware of changes in the boy's behavior as he began to depart from his earlier unquestioning and spontaneous expression of love for his father. Wyzewa and Saint-Foix came to similar conclusions:

> Musically speaking, the months in London mark the end of his childhood. From now on he is a trained musician, aware of all aspects of musical style as practiced by those around him. . . . Throughout his life, Mozart had the feelings and imagination of a child; but after his ninth year, with regard to music, he was a child no longer.

Wyzewa and Saint-Foix leave no doubt about the one to whom Mozart owed this transformation. They call that person a "charming musician, and also the kindest, the most likeable, human being": John Christian Bach. Mozart, they continue, felt his influence soon after the family arrived in London. It was at first combined with other influences, but "increasingly, until 1768 and beyond, it replaced the influence of the father and of Schobert, *so that John Christian Bach became the only, the true teacher of Mozart*" (author's italics).[12]

Of the London Sketch Book the French scholars say that

> the first twenty-five short pieces, written in quick succession during the summer and fall of 1764, reveal perhaps more strikingly than music from any other period in Mozart's life how quickly his talent developed. The child's transformation into a master, a poet, is truly magical.

They believed that the remaining eighteen pieces were written later, probably between January and August of 1765, whereas Nannerl assigned the entire book to the summer months of 1764 in Chelsea.

Pages from the London Sketch Book containing the first preserved attempts at composition by the child Wolfgang, mostly written in Chelsea during Father Leopold's illness.

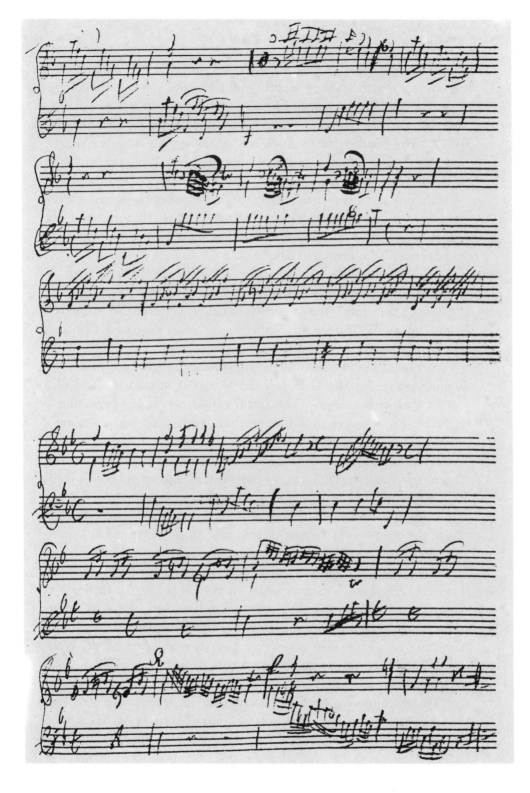

In view of these and other conflicting claims, it may be helpful to reconstruct those important months of the Mozarts' stay in England.

On 8 July 1764, Leopold Mozart came down with a serious illness. According to Nannerl, the children "were not allowed to touch the keyboard." The London Sketch Book was written at this time, at least the first twenty-five pieces. Nannerl also recalled that Wolfgang wrote his first symphony at this time.

On 5 August, Leopold was taken to Chelsea, where he rented a house in the country for his recuperation. The family moved there the next day. According to Wyzewa and Saint-Foix, a few of the sonatas that were soon to be printed were written in Chelsea.

By 13 September, Leopold had recovered sufficiently to write to Hagenauer,[13] giving details of his illness.

On 25 September, the Mozarts returned to London, taking quarters with Thomas Williamson in Thrift Street, Soho, very near Christian Bach's residence.

As mentioned before, this day in September might be considered a turning point. For the eight-year-old Mozart it marked the end of a period of experimentation. Though still a child, he was now beginning to stand on his own feet in musical matters, while still demonstrating a closeness to Christian Bach.

It seems appropriate here to stress Father Leopold's wisdom. At this juncture of Wolfgang's musical development, he did not stubbornly insist on his parental authority, as later writers liked to claim; rather, he gave Wolfgang free rein, even encouraging him to turn to John Christian Bach, the one person to whom the boy was strongly attracted as a musician and a human being.

It is touching to observe how the collaboration between Leopold and his son changed as the years went by. At first Leopold was completely in charge, writing down his son's every note. Gradually, the manuscripts show more sharing. Still, the degree to which Leopold was involved in the actual composing may never be completely established. Finally Wolfgang, out of necessity, wrote down his music himself. Copying music was a task he never relished.[14]

The three sonatas by Christian that Mozart transformed into keyboard concertos are good examples of "mixed" autographs. Their title, *Tre Sonate del Sigr. Giovanni Bach ridotte in Concerti dal Sigr. Amadeo Wolfgango Mozart,* is in Leopold's handwriting. He also wrote out the keyboard parts of all three concertos and supplied the figuration for the two bass parts (string bass and keyboard). The other string parts are in Wolfgang's hand. A fine example of the collaboration of the three musicians!

That Wolfgang turned to Christian for instruction should not be seen as a matter of course, for the spirit of Handel still hovered over the London music scene. One reason was the king's continued esteem for his former music master and his desire to preserve Handel's memory.[15] Handel's music was much performed at the time of the Mozarts' sojourn in England. During Lent of 1765, a veritable festival of Handel oratorios took place in London: no fewer than eleven performances in five weeks.[16] But times and public taste were changing, in spite of the king's championing of Handel. His music seemed noble and dignified, but the younger generation thought it stiff and learned, too heavy to compete with the charm and grace of the new style.

Leopold Mozart must have been aware of the changing tastes. While he may have endorsed Handel's music because of the king's fondness for it, he surely saw that Christian Bach and his style pointed to the future.

Nevertheless, Handel's style made an impression on Wolfgang, who heard not only his music but also that of John Christopher Smith, a composer then much in vogue in London, whose style, according to Wyzewa and Saint-Foix, resembled Handel's. They detected Smith's influence not only in Wolfgang's sonatas of that time, but even in a contrapuntal passage from his *Magic Flute*.

Handel's music affected and occupied Wolfgang throughout his life. Among the early Mozart sonatas just cited, the fourth, in F major, "still speaks of Schobert and the French esprit," while the others "reflect the more masculine, more original and bold beauty of Handel's music."[17] The French scholars viewed the last sonata of the set as a kind of turning point—a work in which the Andante maestoso movement recalls Handel, while the Allegro grazioso is reminiscent of Christian Bach.

Handel's strong impression on Mozart did indeed last. We note it again, more than twenty years later, when in 1788–89 Baron van Swieten in Vienna commissioned Mozart to provide a new orchestration and new recitatives for Handel's *Messiah*. (Prior to that Mozart had provided a new arrangement of *Acis and Galathea*).[18] And in certain portions of his last composition, the Requiem, that are entirely his own, Mozart made use of several Handel themes.[19]

Let us return to 25 September 1764, the day the Mozart family returned to London from Chelsea. By then the boy had not only tried his hand at writing small pieces; he had also, under Christian's tutelage, composed his first symphonies. In spite of Nannerl's recollections,[20] we cannot determine with accuracy which symphony was the first. We do know that, in a letter to Hagenauer, Leopold mentions a concert, planned for 15 February 1765, in which "all the symphonies will be by Wolfgang" but that he, Leopold, had had to write out all the parts. The authenticity of some of the early manuscripts, such as K. 17, has been doubted by Einstein, who believed that at least the first movement of K. 17 was stylistically too far removed from John Christian Bach's type of symphony.[21] Another example of the confusion surrounding these early symphonies is K. 18. Although Mozart's name appears nowhere on the manuscript, it was for a long time considered to have been composed by Mozart. Finally it was discovered that young Wolfgang had merely copied, note for note, the symphony in E-flat major by Christian's friend Carl Friedrich Abel.

Some of these early symphonies clearly show Christian Bach's imprint, especially K. 16 and 19. Of K. 16, Wyzewa and Saint-Foix say that it was "certainly inspired by Bach" and that one glance at the score sufficed "to recognize the closeness to Bach's overtures," meaning his Opus 3. They discuss the similarities in detail, comparing Mozart's Andante in C minor with slow movements by Bach, such as his C minor Andante in Op. 3, No. 2. They also point to the Finale, saying that the last movement of the Bach symphony just mentioned "was surely its godfather." They also call attention to the repetition of individual phrases and the alternating of forte and piano, devices both composers were fond of. They conclude that Bach's influence is clearly heard, along with a distinctly Italian style.

The three-movement layout of Mozart's symphonies also reflects the practice of Bach, who wrote only one four-movement symphony. The three-movement type, related to the Italian *sinfonia avanti l'opera*, was Christian's norm, and Mozart adopted it, even though not only his father but also Joseph Haydn in Austria and Johann Stamitz in Mannheim preferred the four-movement plan. In this regard, Wolfgang may have been catering to the formal precepts of his mentor as well as to the custom and taste found in London at the time. The likenesses are especially evident in his symphony K. 19.[22] This work resembles Christian's Op. 3, No. 1, both in the choice of keys for each movement (which in itself would not be unusual) and in the tempo markings: Allegro—Andante—Presto. The scoring of the two works is identical (two violins, viola, bass, two oboes, and two horns), as is their length. But above all, they are very much alike in musical substance and character.

There are similar fanfarelike phrases and contrasts of major and minor. The fast movements are especially light, spirited, and joyful, featuring the "singing allegro" manner that Bach bequeathed to his young friend. Quite remarkably, a certain elegiac elegance found in Bach's slow movements is even more pronounced in the corresponding movements by Mozart, an eight- to nine-year-old boy!

Wyzewa and Saint-Foix pointed out the startling similarities between Mozart's symphony K. 19 and Bach's Opus 3 symphonies. Other modern investigators, such as Carl de Nys, even speak of Mozart's "perfect imitations." One does gain the impression that Mozart wanted to prove, to himself and to the world, that he was able to write music worthy of the famous Bach. This objective may have been due not so much to burning ambition as to a desire to test his own skills. At this time, in the K. 16 and 19 symphonies, a teacher-student relationship is still evident. Wolfgang would later test himself in similar ways, but then as a master. His new version of Bach's aria "Non so d'onde viene," written for Aloysia Weber, comes to mind.[23]

That Bach adhered to the three-movement form of the opera sinfonia is understandable. As a composer of Italian operas, he made use of the customary Italian overture in three sections, or movements: fast—slow—fast. Such overtures were often heard in concerts away from the theater, too. Again, we cannot be sure which of Christian's opera overtures found their way into the collections of his concert symphonies; very few manuscripts include any relevant indications.

Mozart had ample opportunity to become acquainted with Bach's symphonies. He must have heard the overtures to *Artaserse*, *Catone in Utica*, and *Alessandro nell'Indie*. Though they belong to operas from Christian's years in Italy, the overtures were performed in London, as were those for *Orione* and *Zanaïda*, operas that had been heard in London before the Mozarts' arrival there. Before long, Mozart would also hear the overture to *Adriano in Siria* in its original context, that is, opening a performance of the opera itself. There were also the pasticci; Christian wrote overtures for several.[24]

All along, Mozart had demonstrated an interest in opera. One of his father's earliest letters from London addressed to Hagenauer mentions that "[Wolfgang] keeps thinking about an opera he wants to produce in Salzburg, with lots of young people. He often asks me to list all those whom he might sign up for the orchestra." Soon after their arrival in London, Leopold tried to meet people who might be helpful in connection with Wolfgang's emerging interest in opera. He was unsuccessful, however, because things had changed drastically for the coming 1764–65 season.

Sinfonie in D
KV 19

Mozart: Symphony in D Major, K. 19, written in London early in 1765. This work shows the influence of Christian Bach's symphony Op. 3, No. 1.

In his journal, right after listing "Mr. Bach and Mr. Abel, King Square, Soho," Leopold entered the names of two Italians: Regina Mingotti, still in charge as impresario, and the singer Angiola Sartori, scheduled to appear in the benefit concert of 22 May together with Wolfgang, who, however, had to cancel because of illness. Leopold also called on Mattia Vento, the opera composer who had been engaged by Mingotti and Giardini, and the male singers Giustinelli and Guglietti, whom Leopold had first met in the house of the "musico soprano" [castrato] Giuseppe Antonio Mazziotti in Brewers Street.

It was unfortunate for Leopold that, because of the 1763–64 season's inglorious end, none of them except Vento were destined to remain in London. Things moved rapidly. Giardini's *Enea e Lavinia* was the last opera of the season, premiered on 5 May and fated to have a short run. Five weeks later Mingotti left London, and the entire ensemble disbanded. But the Mozarts' disappointment was lessened because the 1764–65 season promised much, including another opera by Christian Bach. People also eagerly anticipated the arrival of the famous singer Giovanni Manzuoli. Burney remarked on the sensation he created.

> We are now arrived at a splendid period in the annals of the musical drama, when, by the arrival of GIOVANNI MANZOLI [born *c.* 1725], the serious opera acquired a degree of favour to which it had seldom mounted, since its first establishment in this country. The expectations which the great reputation of this performer had excited were so great, that at the opening of the theatre in November [24th], with the pasticcio of EZIO, there was such a crowd assembled at all the avenues, that it was with very great difficulty I obtained a place, after waiting two hours at the door.[25]

Once more problems arose; this time they were differences of opinion between Manzuoli and Bach, the reasons for which are not clear. It appears, however, that Christian was not overly impressed by the successes Manzuoli had reaped during the previous season in Madrid, for he showed himself unwilling to make the concessions demanded by the star singer. The ensuing events give us cause to revise our picture, valid until now, of Christian as being ever obliging.

According to Gertrude Harris, a lady of London society, there were tensions among the personnel of the King's Theatre that eventually disintegrated into a personal feud between Bach and Manzuoli. Things went from bad to worse, so that the singer "made a vow never to sing anything Bach had composed."[26]

The scandal became a chief topic of conversation; everyone wondered whether Bach would compose for Manzuoli and whether Manzuoli would stand by his oath and ignore Bach, London's favorite composer.

A kind of armed truce resulted. Christian took part in the new season, but when it opened on 24 November 1764 with the pasticcio *Ezio*, he merely contributed his old standby, the aria "Non so d'onde viene," which he had previously written for Raaff. Furthermore, Bach gave it, not to Manzuoli, but to Ercole Ciprandi, a lesser member of the ensemble, who was "deservedly applauded and generally encored" (Burney). Manzuoli may have been displeased.

Nor did Christian provide an aria for Manzuoli in the next pasticcio, *Berenice*, given early in January of 1765. Instead he restricted himself to an aria for Teresa Scotti, who had a thin but pleasing voice. She, too, succeeded; the aria "Confusa, smarrita" came from Bach's *Catone in Utica*. Burney deemed it the best of the "Favourite Songs" from this pasticcio.

To be sure, it was risky for Bach to present himself only with old arias sung by second-string singers, especially when other London composers were vying for the honor of writing for the great Manzuoli. Christian's behavior, whatever intrigues may have been involved, reminds us of the stubbornness occasionally shown by his father and brothers. In the disagreements with Mingotti, Christian may also deserve some of the blame.

Eventually everyone simmered down and a reconciliation took place. In Bach's new opera, *Adriano in Siria*, Manzuoli occupied his rightful place, singing the major role of Farnaspe. The excited and curious public made an even greater run on the box office than they had for the opening of *Ezio*. Burney noted that less than a third of those interested were able to gain admission; Walpole added that the house was so full that many were forced to listen to the performance from backstage.

Opinions were divided about the opera's success. While Walpole thought the performance was marvelous, Burney granted this rating only to the arias, saying that the opera as a whole had failed. Perhaps expectations had been too high, or the crush of people interfered with enjoyment. At any rate, *Adriano* was given only seven times, a great disappointment to the composer. According to Burney, this failure was "a great triumph for the Italians, who began to be jealous of the Germanic body of musicians at this time in the Kingdom." Perhaps this jealousy had been the real reason for Manzuoli's earlier refusal to sing anything by Bach. For him, opera was an Italian affair. And, indeed, the next opera at the King's Theatre, *Demofoonte*, was composed by an Italian.

The restored harmony between Christian and Manzuoli was all to the good. It even included the young Mozart, who was beginning to be seen in a different light. Earlier he had been merely a cause for amazement, a child prodigy. Now, after Chelsea, he began to find recognition as a musician in his own right. People valued his opinions; he took part in social gatherings. In his *Memoirs,* William Jackson recalls how, at a gathering in Bach's apartment, people were

> looking over Bach's famous song "Se spiego" in *Zanaïda.* The score was inverted to Mozart who was rolling on the table. He pointed out a note which he said was wrong. It was so, whether of the composer or copyist I cannot now recollect, but it was an instance of extraordinary discernment and readiness in a mere infant.[27]

If, soon after arriving in London, Wolfgang thought continually about opera, this would be understandable: it was the beginning of a season during which Italian opera was most splendidly presented at the Haymarket, featuring an ensemble, headed by Manzuoli, that was unequalled anywhere. Never before or after did the King's Theatre achieve such high standards. It was also fortunate that Manzuoli gave vocal instruction to his young friend Mozart: he, the great Manzuoli, one of the last representatives of the old school of male sopranos, who insisted on teaching comprehensive musicianship as well as vocal technique. No wonder that "Manzuoli-like singing" became an expression Mozart continued to use. When he was only thirteen, he wrote *La finta semplice,* an Italian opera that could stand comparison with those of the best German composers. In the future, Wolfgang would always show sure judgment of the possibilities and limits of voices, applying this knowledge to his own vocal compositions. His talent along these lines was nurtured by the opportunities he had in London to listen to arias by Christian Bach and to receive vocal instruction from Manzuoli.

Baron Grimm, quoted earlier, tells us in his *Correspondance littéraire* that Wolfgang also sang. "He [Mozart] heard Manzuoli during an entire London season. From this he benefited, for although his voice is extremely weak, he sings with feeling and taste."[28] Sister Nannerl also recalled that he "sang arias with much feeling."

The person who gave us the most lively and detailed description of the young Mozart at this time was the English scientist Daines Barrington. A jurist by profession, he was also at home in geology and other natural sciences and in history, as well. Barrington thoroughly examined the nine-year-old in all musical subjects. The boy was not only willing but enthusiastic about being tested, enjoying, in a mischievous way, the opportunity to show what he could do. According to Barrington, opera was the first area in which he displayed "amazing, incredible" talents.

> I carried to him a manuscript duet, which was composed by an English gentleman to some favourite words in Metastasio's opera Demofoonte. The whole score was in five parts, viz. accompaniments for a first and second violin, the two vocal parts, and a base. I shall here likewise mention, that the parts for the first and second voice were written in what the Italians stile the *Contralto* cleff; the reason for taking note of which particular will appear hereafter.
>
> My intention in carrying with me this manuscript composition, was to have an irrefragable proof of his abilities, as a player at sight, it being absolutely impossible that he could have ever seen the music before.
>
> The score was no sooner put upon his desk, than he began to play the symphony in a most masterly manner, as well as in the time and style which corresponded with the intention of the composer. . . . The symphony ended, he took the upper part, leaving the under one to his father. His voice in the tone of it was thin and infantine, but nothing could exceed the masterly manner in which he sung. . . . He not only . . . did complete justice to the duet, by singing his own part in the truest taste, and with the greatest precision: he also threw in the accompaniments of the two violins, wherever they were most necessary, and produced the best effects. . . . When he had finished the duet, he expressed himself highly in approbation, asking with some eagerness whether I had brought any more such music. . . . Happening to know that little Mozart was much taken notice of by Manzoli, the famous singer, who came over to England in 1764, I said to the boy, that I should be glad to hear an extempory *Love Song*, such as his friend Manzoli might choose in an opera.
>
> The boy on this (who continued to sit at his harpsichord) looked back with much archness, and immediately began five or six lines of a jargon recitative to introduce a love song. He then played a symphony which might correspond with an air composed to the single word, *Affetto.* . . . Finding that he was in humour, and as it were inspired, I then desired him to compose a *Song of Rage*, such as might be proper for the opera stage. The boy again looked back with much archness, and began five or six lines of a jargon recitative proper to precede a *Song of Anger*. This lasted about the same time with the *Song of Love*, and in the middle of it, he had worked himself up to such a pitch, that he beat his harpsichord like a person possessed, rising sometimes in his chair. The word he pitched upon for this second extempory composition was, *Perfido.*[29]

In passing, Barrington mentions a little incident that reminds us that Wolfgang, in spite of his amazing musical genius, still was a child:

> While he was playing for me, a favourite cat came in, upon which he immediately left his harpsichord, nor could we bring him back for a considerable time. He would also sometimes run about the room with a stick between his legs by way of a horse.

In London, Wolfgang also composed arias of his own, including "Va, dal furor portata," K. 19c/21, his first preserved vocal composition of any kind. It wasn't enough for Manzuoli; not until seven years later would he appear in Mozart's *Ascanio in Alba*. Instead, Wolfgang wrote the aria for Ercole Ciprandi, a tenor who at the time sang a minor role in *Ezio*. Wolfgang took the text of the tenor aria from that pasticcio. It is doubtful that Ciprandi sang the aria in an actual performance; had he done so, Leopold, a conscientious chronicler when it came to Wolfgang's accomplishments, would surely have mentioned it in his letters.

Mozart's Italian arias, whether early or later, all have one thing in common: they clearly reveal the proximity of John Christian Bach. The relation can even be detected between arias in Mozart's last Italian opera, *Tito*, and arias in *Orione*, *Adriano*, and other Bach works, as Wyzewa and St. Foix pointed out. They also noted that

> the arias are lighter, more natural, and considerably shorter than those of Galuppi and Lampugnani. . . . Melodic phrases are more concise, with cleaner contours. By introducing choruses and small ensembles and by adding new instruments to the orchestra, [Christian] managed to attract and hold the attention of the general public and to bring about a rapprochement of traditional opera and the increasingly popular opera buffa. . . . When it came to opera, Mozart completely absorbed the style and spirit of John Christian Bach. . . . Even if later impressions went beyond Bach's influence, Mozart became his direct successor.[30]

Adriano in Siria was Bach's only opera for the 1764–65 season. Perhaps to satisfy Manzuoli, the managers of the King's Theatre offered works by two other composers, one Italian, the other English. Vento's *Demofoonte*, premiered on 2 March 1765, was fairly well received. Burney found that "the airs are natural, graceful and pleasing; always free from vulgarity, but never very new or learned." Thomas Arne's *L'Olimpiade*, given on 27 April 1765, met with little success. Burney attributed this to the fact that Arne, so successful with comic opera in English, "had written for vulgar singers and hearers too long to comport himself properly at the Opera-house." Another reason may have been that the London public was beginning to tire of opera. Then, too, there was the competing Covent Garden Theatre, where *The Beggar's Opera* attracted large crowds.

A general malaise prevailed, for everyone knew that Manzuoli and Tenducci were leaving London at the end of the season. In early March, Manzuoli gave a benefit performance, for which occasion Giardini had dressed up his opera *Il Re Pastore* with a few new arias. Manzuoli could not complain about the profit; according to the *Gentleman's Magazine*, he

> got no less, after paying all charges of every kind, than 1000 guineas. This, added to the sum of 1500, which he has already saved, and the remaining profits of the season, is surely an undoubted proof of British generosity; one patriotic lady, we are told, complimented the above gentleman with a 200-pound bill for a single ticket on that occasion.[31]

The other star, Tenducci, had to be satisfied with less. He gave his benefit performance at the end of March in the pasticcio *Antigonus*. He was Bach's "bosom pal" (Mozart), the two being connected by a lifelong friendship in spite of the singer's many escapades. Tenducci was one of opera's most colorful personalities; the events of his life sound like the story of an eighteenth-century rogue.

Born in Siena around 1736, he was approximately Christian Bach's age. After arriving in London in 1758, he experienced several unpleasant interruptions of his operatic career. Thus he spent the better part of 1760 in jail because of the debts his carefree lifestyle had led him to incur. Still, he was loved by the public, common and aristocratic opera fans alike. From prison he issued a heart-rending appeal for help (*Public Advertiser*, 13 January 1761).[32] A benefit concert was arranged; directed by Abel, it took place in the Great Music Room on Dean Street, Soho. Everyone was interested and amused to learn how the singer was taken in a locked coach from prison to the concert hall and then, after singing his benefit concert, was returned to King's Bench Prison to serve the rest of his sentence.

Tenducci was a castrato. Nevertheless, a year after the end of the opera season, he abducted and married a student, a certain Dorothy Maunsell. Before long there was a divorce, for which she avenged herself by publishing an account of her marital experiences: "A true and genuine narrative of Mr. and Mrs. Tenducci." Not to be outdone in indiscretion, Tenducci countered by making "amazing" revelations about his *three* marriages, the account being published in Casanova's memoirs.[33]

As an artist, however, Tenducci was outstanding. Unlike many sing-

The singer Giustino Ferdinando Tenducci, Bach's good friend.

Giovanni Manzuoli, shown with another well-known singer of the day, Gaetano Guadagni (right).

ers whose voices begin to deteriorate by the time they reach the age of fifty, Tenducci sang better than ever. He was in such demand that he received a firm appointment at London's Drury Lane Theatre, until his death in 1790. After 1784 he also directed the Handel festivals in Westminster.

Bach and Tenducci got along famously. Though the singer accepted engagements on the Continent, he always returned to London. It also happened more than once that in order to avoid his creditors he fled to Ireland or Scotland. Bach's fondness for Scottish songs may have been stimulated by Tenducci.

No matter what his lifestyle, Tenducci was Bach's true and faithful friend. He was the one, the only one, who four years after Bach's death organized a memorial concert in the Hanover Square Rooms. Together with two female singers, he performed various works by the "justly celebrated master." According to the *Public Advertiser*, "the angelic genius of Bach appeared to inspire the performance in a superlative degree."[34]

Let us return to the 1764–65 season and to Tenducci's and Manzuoli's farewell concerts. They were joined by the singer Clementina Cremonini in a "Concert of Music composed and directed by Mr. Bach." The situation confronting Christian was similar to what he had faced on his arrival in England: the future of London opera was in doubt. Public interest had diminished, for the management's attempt to restore balance in the repertory had failed. (To the German Bach, they had added an Italian and an English composer, as mentioned earlier.) The operagoing public showed more interest in a rather trivial dispute: was it fashionable to attend the Tuesday night performances?

Until then, operas had always been given on Tuesday and Saturday nights, but only Saturday was considered socially acceptable. High society looked down on whatever was presented on Tuesdays—until Manzuoli's farewell performance (in the pasticcio *Il Solimano*) was scheduled for 14 May 1765, a Tuesday. Tradition-bound society was thrown into confusion. Five years earlier, a reader of the *Public Advertiser* had already voiced the same complaint in the form of a poem entitled "The Opera—Tuesday's complaint to her sister Saturday."[35] Now readers urged Mr. Woodfall, the *Advertiser*'s editor, to prevail with Manzuoli to move all other *Solimano* performances to Saturdays. It seems to have been the only topic that caused excitement during this season.

Aware of the situation, Bach soon turned to a genre of music in which his mastery was beyond doubt: the instrumental concerto. As time would tell, it was a genre in which his success was far more lasting. The change made sense. Opera formed only one part, albeit the most brilliant, in the totality of London's musical life. It was chiefly patronized by the privileged upper class, for whom opera was a social event. Music making on a far broader base took place in various middle-class clubs and societies. Perhaps more than any other large European city, London had a rich and varied concert life that took place in the city's major halls or in inns such as The Devil's Tavern on the Thames.[36]

Concert-giving organizations included the St. Cecilian Society, the Academy of Ancient Music, and the Castle Society of Music. Some of the more socially oriented groups, such as the Madrigal Society and the Noblemen's and Gentlemen's Catch Club, had members who enjoyed singing catches (rounds) and glees (simple part songs for male voices). Other societies had been formed to support indigent members and their families, for instance, the Corporation of the Sons of the Clergy. Their annual Founder's Day concerts, including the Handel performances attended by the Mozarts, were high points of London's concert seasons.

From 1760 on, these activities received additional support from an enterprising singer, Mrs. Teresa Cornelys. As Signora Pompeati, she had appeared in 1746 at the King's Theatre in performances of Gluck's *La Caduta de' Giganti*. After another guest appearance at the Little Haymarket Theatre, she settled in London; by then she had married a Dutchman, whose name she took. Mrs. Cornelys resided—one might say, reigned—in the elegant Carlisle House in Soho.

At the time, Soho was a northern suburb of London, near Oxford Street. Originally it had been a residential district preferred by the aristocracy; among others, the earls of Bolingbroke, Carlisle, and Fauconberg lived there. In time, artists, publishers, and instrument makers moved into the area. Soho (or King's) Square consisted of a large, well-kept garden, enclosed by wrought iron fences. It invited strolling: coaches had to remain outside. Four wide footpaths divided the square into four rectangles. A statue of Charles II formed the centerpiece; at his feet, river gods emptied jugs of water into a basin.

New Carlisle House (the old one was located to the West, in King's Square Court) was an imposing corner building right on Soho Square, on the south side of Sutton Street, one of the five streets that bordered on the square. Mrs. Cornelys had made her home "the most magnificent place of entertainment in Europe." A Chinese bridge connected the mansion itself with the ballroom behind it. The large halls had blue and yellow satin wall coverings. Here as many as six hundred dancers might at times be found, having paid two guineas admission each. Dancing, masquerades, and card games seem to have been the chief attractions, until Bach and Abel arranged for entertainment on a higher level. Their subscription concerts were the first of their kind in Europe.

In 1764 or early 1765, Bach and Abel had given up their quarters in Meard's Street for the more prestigious address in Soho, renting an apartment in the house of Domenico Angelo, a riding and fencing master, in King's Square Court. They were only a few steps away from Soho Square and Mrs. Cornelys's residence. Across the street was the house of the Spanish ambassador, a Count de Fuentes. An unusual tenant also lived in that building: the magician Merlin. Terry relates an amusing incident that also gives us some idea of the carefree lifestyle in the district around Soho Square. Merlin enjoyed appearing as a mysterious magician who amazed and frightened his audience with his "magic inventions." His peculiar behavior was the talk of all London. On one occasion he had constructed a pair of roller skates, which he decided to demonstrate in Carlisle House. Holding a violin in one hand and waving a bow with the other, he barged in on Mrs. Cornelys's elegant party, "gyrating nimbly as he played; but, having invented no brake to retard his velocity, dashed with great force into a costly mirror, damaging himself severely and the furniture irreparably."[37]

To be sure, Mrs. Cornelys's plans had been for more serious social gatherings, enhanced by music. On 30 December 1760, she announced in the *Public Advertiser* that the "Society in Soho Square" would have its third and fourth meetings on 1 and 15 January 1761, and invited the subscribers to arrive at seven o'clock. She later planned regular morning and evening concerts, whose direction she entrusted to Gioacchino Cocchi—the same Cocchi who, as Bach's predecessor, had had a rather luckless season as a composer at King's Theatre.

He may have done no better at Carlisle House, for Bach succeeded him there, too. Christian's transition from opera to concert was abrupt. On 23 January 1765, that is, three days before his *Adriano in Siria* was mounted, he presented himself to the public with the first of the soon to be famous "Bach-Abel Concerts." Other concerts followed every Wednesday, during the same period as the six remaining performances of *Adriano*. These events soon became known as the "Soho Subscription Concerts." They were so popular that the thing to do for London society was to go to the opera on Tuesday and attend a concert on Wednesday. Cornelys showed great concern for the comfort of her guests, who had purchased subscriptions for five guineas. To cope with complaints about excessive heat, she had ventilators installed upstairs; she also arranged for

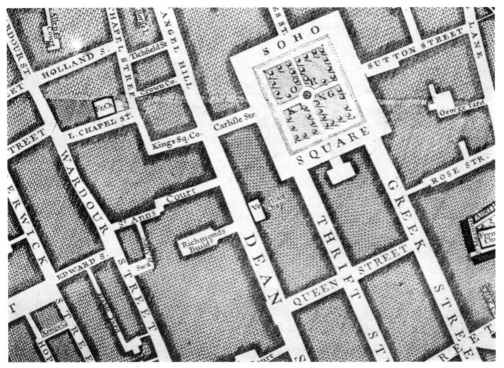

London. Detail of a map showing Soho or King's Square, where Christian Bach lived.

Soho Square from the south. Sutton Street is at the right (east); Carlisle House, where the Bach-Abel concerts were given for some time, is on the S. E. corner.

tea to be served downstairs.

Since the six concerts of the first season were highly successful, their number was increased to fifteen the following year and the year thereafter. For greater comfort in the limited space, the number of subscriptions was limited to two hundred ladies and two hundred gentlemen, though by 1768 it was decided to rent a larger hall to accommodate those who had been turned away.

Details about the programs have not been preserved. Bach probably provided the lion's share of the music, contributing symphonies and keyboard concertos, along with overtures and the most popular airs from his operas. Abel may have presented some of his almost twenty symphonies, and he probably also appeared as soloist. To make the programs as attractive as possible, stars from the opera were billed, including Cremonini, Tenducci, and Ciprandi. Outstanding instrumentalists were also featured, especially a promising young violinist, the twenty-three-year-old François-Hippolyte Barthélémon from Bordeaux. He had served in the French army. In 1764, the earl of Kelly, a friend of his commanding officer and an ardent music lover, had brought him to England, where he soon conquered London's audiences. When the two Mozart children first appeared in public, Barthélémon, together with the cellist Cirri, provided that concert's musical frame. His tone was so exceptionally beautiful that the three-year-old Prince of Wales said to his father, the king: "Papa! Surely there is a flute in Mr. Barthélémon's violin!" which he then eagerly tried to find.[38]

Barthélémon soon became a welcome guest at court; his star rose quickly. Promoted to concertmaster at the King's Theatre in 1766, he also made his debut there as a composer with his opera *Pelopida*. He married the singer Mary Young and belonged to the inner circle of London's musical elite, appearing as a virtuoso at the Bach-Abel concerts. Leopold Mozart, soon after his arrival in London, called on the city's leading instrumentalists. In his journal, Barthélémon's name appears right after that of the singer Cremonini.

The Mozarts had also found lodging in the fashionable district around Soho Square, staying with Thomas Williamson on Thrift Street, close to Bach's residence and to Mrs. Cornelys's establishment. It was a good location for the visitors, who were eager to make a place for themselves in London's concert world. But the Bach-Abel concerts presented formidable competition. They were so well established and prestigious that Father Leopold may well have wondered how his two children might make their mark with concerts of their own. Their first sensational appearances were behind them; the public was now hungry for new attractions.

The royal couple also seemed to be less fascinated; they only showed interest in the upcoming premiere of Bach's next opera, *Adriano in Siria*. They were distracted by political problems; the opposition had been gaining strength ever since unrest in the American colonies had begun, partly because of new laws affecting taxation. The king reacted as he always preferred to do when trouble was brewing: accompanied by his family, he retreated to the country. Disrespectful subjects called him "Farmer George."

Only once more did the king and queen invite the Mozart children to Buckingham Palace. On 25 October 1764, the fourth anniversary of George III's coronation, Wolfgang and his sister again played for the royal family from six to ten o'clock. It would be their last visit to the palace, even though their stay in England extended to July of the following year. In a letter to Hagenauer, Leopold briefly refers to the occasion. For once he said nothing about the gratuity they were offered, but he did mention money in connection with the sonatas dedicated to the queen, who made Wolfgang a present of fifty guineas. Leopold's letter was written in March, whereas the dedication is dated 18 January. Apparently the royal exchequer had been in no hurry to pay the honorarium.

Leopold was beginning to worry about finances. Not only did he have to provide for his family; he also had to think about the continuation of their travels.

Baron Grimm, in Paris, showed himself a true friend of the Mozarts and tried to make use of his good connections. In December 1764, Grimm wrote to Prince Ernst Ludwig of Saxony-Gotha, suggesting that he put in a good word for the Mozarts with his mother, who had good connections to the English court. Grimm explains how the father had been at death's door and how his convalescence had lasted three months. To recapture the summer's losses, they were planning a series of concerts at Mrs. Cornelys's in Soho Square. One of the prominent members of the "Soho Concert" was the Duke of York, the king's brother. "If His Royal Highness would extend his protection to the Mozart children, their concert would certainly succeed and the problem would be solved."[39]

If Prince Ernst Ludwig's mother did intercede, it was to no avail. The king's feelings toward the Mozarts were friendly, but political worries preoccupied him. Moreover, he was not on good terms with his brother. Meanwhile, the public's interest was focused on Bach's new opera and on his forthcoming concerts, scheduled to take place in Mrs. Cornelys's

Mrs. Cornelys.

The New Carlisle House.

establishment, which was fully booked. There is a certain irony in this: Bach, young Mozart's dear friend and mentor, in this way unintentionally kept the Mozart children from appearing in the new, attractive Carlisle House, forcing them to settle for less desirable locales.

To make matters worse, their concert in Little Haymarket Theatre, planned for 15 February, had to be postponed because several participants were needed for a performance of Arne's oratorio *Judith*. A notice to that effect appeared in the *Public Advertiser* on 14 February, and another postponement was announced the following day.[40]

All these setbacks only increased Leopold's financial worries. "Now I must be careful with money. Whatever I plan to do requires money. A long journey lies ahead of me; I must find ways for others to pay our way." In the same letter, Leopold makes a cryptic remark about Christian: "We know what Mr. Bach is like!" This comment may have been prompted by a reference made by Hagenauer to Anton Cajetan Adlgasser.

Adlgasser was Leopold Mozart's colleague in the Salzburg court chapel. The archbishop had granted him a leave of absence for 1764–65 to study in Italy. Perhaps Leopold had urged Adlgasser to ask Christian for a letter of recommendation (to Padre Martini?), which Christian may have failed to supply.

The concert by Wolfgang and Nannerl, which finally took place on 21 February, was not a success, in spite of the announcement that "All the Overtures will be from the Composition of these astonishing Composers [sic], only eight years old."[41] Receipts did not live up to the father's expectations, amounting to a total of 130 guineas, or only 100 guineas after expenses. "This is due to the many amusements here—so many that people tire of them." Leopold then hints darkly: "I know well why we are not being treated more generously; I did not accept an offer made to me." He does not elaborate except to say that "there is no use talking about a matter that I declined to consider, after much thinking and several sleepless nights. It now is behind me. I cannot bring up my children in such a dangerous place, where most people have no religion and where one sees nothing but bad examples."

We can only guess at the reason for this sudden change in Leopold's mood. It suggests that there may have been religious reasons for which he, a Catholic, was not received with open arms. Was he offered a permanent appointment in England, with the condition that he change his religious affiliation? Whatever the problem, he was gravely concerned. In the same letter he reports about a baptism. He was irritated because those present belonged to different denominations. It was "too bad that the gathering did not also include a Jew."

A mysterious reference to Jews occurs in Leopold's travel journal. There is a separate entry, marked "Jews," in which he lists the names "Zuns, Liebmann, de Simon, and Frenck," names of traders or brokers, twelve of whom had been admitted to do business in London, beginning in 1754. This list led to the belief that Leopold, due to his financial predicament, may have considered some monetary transactions,[42] a possibility that cannot be dismissed outright. Thus he wrote to Hagenauer asking him to send sixty copies each of Wolfgang's Paris sonatas to the printers and booksellers Johann Jakob Lotter in Augsburg and Johann Ulrich Haffner in Nürnberg, hoping that they would sell them. He also hoped to derive some income from the children's portraits that had been engraved in Paris, asking Hagenauer to send copies to the same two merchants, and to be sure to obtain receipts.

Other, more down-to-earth, commissions also occupied Leopold as he began to contemplate his return to Salzburg. "Anyone planning to buy nice men's or women's watches . . . should wait till I return." Watches seem to have had a special attraction for Leopold, even if they were expensive. "Gold watches here sell for upward of twelve guineas, depending on whether they are plain or decorated." He would be glad to bring back gold watches for some Salzburg friends, and he asked Hagenauer to contact "Mme. von Robin[43] and ask her to tell him how much she was prepared to pay. . . . I know reliable people here; they would be more than happy to make the best selections for me."

Leopold's interests went beyond such matters. He was fascinated by all that London had to offer. His letters are as detailed and vivid as the descriptions of any travel writer. It is greatly to his credit that he included the children in his explorations, especially at this time, when there were fewer demands for them to perform. Owing to their constant travels, both children were woefully lacking in formal education, and Leopold tried to compensate for this deficiency by broadening their horizons while away from home.

The trio systematically visited the sights of London. Nannerl kept her own diary, less wordy than her father's and amusing to read because of her imaginative spelling of English proper names. She was impressed by a "young elephant in the park" and by "a donkey with white and brown stripes; you couldn't have painted them on any better." The child recorded her visits to all the famous attractions: the pleasure gardens, Westminster Bridge and church, the Greenwich Observatory, the British Museum, and so on.

Leopold used their free time well for these educational activities. At the same time he tried hard to revive the public's flagging interest in the children's concertizing. A tried and true way to do this was to hint at their impending departure. An announcement in the *Public Advertiser* of 11 March tries to do just that:

By Desire

For the benefit of Master MOZART, of eight Years, and Miss MOZART, of Twelve Years of Age,[44] prodigies of Nature, before their Departure from England, which will be in six Weeks Time.

THERE will be performed, at the End of this Month, or the Beginning of April next, a Concert of Vocal and Instrumental MUSIC.

Tickets at Half a Guinea each.

To be had of Mr. Mozart, at Mr. Williamson's in Thrift-street, Soho; where those Ladies and Gentlemen who will honour him with their Company from Twelve to Three in the Afternoon, any Day in the Week, except Tuesday and Friday, may, by taking each a ticket, gratify their Curiosity, and not only hear this young Music Master and his Sister perform in private; but likewise try his surprising musical capacity, by giving him any Thing to play at Sight, or any Music without Bass, which he will write upon the Spot, without recurring to his Harpsichord.

The Day and Place of the Concert will be advertised in the *Public Advertiser* eight Days before.

By the end of the month, however, no concert had yet taken place, and Leopold had to make new concessions. The next announcement, on 9 April, was similarly worded, but the price of admission had been lowered to five shillings. There is also a discreet reminder that "the Sonatas composed by this Boy, and dedicated to her Majesty," are for sale. The announcement still does not mention a date for the concert; only in the 10 May *Advertiser* do we read that it will be given on 13 May.

This, the children's "final" appearance, took place in Hickford's Great Room in Brewer Street. Once more Cremonini, Barthélémon, and Cirri assisted as vocal and instrumental soloists.

What made this event especially important was the instrument on which the children performed. This was the new two-manual harpsichord built by the well-known Swiss maker, Burkhart Tschudi (by then working in England, using the name Shudi) for King Frederick II of Prussia. For Leopold this event occasioned another report to Salzburg. An article in the Salzburg *Europaeische Zeitung* of 6 August 1765 was probably written by the proud father. We read that

It was wise of Herr Tschudi to have this remarkable instrument [Leopold calls it *Flügel*, at this time still meaning harpsichord] played for the first time by the most extraordinary clavier player in the world, namely the very famous . . . nine-year-old master of music Wolfgang Mozart, the remarkable son of the Salzburg Kapellmeister Mozart. It was also enchanting to hear the fourteen-year-old sister of this little virtuoso play the most difficult sonatas on one *Flügel* with her brother providing impromptu accompaniments on another. Their achievements are truly miraculous.

Inspired by this occasion, and at the suggestion of Bach, Wolfgang may have composed the four-hand piano sonata K. 19d, not published until 1921. Leopold assumed that it was the first such work by any composer. "Wolfgangerl wrote his first piece for four hands," he proudly announced to Hagenauer, adding that "up to now, no one has written a four-hand sonata." Whether or not the claim is true, the work holds an important place among those Mozart wrote under Bach's guidance.[45]

Even this little sensation was not enough to ensure the concert's financial success. After the disappointing results of the last public concerts, Leopold had resorted to presenting the children at home; now he found it necessary to move their appearances to a second-rate inn, far from fashionable Soho: the Swan and Harp Tavern in Cornhill. Notices about the event appeared in the *Public Advertiser*.[46] (See page 240.)

All these efforts cause one to wonder: could Christian Bach have done more to help? After all, he was a key figure in London's musical world; he had influential patrons and was *persona gratissima* at court. We may assume that he did all he could but that even his efforts were hampered by the plethora of competing musical events during the winter and spring of 1765.

He was also extremely busy at the time, being in charge of four of the Bach-Abel concerts (23 January, 6 February, 6 March, and 19 March), while Abel directed the other two (30 January and 27 March). He therefore had to supply works of his own, preferably new ones, and line up compositions by others. At that time, he was largely responsible for managing the concerts; later he was entirely in charge.

In addition, as already mentioned, there were seven performances of *Adriano* at the King's Theatre, for which he had at least partial responsibility. And also, for the first time, he contributed arias to a comic opera, to be given at Covent Garden Theatre, a rival institution.

The Covent Garden season had opened on 31 January, only a few days after the first performance of *Adriano*, with *The Maid of the Mill*, which included music by several composers. Busy though he was, Bach contributed an aria, "Trust me," and the duet "My Life, My Joy, My Blessing." (Bach never wrote an entire light opera.) Christian's participation might be seen merely as an example of his industry and versatility were it not that one of the aims of Covent Garden was to challenge the all-powerful reign of Italian opera. Manzuoli was no doubt displeased.

The moving force behind the Covent Garden effort was John Beard, a "very well trained singer with an expressive if not very ingratiating voice,"[47] who had married the director's daughter. When his father-in-law died in 1761, Beard became co-owner of the theater. He had intended all along to establish some equilibrium, to stem the flood of foreign composers and singers by employing local talent. He accomplished this aim with some serious operas but chiefly with lighter fare that could be cast with singing actors and would be sung in English. These works included pasticci such as *The Maid of the Mill* and *Love in a Village*; they consisted of a succession of simple popular songs, for which new texts had often been written. Beard's trump card, however, was *The Beggar's Opera*, first given in 1728; by this time its success had become well established.[48] Beard himself played the role of Macheath (Mack the Knife in the twentieth-century *Threepenny Opera*) and was largely responsible for the success of this mixture of farce, ballads, and opera. As a genre, ballad opera proved extremely successful, presenting to the audience not gods, goddesses, or heroes, but thieves and murderers—a picture of London's underworld never before portrayed onstage. Its music was equally startling. John Christopher Pepusch, the composer, had been born in Berlin and settled in London around the turn of the century. For *The Beggar's Opera*, he provided settings of sixty-nine popular songs, the texts having been modified to fit the plot. The resulting piece of music theater, in English, was enthusiastically received as a welcome change from the traditional Italian opera presented at the King's Theatre.

The Beggar's Opera became socially acceptable when the court attended a performance in October 1764—a daring thing to do, considering that the story includes biting social criticism aimed at the government's ill treatment of the poor. The 1764–65 season, when the work was repeatedly given, was a period of much political unrest.

To witness such unrest may have frightened the Mozarts, especially Father Leopold, who believed in the divinely ordained role of government. During the winter there had been uprisings by the silk weavers, who were protesting the import of French products. Leopold was amazed by what he saw. In a letter to Salzburg, he described the crush of

Some of the satirical paintings and engravings by William Hogarth deal with opera and operatic practices of his time.

Left: the prison scene from *The Beggar's Opera*, parodying Italian opera seria.

Below: a painting from Hogarth's cycle *The Rake's Progress*, here making fun of the castrato Farinelli, surrounded by admirers.

people—thousands in the streets carrying black flags, wearing "their untidy green aprons, just as they did at work." The king's guard was finally able to disperse the protesters. Quite likely Wolfgang saw *The Beggar's Opera* and the uprisings, too, leaving impressions that may have resurfaced when he was working on *Figaro*.

Bach's connection to *The Beggar's Opera* was restricted to his acquaintance with one of the singers, Charlotte Brent. When she was barely twenty years old, she had been spectacularly successful in the role of Polly, her debut. She sang it in thirty-seven successive performances. Perhaps Bach's interest in her was not only professional; at any rate, she provided an ongoing contact with Covent Garden Theatre.

Brent sang to great acclaim in the musical comedy *The Summer's Tale*, a pasticcio. For this occasion, Christian revived for her an aria from *Zanaïde*, "Se spiego le prime vele," providing it (originally a tenor aria) with a new text: "Nature, when she gave us pleasure." It became one of Brent's great hits. (The aria later surfaced for the third time as one of the Vauxhall songs made popular by Bach's favorite pupil, Mrs. Weichsell.) Bach also contributed a new aria, "So profound an impression I bear," sung by the actor Mattocks, and a duet for the star team of Beard and Brent, "Yes, 'tis plain she sees me tremble."[49]

Compared with Bach's busy life, the Mozarts' activities during their last months in England seem insignificant. As mentioned earlier, their appearances (one can hardly call them concerts) took place in humble inns and taverns. One wonders why Leopold, usually a good planner and intent on maintaining high standards, had not decided to leave England much earlier.

No further support from the king could be expected. During the previous winter, the first signs of his mental derangement had appeared; they were to recur at regular intervals and led to his death in 1811. Walpole observed that there was widespread concern. He wrote to the earl of Hertford that the king looked pale but that it was the custom to announce that he was well; "I only wish it were true."[50]

Nothing seemed to go well for the Mozarts; nevertheless Leopold was reluctant to set a departure date. Friends in Salzburg were anxious for them to return; Frau Hagenauer sent word that she hoped they "would not stay in London forever." Leopold replied: "Please allow me to complete what I started out to do with God's help. . . . God will not forsake an honest German." To be on the safe side, however, he asked Hagenauer to have six Masses celebrated, to "calm the waves during our return trip across the sea."

Once again Leopold had inserted three notices in the *Public Advertiser* (8, 9, and 11 July), a last attempt to remind the public of their existence. The wording is especially urgent; in these final notices, addressed "To all Lovers of Sciences," Leopold states:

> The Father of this Miracle, being obliged by Desire of several Ladies and Gentlemen to postpone, for a very short Time, his Departure from England, will give an Opportunity to hear this little Composer and his Sister, whose musical Knowledge wants not Apology. . . . The Two Children will play also together with four Hands upon the same Harpsichord, and put upon it a Handkerchief, without seeing the Keys.[51]

If the public seemed less than eager, admiration was still extended to the children from other quarters. Thus the venerable British Museum requested Leopold to deposit some of Wolfgang's compositions in their collection. Leopold complied by giving to the museum the autograph of an a cappella chorus for four voices, "God is Our Refuge," K. 20. It is Wolfgang's first choral work of any kind and the only one he ever wrote on an English text. Leopold's gift also included one copy each of the sonatas published in Paris and London, and the engraving, based on the portrait by Louis Carrogi, called Caramontelle, which shows the father and the two child prodigies. The museum's secretary acknowledged the gift with thanks to Leopold and the "very ingenious son." Ever since, the autograph, prints, and portrait have been among the institution's most treasured possessions.

Leopold may have postponed the departure several times for a good reason: he was not sure where to turn next. Too many other places beckoned after England. Originally he had planned to go to Milan by way of Paris, probably at Christian's suggestion. Baron Grimm in Paris may have advised a visit to Russia. In her memoirs, Nannerl mentions that "Prince Gallazin tried to persuade me to go to Russia."[52] The Danish ambassadors in both London and Paris were willing to offer the Mozarts an advance payment in order to entice them to go to Copenhagen.

Then there was Karl Wilhelm Ferdinand, the heir-apparent prince of Brunswick, a fine violinist, who had met Wolfgang while the prince was on an inspection trip in France. He became one of Wolfgang's greatest admirers. In Baron Grimm's second report from Paris we read:

> What is most amazing is [the boy's] profound knowledge of harmony and all its subtleties. It caused the prince of Brunswick, a very competent judge in these and other fields, to say that many highly accomplished *maîtres de chapelle* would die without having learned what this nine-year-old child already knows.

After further words of amazement and praise, Grimm predicts: "If these children survive, they will not stay in Salzburg. Sovereigns will soon quarrel over them."[53]

Later, Prince Karl Wilhelm Ferdinand was among the first to perform Mozart's operas in Brunswick; he also became a benefactor to Christian.

On 24 July, the Mozarts left London for Canterbury, where they stayed until the end of the month on the estate of an "English gentleman" (the later Sir Horace Mann). They then left for the Continent. Princess Caroline of Nassau-Weilburg, sister of the prince of Orange, practically forced them to visit The Hague. According to Leopold, the Netherland ambassador in London, Count Walderen, had urged them not to go directly to Paris but to visit Holland first, a request that Leopold did not take seriously. When the ambassador once more came to call on them, they had already left for Canterbury. "Soon [the ambassador] caught up with us and implored me to go to The Hague, since the princess . . . was ever so eager to see this child about whom she had heard and read so much." The offer he made was so advantageous, Leopold continued, that he finally gave in, especially "since one must not refuse the wish of a pregnant woman." And so the family left England on 1 August 1765 and headed for Holland.

In looking back on Wolfgang's months in England, we recall that soon after they arrived, Leopold stated that what Wolfgang knew at that time went far beyond his achievements on leaving Salzburg. Now, as they embarked for Holland, Wolfgang was an accomplished musician. What he had learned during those fifteen months by far surpasses what any other gifted child, at a critical stage of development, might have experienced, before or ever since. His first sonatas had been printed; he had entered his first independent compositions in the sketch book, and he had appeared in public with his first symphonies and arias. A master of Manzuoli's standing had introduced him to the art and skill of Italian singing. Moreover, what the boy had been able to take in—operas and concerts—was richer and more varied fare than what any other European city could have offered. And all this education took place under the guidance of the "famous Bach," John Christian.

Mozart's memories of England were to last. For one thing, he repeatedly met again with friends from the Isles. There was Thomas Linley, whose father was highly esteemed in London as a composer and teacher of voice. Thomas was a talented violinist, and after renewing their acquaintance in Italy, he and Mozart frequently played duos. A close friendship developed, but when they parted ways in Florence, it was for good; eight years later Linley was killed in a boating accident.

The scholar Daines Barrington (1727–1800), who examined Mozart in 1765 and in 1770 reported his findings in a scientific journal.

George Frideric Handel, still a strong influence on London's musical scene at Christian Bach's time.

Mozart's short motet "God is Our Refuge," K. 20. The awkward handwriting suggests an earlier date.

Mozart's friendship with Anna Selina (Nancy) Storace was not clouded in such a way. She sang the role of Susanna when *Figaro* was first given in Vienna. Another British (Irish) friend, Michael Kelly, sang Don Basilio and Don Curzio. Nancy Storace, four years younger than Mozart's wife, Constanze, was the daughter of a bass player at King's Theatre. With her mother and brother, she set out to conquer the stages of Europe. She first sang at the Vienna court opera when she was seventeen and soon achieved stardom. When it came to Mozart, Nancy Storace and Aloysia Lange, née Weber (Constanze's sister), were rivals, both as singers and in private life—a rivalry in which Nancy was the winner.

Another English friend was Thomas Attwood. Before Süssmayr, Attwood had been Mozart's favorite pupil. Scholars attribute importance to the book containing the studies in theory and counterpoint that Attwood composed, under Mozart's supervision and containing his corrections. In his memoirs, Michael Kelly quotes Mozart as saying that Attwood "partakes more of my style than any scholar I ever had."[54]

It was these three—Storace, Kelly, and Attwood—who tried to persuade Mozart to go to England with them during the 1786–87 season. (Mozart's earlier plans to return to the scene of his childhood triumphs had fallen through.) He must have seriously considered making the trip this time, for on 26 December 1786, the Prague journal *Oberpostamtszeitung* reported that "Herr Mozart, the famous composer, intends to visit London next spring, having received most advantageous offers from there. He plans to travel by way of Paris."

This time the plan was squelched by Leopold, who flatly refused to take care of Wolfgang's and Constanze's two children during the parents' absence. As a result, the estrangement between father and son became more serious. Leopold feared that the couple might unduly extend their journey, or even remain in England, leaving him in charge of the children.[55] Once before, in the fall of 1778, Leopold had prevented Wolfgang from visiting England. That was a crucial point in the son's career, a situation to which we shall return later. Wolfgang always harbored friendly feelings toward England; once he even referred to himself as an "Erz-Engelländer" (arch-Englishman).[56]

In 1790, a year before his death, Mozart once more considered a trip to the British Isles. Johann Peter Salomon, the London impresario, had come to Vienna to offer Mozart three hundred pounds if he would go to England as a composer of operas. According to the terms of the contract, Mozart was "to compose two serious or comic operas, at the management's option, by June of next year." Nothing came of the plan; Mozart never saw England again.

Mozart's arrangement of John Christian Bach's keyboard sonata Op. 5, No. 1, as a keyboard concerto, K.

Sr: Giovani Bach ridotti in Concerti dal Sr: Amadeo Wolfgango Mozart. figur. handschift 176_

He may have dreamt of returning to England whenever he became discouraged by professional setbacks at home, which happened often. He also had a lasting strong attachment to John Christian Bach, his musical mentor. When Mozart said farewell to England, he carried with him a substantial parcel containing music by Christian, including the three Opus 5 sonatas that Wolfgang had arranged as concertos. His strong stylistic ties to Christian remained in place, as reflected in Mozart's occasional literal quotations of Bach themes. Certainly there is a seamless connection between Christian's and Wolfgang's styles. Christian Bach may have been the leading proponent of the new melodic style, providing a foundation on which Mozart, more than anyone else, would continue to build. At the point when the Mozarts left England, Christian Bach was at the height of his fame, completely at home in the active musical and social life of the metropolis.

6
Bach, Abel, and Gainsborough

Through his eyes, man enters the world;
the world reaches him through his hearing.
Lorenz Oken (1779–1851)

T HE MANAGEMENT OF KING'S THEATRE had again changed for the 1765–66 season, and again Christian Bach was conspicuous by his absence from the repertory. Two years were to pass before his next opera was given. A new management team (the "opera regency," as Burney called it), consisting of Peter Crawford, cellist John Gordon, and oboist Thomas Vincent, took charge. The ineptitude of this haphazardly assembled trio is evident in their appointment of Cocchi as musical director—the same Cocchi who had already failed twice as director of Mrs. Cornelys's subscription concerts. The season that resulted from their efforts, according to Burney, "interested neither the public nor the publishers" (i.e., the publishers of "Favourite Songs").

Christian must not have hit it off at all well with the new management; otherwise he would surely have contributed some arias for the pasticci in which his old friend Filippo Elisi appeared, works with which the new leadership was hoping to get off to a good start. Elisi was the only singer who could add some glamour to this season; he was still the great vocalist remembered by London from the 1761–62 season. His appearance was majestic, his vocal range enormous. "He was fond of distant intervals, of fourteen or fifteen notes" (Burney). But apparently Bach, who must have felt indebted to Elisi for his help during earlier seasons in Italy, could not or would not take part in the new season. Rather, the action for him now shifted to King's Square Court, Bach's and Abel's new residence. This was a magnificent complex of buildings that comprised thirteen brick houses, most of them four stories high, enclosing a large, attractive courtyard. Bach and Abel occupied the third-largest house, on the west side of the Court. A small garden separated it from the principal building, occupied by the riding and fencing master Domenico Angelo.

"King's Square Court, Dean Street, Soho" is the new address at which Bach offered for sale his Opus 3, the six symphonies dedicated to the king's brother. It should be noted that the music publisher André, in Offenbach, assigned the same opus number to a sextet in C major by Christian Bach, and sold a quartet in G major as Opus 2—the number used, in the English edition, for the six trios Bach had composed for the king's sister. To make the confusion even worse: Huberty in Paris issued as Opus 2 six different trios, which in turn were published by Cramer & Forkel in Germany as Opus 4! In the "official" numbering, Opus 4 refers to the six vocal duets dedicated by Bach in 1765 to Lady Glenorchy.

Such confusion, which characterizes the publication of Bach's entire oeuvre, was common in the case of composers who were popular and famous during their lifetimes but not beyond, for no one bothered to compile an accurate list of their works. In the case of Bach's many vocal and instrumental compositions—not only his symphonies and concertos but also his chamber music and songs, and even the military marches he wrote for the king's regiments—it is seldom possible to establish with certainty the dates of composition and correct opus numbers.

Much of the confusion can be blamed on the complete lack of coop-eration between publishers in England and those on the Continent. They seldom wrote to each other, hence they did not try to agree on the assign-ment of opus numbers. As a result, there are editions published in Berlin, Amsterdam, Paris, The Hague, Vienna, and Offenbach that carry entirely arbitrary numbers.

Opus numbers were customarily assigned to instrumental works, but in Bach's case they were assigned to operas as well. *La clemenza di Scipione* carries the number fourteen, yet this is also the number appearing on Cramer & Forkel's edition of *Trois Grands Concerts pour le Clavecin*.

Aside from *Scipione*, the only other Bach opera to be printed in its entirety was *Amadis*, and that was done close to the end of Bach's career. "Favourite Airs," on the other hand, were published in countless collec-tions, starting right after Bach arrived in England. For the most part, however, publishers showed more interest in his instrumental works. Thus the catalogues of Gerber and of Cramer & Forkel, for the period from 1765 to 1779, list twenty printed editions—not an accurate figure because of the many pirated editions.

Although we know too little about opus numbers and editions, we have better information about Bach's activities in his new home, thanks to Henry Angelo, son of his landlord. To be sure, the boy was only ten

Domenico Angelo, owner of
Old Carlisle House.

Staircase and parlor in
Old Carlisle House.

years old when Bach and Abel moved in to the building adjacent to his
father's, and his later recollections are not always reliable; but they do
give us an idea about the activities of the artists who regularly met in
Angelo's house.

He recalls the "delightful evenings which for years were frequent
events under my paternal roof," evenings when Bach and Abel were welcome guests. He especially remembers parties that were "small and
friendly," with Bartolozzi and Cipriani, the two engravers who designed
the printed cards of admission to the Bach-Abel concerts. Time passed
quickly, with conversations about art and music that continued well past
midnight. Mrs. Angelo delighted everyone "with her gentle voice"; she
was joined by Bach and Abel on harpsichord and viola da gamba.

Larger gatherings included other well-known artists. David Garrick,
the actor, could be found there, as could the popular writers Horn Took
and John Wilkes, and the opera director Thomas Sheridan. Last but by
no means least, there were the great painters: Gainsborough, Reynolds,
and Zoffany.

Gainsborough, in particular, was a constant source of amusement. He
had the strange notion that by borrowing his friends' musical instruments, he would also acquire their ability to play them. Upon hearing a
very accomplished performance, he would readily offer one of his paintings in exchange for the instrument in question. He played the viola tolerably well, but he became the butt of his friends' jokes when he
attempted any other instrument, especially the bassoon, with which he
was fascinated.

> Calling at his lodging in Pall Mall, Bach once found him practicing
> that instrument, his cheeks puffed, his face round and red as a harvest
> moon. "Pote it away, man; pote it away," shouted Bach above the horrid
> sounds; "do you want to burst yourself, like the frog in the fable? De
> defil! it is only fit for the lungs of a country blackschmidt." "No, no,"
> Gainsborough protested, it is the richest bass in the world. Now, do lis-
> ten again." "Listen," yelled Bach, "I did listen at your door, . . . it is just
> for all the world like the veritable praying of a jackass."

Another time Gainsborough wanted to show off his skills at the
harpsichord, playing compositions by Byrd and Purcell.

> Gainsborough would proceed, till, pushing the artist from the harpsi-
> chord, Bach exclaims, "Now dat is too pad! Dere is no law, by goles!
> why the gompany is to listen to your murder of all these ancient gom-
> posers.

With that, Bach himself sat down at the harpsichord and "improvised beautifully."[1]

Thomas Gainsborough was born in 1727; he was thus four years
younger than Abel and eight years older than Bach. He had made a name
for himself as a painter long before the German musicians arrived in London. In his youth, he had devoted himself entirely to landscape painting.
His "Charterhouse" and "Forest of Gainsborough" had been accepted as
gifts by public institutions—an honor. To earn a living, however, he
found it necessary to turn, with great reluctance, to portrait painting. For
this purpose he moved to Bath, the fashionable spa on England's west
coast. There he found enough wealthy patrons who would pay fifteen,
later forty, and eventually sixty guineas for a lifesized portrait with a
romantic landscape as background (what his colleague Reynolds called a
painted fantasy.)[2] While living in Bath, however, he never lost contact
with London, its amenities, and his stimulating circle of friends.

Though Gainsborough lacked a solid technical foundation in music,
he was totally devoted to it. William Jackson—the same Jackson who
had told of meeting the boy Mozart in Bach's quarters—put it well when
he said that "Gainsborough's profession was painting, and music was his
amusement, yet there were times when music seemed to be his employment and painting his diversion."[3] In his style of painting, in the warm,
delicate shades of his "portrait landscapes," Gainsborough revealed his
affinity to Christian Bach's new, often gentle melodic manner.

In the spring of 1773, at the height of his career, Gainsborough wrote
a famous letter to Jackson. Declaring that he was "sick of portraits," he
went on to say,

> [I wish] very much to take my viol-da-gamba and make off to some
> sweet village, where I can paint landskips and enjoy the fag-end of life
> in quietness and ease.[4]

But reality prevented him from doing so—reality being his wife and
two daughters. Gainsborough said of them that they thought of nothing
but "tea drinkings, dancings, husband-huntings etc. etc." Yet we know
that the painter himself, though having an aversion to social life and har-
boring a hatred for aristocratic gentlemen, did thrive on luxury. He
employed a servant and kept a coach. (His fellow painter Zoffany even
owned a magnificent big sailboat on which he entertained guests with
open-air concerts on the Thames.)

Gainsborough felt most at ease in the circle of his musician friends,
where informal music-making alternated with lively conversation that

Thomas Gainsborough, at
about forty years of age.
Painting by Johann Zoffany.

Informal chamber music group.
Chalk drawing by Gainsborough, early 1770s.

often included somewhat risqué humor. His fondness for beautiful women did not go beyond painting them, adorned in silk, satin, and tulle, and bathed in captivating light effects.

He did have a weakness for drink. Often, after dining with friends, Gainsborough would insist on walking home by himself. But inebriated as he was, he would sometimes end up in the gutter. The friendly woman who found him there the next morning and sent him home in a coach to "sleep it off" would be rewarded with a gift of money.[5]

He was generous in thanking his friends with gifts of his paintings. Abel in particular was to profit from this benevolence, since he gave gamba lessons to Gainsborough. As a result, Abel owned more Gainsborough canvases than anyone else; the walls of his home were covered with them. Once, when he gave the painter a not particularly good viola da gamba, Gainsborough returned the favor by presenting his friend with two far more valuable landscape paintings and several sketches. These exchanges were consistently unequal. When Abel's estate was auctioned off after his death, Gainsborough paid forty guineas for Abel's gamba, which he had always admired, while the paintings he had given Abel went for 120 pounds, a much larger amount.

Gainsborough studied the gamba assiduously. According to a story in the *Morning Herold,* a certain Dr. Walcott, on hearing someone in an adjoining room play a minuet by Wanhal, exclaimed: "That must be Abel, for by God, no man besides can so touch an instrument!" The player, however, was Gainsborough.[6]

An amusing story is told about one of the paintings with which Gainsborough paid for Abel's lessons. He painted Abel's dogs and had the canvas delivered to his friend's house. (The painting was later catalogued as "Fox Dogs.") The real dogs, seeing rival dogs in the painting, barked so furiously that Abel had to hang their effigy in a place where they could not see it.

Gainsborough and Abel first met in 1761 (they were not joined by Bach until 1763). Gainsborough, who then lived in Bath, was having his first London exhibition. It was arranged by the Society of Artists, which had been founded the previous year by a group that included William Hogarth, the famous painter and engraver of subjects that represent satirical social criticism. Some of Hogarth's works deal with music: one painting, existing in several versions, is entitled "The Beggar's Opera"; another, "The Enraged Musician," depicts, among others, Castrucci, the eccentric leader of the opera orchestra.

Gainsborough's exhibition took place in the Great Hall at Spring

Gardens, a hall also used for concerts. Bach and Abel held their first joint concert there in February 1764, and the Mozarts used the same hall a few months later to introduce themselves to the public. It is quite likely that on this or other occasions they made the acquaintance of Gainsborough, though the painter is never mentioned in Leopold Mozart's correspondence. Nor is there any record that Wolfgang ever showed a special interest in painting.

Much eighteenth-century writing deals with the interrelationship between music and painting, and between the sciences of acoustics and optics. In 1704, Isaac Newton had published in his *Optics* the results of his experiments with light and color.[7] He related the seven principal colors of his spectrum to the seven steps of a musical scale and to the vibration frequency ratios of musical intervals. His theories and experiments led to many others in England, Germany, and France. Gainsborough's eagerness to excel in both painting and music might be seen as one aspect of the general interest in these relationships.

According to one of Christian Bach's contemporaries, the Belgian composer André-Ernest-Modeste Grétry,

> music that is well organized will detect in all colors the harmonic relations of musical tones. Subdued, low tones affect our ears the same way that dark colors affect our eyes, while high, shrill tones can be compared to vivid, glaring colors. Between these two extremes we have all the colors with which, in music and in painting, a great variety of feelings and character qualities can be expressed.[8]

Gainsborough's interests, however, were not guided by such intellectual considerations. His friend Jackson recalled that Gainsborough read very little. He was an artist with a practical outlook, aware of what was demanded of him.

> In my profession a man may do great things and starve in a garret if he does not conquer his passions and conform to the common eye in chusing that branch which they will encourage and pay for.[9]

That branch, of course, was portraiture, not the landscape painting that Gainsborough much preferred.

The representation of natural beauty was an important concept in mid-eighteenth century aesthetics. Charles Batteux's *Traîté des beaux arts* of 1746, for example, postulates that all true art, whether music, the fine arts, or poetry, represents a combination of the beautiful and the good, a combination only found in the beauties of nature.[10] While it is unlikely that Gainsborough and his friends Bach and Abel knew Batteux's theory of aesthetics, beauty, truth, and goodness are concepts that can easily be related to Gainsborough's paintings and Bach's music. The flowing lines in Gainsborough's paintings correspond to the graceful, flowing lines in Christian's music; Gainsborough's brilliant but always elegant colors are paralleled in Bach's equally brilliant but not overpowering instrumentation; and the painter's famous application of light and shadow is reflected in Bach's changing shades of piano and forte. Gentle, tender tones characterize the styles of both artists. Works such as Gainsborough's *Morning Walk* readily evoke the emotional quality of Bach's typical "singing allegro," just as listening to Bach's chamber music might bring to mind the "grace and lightness" for which Reynolds praised his colleague Gainsborough.

Neither Bach nor Gainsborough ignored the realities of life. Gainsborough, though given to cynical remarks about his portrait painting, regarded it as the source of a comfortable income and therefore a necessity. Christian, by the same token, would entertain and surprise his friends with bold improvisations at the keyboard, commenting that this was the way he would compose if he were in a position to do so. Boldness speaks to us from his symphony in G minor, Op. 6, No. 6, mentioned earlier. Its dramatic, at times melancholic, mood is not unlike that of certain early Gainsborough paintings, such as the several wooded landscapes that show the influence of Risdael. Inspired by the elegance and beauty of Bach's music, the boy Mozart may have discovered similar elegance and grace in some of Gainsborough's paintings. Although we do not know whether Mozart ever met Gainsborough in person, it is safe to assume that he was exposed to the painter's art.

While in The Hague, soon after his family left England, Mozart met Johann Christian Fischer, an oboist from Freiburg who had achieved international recognition. Fischer's composing as well as his playing pleased Mozart greatly. A few years later, Fischer settled in England, became an intimate of the Bach-Abel-Gainsborough circle, and married the painter's daughter (much against Gainsborough's wishes). Mozart selected the Rondo from one of Fischer's oboe concertos as the basis for his own *Twelve Variations for Clavier*, K. 179/189a. He was fond of performing them in public and taught the easier variations to his pupils.

An amusing little incident centers on Fischer's Rondo theme, a minuet. Bach made a bet with Fischer, wagering five guineas that he would be unable to play his own minuet on his own instrument. The oboist, of course, was convinced that he would win with ease. After the first few

Gainsborough, *The Morning Walk*, 1785.

measures, however, Bach stepped directly in front of him and started to suck a lemon so vigorously that the juice ran down his chin. The power of suggestion was too great: Fischer's mouth started watering so much that he could no longer produce a decent tone.

Some time after Mozart's departure, Bach and Abel moved from Mrs. Cornelys's establishment to a building at Hanover Square. Gainsborough decorated their new concert hall with paintings of his own. The auditorium soon became the talk of the town and was described in detail by Mrs. Gertrude Harris in a letter to her son (February 1775):

> Your father and Gertrude attended Bach's Concert, Wednesday. It was the opening of his new room, which by all accounts is the most elegant room in town; it is larger than that at Almack's. The statue of Apollo is placed just behind the orchestra, but it is thought too large and clumsy. There are ten other figures or pictures, bigger than life. They are painted by some of our most eminent artists: such as West, Gainsborough, Cipriani, &c. These pictures are all transparent, and are lighted behind; and that light is sufficient to illuminate the room without lustres or any candles appearing. The ceiling is domed, and beautifully painted with alto-relievos in all the piers. The pictures are chiefly fanciful; a Comic Muse, painted by Gainsborough, is most highly spoken of. 'Tis a great stroke of Bach's to entertain the town so very elegantly.[11]

This high point in Bach's and Gainsborough's collaboration, however impressive, did not last. The illumination of the paintings and statues from behind resulted in the projection of strong colors onto the powdered wigs of people in the audience, causing objections that led to the removal of the art works. At the next concert, one lady voiced her disappointment to Bach: "What? Apollo and the Muses gone?" To which Bach, with his customary wit, replied: "They have acquitted their late stations, madame, but have not absolutely deserted us. When the performance begins, I hope your ladyship will hear them all."[12]

Given the closeness of their circle, it is not surprising that Gainsborough painted portraits of his friends, sometimes more than once. He painted two images of Christian Bach: the "Hillingdon" portrait is in the possession of the family of Lord Hillingdon; the other, a gift to Padre Martini, is now in the Liceo Musicale in Bologna. Both versions, warm and lively, are masterworks. Bach appears as the amiable, elegant man of the world that he was. As seen by Gainsborough, he appears to inhabit a different world from that of Bach's father and brothers, as revealed in *their* portraits.

While Abel was sitting for the painter, there was the usual teasing and quick repartee. The painting shows Abel, writing at his desk, with his viola da gamba leaning against his knee. Gainsborough made sure that the gambist's face would convey something of his epicurean lifestyle. Not happy with the result, Abel observed that "he only lacks a full flask, to complete the picture of a faun!" To which Gainsborough calmly replied, "The only difference between you and him [in the portrait] is that *he* does not drink."[13] Though Gainsborough was still living in Bath at this time (he did not permanently settle in London until 1774), he was in constant touch with Bach and his friends. This was an especially happy chapter in Christian's life.

With Italian opera at the King's Theatre in a state of stagnation, Bach now devoted himself increasingly to instrumental composition.[14] Of interest to us is a journey to Italy by Vincent Gordon, one of the theater's managers. Looking for fresh vocal talent, he hoped to assemble two separate casts, one for serious opera on Saturdays, the other for comic works on Tuesdays. Among the singers he brought back was Cecilia Grassi, Christian's future wife.

Bach, in his thirty-first year, was still a bachelor, and we know nothing of any serious attachments before this time. There is no question that ladies of society were partial to him—and not only as a piano teacher. But there is no indication, beyond vague hints and rumors, that he led a particularly loose lifestyle. One detects a parallel here to Mozart, whose relations to the fair sex were, and still are, the subject of much speculation, the composer being variously pictured as the virtuous darling of the gods, as a rake given to many excesses, or as anything in between.

Although close ties to several women are a matter of record in Mozart's case, this much can be said about both him and Bach: while they certainly were not prudish or straitlaced, there are no indications of any deportment that went beyond what was widely practiced and tolerated at the time.

Such was the situation when the twenty-year-old Cecilia Grassi arrived in England, making her debut on 1 November 1766 in the pasticcio *Trakebarne, Gran Mogul*. Perhaps the English climate did not at first agree with her, for we know of only one other appearance on the stage of King's Theatre, in a repeat performance of *Ezio* on 20 December. The work was given at the court's request, thus providing for Grassi and the new male star, Tommaso Guarducci, an opportunity to shine with Bach's popular arias, "Non so d'onde viene" and "Se il ciel mi divide."[15]

Actually, the young Grassi was not altogether convincing. Those who expected her to live up to Anna Lucia de Amicis's brilliant performances during the 1763 season were disappointed. Burney found that Grassi was "inanimate on the stage, and far from beautiful in her person," which seem rather harsh words. To be engaged at such a tender age to the prestigious King's Theatre, she must have had adequate qualifications. Burney concedes, at least, that she had "truth of intonation, with a plaintive sweetness of voice, and innocence of expression, that gave great pleasure to all hearers who did not expect or want to be surprised."[16]

Perhaps Grassi was temporarily indisposed when Burney passed judgment, for she was no beginner. At only seventeen years of age, she had already attracted attention in the first performance of Gluck's *Il Trionfo di Clelia*, given in Bologna in 1763, in which she played a secondary but demanding role. Dittersdorf, Gluck's young companion, also noticed her "pure, pleasant voice," but observed that she was still a beginner—not surprising in so young a singer.[17]

There are indications that Christian may have known Grassi before she arrived in England. When his *Catone in Utica* was revived in Naples in 1764, the cast included a certain Andrea Grassi. He may have been Cecilia's father or uncle; the exact relationship is not clear. At any rate, he came from a family of musicians at home in Milan.

Cecilia Grassi was growing up there when Christian was in the employ of Count Litta and making a name for himself in Milan music circles. According to the not always reliable Elise Polko,[18] Cecilia's father was a teacher of singing, her mother a German; Luigi, probably her older brother, was a singer, and her younger brother, a violinist. Such a musical family must have been well known in Milan, which makes it likely that Christian and Cecilia met there: he, the opera composer who had been successful in Naples and Turin; she, eleven years younger, the up-and-coming singer.

Her indisposition must have been serious, otherwise she, as prima donna, would surely have sung the role of Cartismandua in Bach's new opera *Carattaco*. As the hero's adversary, this is a major role, but it fell to Signora Moser instead. Cecilia's brother Luigi was cast in both *Carattaco* and in the pasticcio *Sifari* [or *Sifare*] that followed.

Carattaco was well received. At the king's wish it was repeated several times, once in the presence of the five-year-old Prince of Wales. Another event that is indicative of cordial relations between Bach and the royal family had taken place a few weeks earlier when *The Fairy Favour*, sung by children to music by "the celebrated Bach," was given for the young prince at Covent Garden.

Little information has come down to us about Cecilia Grassi's career during the following years. She was not reengaged for the 1767–68 or 1768–69 seasons, which may indicate a serious illness. She returned to Italy in the summer of 1767. We cannot trace her steps there. Her only documented appearance took place on 12 January 1769, in a cantata performed at the Naples San Carlo.

We are better informed about her brother Luigi. Having finished the London season, he went to Berlin by way of Dresden. After his Berlin debut during the carnival of 1768, he was offered a permanent engagement and remained a member of the Berlin company for no less than twenty years. Granted a pension of five hundred taler, he then retired to Pisa in his native Italy. Luigi had an impeccable reputation, a fact to be stressed since claims to the contrary circulated about his sister Cecilia.

A strange, scandalous picture of Cecilia was painted by Henry Angelo, the observer of much that went on in his father's house. He claimed that soon after her arrival in England she became the mistress of Abel, who installed her in an apartment in Frith Street, the street on which the Mozarts had stayed. The walls of her drawing room were decorated with numerous Gainsboroughs, causing visitors (including the painter's son-in-law, the oboist Fischer) to make some pointed remarks. According to Angelo, Cecilia Grassi, "though no beauty, was a wit," and allegedly continued her liaison with Abel until his death in 1787.

An incredible tale! If true, Cecilia would have continued to be Abel's mistress even after she married John Christian Bach. This is most unlikely; certainly Queen Charlotte would never have tolerated such a triangular arrangement and would not have continued to favor the composer under such circumstances. Nor would she have transferred her good will, after Bach's death, to his widow, to whom she in fact granted a substantial pension, enabling Cecilia to retire to Italy. This largess would have been unthinkable had Cecilia led as licentious a life as Henry Angelo claimed in his *Reminiscences*.[19] Furthermore, Mrs. Papendiek, Bach's friend, made a point of calling her a woman "of good character and well-regulated conduct."[20]

Still, one would assume that there was at least some truth to the account. Angelo, after all, was Abel's friend, close enough to accompany him to Paris when Abel temporarily left England—not entirely of his own free will, it was said. Since they were on friendly terms, conversing frequently and intimately, Abel may have been Angelo's source.

As mentioned earlier, Cecilia Grassi had at first spent only a few months in London, from late in 1766 to the summer of 1767. She did not return until 1770. In May 1770, she lived with a Mrs. Margaret Burner, a grocer, at the corner of Panton Street and Leicester Fields, close to the city and in the immediate vicinity of King's Theatre. Three years later, she still lived in the same district, in the house of Mr. Grey, a jeweller in Lisle Street.

On 28 May 1772, Bach's bank account at Drummond's shows a transfer of 105 pounds, payable to "Mrs. Grassi." Bach and Abel, having given up their previous residence in 1771, now lived in Queen Street, Golden Square. They dissolved their common household sometime in 1773, at which time Bach moved to new quarters in Newman Street.[21] In other words, Bach and Cecilia were not married before 1773; otherwise they would not have lived separately.

There are other circumstances to consider. Bach visited Mannheim late in 1772, a visit about which more will be said later. At that time he fell seriously in love with a young girl. His intentions were entirely honorable, as attested to by Mozart's mother. This would not make sense if Bach had already been married at that time, as is claimed by Pohl, the otherwise conscientious chronicler who wrote that Bach and Grassi were married as early as 1767.[22]

All this suggests that Cecilia could have been Abel's mistress only during her first years in England, if at all. The difference in age—he was forty-three, she twenty—is not significant or unusual. Christian's father, Johann Sebastian Bach, was seventeen years older than his second wife, Anna Magdalena. A liaison would not have been unlikely on account of age, but it would have been tasteless, to say the least, for Bach to "take over" the lover of his friend in order to marry her. We can therefore assume that Angelo's memory was faulty and that perhaps two women were involved. The only significant fact to surface from all the gossip is that Cecilia Grassi's first stage appearances in London lasted only a few weeks because unfortunate circumstances prevented her from taking part in Bach's next success, *Carattaco*.

After that work, Christian took leave from King's Theatre, not to return, at least as the composer of a complete opera, for an entire decade. A touch of melancholy can be detected in the review, printed in the *Public Advertiser*, by the anonymous correspondent who signed himself "Harmonicus."

> It was with singular Pleasure I saw every Part of the Opera House so full last Saturday at *Carattaco*, as it had been the previous Saturday. The just Applause it met with on both those Nights prov'd that a Love for Serious Opera is not lessened among us. . . . Encomiums here on Mr.

Bach would be superfluous, as he has already distinguished himself so much among us by the Invention, the Spirit, and Dignity of his Compositions. . . . His Chorusses elevate the Soul and put us in mind of those of the immortal Handel, and of his own favourite *Orione*. With regard to his Airs, several of them are in the noblest Style of Music, and others very pleasing.

But many object to some of the Performers, as unworthy of Mr. Bach's lyre. Tis certain they are not Guarduccis . . . as very few possess his exquisite Talent. Surely Sweetness flows from his Lips, and his Voice steals on the Ear, delicious as the Accents of the Aeolian Harp.

High praise indeed, for Christian to be mentioned in one breath with "the immortal Handel." The choice of an English subject also met with the reviewer's approval, because it avoided the kind of artificiality that had brought serious opera into disfavor. The deserved applause was partly due to that choice.

A few weeks later, on 14 March, "Harmonicus" reports again.

'Tis the Property of all good Music to please the more it is heard. This I experienced the other Night at *Carattaco*. . . . When Carattaco sung the Air at his leaving England [there was] profound Silence. . . . And tho' the Silence was not so deep while the Chorusses were performing, they seem'd to administer vast Pleasure, by the Applause they met with. Being not a Stranger to the Italian Tongue, I was affected by many Parts of the Drama—an English King, his Magnanimity; his Love of Liberty and his native Country; his Abhorrence of Slavery; his Misfortunes as drawn from Tacitus.

How sweetly plaintive is the Air sung by Carattaco when fled from his Enemies to a Cavern! And how deliciously are both the Eye and the Ear entertained when the ill-fated Monarch is a Prisoner in the Court of the Imperial Palace at Rome! When the Emperor, seated in a triumphal Car, advances, attended by sorrowing English Captives, by Priests, and by Roman Soldiers! . . . The noble Style of Architecture, . . . the Splendor of the Lights; with the distant View of Rome, all these, with Carattaco singing his last Air, and the concluding Chorus, formed so sweet an Illusion that . . . will raise some Persons to Rapture, and disengage them, as it were, in certain Moments, so much from their corporeal Part, that they seem all Mind. They are conveyed into Elysium, and the whole is Enchantment.[23]

Another critic agreed, hoping that

Signor Bach may meet with further Encouragement, as his Genius and Judgment seem admirably calculated to reform the present corrupted

Taste of our modern Music and, like a second Handel, once again restore that Elegance and Perfection we have for some Time been Strangers to.[24]

In spite of such critical acclaim, *Carattaco* did not succeed in putting an end to the London public's lethargy. The role of Cartismandua, Carattaco's faithless opponent, would have been a great vehicle for Grassi, especially the highly dramatic aria "Perfidi, non osate." As it was, she had to wait three years before she could shine in arias by her future husband—in a production of Gluck's opera *Orfeo*.

First given in Vienna in 1762, *Orfeo* was now presented to London audiences in a production that opened on 7 April 1770. The version for London was entirely new, an "arrangement" for which the writer of the printed program, Giovan Gualberto Bottarelli, apologized:

> In order to make the Performance of a necessary length for an evening's entertainment, Signor BACH has very kindly condescended to add of his own new composition all such chorusses, airs, and recitatives, as are marked by inverted commas, except those which are sung by Signora *Guglielmi,* and they are likewise an entire new production of Signor GUGLIELMI, her husband.

Although the wording suggests that Bach may have been reluctant to supply additions to Gluck's score, his contribution consisted of seven arias, including two for Cecilia Grassi, who sang Eurydice. When the "Favourite Songs in the Opera Orfeo" were published (always an indication of a work's success), the fifteen pieces included all seven of Christian Bach's arias but only five of Gluck's. The other three were composed by Guglielmi, who directed the opera, for his wife, also a member of the cast.

Predictably there were those who complained about such a mishmash, Burney among them. They pointed out that the added arias unnecessarily slowed down the action, thus impeding dramatic force and obscuring the best qualities of Gluck's opera, simplicity and unity. The work's musical cohesion was further disturbed by the introduction of foreign stylistic elements.

In spite of these objections, this version of Gluck's *Orfeo* turned out to be highly successful on the Continent, where the public often failed to realize that a significant number of the arias were written by Bach. When, a century later, *Orfeo* was first heard in the New World (New York, 25 May 1863), it was in this version, with Bach's arias.[25]

The King's Theatre production was a great success for Cecilia Grassi, largely because of the arias Bach had written for her, and was further enhanced by the performance of the primo uomo, Gaetano Guadagni. His masterful singing and acting elicited torrents of applause, but he then lost the public's admiration because he considered it below his dignity to acknowledge the applause and to grant encores. He may have been miffed because the management showed little appreciation for his sister's singing.

Guadagni left at the end of the season, making room for Ferdinando Tenducci, whom we have met before. Once again Tenducci had gotten into trouble in Italy and had returned to England to escape his creditors.

Before he departed, Guadagni sang in a concert with Grassi. As was customary at the season's end, she appeared in a performance for her own benefit, in this case the pasticcio *L'Olimpiade*. A politely worded announcement that appeared in the *Public Advertiser* on 10 May 1770 stated that Grassi requests

> the kind Protection of the Nobility and Gentry, and hopes the Sub-scribers to the Boxes will not think her remiss in not waiting for them in Person, she being a Stranger in the Method how to proceed, there-fore most humbly desires they will send their Orders for the Boxes to the Office of the said Theatre.[26]

Bach also contributed to this pasticcio—but it was an aria for Guadagni, which suggests that at this time his ties to Cecilia were not yet very close. He did, however, write a major role for her in his only ora-torio, *Gioas, Re di Giuda*, which was given at King's Theatre on 22 March, two weeks before the Gluck-Bach *Orfeo*. But Cecilia Grassi could not take advantage of this opportunity; her state of health apparently left much to be desired. At the first performance, the male soprano Gasparo Savoi had to replace her at the last minute; only in subsequent perfor-mances did she sing. By then, Tenducci had replaced Guadagni.

Constant changes in casting indicate a good deal of confusion and hasty planning. During this spring of 1770, Covent Garden and Drury Lane, the competing theaters, offered oratorios on nights when there was no opera. The King's Theatre management, not to be outdone, had asked Bach not only to prepare Jommelli's *La Passione* but also to contribute an oratorio of his own—this at a time when he was busy with preparations for *Orfeo*. Not surprisingly, *Gioas*, his only oratorio, was a failure. It was given on the last three Thursdays in March and the first in April, but many of the boxes were not occupied. Things were no better at Covent Garden, where Handel oratorios were performed. The public was accus-tomed to hearing oratorios in the concert hall, not the theater.

Moreover, Bach had been ill-advised to appear between the acts as organ soloist, inviting comparisons with John Stanley, a legend even during his lifetime. Performing between the acts at Covent Garden, Stanley set high standards that were beyond Bach's abilities at the organ. Even his friend Mrs. Papendiek voiced mild criticism, observing that

> he had composed for the occasion, and played between the acts, his second concerto. A modern piece was usual, but as it was to be heard on the organ it was ill chosen; for, though beautiful in itself, it did not accord with the sacred performance, and Bach being no organ player, the whole thing rather tended to detract from the success of the evening.[27]

Bach may have been sensitive to such criticism; he had not encountered it so far in his career. This was a hectic period at King's Theatre, where the management was trying everything to counteract the opera public's lack of enthusiasm. Burney paints a gloomy picture:

> At this time crowds assembled at the Opera-house more for the gratification of the eye than the ear; for neither the invention of a new composer, nor the talents of new singers, attracted the public to the theatre, which was almost abandoned till the arrival of Mademoiselle Heinel [the dancer], whose grace and execution were so perfect as to eclipse all other excellence.

Only she, Burney continues, could "seduce" patrons to return to the theater, thus improving its precarious financial condition.

> Her extraordinary merit had an extraordinary recompence: for besides the 600-pound salary allowed her by the Hon. Mr. Hobart as manager, she was complimented with a *regallo* of six hundred more from the Maccaroni Club. Cocchi the composer said: "It is very extraordinary, that the English set no value upon anything but what they pay an exorbitant price for."[28]

All this, along with the capricious behavior of the stars and the audiences' increasing preference for short-lived pasticci supplied by Italian "distributors," did not motivate Christian to do his best. The public's interest was turning to light works; these were now given even on Saturdays, a practice previously frowned upon.

This is not to say that Bach considered himself above contributing to pasticci, for he did so often and willingly. To do otherwise would have meant cutting himself off completely from London's operatic life, indeed from musical life in general, which Bach would have considered unthinkable. Actually, to be asked to contribute was both prestigious and lucrative, even socially desirable. As a composer and contributor of arias in his own distinctive style, Bach was much in demand.[29]

There were also ample opportunities to provide instrumental music. The great popularity of the Bach-Abel concerts, given every year from January to May, not only continued but increased when Bach gave up Mrs. Cornelys's Carlisle House in favor of "Mr. Almack's Room." Mrs. Cornelys, worried about the competition, was unhappy. But Bach and Abel had valid reasons for changing halls: Soho Square was beginning to lose its good reputation, and King Street, near St. James Park, was now a more fashionable address. Furthermore, Almack's had more room, which pleased those who had been unable to gain admission at Mrs. Cornelys's establishment.

Still, there were some problems at Almack's. The building had been finished in 1765 and inaugurated with a gala ball. Apparently the construction was slipshod, done "with hot bricks and boiling water," according to one chronicler. A committee of ladies took charge of scheduling events and tried to provide a congenial setting, but great humidity penetrated the walls and staircases, giving rise to all kinds of macabre jokes. Thus Walpole prophesied to a friend that the duke of Cumberland, who attended the opening, would soon die. "If he died of it—and how should he not?—it will sound very silly, when Hercules or Theseus ask him what he died of, to reply, 'I caught my dead on a damp stair case at the new club-room.'"[30]

Attendance at the concerts did not apparently suffer because of these conditions. Bach's bank account at Drummond's shows much activity, involving substantial amounts. Rent payments to Mr. Almack amounted to approximately 600 pounds per year from 1769 to 1773. Large amounts were paid by Bach to Abel, apparently from the time when he became the exclusive manager of the concerts: 4579 pounds in 1771; 3595 pounds in 1774; 2341 pounds in 1777; 1058 pounds in 1779.

The reasons for other payments to Abel are not certain—1768, 273 pounds; 1770, 270 pounds; 1771, 400 pounds; 1772, 450 pounds; 1773, 773 pounds; 1774, 527 pounds; 1775, none; 1776, 375 pounds; 1777, 100 pounds; 1778, 200 pounds; 1779, 175 pounds—but quite likely these were fees paid to Abel, in addition to box office receipts, for his services as composer and performer.

In June 1768, Bach paid the surprisingly small amount of fifty pounds to the instrument maker Zumpe, yet this transfer is related to an important event. The announcement of the debut of the oboist Johann Chris-

Carl Friedrich Abel. Portrait by Gainsborough.

Almack's concert hall.

tian Fischer does not at first glance seem to contain anything unusual:

> For the benefit of Mr. Fisher . . . will be performed a Grand Concert of
> Vocal and Instrumental Music. First Violin and Concerto by Signor
> Pugnani. Concerto on the German [transverse] Flute, Mr. Tacet. Con-
> certo on the Hautbois by Mr. Fisher. Songs by Sig. Guarducci. Solo on
> the Viola di Gamba by Mr. Abel. Solo on the Piano Forte by Mr. Bach.[31]

But the concert was a historically important event, for it was on this
occasion that Bach introduced the pianoforte to the public as a solo
instrument. (A year earlier, Charles Dibdin had used the new keyboard
instrument for accompanying.) From now on, Bach used the pianoforte
regularly. The title page of his Opus 5 sonatas, published in 1768, calls for
"le Clavecin ou le Piano Forte," a designation that would indicate the
"peaceful coexistence" of the two instruments for years to come.

Another event deserves mention, standing out as it does among the
regular Bach-Abel concerts. Once more a first-rate group of soloists participated: those already known to us are Bach, Abel, Tacet, Fischer, and
Pugnani; new are the cellist Crossdill and Mrs. Barthélémon, the former
Miss Mary Young. She was Manzuoli's pupil and a much applauded singer
at King's Theatre, where she sang in operas by Bach and others.[32] The
event had human as well as musical significance. The notice placed in
the *Public Advertiser* on 23 February 1769 announces a benefit concert for

> Lady Dorothy Du Bois, eldest lawful Daughter of Richard the last Earl
> of Anglesey. Under the Direction of Messrs. Bach and Abel, who, on
> this Occasion, show they are as conspicuously endowed with soft Com-
> passion as unequalled Harmony and Superiority of Genius, having with
> Chearfulness not only consented to exhibit their own Excellence, but
> also to warmly interest themselves for oppressed Innocence.[33]

Lady Dorothy had become the victim of a complex family situation.
Her father, Richard of Anglesey, had secretly married the daughter of a
wealthy Dublin clothier; Dorothy was their child. Before her mother's
death, he had entered into another marriage that produced additional
offspring.

Dorothy's half sisters challenged her right to inherit. They did not
succeed, but the quarrel caused the family to lose their earldom. In the
meantime Dorothy, now without means, had married the violinist
Dubois, who participated in the benefit concert organized by Bach for the
impoverished family. Though of minor importance, the episode does
show Bach to have been a man of compassion.

Of more significance was another event that might have greatly affected Bach's further career, even causing him to return to Germany. This was the visit, in May 1771, of the famous flutist Johann Baptist Wendling, accompanied by his wife Dorothea and his beautiful nineteen-year-old daughter, Elisabeth Augusta. Mother and daughter were singers; they brought with them to London something of the splendor of the Mannheim court. Both had radiant personalities; Bach, not for the first time, readily responded to female charm.

The poets Heinse and Wieland had sung the praises of attractive Dorothea Wendling with a fervor that amounted to "Wagnerian pathos," as Erich Schenk put it.[34] Adding to the poets' praise, Schubart opined that she had "distinguished herself as one of our best singers . . . though in comic rather than serious roles." Schubart was less taken with the daughter. Though admittedly "an outstanding beauty, her cold nature reduced her singing and keyboard playing to virtual insignificance."[35]

Johann Baptist Wendling had many fine human and artistic qualities. Leopold Mozart, who had met Wendling briefly during a 1773 stopover in Mannheim when the family was on its way to London, called him "admirable." Karl Weiss, first flutist in the private chapel of George III, was also partial to Wendling, "the dear, jolly fellow."

Schubart, in his *Gesammelte Schriften und Schicksale*, also praises Wendling the musician, saying that his playing was clear and beautiful, in both the high and the low registers of the flute. Characteristically he adds: "He prides himself on his execution of that which is beautiful and moving, rather than on his playing of what is rapid, difficult, or startling."

Wendling must have been a musician to Bach's liking—and to Mozart's, too. Though not partial to the flute, Wolfgang made an exception in Wendling's case. Wendling's brother teased him because of this, to which Mozart replied:

> Your brother is different. He doesn't just rattle along, and one never worries whether a note is going to be flat, or sharp. His heart, ear, and tongue never fail him. He knows that mere blowing and trick fingerings [*Gabelmachen*] are not enough. Moreover, he knows how to play an Adagio.[36]

When Christian Bach and Wendling met in London, Mozart was no doubt a favorite topic of conversation. It had not been long since Mozart's stay in London, and the Wendlings had known the child prodigy previously. Following his further activities with interest, they were probably aware of his present situation.

At this time Mozart, fifteen years old, was back in Salzburg, waiting "most anxiously" (Leopold) to receive the libretto for *Ascanio in Alba*. He had just completed his first Italian opera, *Mitridate*, and had been honored by the empress Maria Theresia, who had commissioned him to write a Serenata Teatrale, to be performed as part of the festivities for the impending wedding of her son, Ferdinand, to Princess Beatrice d'Este, an event with some political significance. Mozart was understandably concerned about finishing the serenata on time, for with only six weeks until the wedding, he had not yet received the text. All ended well, however; thanks to Mozart's music and the leading singer Manzuoli (Mozart's teacher in London), *Ascanio* was a great success.

Bach and Wendling may have talked about all this, but the most important topics were Wendling's concert, the reason for his coming to London, and Elector Karl Theodor's invitation to Bach to write an opera for the opening of the 1772 season in Mannheim.

Wendling's concert took place on 15 May 1771. Noteworthy was the participation of Maddalena Lombardini Sirmen, an unusual artist. She had just attracted attention as an outstanding violinist, playing her own concertos during the oratorios given at Covent Garden. Earlier, during a benefit concert in April, she had performed a piano concerto. A person of talent and versatility, she also appeared as a singer at King's Theatre in 1773.

Bach's next composition was *Endimione*, a serenata for four voices "with grand Chorusses." Johann Wendling participated in the performance; he and his family must also have made the acquaintance of Cecilia Grassi, who sang the role of Diana. In addition to his participation as a flutist, Wendling seems to have had a part in managing the concert, for he announced in the *Public Advertiser* that tickets for admission were available from him "at Mr. Bach's in Queen Street, Golden Square."

Four arias from *Endimione* later became known as sacred arias. The practice was then quite common: a sacred text was substituted for the original secular one. Thus Endimione's entrance aria "Dimmi che vaga sei" became "Lauda Jerusalem," and his cavatina "Grato sono amato" emerged as "Ave Maris Stella." Twenty-one such *contrafacta* still exist today in the library of Einsiedeln monastery in Switzerland.[37] Among them is Catone's aria from *Catone in Utica*; its text was changed by the local clerics to "O Jesu mi dilecte." Cleofide's aria "Se mai turbo il tuo riposo" from *Alessandro nell'Indie* was sung to the Latin "Confiteor" text. (Bach himself had used this aria again in his *Temistocle*.)

Among Bach's additions to Gluck's *Orfeo*, we find similar substitu-

The Wendling family:
daughter "Gustl" (top);
her parents, Dorothea and
Johann Baptist Wendling.

tions. The aria of Orpheus's father, "Non è ver il dir talora," pleased so much that a new text was provided for church use: "Christum regum adoramus." From the score of *Temistocle*, fourteen arias found their way into the Einsiedeln sacred repertory.

We should not view these transformations as "falsifications"; rather, the process shows the close proximity of sacred music to opera. This was particularly true for, but not restricted to, eighteenth-century Italy. It is well known that Johann Sebastian Bach was also partial to such "parodies," namely, the substitution of secular words to existing church compositions or (more frequently) vice versa. That such arias were made available for church use by Christian Bach and others is also a testimony to their intrinsic musical value.

The arias from *Endimione* must have pleased the Wendlings, too. Less than two years later, the cantata was repeated in Mannheim, with Dorothea Wendling singing the part of Diana, the role Cecilia Grassi had sung at the first performance. Her daughter, "Gustl," who was to be Bach's great love, quite appropriately appeared as Amor.

Hardly a month had passed since *Endimione* had been given when another family of German musicians appeared in London, while the Wendlings were still there. The newcomers, hailing from Christian's Saxon homeland, were Johann Baptist Schröter, oboist in Count Brühl's regiment at the Royal Polish and Electoral Saxon Court, and his children. Johann was on a concert tour; his children were Corona (age twenty-one), Johann Samuel (twenty), and little Johann Heinrich (ten).

Corona in many ways resembled Gustl Wendling. She, too, was a beauty; Goethe, who had met the sixteen-year-old Corona while he was studying in Leipzig, referred to her "super-beauty" (*Überschönheit*). Like the Wendling daughter, who was approximately the same age, Corona early attracted attention as a singer. Another parallel that caused pain to the admirers of both, Goethe of Corona and Bach of Elisabeth Augusta, was that both young women had attracted the interest of their respective employers—an interest that went beyond music. In Corona's case it was Duke Carl August of Weimar, though the seriousness of this liaison has never been established. About the relation between Elisabeth Augusta and Elector Karl Theodor of the Palatinate there can be little doubt.

For the moment, both women still impressed everyone with their brilliant singing. "Still" applies to Corona Schröter. Her father, who also was her teacher, forced her to sing in a register that was too high for her, resulting in irreparable damage to her voice. It was already showing signs of decline when, in 1776, Goethe engaged her for the Weimar court, a lifetime appointment. Her beauty, however, had not faded, and Goethe continued to be passionately in love with Schröter: "An angel; if only God would give me such a woman, such a noble creature." She appeared on stage, together with Goethe, in his *Iphigenie*, and she wrote songs to his poetry, along with duets and the final chorus for Goethe's Singspiel *Die Fischerin*. She was also the first to set his "Erl King" to music.

In the London concert given by the Schröter family, directed by Bach and Abel, Corona made a strong impression. For her, this was the high point of their concert tour, but for her younger brother, Johann Samuel, it assumed even greater significance.[38] Christian Bach took him under his wing, as he had done with the young Mozart. But there was a difference: Mozart soon returned to the Continent, rising to the top, but young Schröter saw this as an opportunity to remain in London, eventually to succeed Bach as music master to the queen.

Was Christian too naïve, too unsuspecting, to sense the threat that this twenty-year-old posed to him during the last decade of his life? He must have been aware of it, to judge by the recollections of Mrs. Papendiek, who described her ambivalent feelings:

> [Schröter] was . . . a young man, fascinating, fawning, and suave; a teacher for the belles, company for the mode, a public performer, or a private player. [He] was brought forward as the new performer on the pianoforte, and although the small instrument was still used for the accompaniment of vocal music in a concert room, as the harpsichord was at theatres, the grand pianoforte was now introduced for solo playing. . . . Bach perceived his excellence in his profession, and assisted him as a friend, for his heart was too good to know the littleness of envy. He gave Schroeder advice from his experience of this country, and was also of great use to him in the theory of his profession. He loved him almost as a son, looking upon his talent with delight, and deploring that his disposition was such as must, in the end, work to his bane.[39]

As Mrs. Papendiek described him, Johann Samuel Schröter must have been spoiled and arrogant. He was an amazingly good pianist, who impressed everyone who heard him, but he did "little or no good to his fraternity in music," playing only when invited to do so. She gives the reason for this: he had married a wealthy student of high social standing, thus gaining financial independence, and no longer had to agree to perform in public. He did not display "fire or energy" in his teaching and showed no interest in his students, which was very different from the way Christian Bach had furthered him.[40]

When young Schröter talked about his successes so far—his concert at Leipzig's Three Swans Inn, for instance—Christian may have been haunted by his own memories of twenty years ago. This was the very inn at which Gottlob Harrer had auditioned to succeed Johann Sebastian Bach, Christian's father, who was then still alive. At the time, Christian was only fourteen, but he was already taking on important business responsibilities because of his father's serious illness. The Three Swans, one might say, had seen the successors of both Bachs: Johann Sebastian and his son Christian.

To talk about a successor to Christian seemed quite appropriate now, for opportunities beckoned elsewhere. It would have been easy for him to leave London for good. In Mannheim, the "paradise of music," a prince who showed great interest in music was awaiting him. (Little did Christian know that they would become rivals for the attentions of beautiful Gustl.) The Mannheim position might have become a lifetime appointment. Given Christian's close relations with the Wendling family, it seemed entirely possible that the trip to Mannheim would turn out to be more than an interlude.

The final event of the season at Almack's, on 2 May 1772, was a concert by Schröter; it was also the last of the Bach-Abel concerts. The two friends now went their own ways: Abel, as we may recall, took young Henry Angelo to Paris in order to find a place for him with "a respectable family" and to attend to his own private affairs.[41] Bach and the Wendlings set out for Mannheim.

7

John Christian Bach and Mannheim

*We honor [John Christian Bach] as a great musician
and love him as one of our compatriots.*

Abbé Vogler in his *Mannheimer Tonschule*

"THE GREAT THEATRE, the ensuing winter, was to be opened
with an opera composed by Mr. J. Bach, who was daily
expected here from London." Burney's remarks were made on 9 August
1772, in eager anticipation of Christian's arrival. The English traveler
and chronicler then goes on with his often-quoted description of what
Christian would find in Mannheim.

> I cannot quit this article without doing justice to the orchestra of his
> electoral highness, so deservedly celebrated throughout Europe. I found
> it to be indeed all that its fame would have me expect: power will natu-
> rally arise from a great number of hands; but the judicious use of this
> power, on all occasions, must be the consequence of good discipline;
> indeed there are more solo players, and good composers in this, than
> perhaps in any other orchestra in Europe; it is an army of generals,
> equally fit to plan a battle, as to fight it.[1]

Bach must have felt honored to have such a famous orchestra at his
disposal, and to have his arrival in this music metropolis so eagerly anticipated. Moreover, Christian did live up to the expectations. He made brilliant contributions to the operatic life of Mannheim, the elector's
residence—this in spite of the fact that the city's musical establishment
was headed by Kapellmeister Ignaz Holzbauer, who had been firmly established there since the 1750s and had made a name for himself as a composer of operas.

Holzbauer's name takes us back to Milan in 1759, when he had
stopped there during a tour of studies in Italy, the third such journey he
had undertaken at the elector's behest. His opera *Alessandro nell'Indie* was

given in Milan's Teatro Regio Ducale. Christian Bach may well have been in the audience, listening with rapt attention.

But times had changed. Holzbauer, now sixty years old, was still held in high esteem but had passed the zenith of his career. It had been three years since his last great opera, *Adriano in Siria*. In Mannheim, as in England, opera seria had ceded much of its sway to comic opera. Only once again did Holzbauer present himself to the operagoing public. This was in 1777; *Günther von Schwarzburg*, the best of his operas, was highly praised by his contemporaries, who greeted it as a victory of German opera over the Italian tradition. The work received unusually high praise from Mozart, who wrote to his father that "Holzbauer's music is most attractive. I marvel at the spirited writing of this older man; his music is full of fire" (letter of 14 November 1777). Two weeks later, Mozart again mentions *Günther*: "I hope I wrote to you that Holzbauer's great opera is in German!"

Holzbauer, however, continued to follow the Italian "operatic" style in his sacred music, featuring many bravura arias with a wealth of melodies. Some disapproved of this style, considering it unsuitable for the church. According to Sulzer, in his *Allgemeine Theorie der schönen Künste* (1774), such melodies "express all feelings equally well, because they express nothing." If Holzbauer's Masses and oratorios were the targets of such criticism, they nonetheless pleased Mozart, who was sorry that he had not brought along some of his own sacred works. "I wish I had taken along [to Mannheim] a copy of at least one of my Masses; I would have performed it here. The other day I heard one of Holzbauer's Masses, which conforms to our taste. . . . If only I had copied my *Misericordias*!" (Letter to his father, 3 December 1777.) In the same letter Mozart states that "the leading musicians here love me and esteem me highly." A few years earlier, Christian Bach had experienced a similar reception in Mannheim. Twenty-four years younger than Holzbauer, Christian might well have returned to Germany to become his successor.

Times seemed promising for Christian. The Holzbauer vogue had lasted some twenty years but was now declining. We do not know whether Holzbauer's gradual loss of hearing was beginning to be a problem, but a search for his successor seemed called for. The elector must have been concerned about preserving the excellent reputation his establishment had enjoyed throughout Europe—and here was Bach, who would surely bring honor to Mannheim.

Bach had many advocates. Holzbauer himself, to judge by his compositions, must have approved of the younger composer's style. And the

Right: Ignaz Jakob Holzbauer, director of the Mannheim Opera.

Left: Elector Karl Theodor of the Palatinate.

Below: The palace theater in Schwetzingen where Bach's *Endimione* was first heard.

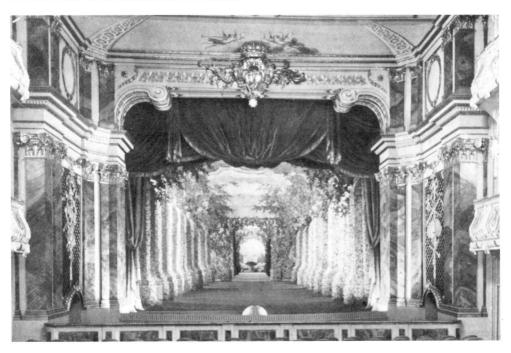

amiable, open Bach must surely have been a good deal more sympathetic as a human being than was Abbé Vogler, who in the end succeeded Holzbauer and who later became a source of trouble.

Another proponent was Anton Raaff, who had substantially contributed to the successes of Bach's first operas at the Naples San Carlo. At that time Raaff had been at the height of his fame. When Elector Karl Theodor invited him to Mannheim in 1770, Raaff was fifty-eight years old. He diffidently replied: "If Your Excellency will be satisfied with the modest remains of my gifts I shall consider myself fortunate to become your subject and to die in your service."[2]

No doubt Raaff did what he could to bring Christian to Mannheim, and not entirely for unselfish reasons. In Mannheim, as before in Naples, Bach could be counted on to write arias for him that were tailor-made. Bach did indeed do so when Raaff sang the title roles in *Temistocle* and in *Lucio Silla*, Bach's second opera for Mannheim. Given Raaff's vocal equipment at the time, this consideration was vitally important to the singer. He needed the same indulgence nine years later when he appeared in Mozart's *Idomeneo*, again at the elector's court, which had by then been established in Munich.

We can understand that the two older musicians (Holzbauer, born in 1711, and Raaff, born in 1714) welcomed Bach in Mannheim with open arms. But a member of the younger generation, twenty-three-year-old Georg Joseph Vogler, also sang Bach's praises.

In spite of his youth, Vogler was a person of some standing at the Mannheim court. He was born near Würzburg and had studied both theology and music. Being an excellent performer on organ and piano, he did not hesitate when he had the opportunity to go to Mannheim, considered the Mecca of music, instead of entering the Franciscan monastery in Würzburg. Karl Theodor had appointed him Almosenier, a title given to clerics who were entitled to distribute alms.

Vogler celebrated his first Mass as court chaplain on 22 November 1772 in the presence of the entire court. (Bach's *Temistocle* had been performed during the same month.) In the years that followed, Vogler rose to a position of authority. To be sure, he was controversial: vain and conceited, he strutted around in the purple stockings that, as a papal protonotary, he was entitled to wear, prompting Mozart to call him an "exasperating musical joker," a person "who has a high opinion of himself but knows little." Nevertheless, Vogler's opinions attracted attention, particularly through his monthly publication *Betrachtungen der Mannheimer Tonschule*. What he printed about Christian, and the way he formulated his thoughts, transcends anything previously written on the subject. Vogler's significance in music history has been questioned, but he must be given credit for being the first and only correspondent of the time to publish a detailed review of one of Christian Bach's cantatas, describing it as "the work of an inspired composer." The significance of the review extended far beyond the confines of Mannheim. Vogler wrote that the cantata in question[3] was written by

> Johann Christian Bach, one of Germany's greatest composers; his fatherland can be proud of him. The cantata consists of two arias and two recitatives. The feelings contained therein afford the singer opportunities to display a variety of affections—gentle and tender ones, but also those representing fire and pathos.
>
> The text is one of the great Metastasio's most felicitous inspirations. Herr Bach chose it in order to demonstrate the power of music, to show how music can eloquently describe even the most contrasting emotions: fright and calm, fear and hope, but also love and tenderness.
>
> His two operas *Catone in Utica* and *Alessandro nell'Indie* received general approval when presented at the royal San Carlo Theater in Naples. [Vogler does not mention the operas written for London.] They caused him to be awarded the poet-musician's laurel wreath. His writing, always enchanting, is simpler and contains fewer notes than works in the sometimes furious Neapolitan style. No sensitive listener can fail to be moved by his tender, ingratiating, *cantabile* writing. There may be passages that sound bold and learned, in the German manner, but Bach employs these sparingly and judiciously, to provide effective contrast to the gentle moods.
>
> This great composer has given us music in all genres. We are hard put to think of anyone else who has written with such facility and success in so many different categories. His many sonatas, trios, quartets, quintets, concertos, symphonies, arias, cantatas, serenades, oratorios, and operas testify to Bach's powers of invention; they are full of fire and imagination. . . . We may marvel at the soulful, true characterization found in Catone's testament, or in the scene showing the desperation of Temistocle's daughter, or the love of Cleofide and Poro [in *Alessandro*]. We may regret all the more that Herr Bach makes many concessions to the fashions and taste of our age, to please the ladies. To do that he sometimes condescends to write keyboard sonatas in the most ordinary, tasteless English style. His circumstances may account for this, but our patriotism causes us to hope that Bach, whose genius has so much to contribute to the arts, will devote himself more to the improvement of music and less to obtaining approval and rewards from insignificant admirers.

Though Herr Bach has published so many greatly dissimilar works, he shows no signs of fatigue [this was written in 1778]. His imagination continues to flourish; his ideas are ever new. In spite of his many musical exertions, which he enjoys, his health seems little affected. Thus we can look forward to many new, wonderful compositions by this great master.

After thirteen pages of detailed description of the cantata, Vogler continues, leading to his next chapter:

It only remains to be said about this work that its vocal writing deserves nothing but praise; that it is simple, natural, and capable of being ornamented. Singers of moderate skill should be able to perform it creditably. Wherever it is heard it should help establish the fame to which Bach has been entitled for a long time. Following the achievements of this great master, a pupil now wants to try his hand at writing for the stage—one who has received his training in this genre in our Mannheim establishment.[4]

Given such encomiums, Mozart's claim that Vogler had "bad-mouthed" Bach might seem unfounded. But there were reasons for this opinion.

Mozart had expressed a desire to have a look at Christian Bach's score of *Lucio Silla* since he had set the same text for Milan. "Holzbauer had told me that Vogler had the score," Mozart wrote to his father on 13 November 1777. Vogler was glad to oblige, saying:

"I'll send it to you tomorrow, but I doubt that you will find much in it that is any good." A few days later when he saw me [Mozart continues], he said with some sarcasm: "Well, did you find anything that was beautiful? Did you learn anything from it? It contains one aria that is quite nice. What is the text?" he asked someone standing next to him; "what aria is it?" "It's that awful aria by Bach, a disgusting piece. *Pupille amate*, that's it; surely he wrote that when he had had too much punch to drink." I felt like taking him by the scruff of his neck.

Here we have the two faces of Georg Joseph Vogler: though a man of the church, he knew how to express himself in a very worldly way. This was a manner that Mozart was not prepared to accept. He felt more comfortable among those musicians who, five years earlier, had helped make Bach's stay in Mannheim so pleasant. (There, as elsewhere, an established circle of friends had surrounded Bach and Mozart.) Mozart thought Holzbauer and Wendling to be "decent, entirely honest" men, though he felt compelled to point out that Wendling "had no religion" and that it was not surprising that Wendling's daughter had at one time been the elector's mistress (letter of 4 February 1778).

After so many years, Mozart still seems to have been disturbed by Gustl's affair. That this attitude may have been due to his sympathy for Christian Bach, whom she had spurned, is confirmed in a letter sent home to Salzburg by Mozart's mother. On 20 November 1777, she wrote:

> We had dined with Herr and Madame Wendling. . . . Their only daughter is very beautiful. Bach, in England, had wanted to marry her. Her health has been poor for about a year and a half. She had a fever that was not properly cured, which is a shame.

A few months later, however, Gustl seems to have recovered enough to take part in the daily musicales. Mozart had nothing against her as far as music was concerned. "Soon after my arrival, I composed a French song for Mademoiselle Gustl. She had given me the text, and she sings it incomparably well. . . . They sing every day at the Wendlings; it's an obsession with them."

Leopold, on the other hand, never could reconcile himself to the Wendlings' morals, and he was highly pleased when Wolfgang gave up his plan to travel to Paris with them in 1778. He vehemently attacked the father:

> How can a father throw away his daughter in this fashion? It is disgusting. Can one trust the friendship of someone who sacrifices his own flesh and blood to self-interest? His honor has thus been compromised, throughout the land and abroad.

Bach's intention of marrying the daughter must have been widely discussed in Mannheim, not only as gossip soon to be forgotten, for five years later, Mozart's mother still brought up the subject. But she is the only one who documented Bach's unrequited love for the beautiful Wendling daughter.

Just when Gustl became the elector's mistress is not clear. Chroniclers of the day had a hard time keeping up with their ruler's affairs, though as Friedrich Walter said, in his *Geschichte des Theaters und der Musik am kurpfälzischen Hof* (History of Theater and Music at the Electoral Court):

> Everyone knew his mistresses. One of them was the daughter of a Mannheim baker named Huber; the elector made her a Countess von Parkstein. The ballerina Seyffert became Countess Haydeck. The elector took good care of his natural children. One of Huber's daughters married a Prince von Isenburg. A Seyffert son became Prince von Bretzenstein; a palace was built for him across from the elector's castle.[5]

Abbé Georg Joseph Vogler.

The Mannheim National
Theater where Bach's *Temistocle*
received a lavish production.

Gustl Wendling was not given such princely treatment, though throughout her life she enjoyed the elector's protection, even after he and the entire court had moved to Munich. Just when he became tired of her is not known, nor is it clear whether Christian knew all along that the attractive Wendling daughter was the elector's favorite—if indeed this was already the case at the time of her family's London sojourn. He may have become aware of the liaison only after he got to Mannheim.

Most likely Gustl, faced with the choice between marrying the famous opera composer, who was seventeen years older than she, or advancing her career by becoming the elector's mistress, opted for the latter. It is consistent with Schubart's description of her as a "cold beauty." She must have made her decision at about the time of the *Temistocle* performance. Until then, Christian may have dreamt of a rosy future with Gustl at his side: he, successor to Holzbauer as Court Kapellmeister and Court Composer; she, a beautiful young woman on the threshold of a promising career. If only the elector hadn't been his rival! The disappointment must have been a great blow to the enamored Christian.

By contrast, everything else looked good. He had the circle of friends already mentioned, including Holzbauer, Raaff, and Wendling. Then there was the gala performance of *Temistocle*, which was the high point of Christian's operatic career. The opera was given in as lavish a manner as was possible in Mannheim, and that meant a really extravagant production.

When it came to presenting Italian opera, the elector was not one to pinch pennies. The increasingly elaborate productions required enormous expenditures, for each opera was given with completely new sets, costumes, and so on. An average of forty thousand gulden was spent on a single opera; special occasions, such as a performance to celebrate the ruler's name day, would cost seventy to eighty thousand gulden. These figures did not include salaries for singers and other personnel.[6]

Most expensive were new costumes (preferably using generous amounts of velvet, silk, and lace) and stage sets, featuring extravagant lighting and machinery. Audiences eventually became spoiled, always expecting new thrills. They were accustomed to three or four scene changes in a single act. This meant nine or ten changes for one opera, not counting special scenery for ballets given between the acts.

For example, one requisition called for 14,965 ells of canvas, to be delivered by boat, for the construction of sets for a new opera production. [A German ell varied in length from fifty to eighty centimeters—trans.] This cost 2230 gulden, even though the court accounting office found the material to be of poor quality and had subtracted 3/4 kreuzer per ell.

The high point of a typical opera production was the finale, for which the set might represent a festively decorated temple where a solemn sacrifice or triumphal chorus would be featured. In addition to such grandiose displays, audiences liked to feast their eyes on garden scenes, fountains, and colonnades, as well as on great palatial halls that revealed impressive feats of perspective in scene painting. By way of contrast there were dark, subterranean dungeons where prisoners languished.

The art of stagecraft was highly developed, producing exquisitely painted backdrops. Costumes were designed by a small army of fashion artists, at times even by the court sculptor. The sophisticated effects of stage lighting would astonish us, given that everything was accomplished by mere candles. Today's stage lighting is electronically controlled; at that time, hinged panels were raised and lowered to produce subtle gradations of light. That way, candles did not have to be continually extinguished and relit. Even so, a staggering number of candles was required; some thirty thousand for a single performance. Among the most spectacular light effects were those produced by chemical flashes or by Bengal fires and other fireworks. Experts from Italy were hired to set these off.

Mannheim's attractions impressed many visitors, among them Voltaire's secretary, Colini.

> The Palatinate court is the most resplendent in all of Europe. One festivity follows another, always attractive and in good taste. There are hunting parties, operas, French stage plays, and musical performances by Europe's foremost virtuosos. In short, the city in which the elector resides offers visitors of some standing the most agreeable sojourn in the world; here he could always count on a cordial and courteous reception.

This was the Mannheim in which Bach's *Temistocle* was given on 5 November 1772. In his diary, Hazard, the elector's *Kammerfournier* (administrator), wrote down his vivid impressions:

> At four o'clock the court assembled in the antechamber of the elector's wife; from there they proceded to the opera house. Many visitors preferred to remain incognito, among them the margraves of Baden with their families and retinue. They were given the grand box in the third tier. The hereditary prince and princess of Hessen-Kassel occupied the *loge grillée* [a box with a grill, for privacy] on the main floor's right side. The corresponding box on the left went to the prince and princess of Nassau-Weilburg and to Countess von Neippberg; next to them were the three Radziwill princes. Many visiting ladies of high social standing

had come incognito; they were assigned the third-tier boxes formerly belonging to the Jesuits. The other boxes were completely full, so that many townspeople were unable to obtain admission and had to console themselves with hopes for a repeat performance.[7]

It was an impressive occasion, and this at a time when Italian opera seria was losing much of its fascination, even becoming the subject of satire. As early as 1774, the elector's name day (which until then had always been observed with an opera seria performance) was the occasion for a "heroic-comic" opera by Mozart's rival Salieri. Its very title, *La seccia rapita* (The Stolen Bucket), suggests a parody of serious opera. Two cities, Modena and Bologna, enter into a feud because of a stolen bucket. Heavy fighting involves counts, field marshals, and Amazons. This, however, does not prevent everyone from indulging in the customary amorous adventures.

In Bach's *Temistocle*, the stars of opera seria had one more opportunity to shine—singing the kinds of arias that were popular in church as well as on stage. In fact, considering that Bach had reused the first and second parts of his *Carattaco* overture for the overture to *Temistocle*, one is tempted to ask whether he might also, for this work, have "recycled" some of the sacred arias he wrote during his years in Italy. But the evidence is to the contrary: on the manuscript copy of every sacred version of an aria from *Temistocle*, the title of the opera aria on which it is based is given first, indicating that the Latin text was added later.

Those who adapted the texts, that is, who substituted Latin words for the original Italian, did not always display great skill. We note distortions that an experienced composer like Bach would never have tolerated. But the music-loving patres of Einsiedeln, who were very partial to Christian's music, occupied themselves for decades with new versions of *Temistocle* arias. The aria "Non m'alletta" also exists in a version with string accompaniment that carries the notation "written at Einsiedeln during the last days of June 1826."[8]

There is some confusion about the casting in *Temistocle* for the part of Roxane (whose arias also exist at Einsiedeln with sacred texts). The role was sung by Elisabeth Augusta Wendling, which some think was not Gustl but her aunt, sometimes called "Lisl," who had the same name. But the assumption that the aunt sang the role of Roxane is not necessarily correct. By this time Gustl had already played leading roles in both Mannheim and Zweibrücken, and as the elector's favorite—if indeed she already was his favorite—she may have been the one to sing Roxane at this gala performance in his honor.

No doubt Gustl did play an important role, off stage if not on, for it must have been around this time that she made her decision against Christian Bach. Her rejection of him would explain why Christian soon left Mannheim. Instead of enjoying his great success there, he promptly returned to London: by early 1773, he had resumed the Bach-Abel concerts. It may well have been the painful experience of being refused by Wendling's daughter that caused him to leave Mannheim so abruptly.

As for Gustl, she continued her career with determination, despite her sometimes frail health. Her parents were always at her side; close family ties were not unusual among musicians (witness the Mozart family).

The meeting of the Mozart and Wendling families in Mannheim during the late 1770s, when Wolfgang composed the French air for Gustl that she sang "incomparably well," has already been mentioned. The next reunion took place in Munich in 1780, during the preparation of Mozart's *Idomeneo*. This time only the Wendling parents were there, along with aunt Lisl. Together with Raaff, they were part of the circle of friends who were present for the opening of Mozart's opera. Gustl had not yet followed the court in its move from Mannheim to Munich. When she finally did arrive there in 1784, it was for her triumphal debut in Georg Benda's *Romeo and Juliet*.

A subsequent letter from Leopold Mozart implies that Gustl had not changed. Nannerl had inquired whether her father might be able to do something for Margarete Marchand, who, together with her brother Heinrich, was living with Leopold in Salzburg. Lepold replied, expressing regrets: "Though March: Gretl had been highly successful singing and acting in operetta, she does not have a chance in Munich, for Augusta Wendling is now the mistress of Count Seeau." ("Gretl" did later become a singer at the Munich court.)

Count Anton von Seeau had been Hofmusikintendant, in charge of court music, since 1753 (Wolfgang called it derisively the "spectacle business" [*Spektakelwesen*]). Malicious observers claimed that Seeau owed his position solely to the fact that he was "the only cavalier at court who knew how to play a Styrian dance on the fiddle." Seeau, an adventurer, had been involved in duels and was fond of wine, women, and song. He became partial to the Wendlings soon after their arrival in Munich. Though Mozart also enjoyed the count's favor, he joked that Seeau was "like wax in the Mannheimers' hands." No doubt this applied especially to the beautiful Wendling daughter. Soon after she was dropped by the elector, Gustl had characteristically transferred her favors to the all-powerful Intendant.

The Concert by Augustin de Saint Aubin, depicting a typical musical event at court.

Strangely enough, she is not listed in the offical court registry as Hof-sängerin, though many years later her obituary refers to her as a singer at the elector's theater. Augusta died in 1794, unmarried, at the age of forty-two. Count Seeau outlived her by five years as did Elector Karl Theodor.

Let us return to Christian Bach. We lack information about his return trip to England; he may have made a detour through Germany to look in on his brothers and sisters, or he may have traveled directly to London. As for his family, the picture is a sad one: they lived far apart from each other, some of them in great poverty.

The sisters, especially, led depressing lives, as their mother had done earlier in Leipzig. Little is known about them; their social standing was inferior. Those who remained unmarried had to shift for themselves, dependent on gifts from charitable persons. Dorothea, the eldest, died at about this time (1774). Regarding Christian's real sisters, Johanne Caro-lina and Regine Susanna, we have only one piece of information, and that from thirty years later. It pertains to Susanna, the only one then still living, for whom a collection was taken up in the year 1800, when she was "aged and destitute." This monetary aid somewhat eased her final years.

There is no record of any assistance from the brothers, except in the case of Elisabeth Altnikol, widowed since 1759. Emanuel apparently sent her money at regular intervals; at least he said so in a letter to Breitkopf, his publisher.

With the possible exception of faraway Christian, Emanuel was the only brother who was financially able to help. Friedemann's life had taken a tragic turn. At this time he lived (vegetated might be a more appropriate term) in Brunswick. He was a recluse, unemployed and bitter. As a composer, he was unwilling to make any concessions to what he considered the trivial tastes of the time, the "ear-tickling" and "bouncy" melodies of others. He was equally isolated as a human being, especially since his two eldest sons had died. The only survivor was his third child, a daughter.

Friedemann had already started on the downward path while he lived in Halle. Having lost all financial security, he auctioned off a parcel of land that belonged to his wife. The professional ruin that followed was of his own doing. He suddenly resigned from his secure position as organist at the Frauenkirche, virtually stopped composing, and barely supported himself by giving lessons. Occasionally, if he felt like it, he would appear in public as an organ virtuoso.

Owing to his desperate financial situation, he was not above selling works by his father as compositions of his own. Johann Sebastian Bach had thought so highly of Vivaldi's music that he arranged some of the Italian's violin concertos for harpsichord. (This may be how Christian had become acquainted with Vivaldi, Italy's greatest musical genius of the early eighteenth century.) Father Bach transcribed Vivaldi's great Concerto in D Minor, Op. 3, No. 11, for organ. In that version it came into the possession of Friedemann, who did not hesitate to add a note on the manuscript: "di W. F. Bach, manu mei Patris descript." In other words, Friedemann claimed that he had composed the work, and that his father had merely copied it.[9]

In spite of his hand-to-mouth existence, Friedemann may have hoped that somewhere and sometime he would find a regular position that would provide security for his old age. He was not likely to find it in Brunswick, the residence of art-loving Duke Carl I. Friedemann applied unsuccessfully for the position of organist at the new town church in Wolfenbüttel and for a similar position at St. Catherine's Church in Brunswick. Why, indeed, should the town fathers bother with a sixty-year-old applicant who was obviously an eccentric loner? He had shown his lack of stability by suddenly walking out on a secure position, without having even the slightest assurance of other employment, and remaining unemployed for seven years. Anyway, as a Bach, he surely would not have been satisfied with a routine assignment, a position that could be filled just as well (and at less pay) by a younger applicant who was apt to be more modest and more cooperative.

The setback must have hurt Friedemann's pride for a special reason. The city of Brunswick apparently did not consider him qualified for the relatively subordinate position of organist, yet their decided preference for his brother Christian was all too evident. Just a few years earlier, in 1768, Christian had brilliantly succeeded as an opera composer with a performance of his *Catone in Utica*. Christian was "the famous Bach," so highly regarded by the ducal family that Field Marshal Ferdinand, one of Duke Carl's brothers, granted him a lifelong pension.[10]

The same Duke Carl had routinely forwarded Friedemann's application to the authorities of St. Catherine's Church, leaving them free to appoint the younger candidate, whom they preferred. That candidate, we read, was "a very skilled organ builder," a skill deemed more important than Friedemann's admittedly expert organ playing.

It was the clearest signal Friedemann had yet received that he was excluded from the new world of music that his brother Christian had successfully entered long ago. The situation seemed hopeless, for Prince Carl

Wilhelm Ferdinand, the successor to the throne, was also completely sold on the new style. Duke Carl had sent his son on a tour of Europe to study the arts. It was then that the prince developed a fondness for the young Mozart and for the "melodists" in general, headed by Christian Bach.

Casting a glance in the direction of nearby Hanover must have revealed to Friedemann that Christian's music was much appreciated there, too. The first concert programs from 1775 that have come down to us are those of January 27 and February 23; both included symphonies by Christian. Nor did his works disappear from the repertory, as evidenced by the program of a *Liebhaberconcert* in 1789, seven years after Christian's death. During the first evening, the audience heard two choruses by Bach, "the late London Capellmeister," as stated in the program. The next concert included one of his symphonies for two orchestras, with one group seated in the hall, the other in the gallery.[11]

Friedemann was embittered and jealous of his half brother's successes, which makes it unlikely that Christian, on his return from Mannheim, would have made a detour via Brunswick. Friedemann had even become estranged from Emanuel, his real brother. Emanuel may have occasionally supported his older brother, but that did not prevent Friedemann from disparagingly referring to Emanuel's compositions as "cute little pieces" (*artige Sächelchen*). Although that remark goes back to Emanuel's Berlin years, not much had changed since then. Even Johann Sebastian, their father, had then voiced some reservations about Emanuel's music, and Friedemann thought himself to be his father's only legitimate successor. In his eyes, both Emanuel, who was well established in Hamburg, and Christian, with his too easily won successes, were defectors.

Emanuel saw things differently. He was the only Bach son who kept some contact with his brothers, especially with Friedrich, the "Bückeburg Bach." His attitude toward his half brother, who was eighteen years younger, was more that of a teacher—a relationship that Friedrich gladly accepted, having followed, as a composer, in Emanuel's footsteps.

Emanuel had left Berlin to become director of church music in Hamburg. His life there was comfortable; he was adequately paid and respected by all. The position may not have offered great potential for the future, but this was not a major concern for Bach, a man in his late fifties. He cherished a large circle of friends and welcomed many visitors from out of town. Being in charge of music in Hamburg's five principal churches, he had ample opportunities for earning extra income; and having good business sense, he made the most of them.

As we learned earlier, Berlin had become less and less attractive to Emanuel, largely because of strained relations between him and the Prussian king. At the end of the Seven Years' War, little remained of Berlin's formerly brilliant musical life. Emanuel therefore had everything to gain when he was invited to become Telemann's successor in Hamburg.

But Hamburg did not altogether satisfy Emanuel either. Burney visited him there in 1773, noting that Bach seemed skeptical and unhappy.

> Mr. Bach received me very kindly, but said that he was ashamed to think how small my reward would be, for the trouble I had taken to visit Hamburg. "You are come here, said he, fifty years too late." He told me at my departure, that there would be some poor music of his, performed at St. Catherine's church, the next day, which he advised me not to hear. . . . After this visit [to the famous poet Klopstock], M. Bach accompanied me to St. Catherine's church, where I heard some very good music, of his composition, very ill performed, and to a congregation wholly inattentive. This man was certainly born to write for great performers, and for a refined audience; but he now seems to be out of his element. There is a fluctuation in the arts of every city and country where they are cultivated, and this is not a bright period for music at Hamburg.

In the course of these conversations, Burney could tell that Emanuel, though highly respectful of his father, no longer shared his taste. When the conversation turned to "learned music,"

> he spoke irreverently of canons, which, he said, were dry and despicable pieces of pedantry, that any one might compose, who would sacrifice his time to them.
>
> He asked, if I had found many great contra-puntists in Italy; and upon my answering in the negative, he replied, nay, if you had, it would have been no great matter; for after counterpoint is well known, many other more essential things are wanting to constitute a good composer.

Emanuel and Burney agreed that music was not like a

> large company, speaking all at once. . . . Instead of reason, good sense, and good humor, [it] makes social intercourse consist of nothing but clamour, impertinence, and noise.

Yet this simile of a "large company" had been quite in line with the views of Johann Sebastian Bach, as we learned from Forkel. Here the son had removed himself from the father's position.

Emanuel thought more highly of the melodists, though they, too,

Wilhelm Friedemann Bach.

Emanuel Bach in Hamburg (standing) with Pastor Sturm and the painter Stöttrup.

came in for some criticism. Burney elaborates:

> He said, he once wrote word to Hasse, that he was the greatest cheat in the world; for in a score for twenty *nominal* parts, he had seldom more than three *real* ones in action; but with these he produced such divine effects, as must never be expected from a crowded score.[12]

Emanuel did have problems with another melodist, namely his brother Christian, but these were personal problems. Christian's carefree lifestyle displeased Emanuel, who may also have gotten wind of some of his half brother's remarks such as "my brother [Emanuel] lives to compose, but I compose so that I can live." Such anecdotes by and about Christian appeared in the Leipzig *Allgemeine Musikalische Zeitung*; the very fact that they were circulated is an indication of Christian's popularity.[13]

Christian had many more printed editions of his music to his credit than Emanuel had. This too may have influenced Emanuel's feelings for his half brother. It also happened at times that someone would seek an introduction to Emanuel, using Christian as a recommendation: Denis Diderot, for example, the leading French philosopher of the mid-eighteenth century and founder of the *Encyclopédie*. Diderot had been in St. Petersburg, where Empress Catherine II had appointed him her librarian, a position that entitled him to a pension.[14] In 1774, on his way home, he interrupted his journey in Hamburg. He had written several letters to Emanuel, asking him for one of his works at a price to be set by the composer. Diderot was even willing to pay a copyist, though he pointed out that "my reputation is greater than my wealth, a fate I share with many men of genius."[15] Emanuel does not seem to have been anxious to comply with Diderot's urgent and repeated requests. It is not known whether Emanuel received him in person and whether he acceded to the wish Diderot had expressed on behalf of his only daughter, Marie-Angélique, who had had thorough musical training.

Emanuel must have been surprised and not pleased by Diderot's stressing that he was "a friend of Johann Bach in London," who had even sent him a piano from England, along with one of his own compositions. Emanuel could hardly believe it: Christian, a good friend of one of France's most distinguished thinkers, who thought so highly of him that he used him as a reference?

We can understand that Emanuel was not elated, especially in view of Christian's seemingly effortless musical successes and his popularity with visitors. But that such feelings clouded his opinions of Christian's music is less understandable. He expressed his views in a conversation with the poet Matthias Claudius, which has come down to us in written form.

Emanuel received the musically interested poet and apologized for wearing his dressing gown. Claudius opined that "virtuosos usually dress like that," but Emanuel disagreed, saying that this was only true of slovenly people. Normally, it would seem, Emanuel was fastidious about his appearance.

The conversation then turned to music.

> *Emanuel:* What can you tell me about music in Copenhagen?
> *Claudius:* It's rather mediocre. The most popular composers are Schobert and your brother Christian, but your music is not greatly appreciated.
> *Emanuel:* I can't help that. Schobert, an intelligent man, is known here, too; but neither his nor my brother's current compositions amount to much.
> *Claudius:* Still, they are pleasant to listen to.
> *Emanuel:* Yes, they please the ear, but the heart remains empty.[16]

Since Christian's brother Emanuel had so little regard for his music, the high esteem of another brother—Friedrich, the Bückeburg Bach—must have warmed his heart. A little later Friedrich would visit Christian in England, bringing along his son, Wilhelm Friedrich Ernst, to become a pupil of the queen's music master. Upon his return to Bückeburg, Friedrich wholly embraced Christian's manner of composing.

In his biography of Friedrich as a "preclassic" composer, Hannsdieter Wohlfahrth has this to say:

> The encounter with John Christian Bach made a lasting impression on the Bückeburg master. His London journey turned out to be a decisive turning point in Friedrich's compositional style. . . . The stimuli he received there, from all kinds of music except opera, henceforth affected and characterized his writing. . . . His London visit lasted only a few months, but the impressions garnered there changed Friedrich's style radically. His compositions, especially those for keyboard, are now so different from what he had composed earlier that the uninitiated might believe that two composers are involved: one from the "pre-London" and one from the "post-London" years.[17]

Christian's relationship to his brothers might be summarized as follows. For different reasons, his half brothers Friedemann and Emanuel did not maintain close ties; this in part can be attributed to their different personalities. Years earlier in Berlin, Emanuel had taken in young Christian, though with some reservations and offering much criticism. But there is no indication that Friedemann had ever been close to Christian; he remained completely aloof. This only left Friedrich in Bückeburg, who thought highly of Christian both as an artist and as a human being.

All brothers were to outlive Christian: Friedemann by two years, Emanuel by six, and Friedrich by thirteen years. The public always showed them respect, partly out of respect for their family name. In Friedemann's case, respect may have been mingled with compassion, with regrets about his wasted life.

Although it may seem obvious that Christian did honor to his father's name, there were those who thought otherwise. Some evaluated Christian solely by comparing him to his father, an attitude still widespread generations later among friends of "Old Bach." Many others, however, interpreted Christian's career more positively; they realized that Christian had to go his own way and that it was to his credit *not* to have walked in his father's footsteps.

Johann Sebastian Bach would surely have continued to be pleased with Christian, just as he had shown himself to be when he paid tribute to his youngest son's talent by bequeathing him three harpsichords as an incentive for the boy's future. Sebastian would also have taken a fatherly pride in Christian, who gave fresh luster to the Bach name during a new epoch in music. And Christian, the composer, enjoyed more public acclaim than any other Bach, Johann Sebastian included.

Christian owed his popularity to himself alone, not to the name Bach, which in some situations was more hindrance than help. His popularity continued, even during the last years of his life. True, the London public was no longer startled by the novelty of his music, and there were also some setbacks. Those, however, were not what brought on his eventual decline; it was caused by a business venture that failed.

8
Last Triumphs

Mr. Bach from London has been here for two weeks. . . .
You can imagine how happy we are to see each other again.

Mozart, writing to his father from Paris

AVING RETURNED TO LONDON from his Mannheim engagement, Bach buried himself in work as though he wanted to forget his painful memories of Gustl Wendling. Early in 1773, he again published an invitation soliciting subscriptions for the Bach-Abel concerts, which were again to be given in Queens Street. The following year's announcement stated that tickets were available at "Mr. Bach's, 80 Newman Street." Abel's name was no longer included; apparently they no longer shared living quarters, though they continued to be closely connected when music making and social activities were concerned. These activities included Gainsborough, who had permanently moved to London in 1774.

After the Mannheim disappointment, Bach became seriously interested in Cecilia Grassi. During the summer and fall of 1773, they undertook extensive concert tours through western England. They appeared in Blandford on 14 July and participated in the Salisbury Music Festival in early October, on which occasion Christian delighted the audience with his fine harpsichord playing.[1] According to Mrs. Papendiek, Cecilia's singing was no longer first-rate, and she appeared in concerts rather than opera.

There has been much speculation as to why Bach married Cecilia, who was eleven years younger than he. Her vocal ability was declining, and she was no beauty. Mrs. Papendiek, usually very partial to Christian, even suspected that he married her for her money, her savings amounting to two thousand pounds. But this is doubtful, for at this time Christian was still quite well off. His bank account at Drummond's amounted to the not inconsiderable sum of 3595 pounds, the result of sold-out Bach-Abel concerts, which had attracted five hundred subscribers. If we add to this the three hundred pounds he was paid yearly for his services to the court, Cecilia's "dowry" seems modest.

There may have been other practical reasons for the marriage. Though her voice was no longer adequate for opera, Cecilia Grassi had a wealth of experience that she could put to good use in assisting Christian with his teaching or in teaching her own students. She continued to have ready access to the royal family. Again according to Mrs. Papendiek, "Madame Bach" and Miss Cantelo (a pupil of both Christian and Cecilia) were often present at court.

Their marriage turned out to be solid and lasting, not weakened by problems of any kind. It remained childless, which may have been a disappointment. Christian's letters of this period contain no family news. This applies to the letter he wrote to Padre Martini in mid-September 1773, after a long silence.

> Reverend Father, Honored Mentor!
> Mr. Waterhouse, a musician in the service of His Royal Highness, the duke of Cumberland, has asked me to give him a letter of recommendation to present to you. Knowing how very kind you are, I took the liberty of complying with his request. Mr. Waterhouse is an accomplished cellist and is anxious to make the acquaintance of such a famous person as you. Please extend your friendship to him and allow him to hear some of your compositions. Hoping that you will grant him this kindness, I remain, Reverend Sir, your most faithful and obedient servant.
> London, 15 September 1773   J. C. Bach

There followed only two more exchanges of letters, both dealing with the same subject. The occasion, in 1776, was a high point in Christian's life: Padre Martini, seventy years old and generally acknowledged to be the grand old man of European music, had asked Christian for his portrait, to be added to his "Gallery of Great Musicians." Christian considered it an honor to be included and replied,

> You are too kind to ask me for a portrait to be displayed next to those of such famous men: I do not deserve it. But my great respect for you, Reverend Father, compels me to obey at once. Moreover, the portrait has been completed, and I am now waiting for an opportunity to send it to you.

Gainsborough had painted his friend with special care; the portrait is one of his best. At Bach's request he made a copy of it, so that two renditions exist today, one in the Liceo Musicale in Bologna, the other in the earl of Hillingdon's collection in England.

As it turned out, two years went by before Christian's portrait reached its recipient in Italy, and only then after Burney, whose help the impatient Padre Martini had enlisted, put pressure on Christian to live up to his promise. The letter that accompanied the canvas was Christian's last to the Padre and is quoted here in its entirety:

> Reverend Father, esteemed Master,
> I have entrusted my portrait to Signor Roncaglia [Francesco Roncaglia, a singer who was Christian's good friend]. It is a very good likeness, done by one of the best painters here. Signor Roncaglia will be traveling through Bologna; I am confident he will deliver the portrait to you. Please accept it as a small token of the debt of gratitude I owe you. I pray that as you look at it you will think of me who will always remain your most faithful and devoted servant.
> London, 28 July 1778   J. Ch. Bach

This letter is the last document of one of the more moving friendships in the history of music; in a sense it concludes the most important chapter of Christian's life.

Romain Rolland's observation about Christian Bach is fitting—that it would be difficult to find a more perfect example of a German artist whose spirit was formed in Italy.[2] In this context the father figure of Martini must not be forgotten.

As an artist-musician, Christian had now reached his maturity, but this cannot be said of his judgment where financial matters were concerned. Turbulent days lay ahead, as Christian, not wise to the ways of the business world, embarked on a financial venture.

It all started with the search for an attractive concert hall. For five years Bach and Abel had settled for Almack's, which had now become too expensive. The hall was spacious but unattractive, and within one year the rent increased by almost 200 pounds to 693 pounds, a price that seemed excessive to Bach, the manager.

The solution was to return to Mrs. Cornelys's Carlisle House. In 1772 she had announced bankruptcy; the complete inventory of her "spacious, comfortable, and splendid house in Soho Square" (as the auctioneer described it) came under the hammer. Though the rent was lower, the public was less than enthusiastic. Mrs. Harris, whom we met earlier, wrote to her son: "[On 12 January 1774] I went to Carlisle House which Bach had selected for his concerts. Things looked very shabby, as they had in Mrs. Cornelys's time; still, I think the hall is more suitable for concerts than Almack's."

Carlisle House, pretty well stripped of its furnishings by the creditors, was only meant to be a temporary solution, for Bach had set his sights much higher, namely, on a concert hall of his own. An elegant estate on the east side of Hanover Square seemed ideal for the purpose. It included the main house, a garden with a concert pavilion, a carriage house, and several smaller buildings. All this was offered for sale by the owner, Lord Plymouth. His asking price was five thousand pounds, which was more than Bach and Abel together could put up.

The sale materialized with the help of a third partner, John Andrea Gallini. As solo dancer of the King's Theatre (later to become one of its directors) Gallini had acquired a small fortune, at least enough to put up half the purchase price. Bach and Abel provided the other half.

Their lifestyle had not been conducive to saving, so that finding enough money to finance even their share was a problem. Bach, it appears, went into debt. His bank statements from 1776 to 1779 show substantial payments to his friend the piano builder Buntebart— payments, presumably, to pay off a loan.

It turned out to be an unfortunate financial venture. Gallini had his own ideas about uses for their newly acquired property. He envisioned an enterprise that would compete with Almack's, offering entertainments that were more social than musical. An evening would begin with a "dinner for gentlemen," following which, around eight or nine o'clock, ladies would be admitted. As for music, there would be singing of glees and catches, without instruments, as was then fashionable. *Festino* was Gallini's name for such an entertainment.

As a result of Gallini's promoting this kind of event, attendance at the Bach-Abel concerts of serious music declined. Box office receipts tell the story: they fell from 3959 pounds in 1774 (the first concert of that year had still taken place at Almack's) to 1505 pounds in 1775. Similar decreases followed. Eventually outsiders had to help. Gallini's father-in-law, the earl of Abingdon, is said to have contributed sixteen hundred pounds so that the concerts could be continued.[3]

With these problems, it was only a question of time before Gallini would tire of the unequal partnership, and this indeed happened after only two seasons. Bach and Abel could no longer contribute financially to the joint venture, so Gallini withdrew, deciding to enlarge and beautify the establishment out of his own pocket. The Bach-Abel concerts continued at Hanover Square for five more years, until Bach's death, but

the public found Gallini's offerings of social entertainments more attractive, and attendance at the concerts suffered.

Abel must have seen the handwriting on the wall. His name no
longer appears in Bach's bank statements, which suggests that he disasso-
ciated himself from the enterprise when the dream of their own concert
hall failed to come true. He had also developed new interests, among
them one of his pupils, an attractive Venetian named Brigida Georgi.

The young lady's career had been truly amazing. As the daughter of a
gondolier, she had first sung in St. Mark's Square in Venice. On her way
to Paris, she had stopped in Lyon, where she appeared in various coffee
houses. She then managed to make her debut in the *Concerts spirituels*,
the leading concert organization in Paris—an amazing feat for someone
who had never had any lessons. She made up for this lack in London,
studying with Abel so intensively that tongues soon started wagging.
Signora Georgi was a frequent guest in Abel's country house in Fulham;
some who could never find him in the city joked that "he was always
going to *Foolish*" (Burney).[4]

In spite of the financial fiasco, neither Abel nor Bach showed any
inclination to reduce their standard of living. Christian continued to
derive some income from various concerts in addition to the subscription
concerts. There were also numerous benefit concerts—no fewer than ten
in May 1777. Further income accrued from lessons given by both Christian and Cecilia, but the total hardly sufficed to cover their substantial
living expenses and loan payments to Buntebart. Eventually there was
bound to be trouble.

Bach had rented a house in Richmond, the royal family's summer
residence on the Thames. That way he was close at hand, free to participate in evenings of chamber music and to give music lessons. Four
princes by now had reached the ages when lessons were called for, keeping Christian quite busy.[5] The house was also close to the residence of
Friedrich Albert, the queen's German chamberlain, who had accompanied her from Strelitz to London. He was the father of the future Mrs.
Papendiek, the source of much of our information about the "London
Bach."

Albert's home was the meeting place of the queen's chamber musicians. In addition to Bach and Abel, these were the oboist Simpson and
the violinist Nicolai. There they would rehearse every Wednesday for the
following day's concert in the queen's chambers. For these occasions
Bach brought along his own small pianoforte. Bach and Abel took turns
providing new compositions or arrangements for each concert.

Mrs. Papendiek recalled one of the rehearsals, at a time when she was only eleven or twelve years old. Bach had completely forgotten that it was his turn to supply a new composition. This, however, did not faze him. After dinner he sat down and composed "an enchanting first movement of a quintet in three flats." He then summoned two copyists who, looking over his shoulder, wrote out the parts from the score, while Christian completed the harmony. The result was a work that "is ranked among the best of his compositions, and the melody is sweetly soothing."[6]

The road to Richmond was not without danger. Highwaymen were a constant problem; coaches were often held up and the occupants robbed. "You are held up every hundred yards!" Walpole lamented. Christian and Gainsborough did not escape such a fate. It happened on 7 July 1775, in the late evening, shortly before they reached Hammersmith. Two bandits stopped them. Christian was the first victim; they had spared Abel, traveling in the coach ahead of them. The robbers, who relieved Bach and Gainsborough of their money and valuables, were eventually caught and tried. Bach was called as a witness. He testified that on the evening in question they had been held up a mile before Hammersmith. One of the robbers yelled: "Stop! Your money or your watch!" The yelling woke him up, for he had fallen asleep in the coach. They took his gold watch, valued at twenty pounds, a chain worth three pounds, and one guinea in cash. "The whole thing was over very quickly. It was about half past nine or near ten o'clock. I would not recognize the person who robbed me."[7] News of the holdup attracted much attention, since it involved threats against the lives of some well-known musicians.

Mrs. Papendiek's recollections also include pleasant events, such as boating excursions on the Thames:

> The nobility, on fine afternoons, came up in boats, other boats being filled with bands of music, to take the Prince to the promenade at Richmond. . . . Mr. Zoffany had a decked sailing vessel, elegantly and conveniently filled up, on board of which we frequently went, the Bachs being of the party. He used to take his pupil, as he wished to give her every opportunity to be heard. She sang with Madame Bach, whose voice was beautiful on the water.[8]

As time went on, Christian and Cecilia faced increasing competition as voice teachers, their chief rival being Venanzio Rauzzini, who had appeared on the scene in 1774. He was an exceptionally good-looking castrato, then twenty-seven years old. A talented musician, Rauzzini was a serious threat to Christian, not only as a voice teacher but also as a composer of operas and as a concert pianist. The *Gentlemen's Magazine* called him one of the best pianists ever to have appeared in London, but Rauzzini's main claim to fame was his undisputed excellence as a singer.

When he was only nineteen, he had entered the service of the elector of Bavaria as primo uomo at the court theater. This was quite an honor for a man his age, joining an ensemble that included stars of Regina Mingotti's calibre. Burney, who had already encountered Rauzzini in Munich, could not praise him enough:

> [Rauzzini] is not only a charming singer, a pleasing figure, and a good actor; but a more excellent contrapuntist, and performer on the harpsichord, than a singer is usually allowed to be, as all kind of application to the harpsichord, or composition, is supposed, by the Italians, to be prejudicial to the voice. Signor Rauzzini has set two or three comic operas here, which have been much approved; and he shewed and sung to me several airs of a serious cast, that were well written, and in exquisite taste.[9]

Once more Mozart enters the picture. When Rauzzini, at the age of twenty, went to Vienna to sing in Hasse's opera *Partenope*, the Mozarts were there. Furthermore, when Rauzzini had to give up his position in Munich because of a love affair, he went to the Teatro Regio Ducale in Milan. There he appeared in Mozart's *Lucio Silla*, playing opposite Anna Lucia de Amicis, Bach's friend from her London days. Rauzzini got along well with Mozart, who composed for him the famous motet *Exsultate, jubilate*, K. 165/158a. In a nonsensical letter to his sister, Mozart, in garbled language, reports that Rauzzini would sing the motet the following day at the Theatiner Church (letter of 16 January 1773).

Anna Maria Schindler, a young German singer, had arrived with Rauzzini.[10] She may have been the cause of his having to leave Munich. Opinions about her differed. Some appreciated her elegant and graceful appearance. In a letter to the *Public Advertiser*, a reader even called her "the best actress ever to have appeared on our Italian stage." Others were critical of her singing; Burney, for example, wrote that "her voice was a mere thread, for the weakness of which there was neither taste nor knowledge to compensate."[11] Still, she must have been popular in London, for posters announcing her appearance simply referred to her as "Schindlerin." But after only one season (1774–75) she was replaced by the famous-infamous Catterina Gabrielli. Once more there is a link to Mozart. Soon after having returned to Vienna, Anna Maria Schindler married the actor Joseph Lange. After her early death in childbirth in 1779, Lange married Aloysia Weber, thus becoming Mozart's brother-in-law. (At that time Mozart was still more interested in Aloysia than in her sister Constanze.)

When it came to writing operas, Christian's only rival in London had been Sacchini. But now Rauzzini became yet another competitor—a formidable one, since he appeared both as composer and star singer. At first Sacchini and Rauzzini were close friends, but they soon became bitter rivals, vying for supremacy at the King's Theatre. Christian, however, did not benefit from this competition, since he contributed only a single aria to the pasticcio *Armida*, Rauzzini's debut. And that aria was only for the second singer, Signor Pasini.

His lack of involvement in the London opera season must have bothered Christian, but it did not threaten him financially. He was much in demand abroad; numerous commissions came his way from Mannheim, Naples, Paris, and elsewhere.

Mannheim had not forgotten the phenomenal success of *Temistocle*, so it came as no surprise that the Mannheim impresario asked Christian for another score. The choice seemed clear. Late in 1772, Mozart had produced his *Lucio Silla* at the Teatro Regio Ducale in Milan. It was well received, in spite of initial difficulties. To have Bach set the same subject seemed like a fine idea. Mannheim had engaged a new court poet, Mattia Verazi, who would write the libretto, and Anton Raaff was available for the title role, a great part. Since he, along with Dorothea and Elisabeth Wendling, had contributed so much to the success of *Temistocle*, a new *Lucio Silla* was bound to succeed.

For once we are in the dark as to the year of performance, since the usual reliable sources of information let us down. Dates given vary from 1773 to 1776. Once source gives November 1773 as the time when Bach's *Lucio Silla* was first given.[12] This is unlikely, for the official court chronicler states that Bach's *Temistocle* was revived during that year. Given that opera's great success at its first production (to celebrate the elector's name day), the revival seems plausible. The same chronicler lists the *Lucio Silla* performance for 1776, as does Christian Bach's biographer Terry, citing the same source. But this date cannot be correct either. In 1775 the singer Francesco Roncaglia was no longer listed on the elector's payroll; he therefore cannot have been a cast member in 1776. All factors considered, 1774 seems the most likely year for the performance of Bach's *Lucio Silla*.

During these years Mannheim heard a great deal of Bach's music.

Aside from the gala operas, *Temistocle* and *Lucio Silla*, several smaller stage works were given. *Endimione*, an "azione drammatico teatrale" that was first performed in London, was mounted in the palace theater. Eight months later, in August 1774, Bach's one-act pastoral opera *Amor vincitore* appeared on the stage of the charming summer theater in Schwetzingen. As usual, Raaff and the Wendlings did their part to ensure that their friend Bach's music would succeed.

The rivalry between Bach and the elector for Gustl Wendling did not cause any problems. In Mannheim, Bach apparently knew how to keep his personal and professional ambitions apart. Indeed, he dedicated the six quintets of Opus 11, which may be his most beautiful works of chamber music, to Karl Theodor. Earlier in this chapter, something about their creation was recounted from one of Mrs. Papendiek's accounts.

It is not known whether Bach attended the *Lucio Silla* and cantata performances. His ties to London had become quite loose, and it may be that in 1774 the forty-year-old Christian was considering a change. Several indications point to Naples, to an offer from the San Carlo Theater that Christian seems to have considered seriously. The offer may have been prompted by plans to give Gluck's *Orfeo* with Bach's additions, a version of the opera that, as we learned, had been successful in many parts of the world. Munich had given it a spectacular production early in 1773; the San Carlo, with Bach's participation, expected to do as well or better. Bach was to direct the performances, but King Ferdinand IV seems to have had further expectations. Recently discovered records in the San Carlo archives indicate that Bach was supposed to arrive in the early summer of 1774 and that he was expected not only to prepare and conduct the *Orfeo* performances but also to reorganize the opera orchestra. The documents in question refer to him as "nuovo maestro di capella." A memorandum issued by minister of state Bernardo Tanucci confirms that problems had arisen about the orchestra's seating plan and about the quality of the string players:

> His Majesty has decreed that the orchestra should abide by the old seating plan, placing the basses in their accustomed location. The harpsichord should occupy the position commensurate with its importance. His Majesty also decrees that the new maestro di capella should hire the best violinists available in the city, for the current players are not among those.
> At the Palace, 1774   Bernardo Tanucci.[13]

Bach, however, did not come. The San Carlo archives contain

Francisco Goya, *Holdup of a Stage Coach*. Highway robberies were not uncommon at the time in England.

another document indicating that he had changed his mind:

> According to His Majesty's wish, Maestro Bach had been invited to compose two operas, for the November and carnival seasons. The maestro has informed the Royal Theater's impresario that unforeseen circumstances have made it impossible for him to leave London and come here as he had promised.

Nothing is known about the "unforeseen circumstances." Certainly Christian would have been cordially welcomed in Naples, by the public as well as by the ruler. According to an anonymous writer, Christian's works were widely acclaimed in Naples. "His arias with harpsichord are known to all music lovers of our city." If Bach was not just making excuses, perhaps he was bound by an order of the queen, who did not want to let her music master go. Actually, there was little going on in London that absolutely required his presence, and he was facing probable difficulties with Catterina Gabrielli, the new prima donna.

Catterina was the daughter of one of Prince Gabrielli's cooks, which accounts for her nickname "La Cocchetta" or "Cocchettina." Undoubtedly she was one of the best singers of her time, but also one of the most capricious and temperamental. Stories about her scandalous behavior on stage are legion; no one was safe from her quick wit and sharp tongue, not even crowned heads. At one time the Russian czarina, also named Catherine, objected to Gabrielli's exorbitant salary demands, telling the singer that, at that rate of pay, she would earn more than the field marshal. The diva, never at a loss for words, calmly replied: "Then why does Your Majesty not ask the field marshal to sing?"[14]

When Catterina arrived for the 1775–76 season, it was prophesied that something like a natural disaster would strike the King's Theatre. But no hurricane materialized, only a stiff breeze. Burney could find nothing more positive to say than that she had "all the grace and dignity of a Roman matron." Others expressed disappointment in her singing. Her admirers thought that she was not in her best form; her detractors complained about her lack of spirit due to her bad moods or the poor condition of her voice. Lord Mount Edgcumbe, who had heard her in Sacchini's *Didone abbandonata*, was puzzled. "It was thought that she never gave herself the trouble to exert her great powers before an English audience. . . . All I can recollect of [her performance] was the care with which she tucked up her great hoop as she sidled into the flames of Carthage."[15]

Georg Christoph Lichtenberg, professor of physics in Göttingen and

Venanzio Rauzzini.

The mansion on Hanover Square that Bach and Abel wanted to purchase as a concert hall.

a talented writer, had heard Gabrielli in England. Having seen Garrick give his famous interpretation of Hamlet at the Drury Lane Theatre, Lichtenberg now wanted to "descend to the glittering world" of Italian opera at the Haymarket Theatre, to hear Gabrielli in the role of Dido. His first and second attempts failed: the diva had a cold. When he finally did hear her, he wrote this report to his friend Boie:

> The curtain rose to an accompaniment of twenty kettledrums and trumpets; this took away my breath. Dido Gabrielli, in gold and white silk, made a grand entrance, applauded by the London audience. It was quite an experience. . . . You must visualize Gabrielli: a smallish, round-faced woman past her prime. Having no talent for acting she relies completely on her voice, facing the audience, even if that means twisting her neck in order to eye someone in a certain box. She sang some of her arias quite well, beginning with "Son Regina, e sono amante" in the first act; but she did not live up to my dreams about her. Hearing her at Drury Lane was not the best way to while away an evening.[16]

Lichtenberg, an astronomer and mathematician, was a frequent guest of King George III, whose newest hobby was astronomy. Lichtenberg had the honor of being invited to attend an evening of chamber music in the royal palace, a performance under Bach's direction. Here we have a scene that is interesting to contemplate: a scientist and a musician, both German, as guest and performer at an intimate gathering arranged by the English royal family, themselves largely of German origin.[17]

Missing Gabrielli's less than brilliant engagement was no great loss for Christian, and the following seasons had nothing more interesting to offer. Neither Sacchini nor Rauzzini nor the newly engaged Tommaso Traëtta was able to add sufficient luster. Bach stayed in the background. When he contributed an overture to the pasticcio *Astarte*, his name was not even listed.

Only once more did Christian's operatic career reach a high point. After an interval of ten years, he composed another work for the King's Theatre: *La clemenza di Scipione*. It was to be his last opera for London. Again the title role was interpreted by a German singer: Johann Valentin Adamberger, who, at the age of thirty, had reached European stardom. Born in lower Bavaria and educated by Jesuits in Munich, he had gained experience in Italy. Modena, Florence, Venice, and Rome were steps in his brilliant career. While in Italy, he adopted the imposing name Adamonti. His Italian successes served as a springboard for London, where the King's Theatre engaged him, initially for two seasons.

Adamberger's teacher, Giovanni Evangelista Valesi (originally Johann Walleshauser), had introduced him to Mozart. In Munich, Adamberger sang the part of the high priest in the first performance of Mozart's *Idomeneo*, other cast members being Raaff and the Wendlings. A close friendship with Mozart ensued when Adamberger's career continued at the Vienna court opera. Mozart admired not only his beautiful voice but also his intelligence and his tasteful interpretations. When the composer encountered many problems during rehearsals for *Die Entführung aus dem Serail*, Adamberger, in the role of Belmonte, was the one on whom he could count. Of the first performance, Mozart wrote to his father that Adamberger sang his opening aria "O, wie ängstlich, o, wie feurig" with more expression than anyone else in the cast, adding that

> this is everyone's favorite aria, myself included. It fits Adamberger's voice like a glove; one can practically see the trembling and hesitating, the throbbing heart [referred to in the text], which is expressed by a crescendo; one hears his whispering and sighing. (Letter of 26 September 1781.)

With such a singer starring in Bach's *Scipione*, success seemed assured, especially since the cast also included Francesco Roncaglia. Bach had known Roncaglia and valued his artistry back in Mannheim, where the singer had appeared in virtually all of Bach's stage works.

It would be a mistake to assume that the London papers printed detailed reports about the splendid event. Most of the public had no contact with operas and concerts; these events were attended by the privileged. Music critics in our sense did not exist. Information can occasionally be gleaned from letters to the editor of the *Public Advertiser*; other than that, the public had to make do with mere announcements of performances.

For *Scipione*, one such letter by a reader is all we have. It reveals enthusiasm but does not go into detail. Strangely enough, Adamberger's name is not even mentioned. About the performance on 4 April 1778, we learn that

> the Fame of Signor Bach, as a Musical Composer, is already well known in Europe. Were it not so, this last Composition would be sufficient to stamp him an Author of the first Merit of his Profession. Signor Sacchini and Signor Bach are undoubtedly two of the best Composers now existing for Serious Opera; and the Managers of the King's Theatre, by engaging both, have occasioned an Emulation between them, and

given a Spur to their Invention, which cannot fail of adding considerably to the Amusement and Satisfaction of all Lovers of Music.

La Clemenza di Scipione is the third new Serious Opera produced this Season at the King's Theatre. They are all excellent in their Kind. Creso is remarkable for its Melody, Erifle for harmony: We do not mean to enter into invidious Comparisons, but Signor Bach seems to have paid a proper Attention to both, though chiefly to the Melody of the Airs, which are finely adapted to the Voices, and are composed with great Learning, Taste, Feeling, Novelty, and Variety.

The writer then lists various arias, duets, and trios, without mentioning Adamberger, who surely must have excelled in the trio at the end of Act II.

The Terzetto at the end of Act II is also admirably composed, and pleased much, though it had the Disadvantage of coming after the very capital Air of Signora Danzi.

Still, no reference to Adamberger here, nor to his arias, such as the "Alma nata" of Act I, or "Frà le catene" of Act II, both highly effective pieces. Roncaglia's Act II aria "Frena le belle lagrime" is praised as being ravishingly beautiful and extremely good for his voice. The new prima donna Francesca Danzi, daughter of the Mannheim cellist Innocenz Danzi, especially impressed the anonymous writer, who considered Bach most fortunate to have such an able interpreter. Equal praise is bestowed on the "masterly Accompanyment of Messrs. Cramer, Cervetto, Florio, and Lebrun," the latter being the oboist whom Danzi would marry before the end of the year. Finally, the writer asserts that "the present Opera Orchestra is infinitely superior to any in Europe."

Eight days later, on 11 April, Scipione was performed again, resulting in new hymns of praise from our reader:

On Saturday last the new Opera of La Clemenza di Scipione, composed by Mr. Bach, was performed for the second Time, with the greatest Applause, to a crowded and brilliant Audience. We congratulate the present Managers on finishing their Reign with such a Chef d'oeuvre as this admirable Opera; and we most earnestly recommend it to their Successors, never to let a Winter pass without employing this great Master in composing at least one Opera.

This wish was not to come true, even though the managers of the King's Theatre had included Bach among the opera composers for the 1779–80 season. Other challenges awaited him, but Scipione was truly the crowning glory of his operatic career in London. It is a measure of its success that almost thirty years later it received a similarly splendid staging. In 1805, Mrs. Billington, daughter of Bach's pupil Mrs. Weichsell, chose *Scipione* for her benefit performance. Once more, according to the *Morning Post*, the performance was "rapturously applauded by a brilliant and discerning audience."[18] After the turn of the century, in the year of the first performance of Beethoven's *Fidelio*, Christian's opera had apparently lost none of its freshness and appeal.

The 1777–78 season in London concluded with six additional performances of *Scipione*, at a time when Bach was finding new opportunities in France. It should not be surprising that the charm of Bach's melodies and the elegance of his "singing allegro" had found a receptive public in France. Indeed, his music was more popular in Paris than anywhere but London, even though he had yet to set foot on French soil. Its popularity was furthered through the many printed editions by French publishers, among them Siéber, Huberty, Chevardière, and Leduc—though some of these editions, and many of the pirated editions, were full of mistakes. Among his compositions of Opp. 1 to 18, there was hardly a single significant work that had not been published in Paris or circulated there in manuscript form. Bach's Opus 1, the six keyboard sonatas dedicated to the queen of England, had been issued by Huberty; Opus 7 by Chevardière. Two of the Opus 9 symphonies were brought out by Siéber, grouped with symphonies by Stamitz and Toëschi. Such couplings indicate the popularity of the works in question. Leduc issued one of the popular overtures while Siéber and Huberty brought out Christian's chamber music— the quartets and trios, along with Bach's best known works in this genre, the Opus 5 sonatas (which Mozart had arranged as keyboard concertos) and the Opus 11 quintets, dedicated to the elector of the Palatinate.

Thus, plenty of Bach's music was available in Paris and was frequently heard in performances, above all in the *Concerts spirituels*. These were the city's most important musical events, featuring what was new and in vogue. Concert programs of the time clearly show that Bach's music was well established. On 1 November 1788, Mademoiselle Carlin, thirteen years old and blind, played a keyboard concerto by Bach. On Christmas Eve 1777, "a new symphony for two orchestras by M. Bach" formed part of a specially festive event. This was probably one of the six *Grand Overtures*, Op. 18; three of them, including the overture to *Endimione*, are scored for double orchestra.

Bach's Italian arias were much in demand; there was hardly a touring virtuoso who did not program them in Paris. Among such singers were

Valentin Adamberger, a star singer who appeared in Bach's last opera, *La clemenza di Scipione*.

A typical design for a stage set, late eighteenth century. Set for Mozart's *La clemenza di Tito* by Giorgio Fuentes, Frankfurt, 1799.

Brigida Georgi (as previously mentioned, one of Abel's favorite students) and Gasparo Savoi, who came from London where he was a mainstay of the King's Theatre. Arias were seldom clearly identified on the programs; the indication "by Bach" seems to have served as an assurance of quality.

We know a little more about Christian's ever-popular "Non so d'onde viene," sung by Raaff during his first appearance at the *Concerts spirituels.* He succeeded so well that he had to repeat the aria in concerts on 13, 15, and 18 April. It has been claimed that Raaff thus prepared the way for Christian's arrival in Paris, but the composer had already been quite popular there before.

It was probably at one of these concerts that Mozart once again heard the aria. "Bach's scena *Non so d'onde viene* [is] my favorite piece," he reported to his father. Mozart and his mother had arrived in Paris late in March 1778; it had been hard for them to become accustomed to the city. Wolfgang composed much. On 18 June, the *Concert spirituel* opened with his Symphony in D Major, K. 296/300a, the "Paris" Symphony. As his mother noted, there were also opportunities to teach. "At this time he has three students; he could have more but cannot accept them, because of the great distances."[19]

Mozart did not like Paris; he complained to his father on 3 July: "One has to languish here for six months, burying one's talent in a city where no money is to be made." He doubted that the French had any musical understanding:

> It really annoys me: these French gentlemen have improved their taste to the point where they can hear what is good—but they don't realize how bad their own music is, or at any rate, they can't tell the difference. . . . And their singing! I might forgive a French singer for doing violence to her own French music, if only she wouldn't sing Italian arias, ruining good music! I simply cannot stand that.

In Paris, Mozart appreciated Raaff all the more, both his company and his musicianship. He wrote to Father Leopold that they saw each other almost daily and that they had become the best of friends. When Mozart's mother came down with an illness that proved to be fatal, Raaff showed great concern for her. In her last letter to her husband in Salzburg, she could not praise Raaff enough:

> Herr Raaff comes to see us almost every day. He calls me "mother" and is ever so loving to us. Often he stays two to three hours. He came just to see me because he wanted to sing for me; he sang three arias, which pleased me greatly. . . . He is truly an honorable man; sincerity personified. (Letter of 12 June 1778.)

Mozart's mother died three weeks later. Strangely enough, Mozart first reported the sad news to a family friend, the Abbé Bullinger in Salzburg. Perhaps he wanted him to prepare Leopold gently. In a letter to his father, written at the same time, Wolfgang merely speaks of her serious illness and says that there was reason to expect the worst. Hence Leopold would write to his wife on 13 July to wish her all the best on her name day, not realizing that she had died on 3 July.

On 9 July, Wolfgang finally wrote to his father about Maria Anna's death. The letter is strangely unemotional. After explaining why he had written to Bullinger first, he blithely goes on to many trivial matters. He informs Leopold that Raaff was leaving Paris, and he mentions an important event: "Kapellmeister Bach will soon be here; I think he is writing an opera." And he adds: "The French are and always will be asses; they know nothing: they always have to turn to foreigners."

At this time, in July 1778, the twenty-two-year-old Mozart's situation was undoubtedly more critical than ever. In his youth he had been extremely close to his immediate family: father, mother, and sister. He cherished close family ties, as he did later, with Constanze, in spite of some escapades. But now, quite suddenly, he found himself completely alone. In Paris, the large, unfamiliar city, he felt terribly lonely, especially since Raaff had left and since Grimm was no longer the ally he once had been. To make things worse, Leopold in faraway Salzburg was deeply hurt because he had not been the first to be informed of his wife's death.

Under such circumstances, the prospect of Christian Bach's impending arrival must have meant a great deal to Wolfgang. On 27 August 1778 he relates the good news to Leopold:

> Mr. Bach from London has been here for two weeks; he is going to write a French opera. He has come now to listen to the singers; then he will return to London, write the opera, and come back to produce it. You can imagine how happy we are to see each other again. Perhaps he is not as glad as I am, but there is no question that he is an honest man who treats people fairly. As you know, I dearly love and greatly respect him. I know for sure that he has complimented me—not in an exaggerated manner, as some have done, but seriously and truthfully. Tenducci is also here; he is Bach's close friend and was also delighted to see me again. Now let me tell you how I went to St. Germain.

The stay there was a welcome change for Mozart, who wrote to his father that "even though I am not being paid, I have made a very useful acquaintance." He was referring to the duc d'Ayen, marshal of France since 1775, who resided in St. Germain. These eight days in stimulating company, with Bach and Tenducci as his companions, inspired a number of Mozart compositions, including a scena for Tenducci, unfortunately lost. Christian may have given Mozart the idea, for he had written a cantata for Tenducci with similar scoring. Tenducci, the "close friend," was traveling once again to escape his London creditors.

The duc d'Ayen had his own musical establishment. Mozart noted specifically that the keyboard, oboe, horn, and bassoon players were "Germans who play very well." He enjoyed their company, and during his Paris stay he repeatedly stressed that he was "an honest German." In an argument with Grimm, he accused him of preferring other opera composers. Mozart was anxious to prove to him that he was "just as good as your Piccinni, although I am only a German."

It appears that Mozart was making plans at about this time to go on from Paris to England. So far, Mozart biographers seem to have been unaware of this intention, for the pertinent reference in a letter from Leopold is rather casual. On 3 September he wrote that "Bach had promised to write to you from England and perhaps to find something for you," though Wolfgang's last letter from St. Germain contains no such hint. The passage implies that Grimm had written directly to Leopold—the two corresponded regularly—about Wolfgang's plans. Being bypassed in this way is likely to have contributed to the deterioration of Wolfgang's friendship with Grimm.[20]

Mozart must have seriously considered moving to England, for Leopold now mustered all conceivable arguments, rational and emotional, to induce his son to return to Salzburg. Surely, he exclaims, Wolfgang would not consider leaving his father, who had just lost his wife; surely he would not deprive him of the support he would need in his old age? He urges Wolfgang to remember that in Salzburg he would command "better pay, higher standing, and greater authority." Wolfgang should decide at once to leave Paris and head back to Salzburg while the weather was still good for traveling. "If you stay on there, I might have to pay for your board and room!"

Leopold feared, and not without reason, that he might lose his influence over Wolfgang; his son, lonesome after his mother's death, might now see a new father figure in Christian Bach. And so Leopold pulls all the stops:

> Everyone wishes you were here! The chief steward [Obersthofmeister] is offering you his horses; you could also have the use of the chestnut mare of Dr. Prex [a Salzburg physician], and Robin Louis [Aloysia von Robinig, one of Mozart's earlier girl friends] surely loves you. As for myself, I

Christian Bach's music was widely performed in Paris. The Opus 6 symphonies, published in Paris, were announced and reviewed in Germany. Smaller works were heard in private homes, such as that of the prince de Luynes (below).

Paris.

Daſelbſt ſind in Kupferſtich heraus gekommen, Six Simphonies à huit parties, compoſées par *Jean Bach.* Oeuvre 6, mis au jour par *Huberty,* cy devant de l'Academie royale de muſique. Man iſt mit den Sinfonien dieſes Herrn Bachs, eines Bruders des Herrn Kapellmeiſters in Hamburg, ſchon hinlänglich bekannt. Das halbe Dußend, das bey Hummeln in Amſterdam geſtochen iſt, fand beſonders viel Beyfall. Die erſten Sätze waren alle ſehr feurig und galant, die zweyten angenehm und ſingbar, die dritten ſcherzhafft und tändelnd: ſo ohngefähr ſind auch die neuern ſechs Sinfonien, die wir jetzt aus Paris erhalten. Bey der erſten und zweyten findet ſich vor dem dritten Satze noch eine Menuet und Trio. Damit man ſehen könne, ob dieſe Sinfonien an jedem Orte neu ſind, oder ob man nicht eine oder die andere davon ſchon habe, folgen hier die Anfänge:

Die Bewegung, daß ſie geſchwind ſey, iſt dabey voraus zu ſetzen, bloß die zweyte Sinfonie fängt mit einem kurzen Adagio an, worauf ein großes Allegro im ¼ Tacte folgt. Die dritte iſt hieſigen Orts in Manuſcript ſchon ſeit ein paar Jahren bekannt; die vierte findet man auch ſchon im Breitkopfiſchen Catalogo, und zwar im Supplem. I. ſub tit. BACH no. V. Uebrigens ſind dieſe Sinfonien ſowohl geſtochen, als auch einzeln geſchrieben bey Herrn Breitkopf zu haben.

would remain in good health, have a long life—all the good things you
might wish for your father. Your sister offers you friendship, love, and
devoted service; Tresel, the maid, has bought thirteen capons for you,
and Amperl [the Mozarts' dog] would lick you a thousand times: what
more could you want?

Leopold's emphasis on all that Salzburg had to offer, his application
of so much pressure, strongly suggests that Wolfgang was ready to respond
to whatever inducement Christian Bach might have offered.

The possible consequences of Mozart moving to England are many
and intriguing to contemplate. A farewell to Salzburg, to Vienna, and to
Prague, a separation from the Continent in general: how might these
have affected the further development of his genius? What if he had not
married Constanze? One can indulge in such speculations, but essentially
they are idle, especially in regard to his further development as an artist.
After all, Christian Bach accomplished a great deal from his home base
in England.

As we know, nothing came of these plans to move to England.
Leopold had one other card up his sleeve: Aloysia Weber. "Your hope
that the Weber family would have 1000 florins a year has been fulfilled.
On 15 September I had word from Munich that Count Seeau had
engaged Mlle. Weber for the German theater for 600 florins." Even a
month earlier, in his letter of 31 August, Leopold had outdone himself to
induce Wolfgang to return to Salzburg. The archbishop "definitely wants
to hear" Aloysia, in which case "they (the Webers) could stay with us."

To make such an offer, Leopold must really have feared that Wolfgang might go to England, for up to then he had taken a dim view of
Wolfgang's love interests. "All young people must do foolish things!" At
any rate, this trump card may have done the trick. Delighted by the prospect of seeing Aloysia again, in Munich or even in the family quarters in
Salzburg, Wolfgang returned home.

But what sounded like a tender romance ended with a grating dis-
cord, reminding us of Christian Bach's experience with Gustl Wendling.
Aloysia was no longer the sweet young thing Wolfgang had admired in
Mannheim. She was now all prima donna, not at all interested in Mozart,
not even moved by his musical declaration of love, the aria "Popoli di
Tessaglia," K. 300b/316, which he had begun in Paris and completed in
Munich. He was deeply hurt, although two different reactions to this
turn of events have been reported: a rather tame one, as relayed by Nissen, and an unprintable one, which Nissen suppressed.[21]

At any rate, Father Leopold had accomplished his objective; the danger of losing his son to faraway England had been averted. Wolfgang decided to return to Salzburg by way of Mannheim (strictly against the father's wish) and Munich, where he met his cousin Maria Anna Thekla, the "Bäsle," who probably accompanied him to Salzburg.

Wolfgang never saw Christian Bach again. As to the Mozart family ties, these became increasingly loose. Actually, Wolfgang had begun to distance himself from his father in 1777, when he left home accompanied only by his mother. The well-known painting by della Croce, painted in 1780–81, once more shows the family together. Mozart's mother is included through her portrait, which is shown hanging on the wall. Wolfgang then moved to Vienna and married Constanze. The last ten years of his life were the most productive ones, right up to the Requiem. Only once again did he mention John Christian Bach in writing—after he received news of Christian's death.

It is unlikely that Bach felt encouraged by the quality of singers available in Paris. He may have shared Mozart's opinion about French singers, especially female ones. But Christian had no choice, for his assigned task was to set a French text, on a French subject, to music. Perhaps he consoled himself knowing that another German composer—the sixty-five-year-old master, Gluck, who had arrived in Paris in November 1778 to prepare performances of his *Iphigénie en Tauride*—would have to make do with the same singers. Little did he then know that he was going to be used as Gluck's rival and adversary.[22]

Paris, more the capital of European civilization in general than in music, had hoped that Gluck would give international prestige to its Opéra. The time seemed just right: the Mannheim opera had closed when the elector and his court and most of his ensemble moved to Munich. After the Seven Years' War, neither Berlin nor Dresden had recaptured its former preeminence. London, as we learned, no longer contributed much that was praiseworthy. This left only the Italians, unassailable, and Vienna, rather far away.

French opera, the traditional *tragédie lyrique*, though incorporating some elements of Italian style, was mainly a French affair, written in French for French audiences. Gluck, however, who had been enticed to come to Paris in 1773 with the promise of commissions for five operas in addition to *Iphigénie en Aulide*, turned out to have a will of his own. For strategic reasons, he at first appeared to be conciliatory, but in the end he remained true to his own vision. To him, opera was a kind of music drama that was neither Italian nor French but supra-national in scope, stressing universal human values. Gluck also demanded exorbitant fees. For *Echo et Narcisse* he asked for twenty thousand livres, but was paid only half that amount. These difficulties with Gluck caused the French to look for another composer who might offer him some competition.

They first turned to Piccinni for this purpose, but this stratagem misfired. His arrival from Naples in 1776 prompted heated controversy. Forkel, no friend of Gluck, gleefully reported in his *Musikalisch-kritische Bibliothek*: "The famous *Capellmeister* Nicolo Piccinni has arrived here and has become director of a singing school for three years, with an annual salary of 2000 *Reichsthaler*. . . . He and the chevalier Gluck will soon provoke a theatrical squabble here."[23]

The "squabble," however, hardly involved the two composers themselves; it was instigated by others who had their own axes to grind. Piccinni was a gentle, agreeable man; he did not have Gluck's monumental stature, which was comparable to Handel's in England. Gluck could afford to give advice to this harmless opponent. "Believe me, in France one thinks only of making money." Poor Piccinni was to learn the truth of these words: he died in poverty, while Gluck, a rich man, died after an overly sumptuous banquet.

Gluck's opponents tried in vain to launch Piccinni as his adversary. The Italian was all too eager to write in the French manner, but this resulted in the fiasco of his opera *Roland*. He had dedicated it to Queen Marie Antoinette, who, while still crown princess, had played on both teams. She had been Gluck's pupil in Vienna, but she had also seen to it that Piccinni was engaged for Paris so that Gluck would not be the undisputed ruler there.

Monsieur de Vismes, the new director of the opera, had his own ulterior motives in dealing with Bach. Not only did he see to it that his brother would contribute the libretto for Bach's new opera, *Amadis des Gaules*; he also tried (after the failed Piccinni coup) to play Christian Bach against Gluck. Such a strategy, if Christian was aware of it, would have been just as foreign to his personality as it had been to Piccinni's.

Little can be reported about Bach at this time, 1778–79, except that, as always, he was involved in various concerts. Again he showed himself to be a true friend of Tenducci, making it possible for him to return to London in spite of his creditors. They had probably been pacified by the announcement of a benefit concert for Tenducci, who even felt secure enough to reveal his London address: Prince's Street, Leicester Fields.

The concert, on 20 April 1779, offered an ambitious program. Bach presented his one-act pastoral *Amor vincitore*, which had had such spec-

Christoph Willibald Gluck.

Nicolo Piccinni.

tacular success years earlier in Schwetzingen. Singers included Abel's pupil Brigida Georgi and Signora Marchetti, prima donna at the King's Theatre in 1774. Bach also contributed a new work of chamber music, a quartet for violin, oboe, cello, and pianoforte, probably one of the four works of Opus 29, which he had dedicated to the earl of Abingdon, who had financed the Bach-Abel concerts.

All would have been well had it not been for an occurrence in Bach's household. Mrs. Papendiek relates the incident that almost ruined Bach, whose financial situation was already shaky.

Bach, trusting as always, had fallen into the habit of advancing to his housekeeper in Richmond ample funds for paying those merchants who customarily extended credit to Bach. The housekeeper provided forged receipts for Bach and pocketed the money. Her fraudulent practices might have gone undetected for weeks and months, but rumors of Bach's impending departure from Richmond had begun to circulate. When merchants confronted Bach with their bills, the scheme was discovered. But the housekeeper by then had left town, leaving Bach with debts between eleven and twelve hundred pounds. "This shook him, and other troubles followed."[24]

Meanwhile, back in Paris, Gluck had tried in vain to solidify his position as an opera composer. Piccinni no longer posed a threat, but Bach did. Everyone impatiently awaited his *Amadis des Gaules*, scheduled for the end of the season. In May, Gluck's *Iphigénie en Tauride* had been a decided success, but *Echo et Narcisse* was a setback. Though not normally given to experimentation, Gluck had attempted to deal with the tense situation by trying out new stylistic devices, hoping to take the wind out of his competitor's sails.

The experiment failed. The love of the nymph Echo for the beautiful shepherd Narcisse was unconvincing, musically speaking, for Gluck had tried to combine pastoral music with the heroic sounds of his earlier musical dramas. But more power was expected from Gluck, and more drama than the pastoral subject called for. In his earlier operas, the public had accepted or even welcomed the unheroic appearances of his heroes, since that had been the convention of the time. Thus in *Alceste*, Hercules wore high-heeled boots, flesh-colored stockings, knee britches of green satin, and a helmet with ostrich plumes that gleamed in all colors of the rainbow. Such things were admired rather than criticized, but admiration did not extend to any music that even vaguely resembled the gentle Piccinni's.

Embittered and no longer in good health—he had suffered several slight strokes—Gluck returned to Vienna late in October 1779, leaving the field to Bach. The Paris journal *L'Esprit des Journaux* noted his arrival with kind words:

> M. Bach, music master to the queen of England and to the royal family, arrived in Paris in August. He brings with him the opera *Amadis des Gaules*, which he chose to compose under an agreement with the management of the Académie Royale de Musique. He has arranged the text in a way that demonstrates his brilliant talent. M. Bach is staying at the Hôtel de Bretagne, rue Croix-des-Petits-Champs.[25]

There is no record of a meeting between Christian Bach and Gluck. Such an encounter might have been fascinating, given their altogether different personalities, but it probably did not occur. Gluck was not a gregarious person; he was also hurt by his recent experiences in Paris ("I was treated like a common thief") and was in no mood to welcome his successor. Nor was he anxious to return:

> But as to my going to Paris again, nothing will come of it, so long as the words "Piccinist" and "Gluckist" remain current, for I am, thanks be to God, in good health at present, and have no wish to spit bile again in Paris. . . . I shall hardly allow myself to be persuaded again to become the object of the criticism or the praise of the French nation. . . . I could wish that someone might come one day to take my place, and to please the public with his music.[26]

When Gluck wrote this, the man who might take his place was already in Paris. Christian's *Amadis des Gaules* was given on 14 December 1779, in the presence of Queen Marie Antoinette and the entire court, an honor for the composer. But *Amadis* did not succeed much better than Gluck's *Echo* at its September performance, which Bach had probably attended.

The *Amadis* production cannot have been the problem; it was a magnificent spectacle with magicians, demons, and good and evil fairies. The two lovers, Amadis and Oriane, are attacked by Arcabonne, the wicked fairy, who, wildly jealous, raises a dagger against Amadis, whom she loves. Needless to say, there is a happy ending: Urganda, the good fairy, descends from on high, accompanied by lightning and thunder, to unite the loving pair.

There are other impressive scenes. Demons are transformed into nymphs, shepherds, and shepherdesses; they lure the unsuspecting Amadis into a pavilion of love that is actually a prison. All this provides Bach with an opportunity to write two moving choruses for the prisoners: "O fortune cruelle" and "Ciel, finissez." In general, the choruses in *Amadis* make powerful dramatic and musical statements. Elsewhere, ballet and pantomime, so important in French opera, advance the action and delight the eyes more than the most beautiful music could delight the ears. A scene from the last act serves as an example.

Amadis must ascend two flights of stairs, one of which suddenly goes up in flames. At that moment, two statues of armed men come to life and attack poor Amadis with their swords and spears. He, of course, subdues them and, accompanied by flower girls, moves on to the second set of stairs. A portal opens, revealing knights and their ladies, who celebrate the happy outcome in a ballet finale. Amidst all these spectacular displays, the aria "Jeunes coeurs que l'amour engage," sung by Amadis and the chorus, assumes secondary importance.

Whatever kind of music the public expected, presumably in a style somewhere between Gluck and Piccinni, they were disappointed. Though the opera's subject and language were French, the music was Christian Bach's own, written in the manner that had brought him success before. He had not tried to cater to the taste of an audience that seems to have expected some kind of a new musical sensation.

The reviews refer to the "tremendous applause" that had followed some of the arias. The writer in the *Correspondance littéraire* expressed regret that Bach succeeded "neither in rekindling the war between Gluckists and Piccinists nor in settling the conflict." The *Mercure de France* blamed the lack of success on singers who were "unspeakably bad," which might be seen as a confirmation of Mozart's views on French singers cited above.

Nevertheless, Bach's music was distinctive enough to provide inspiration, twelve years later, for Mozart's *Magic Flute*. Perhaps the evil fairy Arcabonne served as a model for Mozart's Queen of the Night, although such similarities quite regularly occur in fairy-tale operas of that period.[27] Two hundred years later, in 1983, a revival of *Amadis* was successful enough to prove its lasting intrinsic worth.[28]

Though early reviews reflected some disappointment, the judgment of connoisseurs seems to have prevailed, for soon Bach was commissioned to write a second opera for Paris. Again he was asked to revive an old subject: the tragedy *Omphale* by Houdar de la Motte. It had first been set to music in 1701 by Destouches, then again in 1769 by Jean-Baptiste Cardonne. The fate of Cardonne's *Omphale* had been similar to that of Bach's *Amadis*: it neither satisfied Destouches's followers nor fulfilled the expectations of the progressives.

A modern production of Bach's *Amadis*, Hamburg 1983.

Omphale was the last opera undertaken by Bach. It seems that work on it did not go well; no music has been preserved. Health problems may have stood in the way, or financial concerns, or both. At any rate, the Paris public never had an opportunity to compare Bach's *Omphale* with that of Destouches or Cardonne.

Late in life, Bach began work in a field that was entirely new to him: writing a treatise on how to play the pianoforte, the instrument for which he had done so much as a pioneer composer. After twenty-five years, he thus followed in the footsteps of his brother Emanuel, whose *Versuch über die wahre Art das Clavier zu spielen* around 1750 had become the basic treatise on keyboard playing, including accompanying and musical interpretation. At that time the pianoforte was not yet widely known.

Bach had written *Four Progressive Lessons for the Harpsichord or Pianoforte*. These pieces may have prompted Francesco Ricci, then also in Paris, to invite Bach to collaborate on a teaching manual he was writing for the Naples Conservatory. Ricci had been born in Como, and he returned there as maestro di capella at the cathedral. He had made a name for himself as a composer, some of his works being published in Amsterdam, London, and Paris. Leopold Mozart did not think much of his music, calling him a minor figure, even a "half-composer and scribbler." Yet Ricci deserves credit for having been the first to publish a sinfonia concertante in Paris, and for having written sacred music that was well received, especially in England.

Ricci and Bach may have met in London, if not earlier in Milan. The exact circumstances of their collaboration on the teaching manual are not known. Perhaps Bach had originally written these studies for the Naples Conservatory and later added them to Ricci's manual, which was then making the rounds in Paris. Or their collaboration may have taken place in Paris, after some preliminary work in London. Ultimately the book was published by Leduc with the title *Méthode où Recueil de connoissances élémentaires pour le Forte-Piano où Clavecin . . . Composé pour le Conservatoire de Naple par J. C. Bach et F. P. Ricci.*

The introduction to Part Two is in French; it discusses the one hundred elementary exercises with violin accompaniment found in Part One. The commentary for Part Two is written in both French and Italian. Part Two, for more advanced players, consists of eighteen more attractive studies.

Bach returned to England sometime during the spring or summer of 1780, carrying with him the contract for his next opera, *Omphale*. He revised the score of *Amadis* after its first three performances, but the following four repetitions do not seem to have benefited from the changes. Nevertheless, Bach did not feel financially threatened during these last two years of his life. He had earned ten thousand francs from *Amadis*, he had a commission to write *Omphale*, and he could expect some earnings from his teaching manual. He was also still listed as a composer for the 1781–82 season of the King's Theatre, although this may have been a mere formality.

Christian had made an error in judgment when he left London voluntarily, opening the field to his competitors, though he may not have thought of them as such. At the opera, as we have heard, Sacchini and Rauzzini were the big names, while in the concert hall, the young pianist Schröter dominated the scene. During Bach's absence, many of his pupils changed over to Schröter. Among violinists, Wilhelm Cramer, whom Bach had brought to London, and Felice Giardini drew full houses. One consequence of these developments was that attention was diverted from the Bach-Abel concerts.

Title page of the original edition of Bach's *Amadis*.

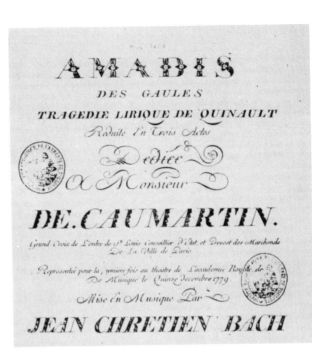

Amadis's aria, from the same edition.

There was another important change. The younger generation of the royal family was growing up, which jeopardized Bach's position as music master for the queen. The crown prince, now eighteen, had become a devoted musical amateur and had, in a sense, succeeded his mother as musical head of the household. He had a pleasant voice, played the cello with good intonation and taste, and would accompany the keyboard part on the cello as his father used to do. The father had become absorbed in his new hobby, astronomy.[29]

Giardini was now in charge of the weekly evenings of chamber music, to which he contributed his own compositions. He had become the royal family's favorite, for Bach, having been away in Mannheim, Paris, and later expected in Naples, had distanced himself from music at court.

None of these circumstances, not even the theft by his dishonest housekeeper, seem to have worried him a great deal. According to Mrs. Papendiek, Bach continued to enjoy life to the hilt, even though he had overdrawn his account at Drummond's. The ten thousand francs from *Amadis* and a possible advance on *Omphale* were not enough to make him solvent again.

There is no factual evidence that alcohol contributed to Bach's downfall, though Bach's biographer Macfarren relates that during his last years "he rarely wrote save under spirituous excitement."[30] Still, we do know of alcoholic excesses by his friends Abel and Gainsborough, which makes it unlikely that Christian would have been the only one to abstain. Alcohol, then, may have contributed to his physical deterioration, which made it imperative for him to seek a change of scene in Paddington.

That his collapse occurred within a few months is all the more surprising when we regard his portrait by Gainsborough, considered to be very lifelike. The painting reveals a robust appearance, similar to that of his father and brothers. But Christian must have felt that the end was near. On 14 November 1781 he drew up his will:

> This is the last will and testament of me John Christian Bach of the parish of St. Mary le bone in the County of Middlesex, Music Master to Her Most Gracious Majesty Queen Charlotte. I give, devise and bequeath unto my dear wife Cecilia Bach, late Cecilia Grassi, all my real and personal estate whatsoever to hold to her, her heirs, executors, administrators, and assigns for ever, but subject nevertheless to the payment of my debts and funeral expenses. And of this my will I do appoint my said dear wife Cecilia sole executrix. In witness whereof I the said

John Christian Bach have hereunto set my hand and seal this four-
teenth day of November 1781.[31]

Only a few days before Christian had prepared this document, and
some ten weeks before his death, an announcement appeared in the *Public Advertiser* of 27 October 1781. In it, opera director Peter Crawford
informs the readers of the composers who will write operas for the next
season: Bertoni, Bianchi, Rauzzini, and Bach. The star that had shone so
brightly in London's operatic firmament had not yet burned out.

During his last days and hours Bach's friends were with him, which
pleased and cheered him. "I believe few days passed without one or the
other of our family seeing him," recalled Mrs. Papendiek, then still Miss
Albert. Mr. Papendiek, her fiance, was among Bach's most devoted students.

> The Zoffanys,[32] poor Abel, and others supplied him entirely with provi-
> sions sent already prepared. Mr. Papendiek saw him every day, and
> assisted him by many kind acts, which are all the more comforting
> when done by the hand of one we love. Here I urged him to close the
> eyes of his beloved friend in happiness, by offering marriage to his *pro-
> tégée*, Miss Cantilo, but on that subject Mr. Papendiek was deaf to
> entreaty. The last visit we paid was together with my father and mother
> [and Mr. Papendiek]. Bach, on taking a final leave, joined our hands [to
> show that he wanted Miss Albert and Mr. Papendiek to be joined in
> marriage]. I think now I see his enchanting smile. Not a word was said;
> we were motionless. On retiring, we could not get Mr. Papendiek away,
> but at last my father prevailed upon him to hasten to the Queen, with
> the news of Bach being so near his end. This roused him, and after this
> painful mission, he obtained leave to return to his friend, who had just
> passed away when he reached this room of mourning.[33]

What happened then must seem incredible to us. As soon as word of
Bach's death had gotten out, creditors began to force their way into the
room in which he had just passed away. Even with the help of a coachman, Mr. Papendiek could barely fend them off.[34]

In her continued account, Mrs. Papendiek relates that the queen sent
some money to Bach's widow, by way of her father, to cover the costs of
the funeral and other urgent necessities. She also paid one hundred
pounds to Bach's faithful coachman, who had served him a long time and
from whom Bach had borrowed that amount—it had come to that.

Bach's debts must have been enormous. The queen was not in a position to erase them, and the sale of Bach's estate did not accomplish that

much either. The queen, at any rate, made it possible for Bach's widow to return to Italy, paying her travel expenses as well as those of her coachman and one other companion. She also granted her a pension of two hundred pounds for life.[35]

Mrs. Papendiek sadly noted that only Schröter, Cramer, and a very few other colleagues appeared "to see and hear." She reproached the other musicians for not having shown the respect they owed Bach. For unknown reasons, neither Abel nor Gainsborough attended the funeral. As to Abel, there is one more brief reference to him in Mrs. Papendiek's diary. Beyond that, we know that during his remaining years he turned increasingly to drink. Often others had to help him to the podium when he was to appear as soloist at a concert. Gainsborough, who also imbibed heavily, remained Abel's friend to the end; the death of Abel in 1787 was a great blow to him. He wrote to his longtime friend, the journalist and publisher Henry Bate:

> If Abel was not so great a man as Handel it was because caprice had ruined [his] music before he ever took up the pen. For my part I shall never cease looking up to heaven—the little while I have to stay behind [Gainsborough was to die a year later]—in hopes of getting one more glance of the man I loved from the moment I heard him touch the string.[36]

Perhaps alcohol had kept both Abel and Gainsborough from attending Bach's funeral. He had died on 1 January 1782, the very day on which the *Public Advertiser*, unaware of his death, had announced another Bach-Abel concert for 23 January. A correction was published a week later, adding that from now on the concerts would be held as benefits for Bach's widow and for Abel. Nothing came of that plan, however; Abel's condition had deteriorated to the extent that he could no longer organize the concerts.[37]

On Sunday, 6 January 1782, Bach, aged forty-seven, was laid to rest in St. Pancras cemetery, Middlesex.[38] It was an ironic twist of fate that Bach, one of music's great masters, was accompanied to his place of interment by only four friends, none of them musicians: Friedrich Albert and Mr. Papendiek, the painter Zoffany, and the piano maker Buntebart.

From faraway Vienna, Mozart reported that at Baron van Swieten's house "they play nothing but Handel and Bach." (Letter of 10 April 1782.) In the same letter, addressed to his father, he asks: "Have you heard that the English Bach has died? What a loss for the world of music!"[39]

Christian Bach's tomb, designed by the sculptor Agostino Carlini, Bach's neighbor at King's Square.

Notes

Sources included in the Bibliography are given here in short form only.

Abbreviations:
Burney, *History* = Burney, *A General History of Music* . . . (see Bibliography).
Burney, *Germany* = Burney, *The Present State of Music in Germany* . . . (see Bibliography).
Burney, *Italy* = Burney, *The Present State of Music in Italy* . . . (see Bibliography).
Deutsch-*Dokumente* = Deutsch (see Bibliography).
MGG = *Musik in Geschichte und Gegenwart*, 16 vols., Kassel, 1949–79.
NMA = W. A. Mozart, *Neue Ausgabe sämtlicher Werke*, Kassel, 1956–.

CHAPTER I

1. Bernhard Knick, ed., *St. Thomas zu Leipzig*, Wiesbaden, 1963.

2. Bernhard Friedrich Richter, *Das Innere der alten Thomasschule*, Leipzig, 1904.

3. Mattheson, *Ehrenpforte*, Preface, xxxii.

4. Terry, [J. S.] *Bach*, 216.

5. Georg Thiele, "Die Berufung des Johann Gottfried Bernhard nach Mühlhausen," *Mühlhäuser Geschichtsblätter, Zeitschrift des Altertumsvereins für Mühlhausen in Thüringen und Umgebung* (1920): 50–54. By the same author: "Die Bach-Familie in Mühlhausen," ibid. (1921): 71–84.

6. Scheibe, sec. 6, 62.

7. Johann Adam Hiller, ed., *Wöchentliche Nachrichten und Anmerkungen die Musik betreffend*, Leipzig, 1769, sec. 17, 127: "Ermahnungen eines Vaters an seinen Sohn, die Musik betreffend."

8. Esteban Arteaga, *Geschichte der italiänischen Oper*, Leipzig, 1789; rpt. Hildesheim, 1973, 42.

9. M. Jakob Adlung (1699–1762) was a professor and organist in Erfurt (*Anleitung zur musikalischen Gelahrtheit*, 1758). See Johann Adam Hiller, "M. Jakob Adlung," in *Lebensbeschreibungen berühmter Musikgelehrter und Tonkünstler neuerer Zeit*, Leipzig, 1784, 1.

10. Paul Benary, *Die deutsche Kompositionslehre des 18. Jahrhunderts*, Leipzig, 1961. This is an appendix to Scheibe's *Compendium musices*.

11. Romain Rolland, *A Musical Tour Through the Land of the Past*, New York, 1922, 77.

12. Mattheson, *Patriot*, 129.

13. Mattheson, *Der vollkommene Capellmeister*, 133.

14. Letter of 13 August 1778.

15. Falck, 1–11.

16. Forkel, cited in *The Bach Reader*, 328.

17. Christian Friedrich Daniel Schubart, *Schubarts, des Patrioten gesammelte Schriften und Schicksale*, Stuttgart, 1839, vol. 6, 183.

18. Hans-Joachim Schulze, "Frühe Schriftenzeugnisse der jüngsten Bach-Söhne," *Bach-Jahrbuch* 64 (1963): 61–69.

19. Karl Pottgiesser, "Die Briefentwürfe des Johann Elias Bach," *Die Musik*, 12 (1912/1913): 43.

20. Otto Kaemmel, *Geschichte des Leipziger Schulwesens*, Leipzig/Berlin, 1909, 305–307.

21. Friedrich Rochlitz, *Allgemeine Musikalische Zeitung* 8 (September 1806): 813.

22. Burney, *General History*, vol. 2, 955.

23. *Auszüge aus Johann Salomon Riemers Leipzigischem Jahrbuche, 1714–1771*, 426.

24. Fritz Reuter, "Die Entwicklung der Leipziger, insbesondere Italienischen Oper bis zum siebenjährigen Krieg," *Zeitschrift für Musikwissenschaft* 5: 1–16 (October 1922); Erich H. Müller, *Angelo und Pietro Mingotti . . .* , Dresden, 1917.

25. Forkel, reprinted in *The Bach Reader*, 305.

26. Karl Heinrich Friedrich Rödenbeck, *Tagebuch oder Geschichtskalender aus Friedrichs des Grossen Regentenleben*, Berlin, 1840, vol. 1, 142.

27. Bach bows even lower to the king in the dedications (really solutions) to his canons: "Notulis crescentibus crescat Fortuna Regis" (As the notes rise, may the king's fortune rise), or "Ascendenteque Modulatione ascendat Gloria Regis" (As the modulations rise, may the king's glory rise).

28. Willi Reich, *Padre Martini als Theoretiker und Lehrer*, Diss., Vienna, 1934, 113.

29. The encounter of Bach with Frederick II is the subject of a controversy between Fritz Müller and Rudolf Steglich in *Zeitschrift für Musik*, Regensburg 1936, 931 and 1368–72.

30. Franz Wöhlke, *Lorenz Christoph Mizler—ein Beitrag zur musikalischen Gelehrtengeschichte des 18. Jahrhunderts*, Würzburg, 1940.

31. Lorenz Christoph Mizler, *Anfangs-Gründe des General Basses*, Leipzig, 1739, rpt. Hildesheim, 1972, 61.

32. Wöhlke, 75.

33. *Bach-Dokumente*, vol. 3, 288 (No. 803).

34. *Bach-Dokumente*, vol. 2, 461–464. See also Ernst Otto Lindner, "Biedermann und Bach," *Zur Tonkunst*, Berlin, 1864, 64–94.

35. Apparently Friedemann entered into the quarrel from Halle; it continued until 1751. This is indicated by a remark by Biedermann, *Bach-Dokumente*, vol. 1, 125f.

36. *Bach-Dokumente*, vol. 1, 209–212.

37. Cited by Schmid, 36, note 1.

38. On returning from St. Petersburg, Denis Diderot stopped in Hamburg in March 1774. In a letter to Emanuel he refers to himself as Christian's friend.

39. Anna Magdalena's dedication reads as follows: "I, Anna Magdalena Bach, née Wülckin, give this magnificent book to my dear son, as a memento and for your Christian edification. 25 December 1749, your loving Mama." *Bach-Dokumente*, vol. 1, 124.

40. Joseph Riepel, *Anfangsgründe zur musicalischen Setzkunst*, Frankfurt/Leipzig, 1752. Quoted in Hannsdieter Wohlfahrt, *Johann Christoph Friedrich Bach*, Bern, 1971, 50. See also Wilhelm Twittenhof, *Die musiktheoretischen Schriften J. Riepels als Beispiel einer anschaulichen Musiklehre*, Halle, 1935.

41. Forkel, quoted in *Bach Reader*, 322.

42. Rudolf Steglich, *Wege zu Bach*, Regensburg, 1949, 53.

43. Rochlitz (note 21), 813f.

44. While Bach was still alive, having suffered his first stroke, Gottlob Harrer played an audition (8 June 1749). He was applying for the position held by Bach, who recovered, however. Harrer had to wait another year.

45. *Bach-Dokumente*, vol. 2, 513 (No. 630).

46. *Bach-Dokumente*, vol. 2, 504 (No. 628). Bach's widow was instructed to "hold on to the remaining instruments belonging to the deceased until a sale had been arranged."

47. An idea of the purchasing power can be obtained from some prices in effect in Berlin at the time:

A garment with vest	50 taler	
An ordinary garment	22 taler	
Trousers and stockings	12 taler	
A pair of boots	5 taler	
A wig	2 taler	
A pocket watch	40 taler	
A bushel of wheat	1 taler	10 groschen
A bottle of Moselle wine		12 groschen

Source: Ernst Consentius, *Alt-Berlin Anno 1740*, Berlin, 1907, rpt. 1980.

CHAPTER 2

1. Three months later, on 25 February 1751, in Halle, Friedemann married the daughter of the customs official in whose house he resided.

2. Johann Sebastian's godparents were: Margrave Heinrich, Margrave Carl, Herr von Happe, Count Keyserlingk, the wife of General von Meyern, and Frau von Printzen. Heinrich Miesner, "Aus der Umwelt Philipp Emanuel Bachs," *Bach-Jahrbuch* 1937, 133.

3. Hermann Wucherpfenning, *J. Fr. Agricola*, unpubl. diss., Berlin, 1922. MGG 1: 159.

4. Siegfried Borris, *Kirnbergers Leben und Werk und seine Bedeutung im Berliner Musikkreis um 1750*, Kassel, 1933.

5. Falck, 52.

6. Rudolf Steglich, "Johann Joachim Quantz," *Zeitschrift für Musik*, August 1936, 920.

7. Schmidt 42; Amalie Arnheim, "Zur Geschichte der Liebhaberkonzerte in Berlin im 18. Jahrhundert," *18. Jahresbericht der Gesellschaft zur Pflege alt-klassischer Musik*, Berlin, 1912–13, 166.

8. Burney, *Germany*, 2: 151.

9. Bitter, vol. 1: 183.

10. *Allgemeine Musikalische Zeitung*, Leipzig, January 1814, vol. 16, column 36.

11. Burney, *Germany*, 2: 234f.

12. Mennicke, 458.

13. A performance of Graun's opera *Mitridate* on 27 March 1751 included a grand display of fireworks and a conflagration. For this the king had brought from Bologna one Angelo Galiani, a fireworks specialist. Ludwig Schneider, *Geschichte der Oper und des königlichen Opernhauses in Berlin*, Berlin, 1852, 135.

14. Mennicke, 467.

15. Albert Mayer-Reinbach, "Carl Heinrich Graun als Opernkomponist," *Sammelbände der Internationalen Musikgesellschaft* 1 (1899–1900).

16. Schneider, 108.

17. Georg Thouret, *Friedrich der Grosse als Musikfreund und Musiker*, Leipzig, 1898.

18. Algarotti, *Essay*, 19.

19. Algarotti, 20; see also Egon Wellesz, "Francesco Algarotti und seine Stellung zur Musik," *Sammelbände der Internationalen Musikgesellschaft* 15 (1913–14), 427.

20. Halberstadt, 1751, 19.

21. Lorenz, 148.

22. Burney, *Germany*, 2: 3.

23. Prince Lobkowitz (1724–1784) himself was an excellent composer. Burney admired several of his works.

24. Burney, *Germany*, 2: 271; Carl von Ledebur, *Tonkünstler-Lexicon Berlin's*, Berlin, 1861, 19; Antoine Cherbuliez, "Carl Philipp Emanuel Bach 1714–1788," *Neujahrsblatt der Allg. Musikgesellschaft*, Zurich 1940, 18.

25. Bitter, 25.

26. Mennicke, 482, note 5.

27. Quoted in a lecture by Carl Friedrich Zelter, 17 January 1808 in Königsberg, East Prussia; Ledebur, *Tonkünstler-Lexikon*, 19.

28. Zelter confirms that during his Berlin years Emanuel Bach wrote canons. See Schmid, 75; Bitter, 112f.

29. Beaujean, 14, note 55; Krause, 35.

30. Schmid, 51, letter of 5 December 1767.

31. Bitter, 84.

32. Johann Friedrich Reichardt, *Musik-Almanach von 1796*, quoted in Bitter, 173.

33. *Bach-Dokumente*, 3: 113 (No. 683).

34. Heinz Döllmann, *Christoph Nichelmann (1717–1762), ein Musiker am Hofe Friedrichs des Grossen*, diss., Löningen, 1938, 25–29.

35. Geiringer, 427.

36. Bernhard Engelke, "Gerstenberg und die Musik seiner Zeit," *Zeitschrift der Gesellschaft für Schleswig-Holsteinische Geschichte*, 56: 429 (Kiel 1927); see also Schmid, 37.

37. C. P. E. Bach, *Versuch*, 123. (See also Engl. transl., 152f.)

38. Bitter, 86, footnote.

39. Bitter, 85.

40. Krause, 89–91, 171, 190.

41. Mattheson, *Capellmeister*, 194.

42. Rudolf Schäfke, "Quantz als Ästhetiker," *Archiv für Musikwissenschaft*, 6: 227 (Leipzig, 1924).

43. In his Easter Cantata of 1756, Emanuel uses his father's chorale settings. They appear unchanged in the concluding chorale "Heut' triumphiret Gottes Sohn." See Bitter, 136.

44. C. P. E. Bach, *Versuch*, Engl. transl., 151.

45. Engelke, 432.

46. Arnold Schering, "Carl Phillip Emanuel Bach und das 'redende Prinzip' in der Musik," *Jahrbuch Peters* 45 (1938): 13–29.

47. Gleim in a letter to Kleist, 23 September 1747, writes that he and Krause will meet with the "starke Geister" and prove them wrong in their statements against Moses and the prophets. Quoted by Beaujean, 10.

48. In the spirit of merriment, Marpurg had written and circulated the canon: "Kirn-, Kirn-, Kirn-berger hat kein Gehirn" (Kirnberger has no brain). Kirnberger was quick to retaliate with "Mar-, Mar-, Mar-purg ist ein Narr" (Marpurg is a fool). Bitter, 105, note 2.

49. Beaujean, 10.

50. Schmid, 39, refers to Ramler's letters to Gleim, 5 May and 14 July 1759.

51. Friedrich Nicolai, *Briefe über den itzigen Zustand der schönen Wissenschaften in Deutschland*, Georg Ellinger, ed., Berlin, 1894, letter 8, p. 8.

52. Gerber, *Historisch-Biographisches Lexikon*.

53. Beaujean, 46.

54. Christian Gottfried Krause, "Vermischte Gedanken," in Marpurg, *Historisch-kritische Beyträge*, 3: 540 (Berlin, 1758).

55. Scheibe viewed the concise genre of the ode as the best counterpart to the "cumbersome and confused manner of some great minds." According to him, "the melody of an ode must flow freely and be pure and natural, so that someone with little musical experience can sing it, easily and at once." *Critischer Musikus*, 594.

56. Albert Jansen, *Jean-Jacques Rousseau als Musiker*, Berlin, 1884, 157, Rpt. Geneva, 1971.

57. Rosemarie Ahrbeck, *Jean-Jacques Rousseau*, Leipzig, 1978, 59.

58. Max Friedländer, *Das deutsche Lied im 18. Jahrhundert*, Stuttgart/Berlin, 1902, 58.

59. The text has been attributed to one B. von Gemmingen. It is not known whether he was related to Otto von Gemmingen-Hornberg (1755–1836), Mozart's friend and benefactor.

60. Friedrich Wilhelm Marpurg, *Historisch-kritische Beyträge zur Aufnahme der Musik*, Berlin, 1754–55, 505.

61. *Verzeichnis des musikalischen Nachlasses des verstorbenen Kapellmeisters C. Ph. E. Bach, Hamburg*, printed by Gottlieb Friedrich Schniebes, 1790, 82f. Christian in Italy probably sent to his brother the "Clavier-Concert nach Tartini's Manier."

62. Schökel, 26–40; see also Arnold Schering, *Die Geschichte des Instrumentalkonzerts*, Leipzig, 2d ed. 1927, 147.

63. Minos Dounias, *Die Violinkonzerte Giuseppe Tartinis als Ausdruck einer Künstlerpersönlichkeit und einer Kulturepoche*, Wolfenbüttel/Zurich, 1966, 245.

64. Ibid., 91.

65. Ibid., 162f.

66. Leopold Mozart used some examples from Tartini's violin method, though

he does not refer to him by name. In one place he writes: "I will put down a few examples which are drawn from the pieces of one of the most celebrated violinists of our time." Engl. trans. by Editha Knocker, London, 1948, p. 201. See also Paul Brainard, *Die Violinsonaten Giuseppe Tartinis*, diss., Göttingen, 1959, 505.

67. Giuseppe Tartini, *Trattato di Musica secondo la vera scienza del armonica*, Padua, 1754, 149. German trans. in Dounias, 176.

68. Dounias, 207.

69. Dounias, 205.

70. Jean-Jacques Rousseau, *Oeuvres*, 7: 131; see also Jansen, 283.

71. Luigi Petrobelli, "La scuola di Tartini in Germania e la sua influenza," *Analecta Musicologica*, published by the music department of the German Historical Institute in Rome, 5 (1968): 1–17.

72. Tartini made the acquaintance of Prince Lobkowitz's family when he was in Prague for the coronation festivities of Charles VI. He wrote to Algarotti: "I can still hear the sound of the lute, which the mother (of Prince Lobkowitz) played so well that I could not distinguish her playing from that of her teacher, Monsieur Vais." Petrobelli, 1.

73. Quantz, Engl. trans., 326.

74. Schäfke, 226.

75. Dounias, 118.

76. Emanuel Bach in his *Nachträge zur Bachschen Familienchronik*: "He traveled to Italy anno 1754." *Bach-Dokumente*, 3: 287. Marpurg, in his *Historisch-kritische Beiträge*, 1: 504 (Berlin, 1754–55): "Herr Joh. Christian Bach, born 1735 in Leipzig, the youngest son of the late Capellmeister. . . . He recently left for Italy."

77. Fredersdorf played flute and oboe. He probably belonged to the crown prince's orchestra in Rheinsberg but, as others, was officially listed as Kammerdiener. See also Heinrich Miesner, "Portraits aus dem Kreise Phillip Emanuel and Wilhelm Friedemann Bach," *Musik und Bild: Festschrift Max Seiffert*, Kassel, 1938, 101–112.

78. As a result, the king supposedly suspended Emanuel and temporarily replaced him by one J. C. Fischer of Freiburg. Bittner, 180.

79. Johannes Richter, *Die Briefe Friedrichs des Grossen an seinen vormaligen Kammerdiener Fredersdorf*, Berlin, 1926, 376f.

80. Heinrich Miesner, *Phillip Emanuel Bach in Hamburg*, Leipzig, 1929, 116f.

81. Burney reports from Hamburg that Emanuel had not played the organ in a long time. *Germany*, 2: 275.

82. Burney, *Germany*, 2: 268.

83. Thouret (see note 17, page 339), 58.

84. Bitter, 142; see also Schwarz, 405f.

85. Elise Polko, "Die beiden jüngsten Söhne Bachs. II. Der Londoner Bach," *Die deutsche Musikzeitung*, Vienna, 1 (1860): 194.

86. Heinrich Miesner, "Ungedruckte Briefe von Philipp Emanuel Bach," *Zeitschrift für Musikwissenschaft*, 14 (Leipzig, 1932): 227.

87. Alessandro d'Ancona, *Friedrich der Grosse und die Italiener*, Rostock, 1902, 7f.

88. Einstein, 17.

89. Francesco Bellati, *Serie de' governatori di Milano dall'anno 1535 al 1776 con istoriche annotazioni*, Milan, 1776, 2 (footnote 64).

90. Rödenbeck (see note 26, page 336), 1: 169; 2: 204, and 215.

91. Letter from Algarotti to the king, 17 September 1749. *Correspondance de Frederic II avec le comte Algarotti*, Berlin, 1837, 71.

92. Ernst Graf von Lehndorff, *Dreissig Jahre am Hof Friedrichs des Grossen*, ed. K. E. Schmidt-Lötzen, Gotha, 1907 with 1913 supplement, 23, 48, 146.

93. Detailed description in *Ewald von Kleists Werke*, ed. A. Sauer, Berlin, 1880–82, 344 and 347. As a prisoner of war, Prince Lobkowitz was brought to Königsberg where he was able to pursue musical interests. H. M. Schletterer, *Johann Friedrich Reichardt*, Augsburg, 1865, 41.

94. Gudrun Busch, *C. Ph. E. Bach und seine Lieder*, Regensburg, 1957, 45.

95. Concerning the Lobkowitz family, see also Alexander Wheelock Thayer, "The Lobkowitz Family," *The Musical World*, London, 1879, 307; also the article "Lobkowitz" in MGG, 8: 1070 (Kassel, 1960).

CHAPTER 3

1. Johann Jakob Volkmann, *Historisch-kritische Nachrichten von Italien*, Leipzig, 1770–71, 280.

2. *Aus der Zeit Maria Theresias. Tagebuch des Fürsten Johann Josef Khevenmüller-Metsch*, ed. Count Rudolf Khevenmüller-Metsch and Dr. Hans Schlitter, Vienna and Leipzig, 1917, 2: 175 and footnote 208, p. 443.

3. Volkmann, 318.

4. Burney, *Italy*, 95.

5. Charles de Brosses, *Lettres familières sur l'Italie*, ed. Ivonne Bezard, Paris, 1931, 2: 336ff.

6. Burney, *Italy*, 80, 96ff.

7. Martini's letter to Litta, 27 July 1757; see also Schwarz, 409.

8. Christian apparently studied Italian thoroughly while still in Berlin. Miesner (see note 86, page 343) mentions that four Italian teachers lived close to Emanuel.

9. Burney, *Italy*, 304, dated 17 October 1770.

10. Ibid, 336f.

11. Ibid, 317.

12. John Mainwaring, *Memoirs of the Life of the Late George Frederic Handel*, London, 1760, rpt. New York, 1980, 53, 48.

13. Brosses, (see note 5, page 344) 2: 328.

14. On 3 September 1757, Hasse wrote to Algarotti: "I am greatly pleased that Padre Martini thinks highly of my modest talent; I shall try all the harder to be worthy of this. I cannot emphasize enough how much I long to make the acquaintance of such a venerable person. . . . I am considering a side trip to Bologna before returning to Dresden." Mennicke, 421, footnote 1.

15. Burney, *Italy*, 145f, 156.

16. K. Chr. Fr. Krause, *Darstellungen aus der Geschichte der Musik*, Göttingen, 1827, 189; see also Walther Müller, *Johann Adolf Hasse als Kirchenkomponist*, Leipzig, 1911.

17. Karl Gustav Fellerer, "Der Wandel der Kirchenmusik in der Geschichte," *Handbuch der katholischen Kirchenmusik*, Essen, 1949, 180; by the same author: "Das Tridentinum und die Kirchenmusik," *Das Weltkonzil von Trent*, ed. Georg Schreiber, Freiburg, 1951, 1: 447–462; see also Karl Emil von Schafhäutl, *Ein Spaziergang durch die Liturgische Musikgeschichte der Katholischen Kirche*, Munich, 1887.

18. Dounias (see note 63, page 341), 107.

19. Mattheson, *Patriot*, 105–108.

20. Ignazio Balbi (birth and death dates unknown) was a Milan priest and composer. Oratorios by Balbi were performed in Vienna (1720) and Milan (1729).

21. Numbering according to Marie Ann Heiberg-Vos.

22. Christian here refers to a gift from Count Litta, who, in his letter of 20 July 1757, announced that he was sending ten pounds of homemade chocolate, with more to follow.

23. Both quotes by Rudolf Ewerhart, referred to by Carl de Nys in the liner notes to his recording of the "Dies Irae" (Musica sacra, Schwann AMS 19).

24. The English couple Vincent and Mary Novello visited Mozart's widow, Constanze, in 1829 and noted this in their diary, published as A Mozart Pilgrimage, London, 1955. See also Heinz Gärtner, Constanze Mozart: After the Requiem, Portland, 1991, 44f, 143, 148.

25. Today the monastery owns eighteen sacred compositions by Christian Bach. Ten of these are of special value since the originals are lost. See Heiberg-Vos, 8–23.

26. Terry (p. 32) prints the letter with the date 8 October 1758. The autograph gives the year as 1757.

27. Terry translates the passage in question as "my Aria cantabile," implying that it is a composition by Christian. The original words are "un' aria cantabile."

28. Terry (p. 28) gives the date as 16 December 1757.

29. Terry (p. 50) believes that Christian's reference to "Parigi" is to the singer Maddalena Parigi; further, he believes that Christian's music was not then in demand in Germany. Yet, in his letter of 14 February 1761, Christian says "tanto per Germania come anche per Parigi" (for both Germany and Paris). By this time Christian was well established as a composer of operas and church music. It seems likely that his instrumental music was also attracting attention in Germany and Paris.

30. J. S. Bach probably wrote this himself in 1735. Additions, which include those referring to Christian, were supplied by Emanuel in 1774–75. Bach-Dokumente, 1: 255.

31. Johann Wilhelm Ludwig Gleim, Briefwechsel zwischen Gleim und Uz, ed. Carl Schüddekopf, Tübingen, 1899, 291.

32. The violinist Franz Benda converted from Catholicism to Lutheranism. He did this secretly after having entered the Dresden court chapel, fearing persecution by the powerful local Catholic establishment. See also Lorenz, 15.

33. Terry's date (7 August 1759) is incorrect, as is the attribution of Rochlitz's words of praise for the "Te Deum" to Schubart. Terry, 34, 46.

34. Nevertheless, Leopold was optimistic. He reports that the copyist was "in a good mood, which in Italy is a good omen. For if the music succeeds, the copyist, by making extra copies and distributing them, sometimes derives more benefit from it than the composer" (letter of 15 December). When the Mozarts left, they were obliged to leave the score with the copyist who had to make at least five complete copies.

35. Burney, *History*, 2: 842, 852f.

36. Wohlfahrt, 61. Georg Schünemann, "J. Ch. F. Bach," *Bach Jahrbuch*, 1914, 50–54. See also Gotthold Hey, "Zur Biographie J. Ch. F. Bachs und seiner Familie," *Bach Jahrbuch*, 1933, 77–85.

37. Terry (p. 40) reproduces this document, made available to him by Signor Vatielli of the Milan Cathedral Archives.

38. Heiberg-Vos, Appendix A, 4–67.

39. Not included by Terry.

40. Gian Francesco de Majo (1732–1770) was the son of the famous Giuseppe de Majo, the primo maestro at the Naples court. He succeeded as an opera composer in Rome, Venice, and Naples and died early of tuberculosis.

41. Francesco Vatielli, "Le opere comiche di G. B. Martini," *Rivista Musicale Italiana*, 40 (1936): 450–476.

42. On 24 February 1762, Naumann wrote to his parents that he would depart in four weeks. He wrote again on 16 June: "I am studying with Padre Martini, to make good use of my time and learn something substantial." In the spring of 1762, Christian, too, was Martini's guest in Bologna, as revealed in his last letter. See also A. G. Meissner, *Bruchstücke zu des Kapellmeisters J. G. Naumanns Biographie*, Prague, 1803–04, Vienna, 1814, 154f.

43. Ibid, 150f.

44. Indignantly, Leopold Mozart wrote to his wife on 4 September 1773: "Herr Gassmann was ill; he now is better. I don't know why this should have anything to do with our stay in Vienna." After Gassmann's death in 1774, his position was given to court composer Bonno.

45. Gustav Donath, "Florian Leopold Gassmann als Opernkomponist," *Studien zur Musikwissenschaft, Beihefte der Denkmäler der Tonkunst in Österreich*, 2. Heft, Leipzig/Wien, 1914, 213–240.

46. Burney, *Germany*, 1: 94.

47. Helga Scholz-Micheltisch, *Georg Christoph Wagenseil als Klavierkomponist*, Diss., Vienna, 1967; Walther Vetter, "Italienische Opernkompositionen

Georg Christoph Wagenseils," *Festschrift Friedrich Blume*, Kassel, 1963, 363–374; id., "Der Opernkomponist G. Ch. Wagenseil und sein Verhältnis zu Mozart und Gluck," *Gedenkschrift für Hermann Abert*, Halle, 1928, rpt. Tutzing, 1974, 165–176.; id., "Der deutsche Charakter der italienischen Oper G. Ch. Wagenseils," *Festschrift Karl Gustav Fellerer*, Regensburg, 1962, 558–72.

48. That this little incident was typical for the boy Mozart appears from the sentence that follows in Nannerl's account: "Praise from great men never caused him to be conceited. When he knew that he was playing for connoisseurs, his playing was all the more attentive and fiery." *Mozart-Briefe*, vol. 4: 201 (No. 1213).

49. Jean-Jacques Rousseau, *Dictionnaire de Musique*, article "Génie," rpt. of 1768 ed., New York, 1969, 117.

50. Mozart makes it a point to indicate that the text was made into "a true opera" by Caterino Mazzolá, the Saxon court poet.

51. Benedetto Croce, *I Teatri di Napoli*, Naples, 1891, 495.

52. In the letter to his father of 17 August 1782, Mozart complains that his talent is not sufficiently appreciated by the emperor in Vienna. "Prince Kaunitz regrets that the emperor does not esteem talented people as much as he should. He recently said to Archduke Maximilian, when the conversation turned to me, that such people came along only once in a hundred years. One should not cause such people to leave Germany, especially when one is fortunate enough to have them right here in the capital. You have no idea how kind and courteous Prince Kaunitz was when I was with him."

53. K. Trautmann, *Kulturbilder aus Alt-München*, Munich, 1914, 97–106; H. Freiberger, *Anton Raaff (1714–1797), sein Leben und Wirken*, diss., Cologne, 1929. Raaff's letters to Padre Martini are included.

54. Walter, 232.

55. Dounias (see note 63, page 341), 122.

56. Stefan Kunze, "Die Vertonungen der Arie 'Non so d'onde viene' von J. Chr. Bach und W. A. Mozart," *Analecta Musicologica, Studien zur Italienisch-Deutschen Musikgeschichte*, Cologne, 1963, 2: 85–111.

57. Raymond Leppard believes that this is one of the first great compositions in this key. (Liner notes for the recording Philips 839 713 LY.) The high point in this development surely is Mozart's G minor symphony, K. 550.

58. Croce, 496f.

59. Anton Ferrante Boschetti, *I cataloghi dell'opera di Pompeo Litta, Famiglie celebri italiane*, Modena, 1930. I am thankful to Signor Giuseppe Baretta,

Biblioteca Nazionale Braidense, Milan, for this information, and for pointing out to me the source quoted in the next note.

60. *Atti della Società Patriotica di Milano*, vol. 2 (1789), vi–ix.

61. On 10 February 1770, Leopold Mozart notes the death of the "old Marchese
    Litta." This is Agostino's father; Walter Gerstenberg erroneously refers to
    him as "Johann Christian Bach's benefactor" (*Neue Mozart-Ausgabe* X/28,
    part 2).

62. Brosses (see note 5, page 344), 2: 579f.

63. Guglielmo Barblan, "Sammartini e la scuola sinfonica Milanese," *Musicisti
    Lombardi ed Emiliani*, Siena, 1958. I am grateful to Professor Barblan, who,
    in his letter of 12 January 1978, shared with me the results of the most
    recent resarch concerning Christian Bach and Sammartini. There is no
    documentary evidence that they met.

64. Burney, *History*, 2: 863.

CHAPTER 4

1. Horace Walpole, *Memoirs of the Reign of King George the Third*, Russell
   Barker, ed., London, 1894, rpt. 1971, 1: 48.

2. Alvin Redman, *The House of Hanover*, New York, 1961, 98.

3. The young duke of Roxbury, while traveling, had made Christina's acquaintance. Their love might have led to marriage. But when it was decided that
   Christina's sister, Sophie-Charlotte, would marry, it was with the condition
   that no British subject would marry the future queen's sister. Christina and
   the duke, who would later become the favorite of George III, died without
   having married. John Heneage Jesse, *Memoirs of the Life and Reign of King
   George the Third*, London, 1891, vol. 1: 127.

4. Terry, who was unable to compare the handwritings, erroneously assumed
   Emanuel's signature to be that of Christian. Terry assumed that on his way
   to England, Christian stopped in Strelitz. Terry, 59f.

5. Burney, *History*, 2: 865.

6. Johann Jakob Volkmann, *Neueste Reisen durch England*, Leipzig, 1781–83,
   365f.

7. Burney, *History*, 2: 864f.

8. The clarinet, said to have been invented by Johann Christoph Denner of
   Nürnberg around 1700, was still in an experimental stage; there were few

expert players. Handel had used the clarinet as early as 1724 in his opera *Tamerlano*. Pohl 72, note 1.

9. Downes, 218–222.

10. Einstein, 48.

11. Karl Ditters von Dittersdorf, *Lebensbeschreibung*, ed. Eugen Schmitz, Regensburg, 1914. Downes (p. 174) compares Gluck's *Orfeo* and Christian's *Catone*, as to their success in Italy. He refutes the claim that no composer before Gluck reached such a record number of performances. He lists at least seven performances of Bach's *Catone* within four years, while Gluck's *Orfeo*, written later, reached only six performances in nineteen years. Actually, both numbers are impressive, considering that in the eighteenth century repeat productions of an opera seria, in another city and with a different cast, were extremely rare.

12. Burney, *History*, 2: 866.

13. Terry, 73.

14. In his travel diary (3–11 August 1763) Leopold Mozart noted that "De Amicis, with her father, sister, and brother, have arrived from London." A lasting friendship grew from this chance encounter. Wolfgang Mozart wrote the female leading role in *Lucio Silla* for Anna Lucia de Amicis. On 12 December 1772, Leopold Mozart in Milan wrote to his wife and daughter: "Signora De Amicis wishes to be remembered to you; she is more than pleased with her three arias. Wolfgang has provided her principal aria with coloraturas that are remarkable and extremely difficult; she sings them amazingly well. We are on very close, friendly terms with her."

15. Pohl, 170–76.

16. Riemann, *Musiklexikon*, 1959. After his separation from Regina Mingotti, her husband Pietro Mingotti tried unsuccessfully to establish an Italian opera company in Copenhagen. He died on 28 April 1759, "on the ruins of his earlier fame. He left nothing but his clothes . . . and an account book, still existing, which reveals that the aged impresario tried to drown his sorrows in brandy." Erich H. Müller, *Angelo und Pietro Mingotti: Ein Beitrag zur Geschichte der Oper im 18. Jahrhundert*, Dresden, 1917, 139.

17. Downes, 164.

18. Walter Knape, *Bibliographisch-thematisches Verzeichnis der Kompositionen von Karl Friedrich Abel*, Cuxhaven, n.d.; see also Marion Helm, *Carl Friedrich Abel, Symphonist: A biographical, stylistic and bibliographical study*, diss., Ann Arbor, 1953.

19. Letter from Herschel, 30 May 1763. The correspondence of the two brothers, so far unpublished, contains lively exchanges of ideas about problems in music theory. Sir John Herschel-Shorland, a descendant of the famous astronomer, was kind enough to make this correspondence available to me.

20. One such business transaction caused Giardini to lose the confidence and favor of the Prince of Wales: he sold him a Cremona violin for a high price—but the instrument was a forgery. In this way he also lost his good reputation at court. See Pohl, 176.

21. Burney, *History*, 2: 866f.

22. *Bach-Dokumente*, 2: 424–426 (Nos. 546, 547, 548).

23. Rosamond E. M. Harding, *The Piano-Forte*, rpt. New York, 1973, 54; Philip James, *Early Keyboard Instruments*, London, 1960, 51.

24. Burney, *History*, 2: 866.

25. Cramer, 553.

26. Terry, 78.

27. Papendiek, 64f; Jesse (see note 3, page 348), 553.

28. Redman, 102f.

29. Volkmann (see note 6, page 348), 237.

30. Pohl, 1–11.

31. It is likely that Bach wrote his Keyboard Concerto in F Major, Op. 7, No. 2, for the organ at Vauxhall. It represents a conscious attempt to follow the style customary at Vauxhall concerts.

32. Hornpipe: an old English dance, usually in 3/2 or 4/4 time. As an instrument, the hornpipe was related to the shawm.

33. Cramer, 194.

34. The French original text is quoted in Deutsch-*Dokumente*, 27.

35. During the early 1740s, Grimm had studied with Gottsched in Leipzig; his lectures were attended by Bach's pupil Doles and others (Scheibe, Mizler, Hiller). Grimm's acquaintance with J. S. Bach goes back to these days in Leipzig; perhaps he then also met Christian Bach. In 1748 Grimm became the secretary of Count Friese, with whom he moved to Dresden. In 1749, both settled in Paris.

36. Wolfgang Plath in NMA, IX/27, vol. 1, "The Notebooks," xx, Kassel, 1982.

37. Concerning Wolfgang Mozart (the son) and Josephine von Baroni-

Cavalcabò, see Heinz Gärtner, *Constanze Mozart: After the Requiem*, Portland, 1991, 142ff.

38. Leopold Mozart: "German composers are most prominent here; among them Schobert and Eckard for the piano. Hochbrucker and Mayr are very popular composers for the harp." Letter of 1 February 1764.

CHAPTER 5

1. Deutsch-*Dokumente*, 34.

2. Ibid., 400.

3. While en route to England, Wolfgang had quickly learned how to play the organ pedals, as the father reported to Salzburg: "To amuse ourselves [in Wasserburg], we went to the organ loft. I explained the pedal board to Wolfgang. He then at once showed that he had understood it, moved away the bench, and played the pedals standing up. His improvisation sounded as though he had practiced the pedals for many months." *Mozart-Briefe*, 1: 71.

4. Deutsch-*Dokumente*, 400.

5. Wyzewa/St.-Foix, 112–116.

6. "Mozart als achtjähriger Komponist." Review of the notebook edited and published by Georg Schünemann (Leipzig, 1909), *Gegenwart* 4 (Berlin, 1909): 52.

7. Alfred Valentin Heuss in *Zeitschrift der Internationalen Musikgesellschaft*, 10: 181.

8. Abert, 52.

9. Wolfgang Plath called attention to this recording entitled *Mozart in Chelsea, Divertimenti and Contra Dances*, played by the Academy of St. Martin-in-the-Fields, Neville Mariner, conductor (Philips 6500367). "Listening to this recording objectively, one thinks that the compositions in this London sketch book are a collection of pieces for a ballet. Thus orchestrated, this music could well be revived." Plath in NMA, IX/27, 1: xxiv, note 77.

10. Théodore de Wyzewa, "La jeunesse de Mozart," *Revue des Deux Mondes*, Paris, 1904. Part 1 (April), 543–580, deals with the years 1756–1762; Part 2 (December), 185–225, covers 1762–1763.

11. George E. Gardner, *The Emerging Personality: Infancy Through Adolescence*, New York, 1970, 101f.

12. Wyzewa/Saint-Foix, 122.

13. Leopold Mozart: "During the coming months I shall be quite busy to win over the nobility. That will take lots of running around, lots of effort. But if I succeed, I will have made a good catch." Letter of 13 September 1764, *Mozart-Briefe*, 1: 169 (No. 92).

14. Wolfgang Plath provides a thorough analysis of Leopold Mozart's handwriting, comparing it with Wolfgang's. On the basis of his study, it is likely that Leopold contributed to these compositions by his son. "Beiträge zur Mozart-Autographie 1—Die Handschrift Leopold Mozarts," *Mozart-Jahrbuch 1960– 1961*, 82–117.

15. King George III liked to be viewed as an expert on Handel's music. He would tell young orchestra leaders to watch him: he would, with his hand, establish the correct tempo. When the violinist Hay took some liberties with interpretation, the king told him that he had come "to hear Handel's music, not Mr. Hay's fiddling." The king also took a lively interest in the publication of Handel's works, forty volumes of which had appeared before George III suffered the second attack of his incurable mental disease. Pohl, 98f.

16. Pohl lists them. 22 February: *Judas Maccabeus*; 27 February: *Alexander's Feast*; 1 March: *Israel in Babylon* (compiled from various Handel works); 6 March: *Samson*; 8 March: *Judas Maccabeus*; 13 March: *Israel in Egypt*; 15 March: *Solomon*; 20 March: *Samson*; 22 March: *Judas Maccabeus*; 27 and 29 March: *Messiah*.

17. Wyzewa/St.-Foix, 94.

18. Reinhold Bernhardt, "W. A. Mozarts Messias-Bearbeitung und ihre Drucklegung in Leipzig 1802," *Zeitschrift für Musikwissenschaft* 12 (1929): 21–45.

19. See Gärtner, *Constanze Mozart*, 164f.

20. Deutsch-*Dokumente*, 426.

21. Later, St.-Foix surmised that for stylistic reasons this symphony might be by Leopold Mozart. *The Symphonies of Mozart*, New York, 1949, 6. Alfred Einstein disagreed with this, as stated in his edition of the *Köchel-Verzeichnis*, Anhang, 869.

22. Einstein attributes two other symphonies (K. 19 a and b) to the London period. He believes 19a to be one of the overtures that were performed in the London concerts of 21 February or 13 March 1765. He groups 19b with 19a because the opening bars "show the typical opening of a John Christian Bach symphony." *Köchel-Verzeichnis*, 34.

23. See page 153.

24. Downes lists two pasticci that include arias by Christian Bach, which the

young Mozart might have heard in London: *Ezio* (24 November 1764) and *Berenice* (1 January 1765). Mozart, of course, might also have heard some of the arias Bach had contributed to five earlier pasticci, which subsequently became very popular. Downes, 70–72.

25. Burney, *History*, 2: 867ff.

26. Mrs. Harris to her son in Oxford, 19 October 1764; Terry, 81f.

27. Deutsch-*Dokumente*, Addenda and Corrigenda, Supplement 1: 109.

28. Original French text in Deutsch-*Dokumente*, 54f.

29. Original text in Deutsch-*Dokumente*, 86–91.

30. Wyzewa/St.-Foix, 123f.

31. Terry, 84.

32. Terry, 81 and 121.

33. Pohl, 179; article "Tenducci" in MGG 13: 230.

34. The concert took place on 17 May 1786. A review appeared in the *Public Advertiser* on 22 May. Terry, 168.

35. Terry, 86.

36. Pohl, 3f., 12–33.

37. Terry, 89.

38. Pohl, 163, note 3.

39. Original French text in Deutsch-*Dokumente*, 38.

40. Original text in Deutsch-*Dokumente*, 40f; see also Pohl, 122f.

41. Wolfgang was by then nine years old. Deutsch-*Dokumente*, 42.

42. Schenk, 115, hints at "risky financial dealings."

43. "Madame von Robini" is Viktoria Aniser Robinig von Rottenfeld, member of a Salzburg noble family whom the Mozarts knew socially. Wolfgang repeatedly mentions the daughter in his letters.

44. Leopold persists in misleading indications of the children's ages. Actually, by then, Wolfgang was nine and his sister fourteen years old.

45. Wolfgang Rehm in his preface to NMA IX/24, sec. 2: vi f.

46. Deutsch-*Dokumente*, 45.

47. Pohl, 79–83.

48. John Gay, the poet, had first offered the work to the Drury Lane Theatre, which declined. It was then given at the Lincoln-Inn-Fields Theatre, directed by John Rich. During the first season it was performed sixty-three times, which gave rise to the saying that the opera made Gay rich and Rich gay. Pohl, 83.

49. Terry, 97; music incipits, 245f.

50. Pohl, 131.

51. Original text in Deutsch-*Dokumente*, 45.

52. Deutsch-*Dokumente*, 405. "Prince Gallazin" refers to Lieutenant General Dimitri Alexevich Prince Golycyn, Russia's diplomatic representative in Paris. The Mozarts had made his acquaintance in Paris. "He loves us like his own children" (Leopold Mozart in his letter of 1 April 1764).

53. Deutsch-*Dokumente*, 54f.

54. Michael Kelly, *Reminiscences*, 2 vols., 2d ed., London, 1826, 1: 225. Excerpts in Deutsch-*Dokumente*, 454–459.

55. Leopold's brusk refusal may have been due to the fact that he already had Nannerl's son to look after, which Wolfgang did not know.

56. On 19 October 1778, Leopold reported the British victory over Spain in the battle of Gibraltar. Mozart replied that he was "glad to hear of England's victory; as you know, I am an arch-Englishman."

CHAPTER 6

1. Terry, 93.

2. Keith Roberts, *Thomas Gainsborough*, Milan, 1965, 2.

3. William T. Whitley, *Thomas Gainsborough*, London, 1915, 360. Jackson also takes up the subject of painting and music in his *Observations on the Present State of Music in London*, London, 1791, 31f. He indicates his preference for painting: exhibitions of art are open to everyone, whereas concert attendance was possible only for relatively few.

4. Oliver Millar, *Thomas Gainsborough*, New York, 1949, 11.

5. Whitley, 367.

6. Whitley, 362.

7. Isaac Newton, *Optics*, Book III, Part 1, Questions 13 and 14.

8. *Grétry's Versuche über die Musik*, Karl Spazier, ed., Leipzig, 1800, 345.

9. Whitley, 387.

10. Walter Serauky, article "Charles Batteux," MGG 1: 1411–1416.

11. Terry, 141.

12. Terry, 142.

13. Pohl, 157.

14. For the 1766–67 season, both Burney and Terry list the pasticci *Gli stravaganti* and *Trakebarne, Gran Mogul*, Piccinni's opera *La buona figliuola*, and the return of the pasticcio *Ezio*. Burney, *History*, 2: 873; Terry, 105.

15. Terry, 105.

16. Burney, *History*, 2: 873.

17. Dittersdorf, *Lebensbeschreibung*, B. Loets, ed., Leipzig, 1940, 108.

18. Terry, 52f.

19. Angelo, 190.

20. Papendiek, 109.

21. Terry, 109f.

22. Pohl, 160.

23. Terry, 107f.

24. Terry, 106f.

25. Downes, 343f.

26. *Public Advertiser*, 10 May 1770; Terry, 119.

27. Terry, 120f.

28. Burney, *History*, 2: 878.

29. Miesner, quoting Landshoff, lists one French and two English pasticci containing arias by Bach, preserved in the Library of Congress, Washington, D. C. They are *Zophilette* (1765), *Tom Jones* (1769), and *Amelie* (1771). They had been given at Drury Lane and Covent Garden. Miesner, 187.

30. Pohl, 5.

31. Terry, 113.

32. In *Adriano in Siria* and *Carattacco*.

33. Terry, 115.

34. Schenk, 271.

35. Christian Daniel Friedrich Schubart, C. F. D. Schubart's, des Patrioten, gesammelte Schriften und Schicksale, Stuttgart, 1839–40, vol. 5: 152.

36. Abert, 473.

37. Andreas Traub and Peter Ross, "Die Kirchenmusik von Johann Christian Bach im Kloster Einsiedeln," Fontes Artis Musicae, Kassel, April–June 1985, 92–102.

38. His brother Johann Heinrich Schröter, who became well known as a violin virtuoso, disappeared during the 1780s under mysterious circumstances.

39. Papendiek, 134.

40. Pohl, 348.

41. Terry, 124.

CHAPTER 7

1. Burney, Germany, 1: 94.

2. Freiberger (see note 53, page 347), 30.

3. The composition in question is the cantata La Tempesta, performed in Mannheim in 1776. Ernest Warburton, article "Johann Christian Bach," The New Grove Dictionary of Music and Musicians, London, 1980, 1: 873.

4. Vogler, 63–79.

5. Walter, 99.

6. Walter, 172–179.

7. Walter, 104.

8. Information supplied by Dr. Andreas Traub, whose assistance is gratefully acknowledged.

9. Falck, 53. Although this work was identified in the early twentieth century as a Vivaldi composition, it is still occasionally performed with Friedemann's name. Walter Kolneder, Antonio Vivaldi, Wiesbaden, 1965, 133f.

10. Carl G. W. Schiller, Braunschweigs schöne Literatur in den Jahren 1745–1800, Wolfenbüttel, 1845, 254, 258.

11. Georg Fischer, Musik in Hannover, Hannover, 1903, 56f.

12. Burney, Germany, 2: 246ff.

13. Bitter, 147, note 1.

14. To help the impoverished Diderot, Catherine II had bought his library, though he had its use for the remainder of his life.

15. Schmid, 44–46.

16. Schmid, 37.

17. Wohlfarth, 75f.

CHAPTER 8

1. Papendiek, 109.

2. Rolland (see note 11, page 336), 223.

3. Terry, 143.

4. Burney, *History*, 2: 885.

5. They were George, prince of Wales, born 1762, who later became King George IV; Frederick, duke of York (1763); William, duke of Clarence (1765), the later King William IV; and Edward, duke of Kent (1767).

6. Papendiek, 77.

7. Whitley (see note 3, page 354), 118.

8. Papendiek, 138.

9. Burney, *Germany*, 1: 128.

10. Emil Karl Blümml, *Aus Mozarts Freundes- und Familienkreis*, Vienna, 1923, 36–47.

11. Burney, *History*, 2: 881.

12. See *Lucio Silla*, NMA II/5/7, Teilband 1, preface by Kathleen Kuzmick-Hansell, xiv. See also Walter, 141 and 367, Downes, 390.

13. Terry, Corrigenda, xlvi and 234. Terry gives the name as "Tenducci."

14. Terry, 53.

15. Richard, Earl of Mount Edgcumbe, *Musical Reminiscences of the Earl of Mount Edgcumbe*, 4th ed., London, 1834, 4, rpt. New York, 1973.

16. *Georg Christoph Lichtenberg: Schriften und Briefe*, ed. F. H. Mautner, Frankfurt, 1983, vol. 2: 65–67.

17. In a letter to Christian Gottlieb Heyne, his colleague in Göttingen, Lichtenberg wrote on 16 August 1775: "This evening, in the king's chambers, I heard several quartets. Bach was at the keyboard, Abel played the

bass, a certain Cramer from Mannheim, a great violinist, played first violin, and Nicolai second. In addition to the king and his children, the listeners included Herr Salgas, Herr Deluc, and me." Wolfgang Promies, *Georg Christoph Lichtenberg: Schriften und Briefe*, Munich, 1967, vol. 4: 241.

18. Terry, 158.

19. This quotation and those following are taken from letters written from April to September 1778.

20. Grimm had corresponded with Leopold behind Wolfgang's back—at least Wolfgang interpreted it that way. Grimm indicated that he no longer considered Paris to be the suitable location for Wolfgang's future—an observation that was probably correct. At this time, however, Mozart was eager to have his beloved Aloysia Weber come to Paris. In a letter to his father (11 September 1778) he criticizes Grimm severely: "He may be able to help *children*, but not grown-ups."

21. According to Nissen's "official" account, Mozart, when spurned by Aloysia, sat down at the piano and sang: "Ich lass' das Mädchen gern, das mich nicht will" (I am glad to be rid of a girl who doesn't want me). Among Nissen's notes, a considerably stronger version exists: "Leck' mir das Mensch im Arsch, das mich nicht will" (If she doesn"t want me, she can kiss my ___). *Mozarts Bäsle-Briefe*, J. H. Eibl and W. Senn, ed., 2d ed., Kassel, 1980, 59.

22. Michel Brenet, "Un fils du grand Bach à Paris en 1778–1779," *Le Guide Musical*, Nos. 29–32, 27 July and 10 August 1902, 551–573.

23. Einstein, 149.

24. Papendiek, 106.

25. Brenet (see note 22, page 358), 572.

26. Einstein, 176. It is strange that Gluck should not have known of Bach's presence in Paris, since *Amadis* was to be the next work produced.

27. Downes points out the similarity of Mozart's aria "Der Hölle Rache" (final measures) to Arcabonne's aria "Mânes plaintifs." He also compares the form and mood of the Pamina-Papageno duet "Bei Männern, welche Liebe fühlen" with the trio (Oriane, Urgande, and Amadis) "Aimés-vous." Downes, 489.

28. Helmut Rilling, church musician and Bach interpreter, deserves credit for the revival of *Amadis* at the Hamburg State Opera in 1983. Critics considered it an "undisputed success." The same applies to the revival of *Lucio Silla* by Fritz Tutenberg in Kiel in 1929, which "delighted a large audience." Fritz Tutenberg, "Johann Christian Bach und seine Oper 'Lucius Silla,'" *Deutsche Musikkultur* 1 (1936–37): 283–85.

29. Friedrich Wilhelm Herschel had stimulated the king's interest in astronomy. Herschel had discovered the planet Uranus; he named it "George Star" in appreciation of the king's support.

30. Terry, 164.

31. Terry, 165.

32. The painter Johann Zoffany, born in Frankfurt in 1733, had been court painter to the Elector of Trier before going to England in 1760.

33. Papendiek, 150f.

34. Such behavior was not unusual at the time. Even if the deceased had only small debts, his family feared that creditors might take possession of the body. By selling it to anatomy students, they hoped to obtain the moneys owed them. Joyce Hemlow, *The Journals and Letters of Fanny Burney*, Oxford, 1973, vol. 4: 301.

35. Well-meaning friends advised Cecilia Bach to organize her own benefit concert at King's Theatre. It took place on 27 May 1782—five months after Bach's death. The ambitious program consisted of Anfossi's opera I *viaggiatori* (first performed on the day of Bach's death) and the ballet *Rinaldo ed Armida*, for which Bach had written the music. The number of tickets sold was insufficient to defray the event's expenses, even though the singers donated their services. Mrs. Papendiek sadly noted that the undertaking was a failure—that Bach, talented, kind, and generous though he was, had been quickly forgotten. Papendiek, 153.

36. Whitley (see note 3, page 354), 282.

37. Abel's last appearance as a soloist took place on 21 May 1787, in a concert given by the singer Mrs. Billington. He died approximately a month later, having been asleep for three days and nights. Reichardt, in the "Berliner musikalischer Almanach," attributed his long sleep to "excessive consumption of alcohol." Pohl, 156.

38. Heinrich Miesner, "Bach-Gräber im Ausland," *Bach-Jahrbuch* 1936, 109–11. Today the graveyard no longer exists; a tennis court occupies the site.

39. In the same letter of 10 April 1782, a few lines before, Mozart writes: "I am compiling for myself a collection of Bach fugues, by Sebastian, Emanuel, and Friedemann." The circle, we might say, is complete: from Father Bach by way of his sons (especially Christian) to Mozart, and back to Johann Sebastian.

List of Works with Opus Numbers

(Numbers according to Terry)

Opus 1/1763
Six harpsichord concertos, dedicated to the queen of England.

Opus 2/1763
Six trios for keyboard, violin (flute), and cello, dedicated to Princess Augusta of Braunschweig-Lüneburg.

Opus 3/1765
Six symphonies, dedicated to the duke of York.

Opus 4/1765
Six canzonettas, dedicated to Lady Glenorchy.

Opus 5/1768
Six sonatas for harpsichord or pianoforte.

Opus 6/1770
Six canzonettas, second series, dedicated to Duke Friedrich of Saxony-Hildburghausen.

Opus 7/1770–75
Six concertos for harpsichord or pianoforte, dedicated to the queen of England.

Opus 8/1770–75
Six quartets for flute, violin, viola, and cello, dedicated to Sir William Young.

Opus 9/1770–75
Three symphonies.

Opus 10/1770–75
Six sonatas for harpsichord or pianoforte, dedicated to Lady
Melbourne.

Opus 11/1772–77
Six quintets for flute, oboe, violin, viola, and cello, dedicated to Elector
Karl Theodor of the Palatinate.

Opus 12/13/1772–77.
Six concertos for harpsichord or pianoforte, third series, dedicated to
Mrs. Pelham. (Published by Hummel in two parts, as Opus 12 and 13.)

Opus 14/1778
Opera *La clemenza di Scipione*.

Opus 15/1779
Four sonatas and two duets for harpsichord or pianoforte, dedicated to
Countess Abingdon.

Opus 16/1779
Six sonatas for harpsichord or pianoforte and violin (or flute),
dedicated to Miss Greenland.

Opus 17/1779
Six sonatas for harpsichord or pianoforte, dedicated to Princess Julie of
Hessen-Philippstal. Published by Hummel.

Opus 18/1781
"Six Grand Overtures."

Opus 19/posthumous
Four quartets, originally written as quintets.

Opus 20/posthumous
Three sonatas for pianoforte or harpsichord and flute.

Opus 21/posthumous
"Three Favorite Overtures."

Opus 22/posthumous
Two quintets, published by Hummel.

CONTENTS OF THE COLLECTED WORKS
(*Scheduled for completion in 1994*)

1. *Artaserse.* Facsimile of an eighteenth-century manuscript score.
648 pages   ISBN 0-8240-6050-4

2. *Catone in Utica.* Facsimile of an eighteenth-century manuscript score.
584 pages   ISBN 0-8240-6051-2

3. *Alessandro nell'Indie.* Facsimile of an eighteenth-century manuscript score.
600 pages   ISBN 0-8240-6052-0

4. *Orione, ossia Diana vendicata and Zanaida.* New manuscript scores and facsimiles of the surviving fragments.
430 pages   ISBN 0-8240-6053-9

5. *Adriano in Siria.* New manuscript score.
550 pages   ISBN 0-8240-6054-7

6. *Carattaco.* Facsimile of an eighteenth-century manuscript score and new manuscript score.
550 pages   ISBN 0-8240-6055-5

7. *Temistocle.* Facsimile of an eighteenth-century manuscript score.
560 pages   ISBN 0-8240-6056-3

8. *Lucio Silla.* Facsimile of an eighteenth-century manuscript score.
584 pages   ISBN 0-8240-6057-1

9. **La clemenza di Scipione and music from London pasticci.** Facsimiles of eighteenth-century prints and new manuscript scores.
488 pages   ISBN 0-8240-6058-X

10. *Amadis de Gaule.* Facsimiles of eighteenth-century prints and new manuscript scores.
432 pages   ISBN 0-8240-6059-8

11. **Gluck's *Orfeo ed Euridice* as arranged by J. C. Bach.** Facsimile of an eighteenth-century manuscript score.
560 pages   ISBN 0-8240-6060-1

12. **Single operatic arias and overtures.** Facsimiles of eighteenth-century manuscript scores.
502 pages   ISBN 0-8240-6061-X

13. **Cantatas.** Facsimiles of eighteenth-century manuscript and printed scores.
336 pages   ISBN 0-8240-6062-8

14. *Endimione.* New manuscript score.
450 pages   ISBN 0-8240-6063-6

15. *Amor vincitore.* New manuscript score.
248 pages   ISBN 0-8240-6064-4

16. **Miscellaneous works to French and Italian texts.** Facsimiles of an eighteenth-century manuscript and printed scores.
272 pages   ISBN 0-8240-6065-2

17. *Gioas, ré di Giuda.* Facsimile of an eighteenth-century manuscript score.
456 pages   ISBN 0-8240-6066-0

18. **Solo motets.** Facsimiles of eighteenth-century manuscript scores and new manuscript scores.
280 pages   ISBN 0-8240-6067-9

19. **Music for the Mass I.** New manuscript scores.
344 pages   ISBN 0-8240-6068-7

20. **Music for the Mass II.** Facsimile of an eighteenth- and nineteenth-century manuscript score and new manuscript scores.
360 pages   ISBN 0-8240-6069-5

21. **Music for the Office of the Dead.** Facsimiles of eighteenth-century scores and new manuscript scores.
608 pages   ISBN 0-8240-6070-9

22. **Music for Vespers I.** New manuscript scores.
350 pages   ISBN 0-8240-6071-7

23. **Music for Vespers II.** New manuscript scores.
400 pages   ISBN 0-8240-6072-5

24. **Miscellaneous church music.** New manuscript scores.
156 pages   ISBN 0-8240-6073-3

25. **Works with English texts.** Facsimiles of eighteenth-century manuscript and printed scores.
428 pages   ISBN 0-8240-6074-1

26. **Symphonies I.** New manuscript scores.
350 pages   ISBN 0-8240-6075-X

27. **Symphonies II.** New manuscript scores.
456 pages   ISBN 0-8240-6076-8

28. **Symphonies III.** New manuscript scores.
480 pages   ISBN 0-8240-6077-6

29. **Symphonies IV.** New manuscript scores.
256 pages   ISBN 0-8240-6078-4

30. **Symphonies concertantes I.** New manuscript scores.
468 pages   ISBN 0-8240-6079-2

31. **Symphonies concertantes II.** New manuscript scores.
476 pages   ISBN 0-8240-6080-6

32. **Keyboard concertos I.** New manuscript scores.
360 pages   ISBN 0-8240-6081-4

33. **Keyboard concertos II.** New manuscript scores.
210 pages   ISBN 0-8240-6082-2

34. **Keyboard concertos III.** New manuscript scores.
272 pages   ISBN 0-8240-6083-0

35. **Keyboard concertos IV.** New manuscript scores.
328 pages   ISBN 0-8240-6084-9

36. Other solo concertos. New manuscript scores.
272 pages   ISBN 0-8240-6085-7

37. Music for wind band. New manuscript scores.
216 pages   ISBN 0-8240-6086-5

38. Music for two instruments. Facsimiles of eighteenth-century printed scores and new manuscript scores.
448 pages   ISBN 0-8240-6087-3

39. Music for three instruments. New manuscript scores.
512 pages   ISBN 0-8240-6088-1

40. Music for four instruments. New manuscript scores.
432 pages   ISBN 0-8240-6089-X

41. Music for five and six instruments. New manuscript scores.
250 pages   ISBN 0-8240-6090-3

42. Keyboard music. Facsimiles of eighteenth-century printed scores and new manuscript scores.
280 pages   ISBN 0-8240-6091-1

43. Librettos I. Facsimiles of eighteenth-century prints.
360 pages   ISBN 0-8240-6092-X

44. Librettos II. Facsimiles of eighteenth-century prints.
335 pages   ISBN 0-8240-6093-8

45. Librettos III. Facsimiles of eighteenth-century prints.
464 pages   ISBN 0-8240-6094-6

46. Librettos IV. Facsimiles of eighteenth-century prints.
280 pages   ISBN 0-8240-6095-4

47. Librettos V. Facsimiles of eighteenth-century prints.
564 pages   ISBN 0-8240-6096-2

48. Thematic catalogue.
ca. 500 pages   ISBN 0-8240-6097-0

Bibliography

Abert, Hermann. *W. A. Mozart*. New enlarged edition of Otto Jahn's *Mozart*. 7th ed., 3 vols. Leipzig, 1955.

———. "Johann Christian Bachs italienische Opern und ihr Einfluß auf Mozart." *Zeitschrift für Musikwissenschaft* 1 (1919): Heft 6.

Algarotti, Francesco. *Essay on Opera*. Engl. trans. of the 1767 edition, Richard Northcott, ed. London, 1917.

Allroggen, Gerhard. "Mozarts erste Sinfonien." *Festschrift Heinz Becker*, 1982.

Angelo, Domenico. *Reminiscences of Henry Angelo, With Memoirs of his Late Father and Friends*. 2 vols. London, 1828–30.

Bach, Carl Philipp Emanuel. *Versuch über die wahre Art das Clavier zu spielen*. Berlin, 1753. Engl. trans. New York, 1949.

Bach-Dokumente. Vol. 1: *Schriftstücke von der Hand Johann Sebastian Bachs*; vol. 2: *Fremdschriftliche und gedruckte Dokumente 1685–1750*; vol. 3: *Dokumente zum Nachwirken Bachs 1750–1800*. Kassel, 1963–1973.

Baierle, Ilse Susanne. *Die Klavierwerke von Johann Christian Bach*. Diss., Vienna, 1974.

Baretti, Joseph. *An Account of the Manners and Customs of Italy*. 2 vols. London, 1769.

Beaujean, Joseph. *Christoph Gottfried Krause*. Diss., Dillingen, 1930.

Bernhard, Reinhold. "Das Schicksal der Familie Johann Sebastian Bach." *Der Bär, Jahrbuch von Breitkopf & Härtel*. Leipzig, 1930.

Bitter, Carl Hermann. *Carl Philipp Emanuel und Friedemann Bach und deren Brüder*. 2 vols. Berlin, 1868.

Bücken, Ernst. *Die Musik des Rokoko und der Klassik*. Potsdam, 1932.

Burney, Charles. *A General History of Music, from the Earliest Ages to the Present Period*. 4 vols. London, 1776–1789. New ed. by Frank Mercer. London, 1935, rpt. New York, 1957.

———. *The Present State of Music in Germany, the Netherlands, and United Provinces*. 2 vols. 2d ed. London, 1775, rpt. New York, 1969.

———. *The Present State of Music in France and Italy*. 2d ed. London, 1773, rpt. New York, 1969.

Cramer, Carl Friedrich. *Magazin der Musik*. Hamburg, 1783–1786.

Daffner, Hugo. *Die Entwicklung des Klavierkonzerts bis Mozart. Publikationen der Internationalen Musikgesellschaft* Beihefte II, Heft 4. Leipzig, 1906.

David, Hans T. and Arthur Mendel. *The Bach Reader*. New York, 1945.

Deutsch, Otto Erich. *Mozart: Die Dokumente seines Lebens*. Kassel, 1961. Addenda and Corrigenda, 1978.

D. J. F. L. *Das jetzt lebende und florierende Leipzig*. Leipzig, 1736.

Downes, Edward O. D. *The Operas of Johann Christian Bach as a Reflection of the Dominant Trends in Opera Seria*. Diss. Harvard, 1958.

Einstein, Alfred. *Gluck*. Engl. trans. by Eric Blom. London, 1936.

Engel, Hans. "Über Mozarts Jugendsinfonien." *Mozart-Jahrbuch* 1951.

Engelke, Bernhard. "Neues zur Berliner Liederschule." *Riemann-Festschrift*. Leipzig, 1909.

Falck, Martin. *Wilhelm Friedemann Bach*. Lindau, 1956.

Forkel, Johann Nikolaus. *Johann Sebastian Bach*. Leipzig, 1802. Engl. trans. London, 1920. Rpt. New York, 1970.

Frotscher, Gotthold. "Die Ästhetik des Berliner Liedes in ihren Hauptproblemen." *Zeitschrift für Musikwissenschaft* 6, 1923–24.

Fürstenau, Moritz. *Zur Geschichte der Musik und des Theaters am Hof zu Dresden*. Dresden, 1861–62.

Geiringer, Karl. *The Bach Family*. New York, 1954.

Gerber, Ernst Ludwig. *Historisch-Biographisches Lexikon der Tonkünstler*. 2 vols. Leipzig, 1790–92.

———. *Neues Historisch-Biographisches Lexikon der Tonkünstler*. 4 vols. Leipzig, 1812–14.

Goldschmidt, Hugo. *Die Musikästhetik des 18. Jahrhunderts und ihre Beziehungen zu seinem Kunstschaffen*. 1915. Rpt. Hildesheim, 1968.

Haacke, Walter. *Die Söhne Bachs*. Königstein im Taunus, 1962.

Heiberg-Vos, Marie Ann. *The Liturgical Choral Works of Johann Christian Bach*. Diss., Washington University, 1969.

Helm, Ernest Eugene. *Music at the Court of Frederick the Great*. University of Oklahoma Press, 1960.

Krause, Christian Gottfried. *Von der musikalischen Poesie*. Berlin, 1753.

Kretzschmar, Hermann. *Die Correspondance littéraire als musikgeschichtliche Quelle*. Leipzig, 1911. Rpt. 1973.

———. "Aus Deutschlands italienischer Zeit." *Jahrbuch der Musikbibliothek Peters* 1901.

Landshoff, Ludwig. *Einführung zu "Zehn Klavier-Sonaten von Joh. Christian Bach"* (Edition Peters, Leipzig). Munich, 1925.

Laux, Karl. *Der Thomaskantor und seine Söhne*. Dresden, 1939.

Lewicki, Ernst. "Mozarts Verhältnis zu Sebastian Bach." *Mitteilungen für die Berliner Mozartgemeinde*. Heft 15, 1903.

Löffler, Hans. "'Bache' bei Bach." Bach-Jahrbuch. Leipzig, 1949–50.

Lorenz, Franz. Franz Benda und seine Nachkommen. Berlin, 1967.

Mattheson, Johann. Der vollkommene Capellmeister (1739). Facsimile rpt. of the 2d ed. Kassel, 1969.

———. Der Musicalische Patriot (1728). Facsimile rpt. Leipzig, 1975.

———. Grundlage einer Ehrenpforte (1740). Facsimile rpt. Kassel, 1969.

McVeigh, Simon. Concert Life in London from Mozart to Haydn. Cambridge, 1993.

Mennicke, Carl. Hasse und die Gebrüder Graun als Symphoniker. Leipzig, 1906.

Miesner, Heinrich. "Terry: John Christian Bach" (book review). Zeitschrift für Musikwissenschaft 16 (1934).

Milhous, Judith, and Robert D. Hume. "Opera Salaries in Eighteenth-Century London." Journal of the American Musicological Society 46 (Spring 1993): 26–83.

Mozart-Briefe und Aufzeichnungen. Edited by W. A. Bauer and O. E. Deutsch. 7 vols. Kassel, 1962–1975.

Nissen, Georg Nikolaus. Biographie W. A. Mozarts. Leipzig, 1828. Rpt. Hildesheim, 1984.

Nys, Carl de. "Mozart et les fils de Jean-Sebastien Bach." Les influences étrangères dans l'oeuvre de W. A. Mozart. Paris, 1956.

Papendiek. Court and Private Life in the Time of Queen Charlotte, Being the Journals of Mrs. Papendiek. 2 vols. London, 1887.

Pauchard, Anselm. Ein italienischer Musiktheoretiker: Pater Giambattista Martini. Diss. Lugano, 1941.

Pohl, Carl Ferdinand. Mozart und Haydn in London. Part I: "Mozart in London." Vienna, 1867.

Price, Curtis, Judith Milhous, and Robert D. Hume. The Impresario's Ten Commandments: Continental Recruitment for Italian Opera in London 1763–64. London, Royal Musical Association, 1992.

Quantz, Johann Joachim. Versuch einer Anweisung die flute traversière zu spielen. Berlin, 1752. Engl. trans. by Edward Reilly, On Playing the Flute. London, 1966.

Redman, Alvin. The House of Hanover. New York, 1961.

Riemann, Hugo. "Die Söhne Bachs." Präludien und Studien III. Leipzig, 1901.

Rudhart, F. M. Geschichte der Oper am Hof zu München. Freising, 1865.

Sadie, Stanley. "The Wind Music of J. C. Bach." Music and Letters 37 (1956).

Scheibe, Johann Adolph. Critischer Musikus. Leipzig, 1745. Rpt. Hildesheim, 1970.

Schenk, Erich. Mozart—eine Biographie. Zurich, 1955.

Schering, Arnold. Bach und das Musikleben Leipzigs im 18. Jahrhundert. Leipzig, 1941.

———. "Die Musikästhetik der deutschen Aufklärung." Zeitschrift der Internationalen Musikgesellschaft 8 (1907).

Schmid, Ernst Fritz. *Carl Philipp Emanuel Bach und seine Kammermusik.* Kassel, 1931.

Schökel, Heinrich Peter. *Johann Christian Bach und die Instrumentalmusik seiner Zeit.* Wolfenbüttel, 1926.

Schwarz, Max. "Johann Christian Bach." *Sammelbände der Internationalen Musikgesellschaft* 2 (1901), Heft 3.

Seeband, Rotraut. *Arientypen Johann Christian Bachs.* Diss. Berlin, 1956.

Sickbert, Murl. 1992. "The Mozarts in Milan, February 9–10, 1770, A Funeral Performance of Johann Christian Bach's Dies Irae and Vespers Music?" *Mozart-Jahrbuch 1991–1992,* 461–467.

Simon, Edwin J. "A Royal Manuscript: Ensemble Concertos by J. C. Bach." *Journal of the American Musicological Society* 12 (1959): 161ff.

Spitta, Philipp. *Johann Sebastian Bach.* 2 vols. Leipzig, 1873–80. Engl. trans. London, 1884–85, 2d ed. 1899, rpt. New York, 1951.

Steglich, Rudolf. "Karl Philipp Emanuel Bach und der Dresdner Kreuzkantor August Homilius im Musikleben ihrer Zeit." *Bach-Jahrbuch,* 1915.

Szabolcsi, Bence. *Bausteine zu einer Geschichte der Melodie.* Budapest, 1959.

Terry, Charles Sanford. *John Christian Bach.* 2d ed. with corrigenda by H. C. Robbins Landon. London, 1967.

———. *Johann Sebastian Bach.* 2d ed. London, 1933.

Tutenberg, Fritz. *Die Sinfonik Johann Christian Bachs.* Wolfenbüttel, 1928.

Vogler, Georg Joseph. *Betrachtungen der Mannheimer Tonschule.* Speyer, 1778–80.

Walter, Friedrich. *Geschichte des Theaters und der Musik am kurpfälzischen Hofe.* Leipzig, 1898.

Warburton, Ernest. *A Study of Johann Christian Bach's Operas.* Diss. Oxford, 1969.

———. "Johann Christian Bach." *The New Grove Dictionary of Music and Musicians.* London, 1980.

———. *Johann Christian Bach, 1735–1782: The Collected Works.* New York, 1985–.

———. "Bach, Johann [John] Christian." *The New Grove Dictionary of Opera* vol. 1, 269–271. London & New York, 1992, with additional bibliography.

Wenk, A. *Beiträge zur Kenntnis des Opernschaffens von J. Christian Bach.* Diss. Frankfurt, 1932.

Werkmeister, Wilhelm. *Der Stilwandel in deutscher Dichtung und Musik des 18. Jahrhunderts.* Berlin, 1936.

Wohlfahrth, Hannsdieter. *Johann Christoph Friedrich Bach: ein Komponist im Vorfeld der Klassik.* Berlin, 1971.

Wyzewa, Théodore de and Georges de Saint-Foix. *W. A. Mozart, sa vie musicale et son oeuvre, de l'enfance à la pleine maturité 1756–1777.* 2 vols. Paris, 1912. 3 vols. added by St.-Foix, 1937–46.

Selected Discography

Adriano in Siria: Overture
 S. Standage, Academy of Ancient Music
 (with Sinfonias, Op. 6, No. 6, and Op. 18, Nos. 1 and 4; Sinfonia
  Concertante in C)
 CHANDOS

Amadis des Gaules (opera in three acts) (1779)
 Sonntag, Hobarth, Verebies, Wagner, Schöne, H. Rilling, Bach-Collegium
  and Gächinger Kantorei Stuttgart [G]
 HÄNSSLER CLASSIC 2

Catone in Utica (opera): "Fiumicel che son de Appena"
 Sonnenschmidt
 HELIKON

Concertos in B-flat and E-flat for Bassoon and Orchestra
 Vajda, Lehel, Budapest Symphony
 (with Hummel: Bassoon Concerto)
 WHITE LABEL

Concerto in B-flat for Bassoon and Orchestra
 D. Smith, P. Ledger, English Chamber Orchestra
 (with Graupner, Hargrave, Hertel, Vivaldi: Bassoon Concertos)
 ASV

Concerto in C Minor for Cello and Orchestra
 Turovsky (cello and conductor), I Musici de Montreal
 (with Sinfonia Concertante; Boccherini: Cello Concerto)
 CHANDOS

Concerto in C Minor for Viola and Strings
 W. Christ, H. Müller-Brühl, Cologne Chamber Orchestra
 (with M. Haydn: Viola-Harpsichord Concerto; C. Stamitz: Viola
  Concerto)
 KOCH-SCHWANN

Concertos for Clavier in A, F Minor, and G
Dreyfus (harpsichord), Tokyo Solisten
DENON

Concerto in D for Flute and Orchestra
K. B. Sebon, H. Müller-Brühl, Cologne Chamber Orchestra
(with C. P. E. Bach: Sonatina; J. C. F. Bach: Sinfonia; W. F. Bach:
    Symphony in F)
KOCH-SCHWANN

Concerto in D for Flute and Orchestra
Martin, Jöris, Hanover Chamber Orchestra
LAVENHAGEN & PARIS TON

Concerto in D for Keyboard and Strings, Op. 1, No. 6
Chalen, Couraud Antiqua Musica Orchestra
PHILIPS

Concerto in D for Keyboard and Strings, Op 13, No. 2
Lukas, Lukas, V.-Lukas-Consort
FONO SCHALLPLATTEN

Concerto in E-flat for Bassoon and Orchestra, Op. 8, No. 13
Thunemann, Müller-Brühl, Cologne Chamber Orchestra
KOCH-SCHWANN

Concerto in E-flat for Trumpet and Organ
Andre, Faerber, Württ. Chamber Orchestra Heilbronn
TELDEC

Concerto in F for Keyboard and Strings, Op. 1, No. 3
Straten, Frieberger, Cappella Plagensis
HELIKON

Concerto in F for Keyboard and Strings, Op. 7, No. 2
Sonnenschmidt, Sephira-Ensemble Stuttgart
HELIKON

Concerto in F for Oboe, Strings, and Continuo
Glaetzner, Pommer, Berlin Chamber Orchestra
(with C. P. E. Bach: Oboe Concerto)
CAPRICCIO

Concerto for Keyboard and Strings, Op. 7, No. 5
London Baroque Ensemble
(with Sonata, Op. 20, No. 2; L. Mozart: Sonata; W. A. Mozart:
    Piano Concertos K. 107)
HARMONIA MUNDI

Concerto for Violin, Cello, and Orchestra
Kantorow (violin and conductor), Fujuwara, Netherlands Chamber
    Orchestra
(with Haydn: Cello Concerto in C; Mozart: Violin-Cello Sonata)
DENON

Concerto Movements in B-flat, E-flat, and F for Organ and Strings
Geffert, J. C. Bach-Akademie
FONO SCHALLPLATTEN

Concert-Rondo in F for Organ and Strings, Op. 13, No. 3
Haselböck, Melkus, Capella Academica Vienna
HÄNSSLER

Duets in A and F for Organ Four-Hands, Op. 18, Nos. 5 and 6 (Allegro / Rondo)
Fagius and Sanger
(with Hesse; Kellner; Merkel; Wesley)
BIS

Duet in C for Clavier Four-Hands
Brembeck, Hartmann
VLEUGELS TONTRÄGER

Duet in C for Clavier Four-Hands
Haselböck, Haselböck
KOCH-SCHWANN

Duet in F for Clavier Four-Hands, Op. 18, No. 6 (Allegro / Rondo)
Klavierduo Keilhack
COLOSSEUM

Duet in G for Two Claviers, Op. 15, No. 5
Blöchliger, Vollenweider
TUDOR

Duet in G for Two Claviers, Op. 15, No. 5
Munich Harpsichord Duo
CAVALLI

Fugue on B-A-C-H
Hamm
MOTETTE URSINA

Fugue on B-A-C-H
Haselböck
HÄNSSLER

Magnificat for Two 4-part Choruses and Instruments
Knubben, Rottweiler Münstersängerknaben, Württ. Chamber Orchestra, Heilbronn, Trumpet ensemble H. Sauter
HÄNSSLER

Marches Op. 17, Nos. 1–9
Zöbeley, wind ensemble of the Munich Motet Choir
CALLIOPE

Overtures, Nos. 1–6
Hogwood, Academy of Ancient Music
DECCA

Progressive Lesson for Clavier No. 6, in F Minor
Menger
ORGANO

Quartet in B-flat for Oboe and String Trio
Freiburg Baroque Soloists
AUDIOFON

Quartet in B-flat for Oboe and String Trio
Holliger, et al.
(with Bach: Musical; Handel: Trio Sonata; Holliger; Mozart: Adagio in C;
Penderecki; Telemann: Fantasies; Suite in G Minor
DENON

Quartet in C for Flute and String Trio
Freiburg Baroque Soloists
AUDIOFON

Quartet in D for Flute, Oboe, Viola, and Cello, Op. 19, No. 2
Freiburg Baroque Soloists
AUDIOFON

Quartet in G for Harpsichord and String Trio
Bamberg Piano Quartet
COLOSSEUM

Quartet in G for Harpsichord and String Trio
Freiburg Baroque Soloists
AUDIOFON

Quartet in G for Harpsichord and String Trio
Northwestern Chamber Ensemble
RBM

Quartets for Two Flutes and Strings, Op. 19, Nos. 1–4
B. Larsen and B. Pedersen (flutes), P. Elbaek (violin), H. Olsen (viola),
B. Holst Christensen (cello) ("Complete Works for Two Flutes and
Strings")
(with Trios in C and G for Two Flutes and Srings)
KONTRAPUNKT

Quintet in C for Flute, Oboe, Violin, Viola, and Continuo, Op. 11, No. 1
English Concert
DEUTSCHE GRAMMOPHON

Quintet in C for Flute, Oboe, Violin, Viola, and Continuo, Op. 11, No. 1
Mannheim Soloists
RBM

Quintet in D for Flute, Oboe, Violin, Viola, and Continuo, Op. 11, No. 6
English Concert
DEUTSCHE GRAMMOPHON

Quintet in D for Flute, Oboe, Violin, Viola, and Continuo, Op. 11, No. 6
Kuijken, Dombrecht, Meer, Meer, Huys
ACCORD

Quintet in D for Flute, Oboe, Violin, Cello, and Harpsichord, Op. 22, No. 1
Leipzig Bach-Collegium
(with Albinoni: Trumpet-Flute-Oboe Concerto; Bach: Sonata BWV 1038;
Finger: Sonata; Stradella: Barchegio; Telemann: Trio)
CAPRICCIO

Quintet in D for Flute, Oboe, Violin, Cello, and Harpsichord, Op. 22, No. 1
M. Munchinger, Ars Rediviva Ensemble ("The Bach Family")
(with C. P. E. Bach: Quartet H. 537; *Siciliano*; J. C. F. Bach: Trio Sonata in
E Minor; J. S. Bach: Bach Program; W. F. Bach: Trio Sonata in A Minor
SUPRAPHON 2

Quintet in D for Flute, Oboe, Violin, Gamba, and Fortepiano, Op. 22, No. 1
Concerto Cologne
RCA

Quintet in D for Flute, Oboe, Violin, Gamba, and Fortepiano, Op. 22, No. 1
English Concert
DEUTSCHE GRAMMOPHON

Quintet in D for Flute, Oboe, Violin, Gamba, and Fortepiano, Op. 22, No. 1
Freiburg Baroque Soloists
AUDIOFON

Quintet in D for Flute, Oboe, Violin, Gamba, and Fortepiano, Op. 22, No. 1
Kircheis, Passin, Gütz, palm, Pfaenedr, Schmidt
CAPRICCIO

Quintet in E-flat for Flute, Oboe, Violin, Viola, and Continuo, Op. 11, No. 4
Freiburg Baroque Soloists
AUDIOFON

Quintet in E-flat for Flute, Oboe, Violin, Viola, and Continuo, Op. 11, No. 4
Mannheim Soloists
RBM

Quintet in F for Flute, Oboe, Violin, Viola, and Continuo, Op. 11, No. 3:
Andante / Rondo [Allegretto]
Ensemble Les Adieux
(with Quintet in G, Op. 11, No. 2: Allegro / Allegro assai)
RCA

Quintet in F for Klavier, Oboe, Violins, and Gamba, Op. 22, No. 1
Freiburg Baroque Soloists
AUDIOFON

Quintet in G for Flute, Oboe, Violin, Viola, and Continuo, Op. 11, No. 2:
Allegro / Allegro assai
Ensemble Les Adieux
(with Quintet in F, Op. 11, No. 3: Andante / Rondo [Allegretto])
RCA

Quintet for Flute, Oboe, Violin, Viola, and Continuo, Op. 11, No. 6
K. Pohlers, A. Sous, G. Kehr, G. Schmid, R. Buhl, unnamed harpsichordist
(recorded in 1957)
(with Cimarosa: Concerto for two flutes; Mozart: Andante K. 315;
Concerto No. 2, K. 314; Salieri: Concerto in C)
VOX / TURNABOUT

Requiem: Introitus, Kyrie, and Dies irae
Auger, Watts, Baldin, Schöne, H. Rilling, Bach-Collegium and Gächinger
Kantorei Stuttgart [G]
HÄNSSLER

Salve Regina for Soprano, Chamber Orchestra, and Continuo
Ewerhart, Marshall, German Baroque Soloists
FONO SCHALLPLATTEN

Sextet in C for Clavier, Oboe, Violin, Cello, and Two Horns
English Concert
DEUTSCHE GRAMMOPHON

Sextet in C for Clavier, Oboe, Violin, Cello, and Two Horns
Ensemble Musica Orphea
GALLO

Sextet in C for Clavier, Oboe, Violin, Cello, and Two Horns
Freiburg Baroque Soloists
AUDIOFON

Sinfonia in D, Op. 3, No. 1
Murphy, Consort of London
COLLINS CLASSICS

Sinfonias, Op. 3, Nos. 1 and 2
Concerto Armonico [period instruments]
(with Sinfonias, Op. 6, Nos. 1 and 6, and Op. 9, No. 2)
HUNGAROTON

Sinfonias, Op. 3, Nos. 1–6
Marriner, Academy of St. Martin-in-the-Fields
PHILIPS

Sinfonia in G, Op. 6, No. 1
Gmür, Franconian Chamber Orchestra
COLUMBIA

Sinfonias, Op. 6, Nos. 1 and 6
Concerto Armonica [period instruments]
(with Sinfonias, Op. 3, Nos. 1 and 2, and Op. 9, No. 2)
HUNGAROTON

Sinfonias, Op. 6, Nos. 1–6
G. Rumpel, A. Raoult, R. Tschupp, Zurich Camerata (recorded in 1969 and
1981)
(with Krommer: Concertino; Vanhal: Symphonies [3])
JECKLIN-DISCO

Sinfonia, Op. 6, No. 6
S. Standage, Academy of Ancient Music
(with *Adriano*; Sinfonias, Op. 18, Nos. 1 and 4; Sinfonia Concertante in C)
CHANDOS

Sinfonia in G Minor, Op. 6, No. 6
Collegium Aureum
(with Sinfonias, Op. 18, Nos. 1, 4, and 6)
EDITIO CLASSICA

Sinfonia in G Minor, Op. 6, No. 6
Lukas, V.-Lukas-Consort
FONO SCHALLPLATTEN

Sinfonia in G Minor, Op. 6, No. 6
Tschupp, Camerata Zürich
JECKLIN-DISCO

Sinfonia in G Minor, Op. 6, No. 6
Concerto Cologne
RCA

Sinfonia in E-flat, Op. 9, No. 2
Lukas, V.-Lukas-Consort
FONO SCHALLPLATTEN

Sinfonia, Op. 9, No. 2
Concerto Armonico [period instruments]
(with Sinfonias, Op. 3, Nos. 1 and 2, and Op. 6, Nos. 1 and 6)
HUNGAROTON

Sinfonia in B-flat, Op. 9, No. 3 (Overture to *Zanaida*)
Sacchetti
EUROMUSICA

Sinfonia in E-flat, Op. 18 ("Six Grand Overtures"), No. 1, for Double Orchestra
Zukerman, St. Paul Chamber Orchestra
(with Sinfonia; Boccherini: Cello Concerto)
CBS

Sinfonia in E-flat, Op. 18 ("Six Grand Overtures"), No. 1, for Double Orchestra
Collegium Aureum
RCA

Sinfonias, Op. 18 ("Six Grand Overtures"), Nos. 1 and 3 for Double Orchestra, and No. 6 for Orchestra
Collegium Aureum
(with Sinfonia, Op. 6, No. 6)
EDITIO CLASSICA

Sinfonias, Op. 18 ("Six Grand Overtures"), No. 1, for Double Orchestra, and No. 4, for Orchestra
S. Standage, Academy of Ancient Music
(with *Adriano*; Sinfonia, Op. 6, No. 6; Sinfonia Concertante in C)
CHANDOS

Sinfonia in D, Op. 18 ("Six Grand Overtures"), No. 3, for Double Orchestra
M. Rodan, Israel Sinfonietta
(with Mendelssohn: Symphony No. 1; Poulenc: Sinfonietta)
OLYMPIA

Sinfonias, Op. 18 ("Six Grand Overtures"), Nos. 3 and 5 for Double Orchestra
Jones, Little Orchestra of London
(with Sinfonia Concertante)
ELEKTRA/NONESUCH

Sinfonia in D, Op. 18 ("Six Grand Overtures"), No. 4, for Orchestra (Allegro con spirito / Andante / Rondo [Presto])
Collegium Aureum
RCA

Sinfonia in D, Op. 18 ("Six Grand Overtures"), No. 4, for Orchestra (Allegro con spirito / Andante / Rondo [Presto])
Lukas, V.-Lukas-Consort
FONO SCHALLPLATTEN

Sinfonia in E, Op. 18 ("Six Grand Overtures"), No. 5, for Double Orchestra
Stephani, Bach-Orchestra Frankfurt
BÄRENREITER

Sinfonia in D, Op. 18 ("Six Grand Overtures"), No. 6, for Orchestra
Collegium Aureum
RCA

Sinfonias (Six) for Winds (1781–82)
Consortium Classicum
MUSIKPRODUKTION DABRINGHAUS U. GRIMM (distr. Koch Internat'l)

Sinfonia Concertante in A for Violin, Cello, and Orchestra
Goltz / Goltz, Graf / Kammerorch. C. v. d. Goltz
AUROPHON

Sinfonia Concertante in A for Violin, Cello, and Orchestra
E. Turovsky, Y. Turovsky (cello and conductor), I Musici de Montreal
(with Cello Concerto; Boccherini: Cello Concerto)
CHANDOS

Sinfonia Concertante in A for Violin, Cello, and Orchestra
Zukerman (violin and conductor), Yo-Yo Ma (cello), St. Paul Chamber Orchestra
(with Boccherini: Cello Concerto)
CBS

Sinfonia Concertante in A for Violin, Cello, and Orchestra
Kantorow / Kantorow, Fujiwara / Niederländ Kammerorch.
DENON, C 37 7867

Sinfonia Concertante in C for Flute, Oboe, Violin, Cello
Galway, Wickens, Armon, N. Jones, L. Jones, Little Orchestra of London
(with Sinfonias, Op. 18)
ELEKTRA/NONESUCH

Sinfonia Concertante in D for Flute, Oboe, Violin, and Cello
S. Standage, Academy of Ancient Music
(with *Adriano*; Sinfonias, Op. 6, No. 6, and Op. 18, Nos. 1 and 4)
CHANDOS

Sinfonia Concertante in E-flat for Two Violins and Orchestra
Forchert, Orlovsky, Lukas, V.-Lukas-Consort
FONO SCHALLPLATTEN

Sonata in D for Harpsichord, Op. 5, No. 2 (Allegro di molto / Andante di molto / Menuetto)
Raynaud
PIERRE VERNAY

Sonatas for Keyboard, Op. 5, Nos. 2, 3, 4 and 6, and Op 17, Nos. 2 and 5
A. Raynaud (pianoforte — recorded 3/91)
PIERRE VERANY

Sonata in G for Harpsichord, Op. 5, No. 3 (Allegro / Allegretto)
Raynaud
PIERRE VERNAY

Sonata in E-flat for Harpsichord, Op. 5, No. 4 (Allegro / Rondo allegretto)
Raynaud
PIERRE VERNAY

Sonata in E for Harpsichord, Op. 5, No. 5 (Allegro / Allegretto)
Black
HELIKON

Sonatas for Keyboard, Op. 5, Nos. 5 and 6, and Op. 17, Nos. 2, 3, and 5
V. Black (harpsichord)
CRD

Sonata in C Minor for Harpsichord, Op. 5, No. 6 (Grave / Allegro moderato [Fugue] / Alegretto)
Black
HELIKON

Sonata in E for Harpsichord, Op. 5, No. 6 (Grave / Allegro moderato [Fugue] / Alegretto)
Raynaud
PIERRE VERNAY

Sonata in E for Harpsichord, Op. 5, No. 6, Third Movement (Prestissimo [Allegretto])
Burnett
AMON RA

Sonata in A for Clavier and Violin, Op. 15, No. 2
Berliner Barock Companey
AARTON

Sonata in G for Clavier with Flute or Violin, Op. 16, No. 2 (Allegretto / Andante grazioso)
Kelver, Ven
COLOSSEUM

Sonata in A for Clavier and Flute or Violin, Op. 16, No. 4
Freiburg Baroque Soloists
AUDIOFON

Sonata for Keyboard, Op. 17, No. 2
I. Hobson (piano) ("The London Piano School, Vol. 1")
(with Burton; Busby; Clementi; Dussek; Wesley)
ARABESQUE

Sonata in C Minor for Harpsichord, Op. 17, No. 2
Black
HELIKON

Sonata in C Minor for Harpsichord, Op. 17, No. 2
Hobson
FONO SCHALLPLATTEN

Sonata in C Minor for Harpsichord, Op. 17, No. 2
Iseringhausen
DABRINGHAUS U. GRIMM

Sonata in C Minor for Harpsichord, Op. 17, No. 2
Leigh
BÄRENREITER

Sonata in C Minor for Harpsichord, Op. 17, No. 2
Raynaud
PIERRE VERNAY

Sonata in C Minor for Harpsichord, Op. 17, No. 2
Schornsheim
AARTON

Sonata in C Minor for Harpsichord, Op. 17, No. 2, Third Movement (Prestissimo)
Iseringhausen
DABRINGHAUS U. GRIMM

Sonata in E-flat for Harpsichord, Op. 17, No. 3 (Allegro assai / Allegro)
Black
HELIKON

Sonata in A for Harpsichord, Op. 17, No. 5 (Allegro / Presto)
Black
HELIKON

Sonata in A for Harpsichord, Op. 17, No. 5 (Allegro / Presto)
Raynaud
PIERRE VERNAY

Sonata in C for Clavier with accompaniment, Op. 18, No. 1
Brauchli, Elizondo
TITANIC

Sonata in D for Keyboard and Strings, Op. 20, No. 2
London Baroque Ensemble
(with Concerto, Op. 7, No. 5; L. Mozart: Sonata; W. A. Mozart: Piano
    Concertos K. 107)
HARMONIA MUNDI

Trio in C for Flute, Violin, and Cello
Rampal, Stern, Rostropovich
(with Mozart: Flute Trios; A. Reicha: Variations; Telemann: Quartet)
SONY CLASSICAL

Trio in C for Two Violins and Viola Basso, Op. 4, No. 6
Achilles, Brauckmann, Brauckmann, Lamke
CAPELLA

Trios in C and G for Two Flutes and Strings
B. Larsen and B. Pedersen (flutes), P. Elbaek (violin), H. Olsen (viola),
    B. Holst Christensen (cello) ("Complete Works for Two Flutes and
    Strings")
(with Quartets for Two Flutes and Strings, Op. 19, Nos. 1–4)
KONTRAPUNKT

	J. C. Bach	Bach Family	W. A. Mozart	Contemporary Events
1735	5 September: Birth of John Christian Bach	Sebastian cantor at St. Thomas School in Leipzig. *Christmas Oratorio*, parts 4–6. *Clavier-Übung* (II). Friedemann organist in Dresden. Emanuel studies in Frankfurt/Oder. Bernhard organist in Mühlhausen.	—	
1736		Beginning of the "battle of the prefects." Sebastian appointed court composer.	—	Death of Pergolesi.
1737		Elias Bach joins the family as secretary and teacher.	—	Publication of Scheibe's *Der Critische Musikus*. Birth of Josef Mysliveczek.
1738		Emanuel appointed harpsichordist to the Prussian crown prince. Bernhard flees to escape his creditors.	—	Gluck studies with Sammartini in Milan.

	J. C. Bach	Bach Family	W. A. Mozart	Contemporary Events
1739		Death of Bernhard. Sebastian resumes work with the Collegium Musicum.	—	Mattheson: *Der vollkommene Capellmeister.*
1740			—	Frederick II, king of Prussia.
1741		Sebastian visits Emanuel in Berlin. Serious illness of Anna Magdalena.	—	Death of Vivaldi. Quantz becomes court composer. Gluck's first opera, *Artaserse.*
1742		Elias leaves Leipzig. "Goldberg Variations."	—	Graun introduces Italian opera in Berlin.
1743			—	First appearance of Carl Friedrich Abel as soloist in the Leipzig Grosses Concert.
1744	Instructed by his father.	Emanuel marries Johanna Maria Dannemann. The *Well-Tempered Clavier* (II).	—	Regina Valentini joins Mingotti's opera company in Leipzig.
1745		Bach attends baptism of his first grandchild in Berlin.	—	Stamitz Kapellmeister in Mannheim. Gluck accompanies Prince Lobkowitz to England.
1746		Friedemann organist in Halle.	—	Batteux: *Traité des beaux arts.*

Year			
1747		Bach visits the king of Prussia; joins the Society of Musical Science. *A Musical Offering.*	Gluck in Leipzig with the Mingotti opera company.
1748	Christian's first preserved manuscript.		
1749	Takes care of ailing father's correspondence.	Bach's first stroke. The "Biedermann affair." *The Art of Fugue.*	Harrer auditions for Bach's position. Handel: *Fireworks Music.* Birth of Goethe.
1750	With Friedemann, visits Emanuel in Berlin.	Friedrich becomes court musician in Bückeburg. Sebastian dies after eye surgery.	Birth of Salieri. Jean-Jacques Rousseau's *Discourse on the Sciences and Arts.*
1751	Studies with Emanuel (to 1754). The first keyboard concertos.	Friedemann marries Dorothea Elisabeth Georgi in Halle.	Handel's last oratorio, *Jephthe.*
1752	Choral ode *L'Olimpe* for the Prussian king's birthday.		Krause, *Von der musikalischen Poesie.* Quantz, essay on flute playing. Rousseau, *Le devin du village.*
1753	Contributes to the *Oden mit Melodien,* published 1755, and to *Neue Lieder zum Singen,* 1756.	Emanuel's essay on keyboard instrument playing. He applies for the organist's position in Zittau.	Krause/Ramler, *Oden mit Melodien;* Rousseau, *Letters on French Music.*

	J. C. Bach	Bach Family	W. A. Mozart	Contemporary Events
1754	Christian goes to Italy, enters the employ of Count Litta.	Emanuel and the Prussian king quarrel about pay.	—	Tartini, *Trattato di musica*; Algarotti, *Saggio sopra l'opera in musica*. Gluck becomes court music director in Vienna.
1755		Friedrich, in Bückeburg, marries Lucia Elisabeth Münchhausen.	—	
1756	Studies with Padre Martini in Bologna.	Emanuel offers the copper plates of the *Art of Fugue* for sale.	27 January: Birth of W. A. Mozart.	Beginning of the Seven Years' War. Leopold Mozart's book on violin playing.
1757	Christian's first known letter from Italy. Successful compositions for the church (Dies Irae).			Death of Stamitz.
1759	Converts to Catholicism. Te Deum. First aria for Elisi.	Friedrich concertmaster in Bückeburg.		Deaths of Handel and Graun; birth of Schiller.
1760	Plans for opera in Turin. Organist at Milan cathedral.	Death of Anna Magdalena.		George III becomes king of England.
1761	*Artaserse* in Turin. *Catone in Utica* in Naples, with Anton Raaff.		Leopold Mozart writes down Wolfgang's first attempts at composition.	Marriage of George III to Sophie-Charlotte of Mecklenburg-Strelitz.

1762	*Alessandro nell'Indie* in Naples. Opera commission for London. Cocchi's successor at King's Theatre. Arias for pasticcios and for Anna Lucia de Amicis.	Emanuel visits Strelitz. Friedemann declines the position of Kapellmeister for the Landgrave of Hesse-Darmstadt.	Wolfgang's first concert tour, with Leopold and Nannerl.	Gluck, *Orfeo* in Vienna.
1763	First opera for London: *Orione.* First public concert for the Society of Musicians. Second opera: *Zanaida.* Music master for the queen (before 1 February 1764). Six trios for harpsichord, violin (flute), and cello, Op. 2. Six harpsichord concertos for the queen, Op. 3.		Second concert tour: to Paris via Mannheim, Frankfurt, and Brussels.	End of Seven Years' War. Anna Lucia de Amicis leaves London.
1764	No operatic activity. Bach-Abel concerts. Royal privilege. Beginning in April: Mozart's teacher and mentor.	Friedemann gives up the organist's position in Halle.	April: Departure for England; first concert at court. June: First public concert at Spring Garden. July: Leopold's serious illness. August: Sojourn in Chelsea. London Sketch Book. First symphonies. Return to London. Voice lessons with Manzuoli. Six sonatas dedicated to the queen.	Death of Rameau. Mysliweczek succeeds Christian as opera composer in Italy.

	J. C. Bach	Bach Family	W. A. Mozart	Contemporary Events
1765	Renewed operatic activity. *Adriano in Siria*. Six symphonies, Op. 3. Six duets for Lady Glenorchy, Op. 4. First collection of Vauxhall songs. Move to Angelo's house. Circle of friends includes Gainsborough. "Soho concerts" at Mrs. Cornelys's. Works for Covent Garden.		Concert in the Little Haymarket Theatre. Hears Handel oratorios. Repeated advertisements of a farewell concert. Meets with Daines Barrington. July: "House concerts" at the Swan and Harp Tavern. Gift of music to the British Museum. September: Departure for The Hague. Arranges three keyboard sonatas by Christian as concertos.	Manzuoli leaves London.
1766	Cecilia Grassi engaged for the 1766–67 season. Angelo's suspicions. Guarducci and Grassi in *Trakebarne, Gran Mogul*.		Paris, Switzerland, Munich. November: Return to Salzburg.	Haydn appointed Kapellmeister of Prince Esterhazy.
1767	New opera *Carattaco*, without C. Grassi. *The Fairy Favour*. Grassi returns to Italy.		*Apollo und Hyazinth*. Journey to Vienna.	Death of Telemann. Haydn, *Stabat Mater*. Lessing, *Minna von Barnhelm*.
1768	No operas. Demonstrates the pianoforte as a solo instrument. Bach-Abel concerts at Almack's. Six keyboard sonatas, Op. 5.	March: Emanuel appointed director of church music in Hamburg.	Again in Vienna. *Bastien und Bastienne*. Waisenhaus (Orphanage) Mass. Return to Salzburg.	Christian's *Catone in Utica* performed in Braunschweig. Goethe in Leipzig.

Year				
1769	Performances at Almack's. Benefit concert for Lady Dorothy Du Bois.	Emanuel: *Die Israeliten in der Wüste*.	*La finta semplice*. Barrington's report. December: Departure for Italy.	Gluck, *Paride et Elena*.
1770	Additions to Gluck's *Orfeo*. C. Grassi returns to London. Oratorio *Gioa, Re di Giuda*. Six canzonettas, Op. 6. 1770–1775: Six keyboard concertos, Op. 7. Six quartets, Op. 8. Three symphonies, Op. 9. Six sonatas for clavier and violin, Op. 10.	Emanuel: *Musikalisches Vielerley*. Circle of friends including Klopstock, Lessing, Claudius.	First concert in Verona. Visits Padre Martini in Bologna. Friendship with Thomas Linley in Florence. Papal audience. Accepted into the Bologna *Accademia*. Friendship with Mysliweczek.	Birth of Beethoven. Deaths of Tartini and Krause.
1771	Wendling arrives with wife and daughter; Christian enamored of "Gustl." Opera commission for Mannheim.	Friedemann's unsuccessful application from Braunschweig (there until 1774). Allows his father's works to be auctioned off.	Honorary maestro di capella in Verona. Empress Maria Theresia commissions opera *Ascanio in Alba* for Milan.	Haydn's "classic" symphonic style.
1772	Cantata *Endimione* with the Wendlings. Christian promotes his successor, Schröter. Goes to Mannheim with the Wendlings. *Temistocle* with Anton Raaff. Unsuccessful marriage plans. Six quintets, Op. 11 (to 1777). Six keyboard concertos, Opp. 12–13.	Burney visits Emanuel in Hamburg.	Returns to Salzburg, *Il sogno di Scipione*. Third journey to Italy. December: *Lucio Silla*, symphonies K. 124, 128, 130, 132–134.	

	J. C. Bach	Bach Family	W. A. Mozart	Contemporary Events
1773	Summer and fall: Concert tours with C. Grassi. Marriage. Abel moves to Newman Street. Letter to Martini.	Emanuel's autobiography in Burney's *Diary*.	*Exsultate, jubilate* for Rauzzini. Return to Salzburg, journey to Vienna. Audience with the empress. December in Salzburg: writes his first piano concerto.	Death of Quantz. Gluck goes to Paris.
1774	Own concert hall (with Abel and Gallini) on Hanover Square. Rauzzini: the new star. A German pupil: Anna Maria Schindler. *Lucio Silla* in Mannheim. *Endimione* and *Amor Vincitore* in Schwetzingen. The king of Naples expects Christian to come.	Friedemann in Berlin; organ recital in the Nicolai church. Repeated changes of residence.	Symphonies, sacred music, serenades, and piano sonatas. December: Leopold and Wolfgang travel to Munich.	Mysliweczek performs Gluck's *Orfeo* with Christian's arias in Naples. Gainsborough permanently moves to London.
1775	C. Gabrielli takes part in the opera season. Bach: *Catone*, overture to *Astarto*. Holdup on the road to Richmond.	Emanuel performs Handel's *Messiah*.	January: *La finta giardiniera*. Return to Salzburg: *Il ré pastore*. Violin concertos K. 207, 211, 216, 218, 219.	Beaumarchais, *The Barber of Seville*. Lichtenberg in London.
1776	Terminates collaboration with Gallini. Loan from Buntebart. Padre Martini requests Christian's portrait. Christian rents a house in Richmond.	Emanuel's church cantata *Heilig*.	Sacred music and serenades. Sends his offertory *Misericordias Domini* to Padre Martini.	Piccinni in Paris as Gluck's opponent.

1777	Giardini directs the opera. Adamberger's debut. May: Ten benefit concerts within one month.		Asks for his dismissal from the Salzburg court. Travels with his mother. In Mannheim with Cannabich and Wendling. No appointment by the elector.	Death of Wagenseil.
1778	Last opera for London: *La clemenza di Scipione*, Op. 14. Last exchange of letters with Martini. August: In Paris with Tenducci to prepare *Amadis des Gaules*. Collaborates with Ricci on a book on piano playing. Reunion with Mozart. Concert in St. Germain. An opportunity for Mozart in England? Christian returns to London.	Friedemann: intrigues against Kirnberger. Publishes his father's organ concerto as his own. Emanuel's son dies in Rome. Friedrich brings his son to Christian.	Writes "Non so d'onde viene" for Aloysia Weber. March: Wolfgang and his mother arrive in Paris. Opera plans. Offer of a position as organist in Versailles. July: Death of the mother. Leopold endeavors to have Wolfgang reappointed in Salzburg. Return from Paris with stopover in Mannheim.	Elector Karl Theodor moves his court to Munich. Gluck prepares his next operas for Paris. The eight-year-old Beethoven is presented by his father as a "prodigy, six years old." Deaths of Rousseau and Voltaire.
1779	April: Benefit concert for Tenducci. Four sonatas and two duets for piano and violin, Op. 15. Six sonatas for piano and violin, Op. 16. Six sonatas for harpsichord or pianoforte, Op. 17. Returns to Paris in August. December: *Amadis des Gaules*. Returns to London with commission for *Omphale*.	Friedemann: plans for a "serious" opera.	Appointed court organist in Salzburg. Coronation Mass, *Zaide*. The Weber family moves from Munich to Vienna. Aloysia at the Vienna opera.	May: Gluck's *Iphigénie en Tauride* in Paris. September: Failure of his *Echo et Narcisse*. Returns to Vienna.

	J. C. Bach	Bach Family	W. A. Mozart	Contemporary Events
1780	Expected to write for the 1781–82 opera season. Gives up his house in Richmond. His housekeeper embezzles funds; Christian at the verge of financial ruin. Giardini now in charge of chamber music for the crown prince.	Emanuel: *Geistliche Gesänge mit Melodien zum Singen bey dem Claviere*.	Guest appearance of Schikaneder's troupe in Salzburg. Concerts at court. Aloysia Weber marries Joseph Lange in Vienna. Travels to Munich to prepare his new opera.	Deaths of Empress Maria Theresia and Batteux.
1781	Six *Grand Overtures*, Op. 18. May: Last of the Bach-Abel concerts. Moves to Paddington for reasons of health. November: Draws up his will.	Death of sister Elisabeth Altnikol.	Performance of *Idomeneo*. Archbishop summons him to Vienna. Rupture with Salzburg. Signs marriage contract with Constanze without the father's knowledge. Work on *Seraglio* and other scores.	Death of Mysliweczek. Gluck suffers another stroke. Herschel discovers the planet Uranus and is appointed court astronomer to King George III.
1782[+]	1 January: Death of John Christian Bach.	Deaths of Friedemann, 1784; Emanuel, 1788; Friedrich, 1795.	Death of Mozart, 1791.	Deaths of Abel, 1787; Gluck, 1787; Gainsborough, 1788.

Index

*numbers in **boldface** refer to illustrations*

A

Aaron, Pietro, *music theorist*, 131
Abel, Carl Friedrich, *gambist*, 39–40, 186, 206, 207, 219, 224, 260, **267**, 274, 304, 310, 316, 324, 330, 331
  financial problems of, 303
  and John Christian Bach
    Bach-Abel concerts, 39, 195, 206-207, 228, 230, 236, 254, 266, 268, 273, 299, 301, 302, 303, 328
    their circle of friends, 250-251, 253, 255, 258
    dissolve their common household, 261
    share living quarters: Hanover Square, 257; King's Square Court, 247; Meard's Street, 181; Queen Street, 261
  performs at English court, 146
  performs under J. S. Bach, 181
  stays away from Christian's funeral, 332
  symphony copied by Mozart, 216
Abel, Christian Ferdinand, *father of Carl Friedrich Abel*, 39
Abel, Sophia Charlotte, *sister of Carl Friedrich Abel*, 39
Abert, Hermann, *musicologist*, xi, 209
Abingdon, earl of, 302, 324
Adamberger, Johann Valentin, *singer*, 311–313, **315**
Adlgasser, Anton Cajetan, *composer*, 233
Adlung, M. Jakob, *music scholar*, 22
Agricola, Johann Friedrich, *composer*, 60, 62, 63, 66, 70, 84, 87, 91, 100, 102, 184
Albert, Friedrich, *father of Mrs. Papendiek*, 303, 332
Albert, Miss. *See* Papendiek, Mrs.
Alembert, Jean le Rond d', *encyclopedist*, 86
Algarotti, Count Francesco, **69**, 73, 95, 98, 105, 119
Almack, Mr., *landlord*, 266

Altnikol, Elisabeth. *See* Bach, Elisabeth Juliane Friederike.
Altnikol, Johann Christoph, *organist, husband of Elisabeth Juliane Friederike Bach*, 33, 35, 52, 55, 100
Amicis, Anna Lucia de, *singer*, 169, 171, 174, **175**, 176–177, 182, 259, 305
André, Johann, *music publisher*, 248
Angelo, Domenico, *landlord of John Christian Bach in London*, 228, 248, **249**
Angelo, Henry, *son of Domenico Angelo*, 248, 260–261, 274
Angelo, Mrs., *wife of Domenico Angelo*, 250
Anhalt-Köthen, Prince Leopold of, 107
Anna Amalia, *princess of Prussia*, 62
Arese, Count Bartolomeo, *member of the Litta family*, 109
Argens, Marquis d', 67
Arne, Thomas Augustine, *composer*, 223, 233
Arteaga, Stefano, *writer on music*, 95
Astrua, Giovanna, *female singer*, 70
Attwood, Thomas, *friend and pupil of Mozart*, 243
August "The Strong," *elector of Saxony, king of Poland*, 30
Augusta, Princess, *mother of King George III of England*, 163, 189
Ayen, duc d'. *See* Noailles, Duc Louis d'Ayen.

B

Bach, Anna Carolina Philippina, *daughter of Carl Philipp Emanuel Bach*, 59
Bach, Anna Magdalena, *mother of John Christian Bach*, 1, 2, 6, 34, 36–38, 52, 54, 58, 81, 136, 137, 261, 290
Bach, Carl Philipp Emanuel, *half brother of John Christian Bach*, ix, 1–2, 4, 15, 28, 32, 34, 38, 39, 47, 52, **57**, 58, **61**, 62, 63, 70, 73,

75–87, 91, 92, 99–100, 103, 106, 136, 137, 166, 167, 183, 202
  appearance and personality of, 76–78, 80, 82
  applies for his father's post, 55–56
  compositions in print, 85
  disapproves of Christian's conversion, 130
  on musical style, 83–84, 86
  position at Prussian court, 79–81, 100, 102, 105, 293
  praised by Hasse, 119
  praises brother Friedemann, 29
  and Prince Lobkowitz, 75–76
  sharp tongue of, 67
  treatise on keyboard playing, **61**, 82, 85, 89, 327
  visited by his father in Berlin, 37, 41, 43
  visited by Friedemann and Christian in Berlin, 59–60
  writes obituary for father, 55, 81
Bach, Catharina Dorothea, *half sister of John Christian Bach*, 1, 2, 34, 38, 290
Bach, Cecilia, *singer, wife of John Christian Bach*, 258, 259, 260, 261, 263, 264, 270, 272, 299, 300, 303, 304, 330
Bach, Elisabeth Juliane Friederike ("Liesgen" Altnikol), *sister of John Christian Bach*, 2, 52, 290
Bach, Gottfried Heinrich, *brother of John Christian Bach*, 2, 37, 58
Bach, Gottlieb Friedrich, *painter*, 3
Bach, Johann August, *son of Carl Philipp Emanuel Bach*, 43, 59
Bach, Johann August Abraham, *son of Johann Sebastian Bach (died in infancy)*, 12
Bach, Johann Christoph Friedrich (the "Bückeburg Bach"), *brother of John Christian Bach*, 2, 35, 37, 51, 52, **57**, 58, 136, 137, 292, 296, 297
Bach, Johann Elias, *cousin of Johann Sebastian Bach*, 22, 28, 32, 36, 37, 38
Bach, Johann Gottfried Bernhard, *half brother of John Christian Bach*, 1, 2, 15, 16, 17, 20, 38, 53, 81
Bach, Johann Nicolaus, *relative of Johann Sebastian Bach*, 20
Bach, Johann Sebastian, *father of John Christian Bach*, 1, **3**, 16, 17, 20, 23, 29–30, 32–34, 36, 39–40, 46, **57**(?), 60, 63, 74, 77, 81, 84, 85, 86, 107, 113, 118, 136, 140, 142, 177, 181, 183, 184, 195, 261, 272, 274, 292, 293, 297
  adversarial relationships of,
    with Ernesti, 12–15
    with Mattheson, 23, 26, 90
    with Scheibe, 20–22
  blindness of, 50–51, 54

death and burial of, 55–56, 58
  employs Christian for writing letters, 51–52
  living quarters in Leipzig, 2, 4–6, **5**, **10**
  as teacher
    of sons, 52–54
    teaching methods of, 32-34
  and Vivaldi, 291
Bach, Johann Sebastian, *son of Carl Philipp Emanuel Bach*, 41, 59
Bach, Johanna Maria, *wife of Carl Philipp Emanuel Bach*, 59
Bach, Johanne Carolina, *daughter of Carl Philipp Emanuel Bach*, 58, 290
Bach, Lucia Elisabeth, *wife of Johann Christoph Friedrich Bach*, 137
Bach, Maria Barbara, *first wife of Johann Sebastian Bach*, 1, 15, 36, 37, 38, 81
Bach, Regine Susanna, *sister of John Christian Bach*, 58, 290
Bach, Vitus, *early member of Bach family*, 130
Bach, Wilhelm Friedemann, *half brother of John Christian Bach*, ix, xi, 1, 4, 15, 20, 33, 34, 38, 40, 41, 51, 52, **57**, 59, 74, 81, 84, 86, 100, **294**
  academic education of, 30
  claims compositions by his father as his own, 136
  not close to Christian, 296–297
  composes in style of his father, 29, 32
  conflicts with Kirnberger, 62–63
  employed in Dresden, 12
  lives in poverty, 290–292
  as organist, 45
  returns to Leipzig because of his father's death, 56, 58
  visits Berlin with father, 43, 45
Bach, Wilhelm Friedemann, *half brother of John Christian Bach*, 43,
Bach, Wilhelm Friedrich Ernst, *son of Johann Christoph Friedrich Bach*, 296
Balbi, *mathematician*, 96
Balbi, Ignazio, *composer in Milan*, 122, 128
Barbarina. *See* Campanini, Barbara.
Baroni-Cavalcabò, Baroness Josephine, 199
Barrington, Daines, *jurist, scientist, historian*, 221–223, **242**
Barthélémon, François-Hippolyte, *violinist*, 230, 235
Bartolini, Cardinal, 121
Bartolozzi, Francesco, *engraver*, 250
Bate, Henry, *journalist, publisher*, 332
Batteux, Charles, *philosopher*, 254–255
Beard, John, *singer*, 237, 239
Beccari, Colomba, *dancer*, 155
Beethoven, Ludwig van, *composer*, 83, 314
Belmonte, Princess di, 152

Benda, Franz, *violinist, composer*, ix, 28, **65**, 67, 74–76, 79, 87, 91, 166
Benda, Georg, *composer, brother of Franz*, 287
Benda, Joseph, *brother of Franz*, 28, 76
Benedetti, *male singer*, 135
Bernacci, Antonio, *teacher of singing*, 151
Bernigau, *city councillor*, 16
Bertoni, Ferdinando Giuseppe, *composer*, 331
Besozzi, Gaetano, *oboist*, 40
Bianchi, Francesco, *composer*, 331
Biedermann, Johann Gottlieb, *rector*, 48, **49**, 50–51, 54, 81
Billington, Elizabeth, *singer*, 194, 314
Birnbaum, Johann Abraham, *professor of rhetoric*, 26, 28
Bitter, Carl Hermann, *writer on music*, xi, 83
Bose, Christiana Sybilla, *godmother of John Christian Bach*, 1
Bose, Georg Heinrich, *father of Christiana Sybilla Bose*, 1
Bottarelli, Giovan Gualberto, *poet*, 171, 263
Breitkopf, Johann Gottlieb Emanuel, *music publisher*, 290
Brenner, *engraver*, 186
Brent, Charlotte, *singer*, 239
Brosses, Charles de, *traveler and chronicler*, 112, 118, 143, 159
Brühl, Count Heinrich, 56
Brunswick, Duke Carl I of, 291
Brunswick, Prince Carl Wilhelm Ferdinand of, *heir apparent*, 240, 291–292
Brunswick, Field Marshal Ferdinand, *brother of Duke Carl I*, 291
Brunswick-Lüneburg, Princess Augusta of, 179
Bückeburg, Count Wilhelm von. *See* Schaumburg-Lippe, Count Wilhelm von.
Buckingham, Samuel Felix, *son of Regina Mingotti*, 176
Bullinger, Abbé Joseph, *friend of Mozarts*, 317
Buntebart, Gabriel, *piano maker*, 185, 302, 303, 332
Burney, Charles, *music historian*, 66–67, 85, 105, 119, 143, 152, 160, 169, 176, 182, 185, 219, 220, 223, 247, 263, 265, 301, 303, 309
  on C. P. E. Bach, 76, 100
  on Cecilia Grassi, 259
  on John Christian Bach, 75, 183–184
    arrival in London of, 167, 275
    Orione by, 171, 174
  on music
    in Mannheim, 145
    in Milan, 110, 112–113, 158
    in Naples, 116-117
    by Lampugnani, 135-136
  on Rauzzini, 305
  visits C. P. E. Bach in Hamburg, 293, 295
Bute, Lord, *lover of Princess Augusta*, 163
Buxtehude, Dietrich, *organist, composer*, 140
Byrd, William, *composer*, 250

C

Campanini, Barbara ("Barbarina"), *dancer*, 70, 79
Campolungo, Anna Loria, *contralto*, 103
Campra, André de, *composer*, 118
Cannabich, Christian, *member of Mannheim orchestra*, 34
Cantelo, Anne, *pupil of John Christian and Cecilia Bach*, 300
Caramontelle. *See* Carrogi, Louis.
Caravaggio, Marchese di, 159
Cardonne, Jean-Baptiste, *composer*, 326, 327
Carignac, Princess de, 105
Carlin, Mlle., *thirteen-year-old blind pianist*, 314
Carlo Emanuele III, *king of Sardinia*, 146
Carmagiani, Giovanna, *singer*, 179
Carrogi, Louis ("Caramontelle"), *painter*, 205, 240
Casanova, Giacomo, *writer and adventurer*, 224
Caselli, Michelangelo, *organist*, 113, 138, 140
Castrucci, Pietro, *violinist and composer*, 253
Catherine II, *empress of Russia*, 295, 309
Cervetto, James, *musician*, 313
Charles VI, *Emperor*, 98,
  tomb of, **129**
Charlotte, Queen. *See* Mecklenburg-Strelitz, Princess Sophie-Charlotte of.
Chiesa, Melchior, *harpsichordist*, 135
Chevardière, *publisher*, 314
Chrysander, Friedrich, *scholar*, 125
Cicognani, Giuseppe, *male alto*, 128
Ciprandi, Ercole, *tenor*, 220, 223, 230
Cipriani, Giovanni Battista, *engraver*, 250
Cirri, *cellist*, 230, 235
Claudius, Matthias, *poet*, 86, 296
Cocchi, Gioacchino, *composer*, 228, 265
Colini, *secretary to Voltaire*, 285
Corbelli, Giovanni, *organist*, 113, 140
Cornelys, Mrs. Theresa, *singer and music patron*, 227–228, 230, 231, **232**, 247, 257, 266, 301–302
Correggio, Antonio, *painter*, 120
Cramer, Carl Friedrich, *music publisher*, 186, 195, 248
Cramer, Johann Baptist, *pianist*, 163
Cramer, Wilhelm, *violinist*, 183, 313, 328, 332
Crawford, Peter, *opera impresario*, 177, 247, 331
Cremonini, Clementina, *singer*, 226, 230, 235
Cricci, Domenico [?], *basso buffo, Potsdam theater director*, 72

Cristofori, Bartolomeo, *originator of hammerklavier*, 184
Croce, della, *painter*, 321
Crossdill, John, *cellist*, 268
Cumberland, duke of, 266, 300
Cuzzoni, Francesca, *female singer*, 176
Czarth, Georg, *Bohemian musician*, 75

D

Dannemann, Johanna Maria. *See* Bach, Johanna Maria.
Danzi, Francesca, *singer, daughter of Innocenz Danzi*, 313
Danzi, Innocenz, *cellist*, 313
Dassio, Carlo, *priest*, 142, 179
Delafosse, Jean Baptiste, *artist*, 205
Della Croce. *See* Croce, della.
Destouches, Cardinal André, *composer*, 118, 326, 327
Dibdin, Charles, *pianist*, 268
Diderot, Denis, *philosopher, writer*, 52, 86, 295
Diderot, Marie-Angelique, *daughter of Denis Diderot*, 295
Dittersdorf, Karl Ditters von, *composer*, 173, 259
Doles, Johann Friedrich, *cantor*, 14, 48, 144
Downes, Edward O. D., *musicologist*, x
Du Bois, Lady Dorothy, *daughter of Lord Richard Du Bois*, 268
Du Bois, Lord Richard, *earl of Anglesey*, 268
Dubois, *male dancer*, 87
Dubois, *violinist*, 268
Durante, Francesco, *composer*, 117

E

Eckard, Johann Gottfried, *musician*, 199, 202
Effingham, Lady, 166
Einicke, Georg Friedrich, *pupil of Sebastian Bach*, 48, 50–51
Einstein, Alfred, *musicologist*, 104, 173, 216
Elisi, Filippo, *singer*, 132, 137, 162, 167, 247
Erdmann, Georg, *friend of Sebastian Bach*, 6–7, 9, 34
Ernesti, Johann August, *rector of St. Thomas School*, 1, 2, 11, 12, **13**, 14–15, 20, 37, 41, 48
Este, Princess Beatrice d', 270
Eugen, Prince Friedrich, *brother of Prince Karl Eugen*, 76
Eugen, Prince Karl, *regent*, 76

F

Fasch, Karl Friedrich, *harpsichordist*, 77
Ferdinand, *archduke of Hapsburg*, 270
Ferdinand IV, *king of Naples*, 307
Ferrandini, Giovanni, *composer*, 132, 151

Fioroni, Giovanni Andrea, *maestro di cappella*, 138
Firmian, Count C., *Austrian official*, 149, 151, 155, 158, 159
Fischer, Johann Christian, *oboist*, 255, 257, 260, 266–268
Fischer, Ludwig Franz, *basso*, 153
Florio, *flutist*, 313
Forkel, Johann Nikolaus, *music publisher*, xi, 22, 29, 32–33, 41, 43, 53, 54, 62, 102, 248, 293, 322
Franz I, Emperor, 146, 149
Frederick II, *king of Prussia*, 6, 29, **42**, 52, 59, 62, 70, 73–74, 76, 91, 93, **101**, 103, 104–105, 119, 143, 144, 166, 195, 235
  and C. H. Graun, 67–68, 70–72
  and C. P. E. Bach, 59–60, 77–78, 99–102, 130, 293
  receives J. S. Bach in Potsdam, 37, 41, 43–45, 184
  and Quantz, 67
  and Tartini, 98
Fredersdorf, Michael Gabriel, *chamberlain to King Frederick II*, 99–100, **101**, 103
Friedrich August II, *elector of Saxony*, 6, 11, 12, 15, 30, **31**
Fuentes, Count de, 228
Fux, Johann Joseph, *Austrian composer*, 109

G

Gabrielli, Catterina, *singer*, 305, 309, 311
Gainsborough, Thomas, *painter*, 182, 188, 191, 250, 251, **252**, 253–255, **256**, 257, 258, 260, 267, 299, 300, 304, 330, 332
Gallini, Giovanni ("John") Andrea, *dancer*, 176, 302–303
Galuppi, Baldassare, *composer*, 146, 169, 171, 223
Garrick, David, *actor*, 311
Gassmann, Florian Leopold, *composer*, 143–144, 145, 146
George I, *king of England*, 163
George II, *king of England*, 163
George III, *king of England*, 162, 163, **168**, 185, 187, 189, 231, 269, 311
Georgi, Brigida, *singer*, 303, 316, 324
Gerber, Ernst Ludwig, *lexicographer*, 33, 102, 248
Gerstenberg, Heinrich Wilhelm von, *writer on music*, 78, 86
Gesner, Johann Matthias, *rector*, 11–12, **13**, 54
Giardini, Felice de, *violinist, composer, impresario*, 174, 176–177, 182–183, 191, 219, 224, 328, 330
Giustinelli, Giuseppe, *male singer*, 219
Gleim, Ludwig, *poet*, 86–87, 105, 130

Glenorchy, Lady, 194, 248

Gluck, Christoph Willibald, *composer*, 103–104, 148, 173–174, 227, 259, 263, 264, 270, 307, 321–**323**, 324–326

Goethe, Cornelia, *sister of Johann Wolfgang von Goethe*, 4

Goethe, Johann Wolfgang von, *writer, poet*, 4, 272–273

Goldberg, Johann Gottlieb, *harpsichordist*, 41

Golycyn, Prince Dimitri Alexevich ("Prince Gallazin"), 240

Gordon, John, *cellist*, 247

Gordon, Vincent, *theater manager*, 258

Görner, Johann Gottlieb, *Leipzig musician*, 56

Gottsched, Johann Christoph, *poet*, 20

Götze, *Leipzig organist*, 16

Goya, Francisco, 308

Graeme, *colonel*, 163–164

Grassi, Andrea, *father or uncle of Cecilia Grassi*, 259

Grassi, Cecilia. *See* Bach, Cecilia.

Grassi, Luigi, *singer, brother of Cecilia Grassi*, 259

Graun, Carl Heinrich, *Kapellmeister and singer*, ix, 6, 28, 60, 63, **69**, 73, 77, 78, 79, 84, 87, 91, 92, 119, 144, 166
  and Benda, 75
  and opera in Berlin, 67–68, 70–72
  views on composing of, 47

Graun, Johann Gottlieb, *violinist, brother of Carl Heinrich Graun*, ix, 28, 63, 72, 74–75, 79, 87, 91–92

Graupner, Johann Christoph, *composer*, 7

Graziani, Carlo, *cellist*, 204

Greenland, Emma Jane, *friend of John Christian Bach*, 125

Grétry, André-Ernest-Modeste, *composer*, 254

Grimm, Baron Friedrich Melchior, 195–196, 198, **201**, 202, 203, 221, 231, 240, 241, 317, 318

Grossatesta, Gaetano, *impresario*, 148

Guadagni, Gaetano, *singer*, **225**, 264

Guarducci, Tommaso, *singer*, 151, 258, 262, 268

Guercino, *painter*, 109

Guglielmi, Pietro, *maestro*, 263

Guglielmi, Achiapati, *singer, wife of Pietro Guglielmi*, 263

Guglietti, *male singer*, 219

H

Haffner, Johann Ulrich, *printer and bookseller*, 234

Hagedorn, Friedrich Wilhelm von, *poet*, 92

Hagenauer, Lorenz, *landlord and friend of Leopold Mozart*, 190, 196, 198, 203, 207, 214, 216, 217, 231, 233–234, 236, 239

Hagenauer, Maria Theresa, *wife of Lorenz Hagenauer*, 239

Handel, George Frideric, *composer*, 43, 46–47, 64, 120, 126, 136, 146, 163, 179, 182, 185, 206, 207, 226, **242**, 264, 322, 332
  compared to John Christian Bach, 262–263
  composes for Vauxhall, 194–195
  and John Christian Bach, 117–118
  and Mozart, 215, 227

Harcourt, Lord, 164

Harrer, Gottlob, *successor to J. S. Bach as cantor of St. Thomas School*, 55–56, 84, 274

Harris, Mrs. Gertrude, *music amateur in London*, 219, 257, 301

Hasse, Faustina, *singer, wife of Johann Adolf Hasse*, 6, 40, 118–119, 177

Hasse, Johann Adolf, *composer*, 6, 28, **31**, 40, 64, 70–71, 73, 84, 117, 126, 127, 130, 143, 144, 148, 149, 177, 181, 195, 295
  and Christian Bach, 118–119
  sacred music of, 119–120

Haussmann, Elias Gottlieb, *painter*, 46

Haydn, (Franz) Joseph, *composer*, 216

Hazard, *administrator*, 285

Heiberg-Vos, Marie Ann, *musicologist*, x

Heinel, Anna, *dancer*, 265

Heinse, Wilhelm, *poet*, 269

Herschel, Friedrich Wilhelm, *musician*, 182

Herschel, Jakob, *brother of Friedrich Wilhelm Herschel*, 182

Hertel, Johann Christian, *violinist*, 166

Hertel, Johann Wilhelm, *violinist, son of Johann Christian Hertel*, 166

Hertford, earl of, 239

Hesemann, Herr, *guardian*, 58

Hetzehen, Johann Gottfried, *organist*, 16

Hildebrandt, Zacharias, *organ builder*, 184

Hillingdon, Lord, 257, 301

Hock, *musician*, 75

Hogarth, William, *painter, engraver*, 253

Holzbauer, Ignaz Jakob, *composer*, 109, 144–145, 146, 275–276, **277**, 278, 281, 284

Homilius, Gottfried August, *organist, composer*, 30, 100

Hook, James, *Vauxhall organist, composer*, 194

Horace, *poet and satirist*, 48

Horzizky, *musician*, 75

Huberty, Antoine, *publisher*, 248, 314

J

Jackson, William, *friend of Gainsborough*, 221, 251, 254

Janitsch, Johann Gottlieb, *musician*, 66

Jommelli, Niccolò, *composer*, 117, 264

Joseph II, Emperor, 144

𝕶

Karl Theodor, Elector, 34, 144, 153, 183, 270, 272, **277**, 278, 290, 307
Kaunitz-Rietberg, Count Wenzel Anton, 149
Kelly, earl of, 230
Kelly, Michael, *singer*, 243
Keyserlingk, Count Carl Hermann, *Russian ambassador to Saxon court*, 41, 43, 45
Kirnberger, Johann Philipp, *composer, violinist*, 62–63, 78, 87
Kleist, Ewald von, *poet*, 86, 87
Klemm, Johann Friedrich, *mayor*, 17
Klopstock, Friedrich Gottlieb, *poet*, 293
Knobelsdorff, Baron Georg Wenceslas, 68
Königsegg, Count, 110
Krause, Gottfried Theodor, *prefect*, 14
Krause, Johann Gottlieb, *prefect*, 14
Krause, Christian Gottfried, *music amateur and writer*, 78, 83, 85, 86–87, **88**, 89–90, 91, 92, 98
Krebs, Johann Tobias, *organist*, 100
Kropfgans, Johann, *lutenist*, 32

𝕷

La Motte, Houdar de, *tragedian*, 326
Lampugnani, Giovanni Battista, *composer*, 134–136, 137, 146, 160, 162, 223
Landon, H. C. Robbins, *musicologist*, ix
Lange, Aloysia. *See* Weber, Aloysia.
Lange, Joseph, *actor*, 306
Lebrun, Ludwig August, *oboist*, 313
Leduc, Alphonse, *publisher*, 314, 328
Lehndorff, Count, 105
Leibnitz, Baron Gottfried Wilhelm von, *mathematician, philosopher*, 30, 46
Lennox, Lady Sarah, 163
Leo, Leonardo, *composer*, 117
Leonardo da Vinci, *painter, sculptor, architect, engineer*, 112
Leopold, Prince. *See* Anhalt-Köthen, Prince Leopold of.
Lessing, Gotthold Ephraim, *critic, dramatist*, 23, 86, 87
Lichtenberg, Georg Christoph, *physicist, writer*, 309, 311
Linley, Thomas, *violinist*, 241
Lippsius, Johann, *writer on music*, 1
Litta, Count Agostino, *employer of Christian Bach in Milan*, 38, 107, **111**, **114**, 126–128, 131, 134, 137, 138, 156, 158, 181, 259
    and Christian Bach, 103, 109–110, 113, 115, 121–122, 125, 128, 132, 137, 140, 141, 151, 158, 160
    concerned about Christian's lifestyle, 155–156
    and Padre Martini, 122, 124, 125, 127, 156

    and Prince Ferdinand Philipp Lobkowitz, 103–104
Litta, Count Antonio, *father of Count Agostino Litta*, 103, 104, 109, 110
Litta, Count Pompeo, *brother of Count Agostino Litta*, 103, 104, 110, 156
Lobkowitz, August Anton, *cousin of Prince Ferdinand Lobkowitz*, 104
Lobkowitz, Prince Ferdinand Philipp Joseph, 75–76, 90, 98, 103, 104, 105, **106**
Lobkowitz, Prince Georg Christian, *uncle of Prince Ferdinand Lobkowitz*, 104
Lobkowitz, Joseph Maria Karl, *cousin of Prince Ferdinand Lobkowitz*, 104
Lobwasser, Maria, *Leipzig citizen*, 51
Lockman, John, *poet*, 166–167
Lohenstein, Caspar David von, *tragedian*, 21
Lolli, Antonio, *violinist*, 141
Lorenzoni, P. A., *painter*, 210
Lotter, Johann Jakob, *printer and bookseller*, 234
Louis XV, *king of France*, 91
Lully, Jean-Baptiste, *composer*, 118

𝕸

Mainwaring, John, *biographer*, 118, 179
Majo, Francesco de, *composer*, 142
Manchester, duke of, 118
Mann, Sir Horace, 241
Mannio, Gennaro, *composer*, 116
Manzuoli, Giovanni, *singer*, 219–222, 223–224, **225**, 226, 237, 241, 268, 270
Mara, *Bohemian musician*, 75
Marchand, Margarete, *singer*, 287
Marchetti, *female singer*, 324
Maria Carolina, Archduchess, 159
Maria Josepha, Archduchess 30
Maria Theresia, Empress, 103, 104, 110, 144, 270
Marie Antoinette, *queen of France*, 322, 325
Marpurg, Friedrich Wilhelm, *music theorist*, 62, 78, 80, 91–92, 99, 103
Martini, Padre Giovanni Battista, *teacher and mentor to Christian Bach*, ix, 38, 96, 120–122, **123**, 135, 138, 140–142, 151–153, 233
    composes a stage work, 142
    and Count Agostino Litta, 122, 125, 137, 138, 155–156
    and Christian Bach
        as teacher of, 45, 52, 113, 119, 121, 125, 131, 134, 142, 158, 162, 169, 185
        correspondence with, 115, 118, 121, 122, 124–127, 128, 130–132, 134, 137, 140–141, 156, 160, 179
        requests and receives portrait of, 257, 300, 301
    and Hasse, 119

international reputation of, 143
other students of, 128, 142–143
and Raaff, 151–153
Storia della Musica of, 134
Mattei, Colomba, *singer, impresario*, 160, 162, 169, 174, 176, 177, 181
Mattei, Trombetta, *husband of Colomba Mattei*, 160
Mattheson, Johann, *writer on music*, 9, 23, **24**, 25, 26, 47, 50, 54, 83, 90, 121
Mattocks, George, *singer-actor*, 239
Maunsell, Dorothy, *wife of Ferdinando Tenducci*, 224
Mazziotti, Giuseppe Antonio, *castrato*, 219
Mecklenburg, Duke Ernst of, 185
Mecklenburg-Strelitz, Duke Adolf Friedrich IV of, *brother of Princess Sophie-Charlotte*, 164, 167
Mecklenburg-Strelitz, Princess Christina of, *sister of Princess Sophie-Charlotte*, 164
Mecklenburg-Strelitz, Duchess Dorothea-Sophie of, *mother of Princess Sophie-Charlotte*, 164, 166
Mecklenburg-Strelitz, *Princess Sophie-Charlotte of, queen of England*, **165**, 167, 179, 181, **188**, 189, 260, 296, 303, 309, 325, 330
and Christian Bach, 166–167
dedicatee of
Christian's Op. 1, 177, 184, 314
Mozart's six keyboard sonatas, 195, **208**
learns of Christian's death and grants pension to his widow, 331–332
leaves for England, 162
love for music of, 164, 166
marriage to George III, 163–164, 166
music masters of:
Christian Bach, 182, 189
Schröter, 273
Mozart performs for, 203–204, 206–207, 231
Melzi, Count, 104
Melzi, Princess Antonia Maria, 159
Merlin, Joseph, *magician*, 228
Metastasio, Abbé (Pietro Trapassi), *librettist*, 95, 132, **147**, 148, 151, 171, 173, 194, 279
Miesner, Heinrich, *music historian*, xi
Mingotti, Pietro, *impresario*, 40, 127
Mingotti, Regina, *singer, impresario*, 40, 119, 127, 162, 174, 176–177, **178**, 182–183, 191, 219, 220, 305
Mizler, Lorenz, *founder of the Society of Musical Science*, 26, 28, 30, 46, 47, 60
Modena, duke of, 130
Molteni, Emilia, *singer*, 62, 102–103
Monticelli, Angelo Maria, *singer*, 119
Moser, *female singer*, 259
Mount Edgcumbe, Lord George, earl of, 309
Mozart, Constanze, *wife of Wolfgang Amadeus*

Mozart, 153, 243, 306, 317, 320–321
Mozart, Leopold, *father of Wolfgang Amadeus Mozart*, 47, 96, 135, 144, 184, 195–196, 199, 202, 203, **205**, 207, 211, 215, 217, 223, 233–235, 240, 243, 254, 260, 269, 270, 282, 287, 316–318, 328
announces final concerts of his children in London, 235–236, 240
assembles collection of keyboard pieces, 146, 198
children of, perform at court, 204, 206, 230-231
describes music in London, 190–191
illness of, in London, **212**, 214
leaves England with his children, 241
meets London musicians, 219, 230
received at court with his children, 203–204
sees Christian as a model for Wolfgang, 26
on Wolfgang's early compositions, 198–199, 216
wants to leave England, 233, 237, 239
wants Wolfgang to return to Salzburg, 318, 320–321
wife of, dies in Paris, 317
writes to Padre Martini on Wolfgang's behalf, 153
Mozart, Maria Anna, *mother of Wolfgang Amadeus Mozart*, 135, 203, 207, 261, 282, 316, 317, 318, 321
Mozart, Maria Anna ("Nannerl"), *sister of Wolfgang Amdeus Mozart*, 146, **205**, **210**, 214, 254, 260, 287, 305, 317, 320
arrives in London, 203–204
keyboard performance of, praised, 236
music manuscript book of, 198–199, 211
performs with Wolfgang, 195–196, 230–231, 233
recalls events in London, 206–207, 215, 221, 234, 240
and Wolfgang perform at court, 204–206, 230–231
Mozart, Maria Anna Thekla (the "Bäsle"), *cousin of Wolfgang Amadeus Mozart*, 321
Mozart, Wolfgang Amadeus, composer, x, xi, 39, 47, 75, 82, 96, 126, 148, 149, 151, 173, 175, 177, 181, **200**, **205**, **208**, 224, 243, 251, 254, 257, 258, 260, 269, 270, 273, 281–282, 286, 292, 305, 306, 312, 326
acquires a piano by Stein, 184–185
admires music of:
Christian Bach, 153, 186, 246, 255, 281, 299, 314, 316, 318, 320
Gassmann, 143–144
Holzbauer, 276
admonished by his father, 26
in Bologna and Milan, 135
La clemenza di Tito, last Italian opera of,

Metastasio as librettist for, 148
relation to arias of Christian Bach, 223
stage set (1799), **315**
comments on Christian Bach's death, 332
departs for London, 202
described by English scientist, 221–223
first compositions, 146, **154**, **201**, 207, **208**, 209, 211, **212–213**, 214, **218**, 223, 236, **242**, **244**
influenced by Christian Bach's music, 179, 214–218
instructed by Christian Bach, 206–207
leaves England, 241
in Paris, 196, 198–199
performs
    at British court, 203–204, 206, 232
    on Continent, 195–196
    for Emperor Franz, 146
    in public, 207, 230–231, 233, 235–236
reports his mother's death, 317
Requiem of, compared to Christian Bach's, 124–125
returns to Salzburg, 321
shows interest in opera, 217
and the Wendlings, 286–287
writes arias for Raaff, 153, **154**, 278, 316
Mozart, Wolfgang Amadeus Jr., *son of Wolfgang Amadeus Mozart*, 199
Müller, Pater Marianus, *archabbott of Einsiedeln monastery*, 126
Münchhausen, Lucia Elisabeth. *See* Bach, Lucia Elisabeth.

N
Nassau-Weilburg, Princess Caroline of, 241
Naumann, Johann Gottlieb, *Kapellmeister, composer*, 142–143
Newton, Isaac, *mathematician, physicist*, 254
Nichelmann, Christoph, *harpsichordist*, 62, 63, 79, 80–81, 87, 91, 100, 102
Nicolai, Frederick., *violinist*, 303
Nicolai, Friedrich, *publisher*, 79, 89
Nissen, Georg Nikolaus, *second husband of Constanze Mozart*, 320
Noailles, Duc Louis d'Ayen, *marshal of France*, 317–318
Novello, Vincent, *publisher*, 125
Nys, Carl de, *writer*, 217

P
Paisiello, Giovanni, *composer*, 117
Pallavicino, Count Gian-Luca, 159
Pannwitz, Fräulein von, *lady-in-waiting at Prussian court*, 105
Papendiek, Mr., *husband of Mrs. Papendiek*, 331, 332

Papendiek, Mrs., *pupil of John Christian Bach*, 38, 194, 260, 265, 273, 299–300, 303–304, 307, 324, 330, 331–332
Parma, duke of, 173
Parma, princess of, 141
Pasini, *male singer*, 306
Pauli, *court Kapellmeister*, 45
Pawlowa, Grand Duchess Helene, 199
Pepusch, John Christopher, *composer*, 237
Pergolesi, Giovanni Battista, *composer*, 91, 117
Perti, Giacomo, *composer*, 124
Petrarch (Francesco Petrarca), *poet*, 95
Petri, Georg Gottfried, *cantor*, 22
Petri, Christian, *mayor*, 16
Piccinni, Nicolo, *composer*, 117, 146, 318, 322, **323**, 324, 326
Piesaque de Non, Count, 176
Pisendel, Johann Georg, *violinist*, 30, 74
Plymouth, Lord, 302
Pohl, Carl Ferdinand, *music historian*, 261
Polko, Elise, *writer*, 102, 259
Pompadour, Mme Jeanne, *singer, mistress of King Louis XV*, 91
Porpora, Nicolo, *composer*, 40, 117, 119, 127
Porporino, *male singer*, 79
Prex, Dr., *physician, friend of Mozart family*, 318
Provacaccini, *painter*, 109
Puchberg, Michael, *friend of W. A. Mozart*, 185
Pugnani, Gaetano, *violinist*, 268
Purcell, Henry, *composer*, 250

Q
Quantz, Johann Joachim, *composer*, ix, 43, 60, 63–64, **65**, 66, 67, 70, 73, 79, 83, 87, 89, 90, 91, 92, 98

R
Raaff, Anton, *singer*, 151–153, **154**, 220, 278, 284, 287, 306, 307, 312, 316, 317
Rameau, Jean-Philippe, *composer*, 90–91, 96, 98, 118, 173
Ramler, Karl Wilhelm, *writer and poet*, 86, 87, 89, 90, 92
Rauzzini, Venanzio, *composer, singer*, **175**, 304–305, 306, **310**, 311, 328, 331
Reichardt, Johann Friedrich, *composer and writer on music*, 137
Reynolds, Sir Joshua, *painter*, 250, 251, 255
Ricci, Francesco Pasquale, *composer*, 327–328
Richmond, duke of, 163
Ricieri, Giovanni Antonio, *Franciscan monk, teacher of Padre Martini*, 120
Riemann, Hugo, *lexicographer, theorist*, 54
Ruisdael, Jacob van, *painter*, 255
Rivinus, Johann Florens, *godfather of John Christian Bach*, 1

Robinig, Aloisia von, *early girlfriend of Wolfgang Amadeus Mozart*, 318
Rochlitz, Johann Friedrich, *journalist*, 39, 77, 113, 134
Rödenbeck, *court chronicler*, 44, 104
Rolland, Romain, *writer*, 301
Rolle, Christian Friedrich, *musician*, 100
Roncaglia, Francesco, *singer*, 301, 306, 312, 313
Rothenburg, Count, 86
Rousseau, Jean-Jacques, *writer-philosopher*, 86, 90–91, 96, **97**, 98, 148
Rowlandson, Thomas, *painter*, 191

S
Sacchini, Antonio, *composer*, 306, 309, 311, 312, 328
Sack, Philipp, *organist*, 66
Saint-Foix, Georges de, *musicologist*, x, 209, 211, 214, 215, 216–217
Salieri, Antonio, *composer*, 144, 286
Salimbeni, *male singer*, 70
Salomon, Johann Peter, *impresario*, 243
Sammartini, Giovanni Battista, *composer*, 104, 113, 125, 126, 141, 158, 159–160, **161**
San Raffaele, Count Benvenuto di, 22
Sartori, Angiola, *singer*, 219
Savoi, Gasparo, *male soprano*, 264, 316
Savoie-Carignan, Princess Marie-Thérèse Louise de, 196
Saxony-Gotha, Prince Ernst Ludwig of, 231
Saxony-Weissenfels, Duke Christian of, 11
Scarlatti, Domenico, *composer*, 117
Schale, Johann Christian, *cellist*, 66
Schaumburg-Lippe, Count Wilhelm von, 51, 52, 137
Scheibe, Johann, *organ builder*, 20
Scheibe, Johann Adolph, *composer*, 20–23, 24, 26, 28, 46, 48, 53, 64, 89, 90, 93
Schenk, Erich, *Mozart biographer*, 269
Schindler, Anna Maria, *singer*, 305
Schmidt, Balthasar, *publisher*, 85
Schobert, Johann, *musician*, 199, 211, 215
Schökel, Heinrich, *musicologist*, xi, 93
Scholze, Johann Sigismund ("Sperontes"), *composer*, 18
Schröter, Christoph Gottlieb, *composer and organist*, 48, **49**, 50–51
Schröter, Corona, *singer, daughter of Johann Baptist Schröter*, 272, 273
Schröter, Johann Baptist, *oboist*, 272
Schröter, Johann Heinrich, *son of Johann Baptist Schröter*, 272
Schröter, Johann Samuel, *pianist, son of Johann Baptist Schröter*, 272, 273–274, 328, 332
Schubart, Christian Friedrich Daniel, *poet*, xi, 145, 152, 199, 269, 284

Schübler, J. G., *engraver*, 44
Schwarz, Max, *musicologist*, xi
Scotti, Teresa, *singer*, 220
Seeau, Count Anton von, 287, 290, 320
Segnitz, Dr., *mentor to Johann Elias Bach*, 36
Shakespeare, William, *playwright*, 66
Sheridan, Thomas, *impresario*, 250
Siéber, Jean-Georges, *publisher*, 314
Silbermann, Gottfried, *master organ builder*, 184–185
Simpson, Redmond, *oboist*, 303
Sirmen, Maddalena Lombardini, *violinist, pianist, singer*, 270
Smith, Eric, *musician*, 209
Smith, John Christopher, *composer*, 215
Sophie-Charlotte, Queen. *See* Mecklenburg-Strelitz, Princess Sophie-Charlotte of.
Sperontes. *See* Scholze, Johann Sigismund.
Stamitz, Johann, *composer*, 216, 314
Stanley, Charles John, *organist*, 265
Stein, Johann Andreas, *instrument builder*, 184–185, 202
Stieglitz, *Leipzig mayor*, 55
Storace, Anna Selina ("Nancy"), *singer*, 243
Sulzer, Johann Georg, *writer, philosopher*, 86–87, 276
Süssmayr, Franz-Xaver, *composer*, 126, 243
Swieten, Baron Gottfried Freiherr van, 45, 215, 332

T
Tacet, Joseph, *flutist*, 268
Tanucci, Bernardo, *minister in charge of Naples theaters*, 148, 149, 151, 307
Tartini, Giuseppe, *composer*, 74, 75, 92–93, 95–96, **97**, 98, 143, 152
Taylor, John, *traveling oculist*, 50
Telemann, Georg Philipp, *composer*, 7, 47, 87, 91, 100, 293
Tenducci, Ferdinando, *castrato*, 224, **225**, 226, 230, 264, 317–318, 322
Teniers, David, *painter*, 109
Terry, Charles Sanford, *biographer of John Christian Bach*, x, ix, xi, 228, 306
Terzi, Antonio, *organist*, 160
Tessé, Countess de, 196
Tibaldi, Giuseppe Luigi ("Pietro"), *singer*, 128, **175**
Toëschi, Carlo Giuseppe, *composer*, 314
Took, Horn, *writer*, 250
Trapassi, Pietro. *See* Metastasio, Abbé.
Traëtta, Tommaso, *composer*, 173, 311
Trier, Johann, *organist*, 100
Tschudi (Shudi), Burckhart, *instrument builder*, 235–236
Tutenberg, Fritz, *musicologist*, xi, 203

Tyers, Jonathan, *Vauxhall concessionaire*, 194

U

Uz, Johann Peter, *poet*, 105, 130

V

Valentini, Michelangelo, *brother of Regina Mingotti*, 127
Valentini, Regina. *See* Mingotti, Regina.
Vanhall (Wanhal), Johann Baptist, *composer*, 253
Vento, Mattia, *composer*, 183, 219, 223
Verazi, Mattia, *poet*, 306
Vincent, Thomas, *oboist*, 247
Visconti Borromeo, Elisabetta, *wife of Count Pompeo Litta*, 110
Visconti Borromeo, Donna Paola, *wife of Count Antonio Litta*, 109
Vismes, M., *opera impresario*, 322
Vivaldi, Antonio, *composer*, 291
Vogler, Abbé Georg Joseph, *organist, composer, theorist*, 275, 278–279, 281, **283**
Voltaire (Francois-Marie Arouet), *writer*, 86, 99, 285

W

Wagenseil, Georg Christoph, *composer*, 144, 145–146
Walderen, Count, 241
Walleshauser, Johann (Giovanni Evangelist Valesi), *teacher of singing*, 312
Walpole, Horace, *writer*, 163, 189, 220, 239, 266, 304
Walter, Friedrich, *historian*, 282
Warburton, Ernest, *musicologist*, x
Waterhouse, William, *cellist*, 300
Weber, Aloysia, *sister of Constanze Mozart*, 153, 217, 243, 306, 320

Weber, Constanze. *See* Mozart, Constanze.
Weichsell, Carl, *oboist*, 191
Weichsell, Mrs. Carl, *singer*, 182, 191, **192(?)**, 194, 239, 314
Weimar, Duke Carl August of, 272
Weiss, Karl, *flutist*, 269
Welcker, *music engraver*, 186
Wendling, Dorothea, *singer, mother of "Gustl,"* 269, **271**, 272, 274, 282, 287, 306
Wendling, Elisabeth Augusta ("Lisl"), *singer, aunt of "Gustl,"* 286
Wendling, Elisabeth Augusta ("Gustl"), *singer*, 269, **271**, 272, 274, 281–282, 284, 286–287, 299, 306, 307, 320
Wendling, Johann Baptist, *flutist, father of "Gustl,"* 34, 269–270, **271**, 274, 281–282, 284, 287
Wieland, Christoph Martin, *poet*, 59, 144–145, 269
Wilkes, John, *writer*, 250
Winckelmann, Johann Joachim, *art historian*, 149
Wohlfahrth, Hannsdieter, *biographer of Friedrich Bach*, 296
Wolff, Baron Christian von, 46
Woodfall, Henry, *editor*, 226
Wyzewa, Théodore de, *musicologist*, x, 209, 211, 214, 215, 216, 217, 223

Y

York, Duke of, *brother of King George III*, 231
Young, Mary, *singer*, 230, 268

Z

Zelter, Carl Friedrich, *composer*, 79
Zoffany, John, *painter*, 208, 250, 251, 304, 332
   painting of Gainsborough by, **252**
Zumpe, Johann Christoph, *instrument builder*, 185, 266